MESSIANIC POLITICAL THEOLOGY AND DIASPORA ETHICS

THEOPOLITICAL VISIONS

SERIES EDITORS:

Thomas Heilke
D. Stephen Long
and C. C. Pecknold

Theopolitical Visions seeks to open up new vistas on public life, hosting fresh conversations between theology and political theory. This series assembles writers who wish to revive theopolitical imagination for the sake of our common good.

Theopolitical Visions hopes to re-source modern imaginations with those ancient traditions in which political theorists were often also theologians. Whether it was Jeremiah's prophetic vision of exiles "seeking the peace of the city," Plato's illuminations on piety and the civic virtues in the Republic, St. Paul's call to "a common life worthy of the Gospel," St. Augustine's beatific vision of the City of God, or the gothic heights of medieval political theology, much of Western thought has found it necessary to think theologically about politics, and to think politically about theology. This series is founded in the hope that the renewal of such mutual illumination might make a genuine contribution to the peace of our cities.

FORTHCOMING VOLUMES:

David Deane
The Matter of the Spirit: How Soteriology Shapes the Moral Life

Messianic Political Theology and DIASPORA ETHICS

Essays in Exile

P. TRAVIS KROEKER

CASCADE *Books* • Eugene, Oregon

MESSIANIC POLITICAL THEOLOGY AND DIASPORA ETHICS
Essays in Exile

Theopolitical Visions 23

Copyright © 2017 P. Travis Kroeker. All rights reserved. Except for brief quotations in critical publications or reviews, no part of this book may be reproduced in any manner without prior written permission from the publisher. Write: Permissions, Wipf and Stock Publishers, 199 W. 8th Ave., Suite 3, Eugene, OR 97401.

Cascade Books
An Imprint of Wipf and Stock Publishers
199 W. 8th Ave., Suite 3
Eugene, OR 97401

www.wipfandstock.com

PAPERBACK ISBN: 978-1-62032-987-0
HARDCOVER ISBN: 978-1-4982-8696-1
EBOOK ISBN: 978-1-5326-4274-6

Cataloguing-in-Publication data:

Names: Kroeker, P. Travis (Peter Travis), 1957–, author.

Title: Messianic political theology and diaspora ethics : essays in exile / P. Travis Kroeker.

Description: Eugene, OR : Cascade Books, 2017 | Series: Theopolitical Visions 23 | Includes bibliographical references and index(es).

Identifiers: ISBN 978-1-62032-987-0 (paperback) | ISBN 978-1-4982-8696-1 (hardcover) | ISBN 978-1-5326-4274-6 (ebook)

Subjects: LCSH: Christianity and politics. | Political theology. | Christian ethics. | History—Philosophy. | Bible—Criticism, interpretation, etc. | Apocalyptic literature—History and criticism.

Classification: BR115.P7 K76 2017 (paperback) | BR115.P7 K76 (ebook)

Manufactured in the U.S.A.   11/07/17

*For Felix, Delphine, Ezra,
and the next generation of peregrini*

Contents

Permissions | ix
Acknowledgments | xi

Introduction | 1

Part 1: Apocalyptic Messianism and Political Theology

1 Living "As If Not": Messianic Becoming or the Practice of Nihilism? | 15

2 The Theological Politics of Plato and Isaiah: A Debate Rejoined | 34

3 Augustine's Messianic Political Theology: An Apocalyptic Critique of Political Augustinianism | 46

4 Messianic Ethics and Diaspora Communities: Upbuilding the Secular Theologically from Below | 64

Part 2: Political Theology and the Radical Reformation

5 Anabaptists and Existential Theology | 83

6 Eschatology and Ethics: Luther and the Radical Reformers | 97

7 Why O'Donovan's Christendom Is Not Constantinian and Yoder's Voluntariety Is Not Hobbesian: A Debate in Theological Politics Redefined | 109

8 The War of the Lamb: Postmodernity and Yoder's Eschatological Genealogy of Morals | 130

9 Is a Messianic Political Ethic Possible? Yoder Critically Considered | 144

Part 3: Messianism and Diaspora Ethics

10 Messianic Freedom and the Secular Academy: Educating the Affections in a Technological Culture | 173

11 Gulag Ethics: Russian and Mennonite Prison Memoirs from Siberia (with Bruce Ward) | 185

12 Mennonite and Métis: Adjacent Histories, Adjacent Truths?
    (with Carole Leclair) | 199

13 Rich Mennonites in an Age of Mammon: Is a Messianic Political
    Economy Possible? | 211

14 On the Difference between Torture and Punishment: Theology, Liturgy,
    and Human Rights | 221

15 Technology as Principality: The Elimination of Incarnation | 235

Bibliography | 249

Index of Subjects | 261

Index of Scripture References | 267

Permissions

I AM GRATEFUL TO the following publishers for permission granted to use the following materials:

"The Theological Politics of Plato and Isaiah: A Debate Revisited," *The Journal of Religion* 73/1 (1993) 16–30.
"Living 'As If Not': Messianic Becoming or the Practice of Nihilism?," in *Paul, Philosophy and the Theopolitical Vision*, edited by Douglas Harink (Eugene, OR: Cascade, 2010) 37–63.
"Augustine's Messianic Political Theology: An Apocalyptic Critique of Political Augustinianism," in *Augustine and Apocalyptic*, edited by John Doody et al. (Lanham, MD: Lexington, 2014) 129–49.
"Messianic Ethics and Diaspora Communities: Upbuilding the Secular Theologically from Below," in *Religious Voices in Public Places: Religion and Liberal Reason*, edited by Nigel Biggar and Linda Hogan (Oxford: Oxford University Press, 2009) 110–30.
"Anabaptists and Existential Theology," *Conrad Grebel Review* 17/2 (1999) 69–88.
"Eschatology and Ethics: Luther and the Radical Reformers," *Consensus* 27/1 (2001) 9–25.
"Why O'Donovan's Christendom Is Not Constantinian and Yoder's Voluntariety Is Not Hobbesian: A Debate in Theological Politics Redefined," *The Journal of the Society of Christian Ethics* 20 (2000) 41–64.
"The War of the Lamb: Postmodernity and John Howard Yoder's Eschatological Genealogy of Morals," *Mennonite Quarterly Review* 74/2 (2000) 295–310.
"Is a Messianic Political Ethic Possible? Recent Work by and about John Howard Yoder," *Journal of Religious Ethics* 33/1 (2005) 141–74.
"Messianic Freedom and the Secular Academy: Educating the Affections in a Technological Culture," *Consensus* 32/2 (2006) 41–57.
"Gulag Ethics: Russian and Mennonite Prison Memoirs from Siberia," with Bruce Ward, *Journal of Mennonite Studies*, special issue on "Mennonites in Siberia," edited by Royden Loewen and Paul Toews (2012) 249–66.
"Mennonite and Metis: Adjacent Histories, Adjacent Truths?" with Carole Leclair, *Journal of Mennonite Studies* 28 (2010) 187–202.
"Rich Mennonites in an Age of Mammon: Is a Messianic Political Economy Possible?" *Journal of Mennonite Studies* 27 (2009) 168–78.
"On the Difference between Torture and Punishment: Theology, Liturgy and Human Rights," in *Theology, University, Humanities: Initium Sapientiae Timor Dominis*, edited by Christopher Brittain and Francesca Murphy (Eugene, OR: Cascade, 2011) 19–38.
"Technology as Principality: The Elimination of Incarnation," *Pro Ecclesia* 24/2 (2015) 162–77.

Acknowledgments

THERE ARE SO MANY to thank and too few will be mentioned by name. I'm grateful to Charlie Collier and Rodney Clapp for their gentle persistence in getting these essays under one cover; it wasn't easy and they were patient and encouraging. Without the mentorship of Jim Gustafson and the friendship of Stanley Hauerwas, this book would not exist. Each has been a remarkably generous, formidable interlocutor over the years and a model of encouragement in season and out of season. Maureen Epp did superb work editing and indexing the manuscript. McMaster University has been a congenial, nurturing academic hostel for this theologian in exile, allowing me to work incognito or under various pseudonyms: ethics, religion and politics, religion and literature. My most challenging and sustaining companions throughout my sojourn at Mac have been my graduate students, many of whom have become true friends. All of the work in these pages has been worked out in their company, and I'm profoundly grateful for the quality of their engagement. None of this work could have been completed without friendships, and in particular those connected with the Society of Christian Ethics—my friends Per Anderson, Nigel and Ginny Biggar, John Burgess, Carolyn Chau, Eric Gregory, Jerry McKenny, Steve Pope, and Cristie Traina, among others—and those attached to the research group on Saint Paul's Secular Destinies and the AAR group on Theology and Apocalyptic: Doug Harink, Mark Reasoner, Gord Zerbe, and Phil Ziegler. Bruce Ward, Steve Westerholm, Jim Reimer, Fred Bird and Frances Westley were there from the beginning. My coauthors in chapters 11 and 12, Carole Leclair and Bruce Ward, have been generous and challenging interlocutors and I'm ever so grateful for their collaboration. What could one be or do without family? My parents, Peter and Anna, and my children, Sarah (and Tom), Miriam (and Ian) and Peter have freely and so graciously given themselves to also being my friends on the journey; this book is dedicated to my grandchildren and the next precious generation of pilgrims. Grace (my own TGV) picked me up, bound up my wounds, poured on oil and wine, and we have taken care of each other in the way stations ever since, *Gott sei dank*.

Introduction

I BEGIN WITH THE terminology of my title: *Messianic Political Theology and Diaspora Ethics*. Political theology is a normative discourse rooted in the conviction that political crises—in the complex etymological sense of events, issues, judgments and decisions related to crucial "turning points"—may be best accounted for with reference to theological terms. Indeed, it holds that this is true even in secular political discourses and practices in which these terms continue to resound. "Messianic Political Theology" in the Christian sense is committed to the claim that these terms are revealed in the messianic anointing and worship of Jesus as sovereign, in keeping with the complex political theological narratives of the Bible. These are controversial claims, and not only for secular political philosophers such as Mark Lilla, who rejects this normative discourse as destructive: "We find it incomprehensible that theological ideas still inflame the minds of men, stirring up messianic passions that leave societies in ruins."[1] Political theology is also controversial for Christian theologians and political thinkers who have interpreted those terms in vastly different ways, only some of which might be identified as messianic in an apocalyptic register, with important implications for ethics. That I am using the term "Diaspora" to describe messianic ethics is related to my agreement with Ivan Illich that we still live in an apocalyptic world in which the mystical body of Christ is constantly being crucified (in the church no less than in the world), and that theologians make their particular, embodied critical judgments as pilgrims in a providential world.[2]

I have chosen as my subtitle "Essays in Exile." What could this possibly mean and how is it warranted? Surely it is no more potentially offensive than the main title but perhaps sounds somehow more presumptuous in a time of wrenching displacement—political, economic, and cultural—in our current world. Am I not a tenured professor in a research university in Canada who carries only one passport (and always have)? I was for a time as a graduate student designated a "resident alien" in the United States, so was I hoping to land there and instead found myself "exiled" in the Canadian academic backwater? Or am I showing my political theological colors as a "Hauerwasian," eager to renounce any affiliation not only with American civil religion (and all its "empire" copies, including Canadian multicultural "exceptionalism") but indeed the whole sordid experiment of Christendom? Given the terms of the primary title of this volume, that would come closer to my intended meaning—in opposition to the architectonic political

---

1. Lilla, *Stillborn God*, 3.
2. Illich, *Rivers North of the Future*, 179.

theology of Christendom articulated in the "two roles" model (different, yet "balanced" authorities of church and state) of Oliver O'Donovan that for O'Donovan represents the Christian conversion of the Roman empire. I will argue, moreover, that these colors also cohere with the political theology of Augustine, for whom citizenship is not to be identified with any earthly republic but rather with the messianic body on pilgrimage in this age, and thus political or public life in general may be best characterized as "exilic."

And yet, identities as modes of worldly belonging—national, cultural-linguistic, ethnic and ecclesial—seem unavoidable. As these essays demonstrate, perhaps ironically, I identify in many ways with that ethnic (because persecuted) and religious (thus also triumphalistic) community called "Mennonite."[3] Does the language of exile disavow all others?[4] Does it, as Edward Said suggested it might, "make a fetish of exile, a practice that distances one from all connections and commitments?"[5] No; I suggest it cultivates an alternative imagination to that of possession, including the possession (fetishization) of exile. The Pauline language of living life *hōs mē*, "as if not" possessing it (1 Cor 7) thus entails a certain practice of messianic detachment in all domains and vocations of worldly existence. The theological and political significance of the symbolism of exile-exodus-diaspora in the biblical imagination is beyond question. The origin stories of Genesis 1–11 begin with the exile of the primordial couple from their garden home (the first *oikos* and its *nomos* of immediate obedience to the divine word in naming the world). This exile follows from their communal possessive grasp after godlikeness that alienates them from an umbilical cosmic unity and begins the arduous, increasingly violent narrative journey that culminates in that most evocative biblical image of political empire, Babel. "Come, let us make bricks, . . . let us build ourselves a city, and a tower with its top in the heavens, and let us make a name for ourselves, lest we be scattered abroad upon the face of the whole earth" (11:3–4). The monolinguistic human naming entailed in empire-building resists the creation mandate to "fill the earth and multiply," and while the divine response in Genesis 11 (to scatter the people by confusing their language), like the exile from the garden in Genesis 3, is often interpreted as divine punishment, the motive terms of the narrative—a divine setting of limits on possessive human godlikeness—may be equally described as a liberation. In both cases the conditions for an immortal imperial human sovereignty rooted in the presumptive grasping of power are foiled so as to make possible a new, possibly more promising beginning such as the call of Abraham represents in Genesis—though that beginning also "ends" in Genesis with the people enslaved to an empire in Egypt.

The Exodus narrative may be viewed as paradigmatic for Israel's political theology: YHWH's sovereignty confronts the godlike tyrannical power of the imperial Pharaoh in an unlikely power struggle that nevertheless bears witness to a radically alternative

---

3. For paradoxical biographical clues, see chapter 12.

4. At times O'Donovan suggests it does so: "As the eschatological society, the church is entered only *by leaving* other, existing societies" (*Desire of the Nations*, 178); at other times he does not: "But for its completion in the public realm, the church needs 'the great city'. The curious thing about the two cities in the Apocalypse, Babylon and Jerusalem, is the continuity between them" (*Desire of the Nations*, 155).

5. Said, "Reflections on Exile," 183.

political economy.⁶ Messianic political theology (both Jewish and Christian) is rooted in this affirmation, but the question remains: how is this anti-imperial sovereignty humanly mediated on the earth? The mediation question is closely tied to the question of worship—that which is liturgically enacted in everyday life as worthy of authority, imitation, and good judgment. This goes beyond limitation. It is also closely connected to the question of political education; that is, who is leading us out (*e-ducere*) of bondage into a more liberating, peaceful and just form of communal life and vision? And how is this accomplished? Let us remain, briefly, with the Exodus narrative. When Moses is called by YHWH, in the place of exile, to be the human agent of political liberation, this is not based upon his great abilities but solely upon the promise of divine presence. And when Moses logically inquires after the identity (name) of this divine presence he is told it is "I am what I am" or "I will be what I will be" (Exod 3:14). This is a divine presence shrouded in mystery whose ways can only be revealed as part of an ongoing arduous, seemingly insane journey. Pharaoh's response articulates the perspective of empire sovereignty: "Who is this sovereign? I do not know this Lord. Go and make more bricks." The Pharaoh, also worshipped as a god, governs in the terms of political economic realism: productive labor, large-scale building projects, and military security. The people have become enslaved to the same brick-building economy aspired to at Babel and thus must be liberated not only from an external tyrant but also from an economic logic internal to their own religio-communal history. It would be false for anyone to imagine themselves as un-implicated in the empire political economies of their own time and place, and the essays in Part 3 are attempts to name certain complicities from which would-be or so-called messianic communities might seek liberation.⁷

The language of liberation in Exodus—"let my people go"—is often politically truncated from the full theological slogan: "Let my people go so they might *sheret* me." The Hebrew word *sheret* has multiple meanings (serve, worship, feast, sacrifice) and is translated in the Septuagint (LXX) as *leitourgia* (*laos*, people + *ergon*, work). This often painful and difficult work of liberation is therefore not the mere absence of slavery nor is it self-determination. It is related to coming to know a very different imitation of godlikeness, and the kind of work and building-up it requires, than that provided by Pharaoh, a regime to which the people remain captive in significant habituated forms of desire, thought and practice. If the people are to recognize a new possibility of godlikeness they must first be reeducated by worshipping a mysterious God in the difficult circumstances of everyday life in the wilderness, learning patiently, through liturgical practice translated into life, a new vision and new skills—a new ethics—by which to inhabit a more just economy. This vision of political theology and political economy is the seedbed of messianism that pervades the New Testament. Hebrews 8 suggests that the Messiah Jesus is the *leitourgos* who mediates a new and better liturgy and the "true tent" of divine dwelling, not realized in the Mosaic law but in a *nomos* written in the minds

---

6. See Brueggemann, "Scripture: Old Testament," 7–20.

7. In my 2013 J. J. Thiessen lectures at Canadian Mennonite University, given as "Mennonites and Mammon: Economies of Desire in a Post-Christian World," now published as *Empire Erotics and Messianic Economies of Desire,* I offer a cohesive dramatic account of the messianic vision that also underlies these essays.

and hearts of the people, in fulfillment of Jeremiah 31:31–34. In Hebrews we also get the first Christian elaboration of Melchizedek, the priest-king so important for Augustine's account of messianic political theology. Also in Hebrews, this is explicitly tied to an exilic vision of messianic faith so central also for Augustine's Pauline claim (rooted in the Hebrew scriptures) that "the just shall live by faith."

Among the most interesting recent interventions in political theology are those that identify the importance of Henri de Lubac's Augustinian *Corpus Mysticum* for critically revisiting significant visions of the western political tradition. Jennifer Rust argues that both Carl Schmitt and Ernst Kantorowicz flatten out theoretically (and non-theologically) what de Lubac presents as an originally dynamic and performative, doxological and ethical, relation between *ekklēsia* and Eucharist so as to further their own genealogical projects of secular political order.[8] Schmitt in particular seeks to recover a role for the secular power of Christendom as imperial "restrainer" (*katechon*, 2 Thess 2:6–7) of antinomian evil through the exercise of state sovereignty modeled on Romans 13. Erik Peterson criticized this on Augustinian grounds, arguing that a Trinitarian theology resists all attempts to ground a human politics.[9] I believe de Lubac's sacramental ecclesiocentrism, rooted in the Pauline and Augustinian vision of the messianic body as fully divine and fully human, both mystically hidden and fully public, offers a more compelling critique of Carl Schmitt's secularized Christendom political theology than that offered by Erik Peterson—not least because it is finally more Augustinian. Jacob Taubes, in keeping with Peterson's position, suggests that Augustinian Christianity rejects the "problem" of political theology by "eschatologizing" the apocalypse—i.e., "domesticating" messianic sovereignty by restricting it to the church.[10] As I hope will become clear, I do not consider this to be an accurate portrayal of Augustine.

Now it is true that Peterson's critique could be read another way; that is, he wants to subvert any and every compromise of the public witness of the messianic community entailed in shoring up a secular polis that does not liturgically participate in the messianic sovereignty of the heavenly Jerusalem. As neither Jewish nor pagan, at home in no earthly city, the Christian's citizenship is in heaven, the public cult of which on earth is the *ekklēsia*. On Peterson's reading of the Book of Revelation, Hebrews and Paul, the liturgical political worship of the church is a participation in the cosmic sovereignty of its heavenly imperator, Christ, whose eschatological *imperium* is "opposed to all *imperia*

---

8. Rust, "Political Theologies of the *Corpus Mysticum*"; see also Pecknold, "Migrations of the Host: Fugitive Democracy and the *Corpus Mysticum*," who argues that Sheldon Wolin's "fugitive democracy" (or democracy "in exile") critique of liberal democracy owes much to de Lubac's work because "de Lubac imagined a 'mystical body politics' that was more inclusive, more humanizing and ultimately more social than the isolating politics of the modern, liberal state" (99), but that ultimately this cannot be detached from de Lubac's Augustinian ecclesiology of a visible, public messianic body.

9. Peterson's famous rejection of political theology is found in an essay that begins and ends with appeals to Augustine, "Monotheism as a Political Problem": "In this way, not only was monotheism as a political problem resolved and the Christian faith liberated from bondage to the Roman Empire, but a fundamental break was made with every 'political theology' that misuses the Christian proclamation for the justification of a political situation." Peterson, *Theological Tractates*, 104.

10. Taubes, *Political Theology of Paul*, 109; Taubes, *Occidental Eschatology*, 79–80, 86. Another recent version of this story is told by Northcott, "Revolutionary Messianism and the End of Empire," in *A Political Theology of Climate Change*, esp. 277ff.

of this world," and whose *militia* on earth is made up only of martyrs.[11] This mirrors O'Donovan's church as "eschatological society"; it is, by definition, otherworldly or "afterworldly" and represents in its cultic worship the hidden kingdom of the ascended Christ. O'Donovan's reading of Colossians 2:15, Paul's claim that the principalities and powers that govern the world have been publicly subjected to divine sovereignty through the messianic rule of Jesus, qualifies this Pauline claim. While Paul claims that the messianic "disarming" (*apekdusamenos*: "stripping off the clothing") of these authorities has been accomplished by the cross in "full public openness" (*en parresia*), thus founding a new cosmic sovereignty, O'Donovan argues that until the final *parousia* of Christ, Paul's messianic political theology must be content to authorize a "stripped down" version of secular authority (Rom 13) whose judicial task is to protect the social space for Christian mission. In this way does O'Donovan also agree with Schmitt regarding the *katechonic* (2 Thess 2) role of the state as restraining evil through judicial authority.[12]

Giorgio Agamben provides yet another reading of Peterson that may help bring us back to why de Lubac is so important.[13] In contrast to the political theology of Carl Schmitt that emphasizes the transcendent sovereignty of the one God, Peterson's emphasis on the public liturgical participation in the trinitarian divine economy opens the door for an "economic" political theology and an exploration of the doxological role of divine glory in the messianic *oikos* that may help break down the classical distinction between the private *oikos* and the public *polis,* between governmentality or pastoral household management and public juridical sovereignty. Such a broadening of the political and economic, Agamben argues, may be traced back to early Christianity—and especially to Paul, who calls himself an "economist of the mysteries of God" (1 Cor 4:1; cf. 9:17; Col 1:25). That is, Paul understands his messianic mission (and that of the body of Christ) as one of servanthood or stewardship of the economy of divine mystery, an ongoing apocalypse of the recapitulation of "all things" in Christ (Eph 1:10).

Agamben, like Peterson, suggests that this Pauline language is not really political but rather more accurately an economic theology—Paul is interested in "building up" (*oikodomei,* 1 Cor 8:1; 10:23) the messianic body, which is a liturgical community but not a *polis.*[14] Here again Agamben radically divides what Paul unites, and it is because he remains unattuned to Paul's *theological* claims. When Agamben claims that the overtly political language of Philippians 1:27, 3:20, and Ephesians 2:19 is "exceptional" and "decidedly impolitical," he misses the apocalyptic mood and substance of Paul's messianic political theology. The building Paul refers to in 1 Corinthians 3:10f. has a messianic foundation, the mystery disclosed in the crucified "Lord of glory" (1 Cor 2:7) that the

---

11. Peterson, "Christ as *Imperator,*" in *Theological Tractates,* 147.

12. Regarding O'Donovan's attempt to use Rom 13:1–5 as the Pauline authorization of a new christological grounding for the judicial role of the secular state, I find the following counter-reading (originally against Oscar Cullmann) by G. B. Caird useful: "The powers of state are to be obeyed not because they have been made subject to Christ but simply because they exist, and because no authority can exist apart from God's decree. . . . Paul achieves the universal centrality of Christ not by making the authority of the powers depend on the Cross but by declaring that Christ is God's agent in creation." Caird, *Principalities and Powers,* 25.

13. Agamben, *The Kingdom and the Glory.*

14. Ibid., 24–25. By contrast, see Blumenfeld, *The Political Paul.*

"rulers of the world" failed to see but that is pneumatically disclosed to all who share in the "mind [*nous*] of Christ" (2:16). The more intimate sphere of *oikos* is also public and political, which is why the "household relations" addressed in Paul's letters are politically constituted in the same messianic mystery, which is also a "mind." When Paul says "be citizens [*politeuesthe*] worthy of the constitution, the gospel"[15] (Phil 1:27), he makes references to the *politeuma* founded in heaven (Phil 3:20) where the messianic power governs. Hence the appropriateness of Paul's conjunction of political and economic language in Ephesians 2:19: "you are fellow citizens [*sympolitai*] with the saints and members of the household [*oikeioi*] of God" as a building being built for divine dwelling. The point is that for Paul, as for all the New Testament authors, heaven is not a "place" or "other world" (as Nietzsche's *hinterwelt* implies) but an invisible presence in continuity with the visible world ("on earth as it is in heaven") in a shared messianic political economy.

The point of continuity, however, is consistently the cross. If one is to speak of an economy of glory, therefore, it must be related to the ignominious death of the Messiah crucified by all forms of worldly authority—religious, political, economic, cultural. The only access to the *theologia* is the *oikonomia* of its visible human and earthly representative,[16] the messianic *ekklesia* that corporately shares the "mind [*phroneite*]" (Phil 2:2, 5ff.) of Christ characterized by humility and obedience to death on a cross. In the crucial book 10 of *City of God*, Augustine cites Romans 12 to formulate the embodiment of the "living sacrifice" in the world in conformity with the "form of a servant" offered in the crucified Messiah.[17] There is no radical division between "being" and "acting," between "theology" and "ethics" in this messianic enactment of the mysterious divine reconciliation of "all things" in Christ. For de Lubac this is the sacramental heart of the mystical body of Christ, where "mystical" means more than "moral," but may not, because embodied and enacted in the everyday life of the world, "be in any way taken as synonymous with 'invisible.'"[18]

This allows de Lubac, following Augustine,[19] to call all members of the messianic body both "Christs" and "priests," and it allows me to dare place Mennonites (and the Radical Reformation), with their emphasis on the visible priesthood of all believers, into the Augustinian tradition of political theology understood as *corpus mysticum*. Eucharistic realism and ecclesial realism are united in the sacramental realism of the messianic body,[20] which has implications for political theology. It should be noted that in Augustine's biblical-exegetical formulation of messianic political theology in books 15–18 of *City of God*, which establishes the context for interpreting book 19 (itself placed into

---

15. Blumenfeld's translation, *Political Paul*, 138.

16. This is Hans Urs von Balthasar's account of Henri de Lubac's "ecclesiocentrism," to which we shall return. See *Theology of Henri de Lubac*, 115ff.

17. See especially Augustine, *City of God* 10.6 and 10.20. Cf. Augustine, *The Trinity* 14.22 where this same transformative process according the the "form of a servant" is related to Romans 12.

18. de Lubac, *The Splendor of the Church*, 91. Cf. *Corpus Mysticum*, chap. 3.

19. *City of God* 20.10

20. de Lubac, *Corpus Mysticum*, 248–56.

Augustine's apocalyptic conclusion, books 19–22),²¹ the priest-king of Salem, Melchizedek, plays a more prominent prophetic and figural role than does Israel's king David.²² This is significant for Augustine's claim that the messianic body must take the form of its priest-king, namely the form of the servant—a form prefigured in Melchizedek's offering of bread and wine to Abraham (Gen 14:17–18), taken up in the royal messianic Psalm 110:4, and applied to Christ in Hebrews 5–7. The righteousness of this royal figure, also attached to "Salem," or the city of peace that David renames Jerusalem (the possession of no tribe), is one that rules through the sacrifice of humility displayed above all in Christ and the martyrs. Augustine crucially and consistently relates the political question of peace to the apocalyptic question of worship, a liturgical worship that is also always represented as an incarnational ethic that takes the servant form of diaspora or pilgrimage in the secular world.

The diaspora ethics that I am here relating to messianic political theology is nicely characterized by Augustine as one of proper use and enjoyment: a secular life in which we "make use of earthly goods like pilgrims, without grasping after them."²³ But this use is sacrificially offered up with reference to God so that "inflamed by the fire of divine love," the form of worldly desire may be messianically reformed to reflect divine desire.²⁴ This is what it means to be economists of the divine mystery, and one of the great witnesses to this ethic of political economy in our time is Wendell Berry, who resurrects the term "usufruct" as the measure of good stewardship.²⁵ He suggests that the biblical passage most valuable in displaying this relationship is Revelation 4:11, in a suitably archaic translation: "Thou art worthy, O Lord, to receive glory and honor and power: for thou hast created all things, and for thy pleasure they are and were created."²⁶ The term *thelēma*, here translated "pleasure," is often translated "will," but the ambiguity is nicely Augustinian—where will and love, and indeed pleasure, are closely related to represent motive power, and Berry calls it "affection in action."²⁷ The same word is used in Romans 12:2 in terms of proving the *thelēma* of God as the measure of the completion of "all things," and Jesus himself prays: "thy *thelēma* be done on earth as it is in heaven" (Matt 6:10). The liturgical agency of worship entails attending in our use ("as if not" possessing) of worldly goods to God's pleasure in all things so as to bring about a divinely informed affection in action called "peace" or "wellbeing" or "shalom." Such messianic

---

21. I fully agree with Gregory Lee's argument that *City of God* 19 requires the apocalyptic contextualization of the earlier books to show that "the difference between the two cities on the *summum bonum* is, in fact, the difference between heaven and hell." Lee, "Republics and Their Loves," 558. This is related to Lee's point that a better metaphor for interpreting Augustine's treatment of the relation between the two cities in *City of God* 19.17 than the authority of institutional political offices is Augustine's repeated comparison of the Christian situation to the Israelites in the Babylonian captivity (571); hence, "Augustine's primary metaphor for the church's relation to the world is not citizenship but captivity" (574).

22. Augustine, *City of God*, 16.22; 17.5, 17, 20; 18.35; 20.10, 21.

23. Ibid., 1.29; in 1.10 he provides Paul's apocalyptic warrant for this ethic, given in 1 Cor 7:31: "make use of the world as if not [*hōs mē*] using it," for the form of this world is passing away.

24. *City of God*, 10.6. Augustine cites Romans 12:2.

25. Berry, *What Are People For*, 98ff.

26. Ibid., 100, 136.

27. Ibid., 136.

passion, far from ruining the world (as Lilla thinks it does), will attend to the exhortation of the seer: "Awake, and strengthen what remains and is on the point of death" (Rev 3:2).

Mennonites as a people came into being by the desire, even unto martyrdom, of taking this messianic posture and practice seriously in all aspects of everyday human life, the *oikia*. I have called this stance (Part 2) "Radical Reformation" in recognition of George Hunston Williams's nice historiographical observation, picked up by Mennonite historians, that this movement may be just as well if not better understood as a worldly or "secular" vocational continuation of medieval monasticism, a monasticism in the world. This is not simply a matter of a voluntary ecclesial identity or commitment to "pacifism," but of a coherent and interrelated pattern (let's call it *nomos*) of communal discipleship that includes economic simplicity and the renunciation of possessive desire. This is also in keeping with a Pauline economy (*oikonomia*, sometimes translated "commission," 1 Cor 9:17) that inhabits the mysterious freedom of messianic slavery in order to build up (*oikodome*,[28] 1 Cor 8:1; 10:23) the common world that is nevertheless passing away (1 Cor 7:31). The *nomos* of economic language here helps break down the sharp distinction between *oikos/oikia* (household) and *polis* (politics) that has long prevented the exploration of a more radical biblical political theology in which so-called "domestic" (or indeed "private") relations and institutional orders may not be separated from or opposed to "public" or "political" forms of organization and authority. We all know how our everyday, intimate decisions are also very much tied to public, political judgments. This "love-knowledge" also opens up the entire Bible to a more figural political-ethical interpretation of the sort that I'm attempting in these essays. It would require the church, as an institutional ordering—the particular embodiment of the "messianic body"—to relate itself actively and critically to all aspects of the economy of divine government which presides providentially over "all things." This might enable Mennonites, with their long-term intimate preoccupations with land and family, to become more openly and critically engaged with the ways in which these orderings are implicated in the wider "principalities and powers" of fallen created existence. It would also make it more difficult for mainstream Christian theology to marginalize the Anabaptist-Mennonite perspective as "a-political" or sectarian.

Here might be the place to reflect upon the controversial political theologian whose work features significantly in these pages, especially in Part 2; namely, John Howard Yoder. Yoder will not be forgotten, as much for his prodigious failures as for his prodigious gifts, and we should continue to be instructed by both. While the essays in part 2 were written prior to the unveiling in full public openness of Yoder's furtive and powerfully destructive "pilot projects" in human sexuality,[29] they already identify a theological problem in his revolutionary account of the performative doxological practices of communal discipleship entailed in the messianic politics of Jesus. That problem has to do

---

28. *Oikodomein*, an important verb for Paul, is primarily an apocalyptic and messianic concept, the *Theological Dictionary of the New Testament* tells us (vol. 5, 139). It is simultaneously theological as well as political and ethical.

29. See Goossen, "Defanging the Beast," and the entire issue of *The Mennonite Quarterly Review* 89/1 (January 2015). Yoder's long-term international pattern of sexual "experimentation" and violation included the unwanted sexual harrassment and abuse of dozens of women, including his students, over the course of his career.

with an inadequate account of desire and its messianic reconfiguration in both the self and the wider social body, a problem rooted, I contend, in too limited an interpretation of apocalyptic messianic sovereignty. Yoder it seems could not or would not bring his sexuality in obedient weakness to the power of the cross, nor was he required to do so by his accommodated church and Christian educational institutions (let us not limit the denominational "jurisdictions"). And, let's be honest, this is no easy task, personally or communally. The apostle Paul thought it required daily death.

While this is too confined a space in which to elaborate this, let me briefly engage the recent work of Paul Martens to gesture at my meaning.[30] Martens develops a critique of Yoder in tandem with a critique of contemporary Anabaptism: its self-righteousness based on an impossible perfectionism, an overly stark contrast between church and world, and an excessive confidence in the visibility of soul or spirit in embodied temporal life—all of which may contribute to religious and social violence. He cites Jean Calvin's critique of Anabaptists—"one will scarcely find an Anabaptist who is not tainted with fantasy"—to argue that Yoder's pernicious exercise of the freedom of a messianic ethicist requires a limit to that freedom which should not be entrusted to an ecclesial politics rooted in appeals to "the perfection of Christ" (such as that found in the *Schleitheim Confession*). Tellingly, Calvin's critique was directed not so much at the practice of believer's baptism but at the ineffectual and unrealistic Anabaptist practice of the ban as a form of church discipline modeled upon Matthew 18; a form, Martens argues, that "did not stop Yoder."[31] Perhaps, Martens implies, it is time for Anabaptists to consider again the more "balanced" model of Christendom political theology where the spiritual authority of the church is limited (and chastened) by the embodied, sword-bearing authority of the state as a necessary restraint.

I am in complete sympathy with a strong critique of Yoder's behavior and of the self-righteous triumphalism of a Mennonite perfectionism rooted in spiritual arrogance that claims to possess messianic authority due to some kind of pacifist "purity," while underneath the hidden beast rages. Nietzsche was right to sniff out the hypocrisies of the Christian power game that would love to rule in world-historical humility with its crucified heavenly king. However, would "calling the police" (as Martens suggests) have resulted in a more effective agency for protecting potential victims and dealing with a powerful perp such as Yoder? Could not a case be made that the mainline, acculturated North American institutional authorities did not even attempt to practice the more transparent communal disciplines related to accountability, violation and forgiveness entailed in Matthew 18? Could the Yoder case be equally illustrative of the failures of accommodated, antinomian liberalism as it is of the failure of the ban—which, it might be argued, was practiced (if at all) only in the most half-hearted, non-transparent, and cowardly institutional of ways? What is perhaps most shocking is how complicit, secretive and hypocritical Yoder himself was about it—not at all in keeping with a "revolutionary"

---

30. Martens, "Anabaptist Ethics After Yoder"; see also Martens, *The Heterodox Yoder*. I have responded to the latter in more detail in the symposium on it: "Overcoming Historicism: Weak Messianic Apocalypticism," for *Syndicatetheology.com* (June 2014). Print version in *Syndicate: A New Forum for Theology* 1/1 (May–June 2014) 87–93.

31. Martens, "Anabaptist Ethics," 120. On this, see especially, painfully, Chapter 7.

messianic politics. Lamentable as it is, I do not believe that any external or formulaic "limitation" of Christian freedom (so conceived it is in fact no freedom at all from a messianic perspective) will protect victims from perpetrators or perpetrators from their most pernicious desires. The most important issue in Martens's helpful analysis of the logic of Christian freedom is the question of messianic *obedience*. Only obedient imitation of the form of the servant which liberates desire from its clinging, possessive, self-righteous ways will lead to the renewal of mind via discipleship that may prove the *thelema* of God as the perfection or completion of all things. This is a logic defined by messianic *imitation* not the balanced *limitation* of institutional authorities in a power game. It requires more justice, not less; more challenging practices, not less righteous ones. This "more" (*perisson*, Matt 5:20, 47) is spelled out in the constitutional messianic "new law" of love given in the Sermon on the Mount, delivered by Jesus after his exodus in the wilderness where he undergoes temptation concerning the political theological terms of his vocation. This *nomos* is not an external moral code; it is rooted in a cosmic drama of divine-human intimacy in which the terms of divine justice or shalom may be realized on earth as in heaven. The Sermon on the Mount represents a parabolic elaboration of these terms of divine governance in which the desire of the heart is central.

How does this depict the drama of self-emptying desire? First of all, it has something to do with the baptism of humble repentance, mercy and forgiveness rather than self-righteous reliance upon inherited religious identities. Secondly, it has something to do with a righteousness or justice that exceeds a presumptive religio-cultural knowledge of good and evil that parades itself hypocritically in order to be seen and praised by an adoring human public. In other words, the six antitheses in Jesus's Sermon, which are sometimes called "counsels of perfection" because they seek conformity with the perfection of the heavenly Father (Matt 5:48; cf. 19:21 where it is given an explicitly economic meaning!), are not intended to provide a new visible code of external moral conformity. Rather they are parables of the total motivating orientation ("desire") of the whole human person in the divine-human economy of heaven and earth: not simply the prohibition of *porneia*, but complete lived fidelity to others drained of the possessive desire called lust; not mere prohibition of swearing ostentatious public oaths but complete truthfulness emptied of the desire to appear trustworthy; not mere prohibition of insult and retributive desire but complete love, even of enemies and persecutors, emptied of legal claims and counterclaims. All of this assumes the self-emptying of the desire to possess righteousness or even the reputation for being righteous and the political and personal power that might go along with it, through the messianic imitation of divine perfection.

Yoder the political theologian emphasized the apocalyptic character of messianic sovereignty but Yoder the powerful professor perhaps liked his "reason" (and brilliant reputation for rational domination) a little too much—perhaps like a belt around his neck[32] overly demarcating the separation of his head from the rest of his body. His preferred mode of reason, as Martens says, quoting Yoder himself, was "less dogmatic than

---

32. Martens, *Heterodox Yoder*, 19, refers to Yoder's youthful breaking of dress conventions, wearing a necktie with a T-shirt or a necktie as a belt.

Introduction

sociological,"[33] that is, Yoder's own account of the *damnamus* of Anabaptist orthodoxy and heterodoxy had to do with "the expressions of wrong community: apostate worship, alcoholic partying, commitments of bad faith, and violence." We notice Yoder's (ostentatious?) omission of *porneia* on this list, though it is high on the list of biblical "wrong expressions," and would get us figurally closer to the radical intimacy of the personal, communal, and cosmic dimensions of divine sovereignty in apocalyptic political theology.[34] That is, the embodied, intimate "desire" question touches more nearly the mysterious heart of this theological-political nexus than do sociological markers, inductively derived and straightforwardly translated into the social ethical "sacramental practices" of the church. Yoder's "sacramentality" is too lacking in *mysterion* (the Greek word that *sacramentum* translates), about which Paul has much to say, precisely with reference to the crucified Christ. Augustine's constant correlation of *exemplum* (outer example) and *sacramentum* (inner mystery) in terms of the inner-outer, visible-invisible tensions of messianic existence make it clear that the sacramental may not simply be translated or collapsed into the exemplary, and none of this is amenable to "direct" witness, whether in speech or in practice. This is a question of how the messianic measure is mediated, and how that mediation becomes "accessible." The essays in this book are an attempt to bear witness to this question.

I am not sure when it became clear to me that this book would be a collection of essays as the proper form in which to express the meaning of messianic political theology and diaspora ethics. I think it was around ten years ago, as most of my writing came in response to invitations that I felt called to accept in order to clarify for myself and others what I thought this might mean. If readers experience a sense of déjà vu, it means they will have read more than a few chapters in this book, and I hope the repetition in places will not be annoying or distracting but possibly also illuminating. It was not until I had completed the final essay, "Technology as Principality," that I felt a sense of completion for this project. In it I come round to a number of themes reiterated throughout these essays having to do with messianic political theology as the quotidian embodiment of divine love. Only a messianic materialism will restore to us the divine mystery of our created embodiment, our "personhood" so as to resist movements of disincarnation that would eliminate divine mystery from the world so as to control it on their own terms. For the messianic Christian tradition, Torah or *nomos* ("law") must be construed in personal or existential terms, in keeping with the personal God whose image it bears. The ordering of creation is the dynamic ordering power of love, which means there are no "fixed" orders of creation but rather a dramatic, contingent "economy" of salvation. For Christians there can be no sharp division between the immanent and the "economic" trinity. Servants of the Messiah are also by definition economists of the messianic economy of divine mystery, the process by which the temporal created order is being reconciled

---

33. Ibid., 92.

34. De Lubac rightly notes that for Paul and Augustine the Eucharistic mystery offered in the ecclesial sacrifice is an enactment not only of the mystery of the Cross but also the nuptial mystery identified by Paul as the "great mystery," the "one flesh" of Bridegroom and Bride (Eph 5:32)—a mystery that is indefusably spiritual and embodied. *Splendor of the Church*, chap. 4; *Corpus Mysticum*, chap. 1. Wendell Berry is more explicit when he says that "sexual love is the heart of community life" and he means this sacramentally, as I argue in "Sexuality and the Sacramental Imagination."

to eternal love. If this is so, then perhaps the process of manifesting this economy in personal and political terms is more a parabolic practice of the messianic enactments of divine mystery than an institution-making science. Perhaps the embodied "living sacrifice" as the "rational worship" (*latreia logikē*, Rom 12:1) that frees the messianic mind from conformity to a world of rampant disincarnation may continue to find ways of breaking down economic dividing walls of hostility based on nature (male/female), religion (Jew/Greek), and sociopolitical status (slave/free). In his famous address to the Athenians (Acts 17:16–31), Paul relates the teaching that all human beings are generated by the divine as God's offspring to the teaching about the resurrection of the body. The resurrection is the vindication of the mystery of divine incarnation, and it is celebrated in the sacrament of this sacrificial embodiment—not only as a ritual liturgical event, but in all events that bear witness to the death of the self-desiring ego in order to be reborn into the "one mind" of messianic kinship where in humility we work to build up this divine economy in our shared mortal flesh.

PART 1

Apocalyptic Messianism and Political Theology

1

Living "As If Not"

Messianic Becoming or the Practice of Nihilism?

Where is the wise? Where is the scribe? Where is the debater of this age? Hath not God made foolish the wisdom of the world? . . . But God has chosen what is foolish in the world to confound the wise; God has chosen what is weak in the world to confound the things which are mighty. And base things and things which are despised in the world hath God chosen, yea, and things that are not, to bring to nought things that are. (1 Cor 1:20, 27–28)

WHAT MIGHT THIS CONFOUNDING messianic wisdom have to say to contemporary political philosophy? In *The Antichrist* Nietzsche cites this passage at length to show how completely out of touch with reality the dysangelist Paul really was. He calls Paul the greatest of all apostles of revenge, an insolent windbag who tries to confound worldly wisdom—but to no effect, says Nietzsche.[1] Nietzsche notwithstanding, certain recent Continental philosophers have been reading Paul the Apostle's confounding letters to great effect, allowing his messianic message to disrupt certain modern conventions, political ontologies, and habits of mind; to challenge the technological globalizing wisdom and rulers of this age and suggest a hidden messianic counter-sovereignty not conceived in any human heart. Modern political theory has often regarded messianic political theology in particular as a dangerous threat to secular liberal democracy—and not without reason. Yet it is also the case that the first theory of the *saeculum* in the West, Augustine's *City of God*, was developed precisely within a Pauline apocalyptic messianic understanding of history and the political. It is also the case that notions of neutral technology and juridical state sovereignty that underlie current conceptions and embodiments of the secular are themselves dangerously totalitarian, exclusivist, and violent, though this is often hidden beneath the veneer of progressivist liberal assumptions.

1. Nietzsche, *Antichrist*, sec. 46.

PART 1: APOCALYPTIC MESSIANISM AND POLITICAL THEOLOGY

This is the position articulated in the apocalyptic messianism of Walter Benjamin, whose position is closely related to that of Paul's in the New Testament on the question of sovereignty, which is the central focus of this essay. The political theological concept at the heart of modern secular politics and political theory was given its classical formulation by Carl Schmitt. "Sovereign is he who decides on the exception," says Schmitt, which requires that sovereignty be seen not in strictly juridical terms but as a limit concept in which there is an agential power behind the law who decides on the "state of emergency" that suspends the normal rule of law.[2] This founding notion of sovereignty must be read together with Schmitt's founding definition of the political, namely, the distinction between friend and enemy.[3] For Schmitt the ultimate challenge to this basic political principle is found in the words of Jesus: "Love your enemies" (Matt 5:44)—which Schmitt, in keeping with conventional Christendom ethics, regards as a private ethic, a spiritual and individual, not a public political, ethic. Surely former President George W. Bush would agree. So also would ultraliberal Canadian Prime Minister Pierre Trudeau have agreed when he invoked the War Measures Act in Canada during the FLQ (Front de Libération du Québec) kidnapping crisis of 1970, thus deciding the exception that suspended "normal law" in the face of an "emergency situation."

Walter Benjamin had precisely this definition of sovereignty in mind when he wrote his eighth thesis on the philosophy of history:

> The tradition of the oppressed teaches us that the "state of emergency" in which we live . . . is the rule. We must attain to a conception of history that is in keeping with this insight. Then we shall clearly realize that it is our task to bring about a real state of emergency, and this will improve our position in the struggle against Fascism. One reason why Fascism has a chance is that in the name of progress its opponents treat it as a historical norm. The current amazement that the things we are experiencing are "still" possible in the twentieth century is *not* philosophical. This amazement is not the beginning of knowledge.[4]

Benjamin clearly sets himself against this secular progressivist politics to which all seeming political options are conformed, and he does so in the name of a "*weak* Messianic power" in which each day is lived as the day of judgment on which the Messiah comes, "not only as the redeemer" but also "as the overcomer of Antichrist."[5] Such a "Messianic time" may not be thought of within the categories of historicism but only from the perspective of a *Jetztzeit* (Thesis 18), a "real state of emergency" that calls into fundamental question the normal state of emergency—the politics of modern secular state sovereignty—in which we live. It will bring into view the violent and destructive foundation of this sovereignty with its homogeneous and totalitarian order by remembering another sovereignty, a messianic counter-sovereignty that reorders the secular on completely

---

2. Schmitt, *Political Theology*, 15.
3. Schmitt, *Concept of the Political*, 26–37.
4. Benjamin, "Theses on the Philosophy of History," Thesis 8.
5. Ibid., Theses 2 and 6.

different terms, terms compatible, argue certain recent Continental philosophers, with Paul's gospel.[6]

The apostle Paul stands in the messianic tradition of biblical political theology, where the central overriding claim is "Yahweh is sovereign," a claim that subverts any merely human claim to sovereignty and political authority. This includes, as Jacob Taubes points out, any claims for the sovereignty of law—whether that law be the Torah mediated by Moses or the nomos mediated by Greco-Roman philosophy, or (we might add) the Christendom tradition of secular juridical state sovereignty and its many modern liberal copies. "We preach Messiah crucified," says Paul, "to the Jews a stumbling block and to the Greeks foolishness" (1 Cor 1:23), and to triumphalist globalizing Christians, one might add, a foolish scandal. Paul's messianism will not accommodate conventional discourses of human mastery—which is to say, all conventional political discourses. As Alain Badiou puts it, for Paul the "becoming subject" founded by the messianic event "is a-cosmic and illegal, refusing integration into any totality and signalling nothing."[7] For Badiou, Paul's relevance for the contemporary political situation is precisely to counter the relativism of postmodern identity politics, the multicultural consensus of neoliberal progressivism that has become conscripted to the globalized logic of capital. Here the only common currency is the abstract imperialist count of commercial and economic homogeneity—an empty universality that cashes out all communitarianisms. The beneficence of contemporary French cosmopolitanism that gets worked up at the sight of a young veiled woman nicely displays this problem.[8]

Into this political context Badiou proposes the radical disruption of Paul's messianic proclamation concerning the conditions for a "universal singularity" that defies the globalizing logic of the count, and its prevailing juridical and economic abstractions. It does so by an appeal to what Badiou calls an "evental truth" that reconfigures the universal messianically with reference to the resurrection, as a human "becoming subject" in relation to a truth that is universal but not abstract.[9] For Badiou, Paul is a "poet-thinker of the event" that neither constitutes nor claims authority from an identity or a law. It cannot therefore be a logic of mastery. Rather it is a discourse of rupture, a discourse of the sending of the Son that is detached from every particularism and every form of

---

6. See especially Taubes, *Political Theology of Paul*; Agamben, *Time That Remains*; Agamben, "The Messiah and the Sovereign."

7. Badiou, *Saint Paul*, 42.

8. Ibid., 9–11.

9. In using this language of "becoming subject," Badiou recalls Martin Heidegger's phenomenology of the religious life, in which Heidegger meditates on the meaning of Paul's "having become" language in 1 Thessalonians 1–2, which Heidegger relates to the "coming" of Messiah. See Heidegger, *Phenomenology of Religious Life*, pt. 1, 65–67. That is, for Heidegger as for Badiou, Paul's central concern is with the *how* of subjective enactment, not the *what* of a theoretical teaching, and is therefore characterized by proclamation and not the theorization of objective content (*Phenomenology of Religious Life*, 83–87)—which is what Badiou means when he calls Paul "an *antiphilosophical theoretician of universality*" (*Saint Paul*, 108) that must not conceptualize but rather must subjectively enact the universal. Behind Heidegger, of course, lies Kierkegaard's Pauline emphasis on subjective enactment, though Kierkegaard will radically integrate and not divide the christic "how" and "what" of messianic becoming. That is, Heidegger's (and Badiou's) reading is influenced on this point more by Nietzsche than by Kierkegaard. I hope my essay will help to show why this is significant.

PART 1: APOCALYPTIC MESSIANISM AND POLITICAL THEOLOGY

mastery. Paul's apostolic calling is characterized by "militant peregrinations,"[10] a "nomad leadership"[11] that is equally out of place everywhere, a "nomadism of gratuitousness"[12] that exceeds every law and therefore disrupts every established identity and difference. Evental grace has a particular site, of course, but the "becoming subject" that it founds is one that must "displace the experience historically, geographically, ontologically": it can do that not by escaping the embodied particularity of customs and differences, but rather by "passing through them, within them."[13] As Paul puts it in 1 Corinthians 9:19–22, "For though I am free from all . . . I have become all things to all people."

For Badiou, then, Paul's messianic logic offers a critique of all onto-theologies, all discourses of mastery rooted in appeals to wisdom and power as divine attributes. It does this by making possible an advent of subjectivity as "becoming son," a process of messianic filiation rooted in the foolish and scandalous power of weakness (1 Cor 1:17–29). This means that, contra Nietzsche, such a messianic becoming may not become a subject discourse of glorification that builds a new economy of power and wisdom on the strength of the ineffable. Paul will not glory in his mystical visions or try to tell "things that cannot be told"; he will glory only in his weakness, "for when I am weak, then I am strong" (2 Cor 12:1–10). But what is the "real content" of this "naked declaration" that is borne in militant weakness by messianic earthen vessels?[14]

Here the Continental clouds of fabulation begin to obscure the figure of the real, of the truth procedure that is in question. Badiou is deeply suspicious of any messianic appeal to the way of the cross. While he wants to insist on a Pauline "subjectivity of refuse," of abasement (cf. 1 Cor 4:13), this subjectivity must be detached from any historical particularity that would make of Christ a "master" or an "example."[15] The truth that founds the Christian subject is not a matter of historical content; it is a birth, a filiation in which subjects are founded equally and universally as "sons" insofar as they take up the work of filiation. For Badiou's Paul, the law organizes life according to the dictates of death, whereas messianic filiation dwells only in life; this is the meaning of resurrection.[16] Paul himself, however, would have refused Badiou's account of the messianic event. This new gnostic politics of fabulation divides what Paul's messianism unites: the cross and resurrection. Like any good worldly philosopher, Badiou too is finally scandalized by both the cross and a resurrection that testifies to a Messiah raised up by divine agency, the Holy Spirit. That is, like Nietzsche and possibly also Heidegger (to whom Badiou is finally indebted for the "becoming son" language), Badiou is scandalized by Paul's messianic appeals to *pneuma* and the pneumatic. Here I want to turn to Jacob Taubes and his claim that "Nietzsche has been my best teacher about Paul,"[17] precisely because Nietzsche sees Paul correctly as the greatest enemy of his philosophy. Nietzsche

10. Badiou, *Saint Paul*, 19.
11. Ibid., 67.
12. Ibid., 78.
13. Ibid., 99.
14. Ibid., 54.
15. Ibid., 60.
16. Ibid., 62.
17. Taubes, *Political Theology of Paul*, 79.

discerned what is at issue between a "decadent" nihilistic Christianity (founded by Paul) and his own Dionysian higher humanity: the meaning of martyrdom and suffering.[18] Nietzsche's claim is that Paul's invention of the great lie of the messianic "redeemer" trades on the false currency of spiritual causality, a counterfeit transcendence (*Jenseits*) most evident in the nihilistic doctrine of resurrection—a denigration of the "wisdom of this world" that is in fact a slanderous negation of the natural suffering endemic to the realm of human becoming.[19] I shall here examine this central engagement of the question of nihilism and messianic "becoming" in Paul—which is of crucial importance to the current philosophical interest in Paul's political theology, especially on the question of messianic sovereignty.

At the heart of the conflict between Paul's messianic political theology and Nietzsche's Dionysian *Übermensch*, argues Taubes, lies the question of *pneuma*, or spirit.[20] The importance of *pneuma* for Paul is displayed in two crucial distinctions developed in 1 Corinthians 2:

1. between the *pneuma tou kosmou* (spirit of the world) and the *pneuma ek tou theou* (spirit from God) (2:11–12); and

2. between the *pneumatikos* (spiritual human being) and the *psychikos* (sometimes translated "natural human being," who judges not according to the spirit of God but according to the flesh, the immanent spiritual measure of worldly wisdom attuned to the spirit of the world) (2:14–15).

Paul suggests that only those who discern according to the "spirit from God" are able to see in the crucifixion a mysterious and hidden divine wisdom, "not conceived in any human heart" (1 Cor 2:6f.; Kierkegaard's refrain in *Philosophical Fragments*), that counters all human sovereignties which Paul says "are doomed to pass away" (*katargoumenon*, 1 Cor 2:6)—the key word here being one of Paul's favorite apocalyptic verbs: *katargeō/ katargēsis*.[21] Before looking more closely at this verb, however, I want to note that Paul's appeal to the messianic mind, or *nous* (1 Cor 2:16, 1:10) closely relates this spiritual judgment to the mysterious "mind" of the Lord (*kyrios*, sovereign). In 1 Corinthians 2, as in Romans 11:34, Paul is quoting Isaiah 40: "For who has known the mind [*nous*] of the Sovereign?" The Greek *nous* is used in the Septuagint to translate the Hebrew *ruah*, or spirit, so closely linked to understanding in the Torah. The pneumatic messianic mind is therefore an apocalyptic discernment given by divine Spirit, and it is this that scandalizes a natural human wisdom attuned to the spirit of the world, Nietzsche's warrior wisdom which more clearly than Badiou sees what it is up against.

In *Daybreak*, Nietzsche gives us an early indication of his assessment of Paul: Paul's appeals to the "Holy Spirit" and the messianic *katargēsis* of the law through the crucifixion reveal "a mind as superstitious as it was cunning."[22] It is closely related to Christian

---

18. See Nietzsche, *Writings from the Late Notebooks*, 250.
19. See Nietzsche, *Antichrist*, secs. 38–43.
20. Taubes, *Political Theology of Paul*, 43–46.
21. See the excellent discussion in Agamben, *Time That Remains*, 95–97.
22. Nietzsche, *Daybreak*, 68.

philology and the "art of reading badly,"[23] which is to say, the art of spiritual or figural reading.[24] By the time he writes *Der Antichrist*, Nietzsche is much more bitter: "A religion like Christianity, which is completely out of touch with reality, which immediately falls apart if any concession is made to reality, would of course be mortally opposed to the 'wisdom of this world,' which is to say *science* [*Wissenschaft*]."[25] More specifically, this anti-realist Christianity is Paul's invention, of a god who ruins the wisdom of the world in its specific forms of philology and physiology, the two great adversaries of all superstition. "Indeed," says Nietzsche, "one cannot be a philologist or a physician without at the same time being *anti-Christian*."

This we must try to understand before we turn to Paul, for it represents the common sense of our age, as it did for the age of Paul. Let us not forget Nietzsche's comment that there is only a single figure who commands respect in the New Testament and that is Pilate, the Roman governor: "The noble scorn of a Roman, confronted with an impudent abuse of the word 'truth,' has enriched the New Testament with the only saying that *has value*—one which is its criticism, even its *annihilation* [*Vernichtung*]: 'What is truth?'"[26] The greatest crime against humanity committed by Pauline Christianity is the destruction of natural causality by spiritual causality, the replacement of truly philosophical knowledge (human, worldly wisdom) by religious superstition (hidden, "divine" wisdom)—a decadence represented above all by the Pauline teaching on the spiritual resurrection of the body, thus turning away from the natural nobility of this world in favor of a weaker spiritual one. "Once more I recall the inestimable words of Paul: 'The *weak* things of the world, the *foolish* things of the world, the *base* and *despised* things of the world hath God chosen.' This was the formula; *in hoc signo* decadence triumphed."[27] The teaching of the resurrection, of course, puts the scandal of miracle at the heart of reality: God creates the world *ex nihilo* at each moment; the world is not an immanent becoming according to causal laws of nature. Nietzsche's use of the *in hoc si-*

23. Ibid., 84.

24. See the illuminating accounts of Paul's typological hermeneutics as spiritual or figural, not allegorical, reading in Breton, *Saint Paul*, chap. 2; Taubes, *Political Theology of Paul*, 38–54; Agamben, *Time That Remains*, 62–87. Erich Auerbach has provided an important account of "figural interpretation" as the connection between two historical events in their spiritual relation to divine providence—a relation that therefore cannot be reduced either to historical causality or semiotic representations of meaning. Figural interpretation relies on a mimetic discernment understood as a spiritual act that deals with historical events experientially rather than in conceptual abstraction. The temporal participates in and points toward the eternal for its meaning, which therefore requires spiritual attentiveness and imitation if it is to be apprehended—as an enactment. See Auerbach, *Mimesis*. We are reminded here of Benjamin's description of the messianic *Jetztzeit* as coinciding precisely with "the" *Figur* that human history has in the universe: "*Die Jetztzeit, die als Modell der messianischen in einer ungeheueren Abbreviatur die Geschichte der ganzen Menschheit zusammenfasst, fällt haarschaft mit der Figure zusammen, die die Geschichte der Menschheit im Universum macht*"; and again "*der Jetztzeit, in welcher Splitter der messianischen eingesprengt sind*" (Thesis 18; Benjamin, "Über den Begriff der Geschichte," 261). This description established for Benjamin the manner in which Jews experience their liturgical "remembrance" (*Eingedenken*) of the past: "Every second of time was the narrow gate through which the Messiah might enter" (my translation).

25. Nietzsche, *Antichrist*, sec. 47.

26. Ibid., sec. 46.

27. Ibid., sec. 51.

gno is an ironic reference to the *in hoc signo vinces* of the Constantinian slogan, in which the sign of contradiction and weakness, the cross, becomes attached to triumphalistic state religion, the cross and the sword, Christian sovereignty religion—a development for which Nietzsche holds Paul responsible.

In *Twilight of the Idols* Nietzsche clarifies his alternative to Pauline spiritual causality when he states flatly that there are no spiritual causes, only instinctive ones.[28] While he agrees with the Pauline displacement of the human ego (i.e., "will" for Nietzsche is not rooted in spiritual consciousness or subjective ego),[29] he argues for the primacy of instinctual drives, or the will to power. His argument against Pauline Christianity is that it privileges weak and decadent instincts by cultivating a divinely willed pity that "makes suffering contagious"[30] and persuades human beings to *nothingness*, the practice of nihilism. As such, Christian culture loses its natural, noble instincts, its rootedness in "life itself" as "the instinct for growth, for durability, for an accumulation of forces, for *power*: where the will to power is lacking there is decline,"[31] there is decadence.[32] In keeping with this analysis, Nietzsche argues for the revaluation of all Pauline values by posing the problem of what type of higher human being may be bred and willed that is worthier of life, more attuned to strong natural instincts. This is his Dionysian *Übermensch*, to which I shall return later.

First let us now consider more carefully Paul's apocalyptic verb, *katargēsis*, rooted as it is in a *mē*-ontology that so offends Nietzsche. I wish to show that Paul might be considered not so much a nihilist as a messianic "*ex nihilo*-ist" who at every moment seeks to dwell in the power of divine life, a power displayed above all in the crucifixion, that emblem of worldly weakness and failure (Constantine and triumphalist Christendom notwithstanding). *Katargēsis* is the verb Paul uses in 1 Corinthians 1:28 with reference to the cross, God choosing the things without being (*ta mē onta*) in order to bring to nothing (*katargēsē*) the things with being (*ta onta*). The same verb is used also in 1 Corinthians 15:24, where Paul with reference to resurrection says Messiah will *katargēsē* every earthly rule and authority and power, including death. Nietzsche is right to detect here Paul's understanding of sovereign divine freedom as a power realized in weakness; that is, as Stanislas Breton puts it, "it is nothing of what we would like it to be."[33] God does not inhabit our human dwellings, and to discern the passage of God in a world that is passing away requires a mortification of natural inclination—the sort of inclination displayed by Paul in Romans 1 (the desire to worship the creature rather than the Creator), but also the sort aroused or "energized" by the law (Rom 7). While Nietzsche admires the sovereign divine freedom here, he despises and suspects Paul's tying this to the mortification of the flesh as another worldly power play, despicably hypocritical be-

---

28. Nietzsche, *Twilight of the Idols*, 495.

29. Nietzsche, *Writings from the Late Notebooks*, 59: "All deeper men—Luther, Augustine, Paul come to mind—agree that our morality and its events do not correspond with our *conscious will*—in short, that an explanation in terms of having goals [teleological causality] is *insufficient*."

30. Nietzsche, *Antichrist*, sec. 7.

31. Ibid., sec. 6.

32. Ibid., sec. 17.

33. Breton, *Word and the Cross*, 50.

cause it uses the crucified Christ to establish a new, anti-natural and therefore decadent law. Nietzsche of course *has* to take this line, since he refuses the realism of faith in the miracle of pneumatic divine creation *ex nihilo* as expressed, for Paul, in the Messiah Jesus.

In Romans 7 Paul talks about "dying to the law through the body of Messiah" in order to live in the life of the Spirit. His argument is that the law goes to the heart of desire, and indeed Paul quotes the summing commandment in Exodus 20:17, "You shall not desire [Septuagint, *epithumēseis*]," which echoes Eve's response to the prohibition pertaining to the tree of knowledge of good and evil: "The tree was to be desired to make one wise" (Gen 3:6). The law thus addresses the root of sin, violence, and death: my desire to possess for myself, my "ego," my flesh, all the goods belonging not only to my neighbor in the socio-mimetic cult of desire, but also all the goods belonging to God in the ethico- and religio-mimetic cult of judicial, moral, and spiritual desire for sovereign divine perfection/wisdom/authority. For Paul there is no escape from the fallen desire of the human condition which is held captive and might indeed find expression in Zarathustra's "Yes and Amen Song" (itself a parody of 2 Cor 1:20): "*Doch alle Lust will Ewigkeit—will tiefe, tiefe Ewigkeit.*"[34] For Nietzsche's Dionysian higher humanity, facing up nobly to this tragic ring of recurrence is all-important, and he correctly discerns in Pauline messianism a mortification of this erotic will to power.

Paul says in Romans 7:6, "Now we are *katērgēthēmen* from the law, dead to that which held us captive." The law's energy to arouse sinful desire is rendered inoperative (see Agamben[35]) or transfigured messianically away from juridical codes to the service of love in the new life of *pneuma*. The apocalyptic messianic meaning of this is explored by Paul in 2 Corinthians 3:12–18, where the veil of the written law is removed and we are transfigured by the divine *pneuma* of freedom into the *eikōn* of God, which is the created human destiny. Mimesis is now shaped not by the *psychikos* of fallen desire but by the messianic *pneumatikos* that takes the form of the cross—that is, the kenotic form that is also the human becoming that relinquishes possessive divine power in order to take the form of the servant as a suffering passage in the world that is passing away.

This unveiling is not simply an external matter, though it is the case that messianic becoming (the *parousia* of Messiah in 1 and 2 Thess) forces a decisive choice between a relational enactment of the messianic way of life that entails waiting and suffering, and satanic power that is revealed in terms of external worldly signs and wonders. Even the restraint (*katechōn*, 2 Thess 2:7) of this latter power, however, is not a messianic task, contrary to conventional Christendom political theology. The messianic enactment, the *parousia*, is not the creation of a better world (it is not a "what" or a "when") but a bearing witness to the world's passing away and transfiguration via divine love (it is a "how") that builds up not external edifices, but only (as Kierkegaard emphasized in *Works of Love*) builds up love—and thus fulfills the law![36]

34. Nietzsche, *Thus Spoke Zarathustra*, pt. 3.

35. Agamben, *Time That Remains*, 95.

36. Kierkegaard also notes the connection between *katargēsis* of the law and messianic enactment in *Works of Love*, 97; the connection is the *kenosis* of Christ, a love that gives up heavenly perfections in order to come down and love changeable, mortal persons in all their changeable imperfection (ibid., 173).

Nietzsche, as I said, also seeks a trans-juridical sovereignty beyond good and evil, but he will posit this in an anti-messianic human becoming, a sovereignty of instinct in the value-positing creative will, Paul's *pneuma tou kosmou*. Nietzsche's analysis of an ethic of reactivity and *ressentiment* in Christendom political theology is astute precisely to the extent that he follows the messianic, but his flawed reading of Paul as a priestly moralist is rooted in something deeper than historical or philological error. It is rooted in his attunement to what is at stake and entailed in the claims to a divinely revealed sovereignty of the slain Lamb; hence Nietzsche's declaration of war in *Ecce Homo*: "Dionysus *versus* the Crucified."[37] The only spirit Nietzsche can finally accept is the human *psychikos* attuned to the *pneuma tou kosmou*, the spirit of the world. No less than the crucified Messiah is the Dionysian *Übermensch* given to suffering and martyrdom; the difference, as Nietzsche says, lies in the meaning of it: whether a messianic meaning or a tragic meaning. "The tragic man says Yes to even the bitterest suffering: he is strong, full, deifying enough to do so. The Christian says No to even the happiest earthly lot: he is weak, poor, disinherited enough to suffer from life in whatever form."[38]

Kierkegaard rightly points up the difference between Paul and Nietzsche in his short piece "Of the Difference between a Genius and an Apostle" when he suggests that only if one may reintroduce the distinction between the sphere of immanence and the sphere of transcendence will one be able to discern Paul's apostolic message—it is a revelation, not a philosophical teaching; it is rooted in a divine, not a human authority; it cannot be rationally penetrated, only spiritually discerned in a complete submission to the *logos* of the *stauros*.[39] Attuned, that is to say, not to a human-to-human "pathos of distance,"[40] as between a noble warrior and a slave, but to a divine-to-human pathos of distance that Kierkegaard calls the "passion of faith"[41]—a passion intensified when the divine becomes a slave. Here we have the difference between the Dionysian tragic hero and the messianic knight of faith. By faith in the miracle of divine passage, the knight of faith performs the movement not only of relinquishment in the face of suffering (and does so without noetic or ontic protection of any kind from tragic reality); he or she performs the added movement, a movement given as a breathing room[42] from beyond the immanent sphere, of conforming the self to a messianic becoming that dwells in a love that exceeds death. This is what Paul struggles to express in 1 Corinthians 13 and 15.

In order to pursue this I want to turn to a concluding comparison of Walter Benjamin's "weak messianic power" (which both Taubes and Agamben rightly, in my view, call Pauline) and Nietzsche's will to power on the question of redemption. We could also discuss this contrast in terms of the different *Untergangen*: Dionysian abundance or messianic emptying? I begin with Nietzsche's Zarathustra, the *Fürsprecher*, the advocate or forerunner who prepares the way of the Dionysian "overman" who alone can overcome the nihilistic becoming of the Platonic Christian division between immanence and

---

37. It is the final sentence of Nietzsche's *Ecce Homo*, 151; cf. *Writings from the Late Notebooks*, 249–50.
38. Nietzsche, *Writings from the Late Notebooks*, 250.
39. Kierkegaard, "Difference between Genius and Apostle," 174–77.
40. Nietzsche, *Antichrist*, sec. 43.
41. Kierkegaard, *Fear and Trembling; Philosophical Fragments*.
42. Kierkegaard, *Sickness unto Death*, 38–40.

transcendence in order, as Heidegger tellingly puts it, to "let becoming *be* a becoming."[43] Nietzsche thus creates poetically the thinker of the most burdensome thought, the tragedy of time, who is able to say "Yes" to the supreme "No." Here again Heidegger helpfully shows us that Zarathustra's teaching of the eternal recurrence in keeping with a Dionysian anthropology is not a "what" or a "when" but a "how," a "how to become"—no less than Paul's discussion of the *parousia* of Messiah in 1 Thessalonians, in which it is a shared form of becoming and not an abstract doctrine that is communicated. This becoming is above all an agonistic struggle in keeping with the agonistic becoming of all things. Though Zarathustra's *Untergang* is described as a *kenosis* in a parodying reference to Philippians 2,[44] what he seeks is not to empty himself of divine attributes in order to lovingly serve human beings; he rather seeks to bring human beings the gift of Dionysian superabundance.[45] As he puts it in the section "On the Higher Man": "All great love does not *want* love: it wants more."[46] In contrast to the messianic *Fürsprecher* of and for "the little people," who had to die because of the "overpitying" nature of his self-emptying love,[47] Zarathustra seeks the overcoming of such a love (an overrated "neighbor love"[48]) in order to become divine earthly creators once again—higher, stronger, more worthy human beings. Let us not forget that Zarathustra's animals are the craftiest serpent and the proudest eagle, and that he counters "neighbor love" with "love of the farthest" in overflowing (not self-emptying), creative, warring (not other-serving) friendship.

In order to overcome the nihilistic becoming of the slavish, spiritual messianic revaluation of natural noble values, so as to make possible an affirming, creative earthly becoming humanly possible once again, Zarathustra faces a self-overcoming represented in his "most abysmal" thought. This thought is the very heart of the tragic condition found in the "passing away" of earthly life and all the "no-sayers" who deny the temporality of human becoming (and with this, the highest earthly values) with their theological appeals to eternity. This thought is "the vision of the loneliest,"[49] and it is a vision of self-redemption through creative willing that accepts its suffering, above all the suffering of time, impermanence.[50] The greatest challenge here, the only pathway to the creative, yes-saying will, is how to overcome the spirit of revenge: "the will's ill will against time and its 'it was.'"[51] This is not a reconciliation between time and eternity (that would be to go beyond tragedy via superstition), but something higher than reconciliation: the meeting of time running backward (the past) and time running forward (future)

---

43. Heidegger, *Nietzsche*, 1:218.

44. Nietzsche, *Thus Spoke Zarathustra*, 122; see also the *kenosis* of love, 196, and the descent of power into beauty, 230. On *kenosis* as parody, see Gooding-Williams, *Zarathustra's Dionysian Modernism*, 55–57.

45. *Thus Spoke Zarathustra*, 123; cf. 334–36.

46. Ibid., 405.

47. Ibid., 378.

48. Ibid., 172–73.

49. Ibid., 268; cf. Nietzsche, *Gay Science*, sec. 341.

50. Ibid., "On Redemption," in *Thus Spoke Zarathustra*, 249–52.

51. Ibid., 252.

in the *Augenblick* of the eternal "now."⁵² This, for Nietzsche, can only be understood parabolically:⁵³ the doorway called *Augenblick* has two faces that contradict each other and "offend each other face to face."⁵⁴ The challenge for the *Übermensch* is to face the "spirit of gravity" that proclaims all truth to be crooked and all time a circle,⁵⁵ and to will nevertheless to affirm the human creativity and uniqueness of one's life in a joyful, innocent forgetting of the "all is vanity" of eternal return. The redemption here is not penitential; it is not received as a messianic reconciliation. It is a decision to become a warrior self who engages the agon of saying yes to all suffering and all destruction, life in all its chaotic contradictions. This parabolic becoming stands opposed to the messianic: "The god on the cross is a curse on life, a signpost to seek redemption from life; Dionysus cut to pieces is a *promise* of life: it will be eternally reborn and return again from destruction."⁵⁶

Benjamin's messianic *Untergang*, by contrast, pays attention to the implications of the cruciform curse for the tragic abundance of Dionysian becoming that is motivated by the desire to transform humanity but not through the love of particular humans. Like Paul, Benjamin does not see weakness or the kingdom of God as a curse on life, but rather as a scandal for those seeking ontological strength. This is because, as Benjamin puts it in his "Theologico-Political Fragment," only the Messiah consummates (*vollendet*) all historical becoming "in the sense that he alone redeems, completes, creates its relation to the Messianic," something that nothing historical can do "*von sich, aus sich*."⁵⁷ Historically speaking, the kingdom of God is not a *telos* of historical becoming—Benjamin is very clear that the messianic can have nothing to do with a humanist progressivism—but is rather is the transfigured "end" of history. Messianic becoming is apocalyptic, an interruption of the natural that suspends its immanent laws ("flourishing of the fittest") so as to point to its hidden divine passage through it, its truest becoming and indeed its truest, eternal "happiness." The messianic parable, in Benjamin as in Kierkegaard and in Paul, is not that of the poetic thinker making up an entertaining fable; rather, the Messiah is the second Adam, the man from heaven who became in the flesh a life-giving spirit (1 Cor 15:45–49), and did so in self-emptying servanthood. It is a divine enactment in time, and this is only possible if history is not reducible to the endless repetition of natural causality—or, as in Benjamin's "Fragment," "nature is Messianic by reason of its eternal and total passing away."⁵⁸

---

52. Ibid., 270. It bears noting that Kierkegaard too understands the gateway of human willing as a "Moment," which he calls *ojeblikket* in *Concept of Anxiety*, 87, but unlike Nietzsche and like Benjamin, the paradoxical face of this moment is for Kierkegaard messianic.

53. "It is of time and becoming that the best parables should speak: let them be a praise and a justification of all impermanence [*Verganglichkeit*]." Nietzsche, *Thus Spoke Zarathustra*, 198–99.

54. Ibid., 269–70.

55. This spirit of gravity ("all is vanity"), articulated by the dwarf, is the message of *Qoheleth*: "What is crooked cannot be made straight" (Eccl 1:15; cf. 7:13); and the circular nature of time in Ecclesiastes 3. These slogans pervade *Zarathustra* (e.g., pp. 198, 245, 270, 316, 330).

56. Nietzsche, *Writings from the Late Notebooks*, 250.

57. Benjamin, "Theologico-Political Fragment," 312.

58. Ibid.

PART 1: APOCALYPTIC MESSIANISM AND POLITICAL THEOLOGY

And yet this becoming is not somehow happening behind the back of history or the order of the profane; it is happening within it as a mysterious redemption for those with eyes to see. The "eyes to see" are attuned to a messianic intensity marked not by a "No" to this world but by a "Yes and Amen" happiness in which the earthly seeks its *Untergang* and indeed its transfiguring "*zu Grunde gehen.*" Like Kierkegaard, Benjamin stresses the paradoxical character of this becoming: in immediacy, this messianic "intensity of the heart" of the single one passes through an unhappiness, as "suffering." It is a complete giving away of itself in nihilistic, loving service to what is passing away. And yet in this spiritual service it experiences a worldly restitution of the true form of the world—its passing away as a becoming not unlike Paul's portrayal of *agapē* in 1 Corinthians 13: while all human actions and words, even the highest and most noble, will pass away (again the verb is *katargēsis*), *agapē*, the divine passage in the world, never ends. There is a close, transfiguring connection between worldly *katargēsis* and divine agapic agency. Indeed, in contrast to human *gnosis* which "puffs up," divine *agapē* "builds up" (*oikodomei*, 1 Cor 8:1–2); the difference is that agape is divine, not human knowing, and what is built up is the relation to divine completion of "all things" (*ta panta*, 1 Cor 15:28; Rom 11:36).

This agapic messianic movement, as Benjamin shows in his "Theses on the Philosophy of History," is rooted in the power of weakness, both spiritual and material, that will not conform to triumphalist progressivist politics of the world. "The Messiah," says Benjamin, "comes not only as the redeemer, he comes as the overcomer of Antichrist" (Thesis 6). Here there can be no historicist siding with the victors; a messianic historical materialist must "brush history against the grain" (Thesis 7) on the side of oppressed victims: the weak, the foolish, the lowly and despised (Benjamin, like Paul, imitates Messiah in being a *Fürsprecher* for the weak, "*die kleine Leute*").[59] This goes against the triumphalist politics of social democracy and Marxist belief in the technological mastery of nature no less than against Fascism, insofar as these are rooted in anti-messianic conceptions of human sovereignty that do not recognize that the form of the world is "passing away." Benjamin identifies anti-messianic triumphalism with an immanent natural causality, the concept of a progression through homogeneous time (Thesis 13). To this must be counterposed a messianic time as apocalypse, "time filled by the presence of the now [*Jetztzeit*]" (Thesis 14). Such a time can only be understood and lived figurally, in which one's own time is lived in relation to the whole of time, namely eternity, in such a manner that I comprehend myself and my time in critical relation to a spiritually discerned past and future. As Paul puts it in 1 Corinthians 10, where he complicates the position of the "strong" by appealing to the Exodus in the kind of figural interpretation that drove Nietzsche crazy, "all our fathers were under the cloud, and all passed through the sea, and all were baptized into Moses, . . . and all ate the same spiritual food and all drank the same spiritual drink. For they drank from the spiritual Rock which followed them, and the Rock was Messiah. . . . Now these things happened to them as a warning, but they were written down for our instruction, upon whom the ends of the ages has come. Therefore let any one who thinks that he stands take heed lest he fall" (1 Cor 10:1–4, 11–12). That is, any particular historical event or time is passing away and points for its

---

59. Cf. Nietzsche, *Thus Spoke Zarathustra*, 378.

completion to the *Figur* of history as a whole, which both Paul and Benjamin identify as messianic. But life can only be lived in such a relation to the messianic figure, both past and future, in the kairotic "now"—the *Jetztzeit* (Thesis 18). Why? Because, as Benjamin quoting the rabbis puts it, "every second of time [is] the small gateway through which the Messiah might enter" (18, B). In such an enactment, in which my life and time becomes a spiritual attentiveness to and mimesis of messianic becoming, the actual meaning of the deed remains mysterious—it "passes away" as do all human deeds. And yet it becomes, in a material and worldly way, a "building up" of the messianic passage of God in the world. In this way is the lived deed both retained in a remembering and, as Benjamin puts it (Thesis 17), *aufgehoben*—using Luther's German translation for Paul's apocalyptic verb *katargēsis*[60]—into the movement of all things to their "end." I note in passing that for both Paul and Benjamin this figural messianic becoming is closely tied to liturgical and sacramental participation. This is not accidental insofar as the liturgical and sacramental are emblematic precisely of the parabolic, figural, trans-immanent character of all reality.

But precisely here we face the daunting challenge identified by Taubes, for the liturgical and sacramental heart of the messianic emblem of redemption for Paul is the crucifixion: "Messiah redeemed us from the curse of the law, having become a curse for us" (Gal 3:13). This is what so scandalizes Nietzsche: the earthly parabolic symbolism of mantic Jesus (the "Jesus seminar" Jesus) is turned by Paul into a messianic cosmic mystery, a divine *sacrifice* of atonement[61] that undergirds a vast priestly power structure called "Christendom," used to tyrannize the masses and form moralistic herds via the painful, life-denying creation of conscience.[62] Let us hear Taubes on Nietzsche's view of this:

> Christianity hypostatizes sacrifice rather than abolishing it, and thus perpetuates it. Let someone come and really theologically challenge this! This is in Nietzsche a deeply humane impulse against the entanglement of guilt and atonement, on which the entire Pauline dialectic—but even already that of the Old Testament—is based. This continually self-perpetuating cycle of guilt, sacrifice, and atonement needs to be broken in order finally to yield an innocence of becoming (this is Nietzsche's expression). A becoming, even a being, that is not guilty. Whereas Paul really does believe that humanity and the cosmos are guilty [Rom 7:7–25]. A guilt that can be redeemed by means of sacrifice and atonement. Justified. But what a terrible price is paid in this entanglement! What terrible cruelty, from which there is no escape![63]

At this point Taubes breaks off the engagement with a fizzling excursus on Freud rather than take up the parabolic pattern of messianic atonement and martyrdom in Paul. And as far as I can tell, the current Continental philosophical interpretations of Paul want to remain indirect about this as well. Of course I'm going to fizzle here too, but let me gesture to Kierkegaard and Dostoevsky as nineteenth-century thinkers who engaged

---

60. See Agamben, *Time That Remains*, 99–101.
61. Nietzsche, *Antichrist*, sec. 41.
62. This is the story of Nietzsche's *On the Genealogy of Morals*.
63. Taubes, *Political Theology of Paul*, 87–88.

this Nietzschean critique, albeit indirectly, before ending with some reflections from the recent literature on the implications of this for political sovereignty. Nietzsche proposes the abolition of Christendom atonement theory by abolishing Pauline messianism with its spiritual causality and divine passage. In his parable of "The Madman" in *The Gay Science*, Nietzsche's solution to this whole idolatry of the "holy lie" is to proclaim unabashedly the murder of God, a recognition that God is already dead as a result of the collective murder in which all of us moderns are implicated:

> God is dead. God remains dead. And we have killed him. How shall we, the murderers of all murderers, comfort ourselves? What was holiest and most powerful of all that the world has yet owned has bled to death under our knives. Who will wipe this blood off us? What water is there for us to clean ourselves? What festivals of atonement, what sacred games shall we have to invent? Is not the greatness of this deed too great for us? Must not we ourselves become gods simply to seem worthy of it? There has never been a greater deed; and whoever will be born after us—for the sake of this deed he will be part of a higher history than all history hitherto.[64]

Nietzsche thus violently reverses Christendom atonement theory with yet another murderous sacrifice. By contrast, Kierkegaard and Dostoevsky draw a crucial distinction between the sinful violence of Christendom atonement theory and practice, to which Nietzsche rightly objects but then imitates, and the penitential movement away from this violence (moral, political, religious) in the messianic becoming witnessed to by Paul. That is, they will not seek to become worthy of the divine creativity after which Nietzsche sovereignly grasps. Indeed, for Pauline messianism, that is precisely the sinful heart of the human unlikeness to God that leads invariably to further violence, from which those who seek to participate in a truly human becoming must repent. It is a repentance that is provoked paradoxically in the messianic apocalypse that joins human beings in this unlikeness in order to nullify it. To understand this requires the downfall of worldly human understanding, a reshaping of desire that is so radical it can only be described as a "rebirth" or a "new creation," a *metabasis eis allo geno* (transition to a different becoming, as Kierkegaard puts it[65]). No less than for Nietzsche does this entail an act of willing in time, in the "moment" in which time and eternity touch each other. But here Kierkegaard makes reference to the spiritual causality displayed in the resurrection and to Paul's language in 1 Corinthians 15:52, in which Paul speaks of the "moment" as the "twinkling of an eye" in which the perishability of mortal nature puts on the imperishability of the immortal.[66] No naturalization of this miraculous paradox is possible by which the scandal may be removed[67]: it remains foolish to worldly wisdom precisely insofar as worldly wisdom seeks its own sovereignty.[68]

---

64. Nietzsche, *Gay Science*, 95.
65. Kierkegaard, *Philosophical Fragments*, 73.
66. Kierkegaard, *Concept of Anxiety*, 87–88.
67. Kierkegaard, *Philosophical Fragments*, 95–96.
68. And thus, as Benjamin puts it, must perpetuate the violence both mythically and juridically; see Benjamin, "Critique of Violence."

In conclusion, let me return to where we began. Badiou is faithful to Paul's messianic logic when he says it critiques all onto-theologies, all discourses of mastery rooted in human appeals to wisdom and power as divine attributes. A messianic identity or movement may not become a discourse of glorification that builds a new economy of power and wisdom on the strength of the ineffable. Paul will glory only in his weakness, in a subjectivity of abasement that continually goes outside itself in loving service. Badiou is very nervous about Christian triumphalism that "glories in the cross," coercively trading in the political capital of sacrificial victimhood. This is an understandable worry, but for Paul one cannot address it simply by doing away with scandalous messianic content. "Jesus the crucified Messiah is cosmic sovereign" is Paul's claim, one that Badiou doesn't really engage. Badiou's portrait of Paul is indebted to that of another French philosopher, Stanislas Breton, a Catholic philosopher,[69] who argues that for Paul the messianic call to dispossession and critical detachment from prevailing orders of human sovereignty cannot bypass the path of the cross as Badiou does. For Paul the *logos* of the *stauros* (the word of the cross, 1 Cor 1:18) is the very power of God; precisely the scandal of the cross disrupts the humanist appeals of the wise and the strong. In Jesus the crucified Messiah, the sovereignty of history and all creation is disclosed in the form of the suffering servant, and only those willing to empty themselves of possessive desires that cling graspingly to the eternal form (whether it be a teaching, an ethic, or an identity), only those who take the kenotic form of the servant may journey messianically with the eternal in time. Here we may be reminded of Badiou's worry about a morbid and *ressentiment*-laden glorying in the suffering of the cross. Does not this "path of the cross" simply constitute a reversal of worldly values, in which obedient Christians build up heavenly treasures by trading on a divine spiritual economy that denigrates this world only to gain preeminence in the other world? Breton is fully aware of this danger; he says, "The God of the Cross is not the God of desire, and that is why this God does not know how to be a God of the superlative."[70] What is scandalously revealed in the resurrection event is precisely that the superlative God has died on the cross; the power of the cross thus confounds every "what is" that may be desired by the weakness of "what is not," and this "meontological mission" is the focus of Paul's gospel. The power of the cross is therefore a performative act, a mission that continually moves outside itself in unseen, quotidian service to the least, the lowly, the despised, even those who are not—and thus becomes a foolish spectacle, the refuse of the world, the offscouring of all things. Such a dispossessive, exilic love serves "what is not" not out of resentment or impotence but because God creatively acts *ex nihilo* in a love that is endlessly kenotic and dispossessive rather than acquisitive and accumulative.

---

69. And therefore perhaps of all philosophers these days most to be despised. Most conventional philosophers are tempted, following Kant, to join the company of liberal Protestant scholars who domesticate Paul's messianism by (*a*) controlling it through scholarly contextualization that gets rid of its political incorrectness, its scandal factor; and (*b*) aligning it with the most progressivist of modern humanisms—liberal democracy and all its colonizing works carried out in the name of sacrificial victims and human rights. In which case, who needs Paul? He really is only finally an embarrassment—and it is the embarrassment factor by which the unconventional philosophers I am interpreting are intrigued.

70. Breton, *Word and the Cross*, 9.

PART 1: APOCALYPTIC MESSIANISM AND POLITICAL THEOLOGY

Of course we may ask, what has all this got to do with politics and sovereignty? Is this but a story of the exodus of the soul or the postmodern diaspora self? Breton is clear that the *logos* of the *stauros* may not be so understood—it is very much related to an *ekklēsia*, those called out to a body politic that cannot be reduced to an experience of the individual soul nor to a church that lives unto itself (whether in a liturgy of adoration or in a separatist isolationist sect). The dispossession displayed in Acts, represented in the sharing of the fractured eucharistic body, must be continued in the diasporic messianic body: "Instead of persisting as establishment," Breton writes, "the church must in the final analysis be forgotten in the service of the poor, that is to say, in Paul's very language, in unconditional devotion to 'those who do not exist.'"[71] Whatever else this might mean, it cannot mean anything like a Christian nation or any other self-enclosed political entity. Breton suggests that it will be a politics of *hōs mē*—making use of the world "as if not" (*hōs mē*) using it (1 Cor 7:29–31).

This *hōs mē* political theology is further developed in the interpretations of Paul by the German Jewish philosopher Jacob Taubes and the Italian philosopher Giorgio Agamben.[72] Of course it is fashionable these days to reclaim the Jewish Paul, but Taubes and Agamben, like Walter Benjamin, are not interested in what is fashionable. At the center of Paul's messianic logic is his declaration of faith in the crucified Messiah as the divine act of atonement by which "all Israel" shall be saved. For Taubes this is neither a noetic universalism nor a liberal *nomos* universalism: "Sure, Paul is also universal," says Taubes, "but by virtue of the 'eye of the needle' of the crucified one, which means: transvaluation of all the values of this world . . . This is why it carries a political charge."[73] The death of the Messiah as a scapegoat, a criminal, signals for Paul nothing less than the end of righteousness based upon law. "Outbidding Moses," Paul's political theology believes the Messiah, condemned according to the Law, accomplishes what the Law cannot, namely, the healing of the nations. Hence the place of Moses and the Law is transfigured messianically in the direction of "all Israel," an Israel whose definition can no longer be restricted only to Jews.

This transfiguration, moreover, takes the election of Israel seriously in a manner that is perhaps all the more embarrassing for modern Christianity. The Messiah redeems Israel by extending divine mercy to the unrighteous enemy, even calling "my people" those who were not a people and "beloved" those who were not beloved. In Romans 9–11 this is linked to a mysterious "drama of jealousy" that is paradoxical: "all" will be saved, but only by the messianic "remnant" who proclaims mercy to the enemy and to those who are *not* a people. Hence the central importance of enemy love in Paul's political theology, in a (contra Nietzsche) completely non-moralistic way. The sovereign Messiah, by suffering death, bears witness to the breakdown of every human moral claim to self-sufficiency or righteousness. It is *God* who elects a people for the sake of redeeming all, in a politics of messianic suffering and martyrdom where, in the "time that remains" the "called" live *hōs mē*, as if not. Only such a messianic politics will be able to discern that the "state of emergency" in which we live is the norm, and that its task is to bring

71. Ibid., 56.
72. I develop a fuller account of this in Kroeker, "Whither Messianic Ethics?"
73. Taubes, *Political Theology of Paul*, 24.

Living "As If Not"

into view the "real state of emergency" in which divine sovereign action proclaims the messianic exception.

Giorgio Agamben helps us pursue this further. Like Taubes, he emphasizes that Paul is a diaspora Jew whose Greek is neither properly Jewish (Hebrew) nor Greek. He cites Taubes's wonderful story of his student days in Zurich when his teacher in classical Greek, Emil Staiger, confided: "You know, Taubes, yesterday I was reading the Letters of the Apostle Paul. To which he added, with great bitterness: But that isn't Greek, it's Yiddish! Upon which I said: Yes, Professor, and that's why I understand it!"[74] Paul speaks the language of Jews in exile in a manner that works over the host language from within and confounds its identity. The messianic is precisely related to this diaspora linguistic situation. In order to understand how this relates to the politics of a messianic community, Agamben reflects first on what he calls the structure of messianic time, expressed in 1 Corinthians 7:29: "The kairos has been contracted; in what remains, let those who have . . . live *hōs mē* as though they have not." This is Benjamin's *Jetztzeit*—the time of the "now" in which the accumulative flow of *chronos* is interrupted, burst open, or "contracted" by a messianic event that coincides with the very *Figur* that reveals human history.

For example, Paul refers to himself frequently as *doulos*, slave of the Messiah (the term that so offends Nietzsche). This is a juridical term that Paul now confounds from within, since the sovereign Lord whom the *doulos* serves is a crucified Messiah. As such the condition of *doulos* is itself transformed, and it stands for a general transformation of worldly-political-social conditions, here blasted out of the continuum of history. This also has everything to do with the language of "calling"—Paul's calling as *doulos* of the Messiah but also the calling (*klēsis*) of the *ekklēsia* (further described in 1 Cor 7:17f.) in confounding the relation to worldly "callings"—"remain with God in the calling in which you have been called"—including that of a slave. Contrary to Weber's secularization thesis (influenced by Nietzsche), in which "calling" indicates an eschatological indifference to the worldly, Agamben shows that for Paul "calling" is the language of messianic transformation.[75] Above all, it stands for the nullification and revocation of every vocation.[76] The nullification of every worldly vocation here is not abandoning the world for an "elsewhere" but is a dwelling within it in dispossession, thus confounding its identity from within and allowing the power of God to transform it in keeping with its true condition or "figure," that is, its "passing away" toward an end that lies beyond it. In other words, the messianic is not a new identity with its own set of rights; it is rather the power to use without possessing. In this way worldly vocations and identities are never "replaced" by something new, but there is rather a "making new" that occurs within them that transfigures and opens them up to their true use in keeping with their true condition.[77] In effect, this is a slavery liberated from juridical bondage to worldly possession for free creaturely action in a world that is passing away.

---

74. Ibid., 3–4.

75. Agamben, *Time That Remains*, 19–23.

76. Ibid., 23–26.

77. Ibid., 26.

PART 1: APOCALYPTIC MESSIANISM AND POLITICAL THEOLOGY

For Benjamin this weak messianic power accomplishes what Marx's proletariat revolution cannot. It hollows out the progressivist, abstracting grip of the capitalist count from within, and yet with reference to the very sovereign power of creation, that is, redeeming love.[78] For Paul the *ekklēsia* is precisely this classless society where all are freed by becoming slaves of the Messiah. They become free not by possessing rights nor by taking over the instruments of power for their own superior Christian control, but precisely by using the world "as if not," in a dispossessive manner that assesses the value of each particular thing or relation with reference to the passage of God in the world. This "as if not" messianic ethic thus also stands in opposition to Kant's "as if" (*als ob*) moral universal that strives to possess an ideal (Kant says: act *as if* God, immortality, and freedom exist as regulative ideals). Paul's position is rooted in a kenotic movement of dispossession that cannot become yet another act of (self-)legislation; it relinquishes its moral striving and its hold—whether of the technological means of progressive liberation from the decay of nature, or the political means of liberating particular identities from the burdens of oppression. The point is rather to open up all worldly callings to the transfiguring passage of God—through slavery to the sovereign crucified Messiah. Here it is necessary to get beyond possessive identities and aspirations altogether via messianic healing. With Karl Barth and Franz Kafka, the Pauline messianic subject "knows that in messianic time, the saved world coincides exactly with the lost world"[79]—there is no path to salvation except via self-losing service to what cannot be saved. This is why both Kafka and Barth emphasized the secular language of the parable as the proper discourse for ethics: the parabolic reversal of conventional criteria by which we measure strength and weakness, success and failure.[80] It does this by discerning the passing action of God, not from above in world-historical dominance, but from below—in exile. Only

---

78. I realize this claim with regard to Benjamin is controversial. Yet it is how I read his "Theses"—not as advocating a cheap, empathic love rooted in an "indolent heart" (Thesis 7) but as a love that is referred to "redemption" (Thesis 2), a happiness beyond either envy or conformity to a history defined by "victors." That is, it is love as a struggle for a redeemed humanity in the apocalyptic "fullness" of each historical moment (Thesis 3), which brushes history "against the grain" of its violent progressivist myth (Theses 7f.) in which past victims are expendable.

79. Agamben, *Time That Remains*, 42.

80. For Barth the language of parable, in the section of *Epistle to the Romans* called "The Problem of Ethics," is tied explicitly to 1 Corinthians 7:31, "the form of the world passes away," and therefore the only ethical form that bears testimony to divine action is one that is "offered up" sacrificially in self-dissolution or worldly failure or brokenness (see Barth, *Epistle to the Romans*, 433–36, 445, 462–65.). Kafka's discussion of parables, of course, is parabolically mediated in Kafka's inimitable "On Parables," 158: "Many complain that the words of the wise are always merely parables and of no use in daily life, which is the only life we have. When the sage says: 'Go over,' he does not mean that we should cross to some actual place, which we could do anyhow if the labor were worth it; he means some fabulous yonder, something unknown to us, something that he cannot designate more precisely either, and therefore cannot help us here in the very least. All these parables really set out to say merely that the incomprehensible is incomprehensible, and we know that already. But the cares we have to struggle with every day: that is a different matter. Concerning this a man once said: Why such reluctance? If you only followed the parables you yourselves would become parables and with that rid of all your daily cares. Another said: I bet that is also a parable. The first said: You have won. The second said: But unfortunately only in parable. The first said: No, in reality: in parable you have lost."

thus is the world hollowed out (and "hallowed out") for its reconciliation in the divine passage through it.

In the secular present, all knowledge and prophecy is "in part," but the messianic body looks forward in hope to the "all in all." The only way to relate "in part" to the all, in Paul's view, is through self-sacrificing love. It is the patient, non-possessive "waiting" of love that constitutes the messianic time in which the messianic body is called to live. The remnant therefore is not the possessive object of salvation so much as its instrument in the ministry of reconciliation, and it is precisely the kenotic movement toward the "unsavable" that effects salvation. In the time that remains, then, the messianic ethic of the *hōs mē* is the time in which time and eternity coincide transformatively—as the caesura of *chronos*, but not yet eternity. It is therefore a time of judgment, "the time that time takes to make an end,"[81] the only time we have as creatures (in Breton's words, borrowed from Meister Eckhardt[82]) to exercise our calling as "adverbs of the Verb," the divine speech that is the hidden life of each created being. And so Paul urges, "Make the most of the time [*kairos*]"(Gal 6:10; Eph 5:16; Col 4:5), seizing it not as a proprietary possession but as a loving "bringing to fulfillment" (the "fullness [*plērōma*] of time," Eph 1:9–10) in keeping with the messianic agency of the *hōs mē*. It is also here that the ethical importance of Paul's typological approach to Scripture becomes clear as figural rather than allegorical. There is a relation between the ages that is messianically configured for Paul—a parabolic configuration, not a noetic one. Paul insists, "If anyone imagines that he knows something, he does not yet know as he ought to know. But if one loves God one is known by him" (1 Cor 8:2–3). To be known by God is to participate in the messianic motion of kenotic love, a "fullness of time" that unites, literally "recapitulates," all things in heaven and on earth (Eph 1:10; cf. Col 1:17–20). Such a process is not a hermeneutics that seeks to "replace" one meaning with another in a movement from particular to universal possession of meaning. It is rather the dispossessive process of "becoming parabolic" in a manner that allows the redemptive aim of the law to come to fulfillment in a world that is passing away; for Paul, above all, each commandment is recapitulated in the "love your neighbor as yourself" (Rom 13:8–10).

---

81. Agamben, *Time That Remains*, 67.
82. Breton, *Saint Paul*, 29–30.

2

The Theological Politics of Plato and Isaiah

A Debate Rejoined

IN HIS INAUGURAL LECTURE at Hebrew University in 1938, Martin Buber developed his understanding of the vocation of the social philosopher through extensive reference to a comparative analysis of Plato and Isaiah.[1] The published title of Buber's essay in English is "The Demand of the Spirit and Historical Reality," and in it he plays with the contrast between spiritual power and historical efficacy, in opposition to ideological identifications of the two. Knowledge, states Buber, is an *ascetic* act by which, "through the concentration of spiritual power," the social thinker can be freed from the immediacy of social ties in order to achieve "free vision,"[2] a vision that enables one to assert the demands of historical *reality* in a non-ideological manner. But such spiritual insight into the true nature of reality does not guarantee historical effectiveness against the power politics of ideologues. Indeed, experience seems to suggest the overwhelming helplessness and failure of the spirit in the face of history.

Buber's comparative analysis therefore concerns Plato and Isaiah as two representatives of spirit who experienced historical and political failure in different ways that were rooted in different spiritual visions of reality. However, in his attempt to vindicate the theological politics of Isaiah's prophetic consciousness, Buber falls into a major pitfall of comparative studies. He is unable to free himself from an ideological (or at least idealist) reading of Plato, reifying the symbolic and philosophical account of true experience in the *Republic* as a doctrine of ideas and a utopian model of the state. The political failure of Socrates and Plato can then be presented in terms of the disappointments of utopian idealism, in contrast to Isaiah's failure, which is rooted in a spiritual discernment of the divine purposes in historical reality. In the first part of this essay I point out the problems with Buber's dogmatic and caricatured reading of the *Republic* and argue that a better

---

1. Buber, "Demand of the Spirit," 177–91; an excerpted section of Buber's essay dealing with the comparative analysis of Plato's *Republic* and First Isaiah is published separately as "Plato and Isaiah."

2. Buber, "Demand of the Spirit," 181.

interpretation of Plato brings the religio-political visions, vocations, and "failures" of the Greek philosopher and the Hebrew prophet much closer together.

The structural symmetry of this essay benefits greatly from the fact that a comparative analysis of the religious politics of Plato and Isaiah was also undertaken by a renowned Platonic philosopher, Eric Voegelin.[3] Voegelin interprets Isaiah as the purveyor of a "metastatic faith" whose political counsel to the kings of Judah suggests that the structure of reality can be changed magically by an act of faith in divine intervention. In this interpretation is an interesting reversal of the same temptation in comparative work that led to Buber's flawed reading of the *Republic*, namely, a caricatured interpretation of the comparative contrast so as to make one's own preferred symbolism (for Voegelin, the Platonic vision) appear to be vastly superior. In the second part of the essay, then, I argue that Voegelin's undialectical reading of Isaiah falsely reifies the Yahwistic symbolism and measures it dogmatically by the noetic symbolism of Greek philosophy.

The modest aim of this essay is to prepare the way for a more accurate and illuminating comparative dialogue on the theological politics of Plato and the Hebrew prophets by correcting the distortions present in dogmatic misreadings of Plato's *Republic* and Isaiah. I suggest, furthermore, that the decisive difference between Plato and Isaiah lies in the contrasting religious symbolizations they employ to represent their experiences. Plato's noetic theology is rooted in a theophany of the intelligible ground of the cosmos and leads to a philosophical critique of sophistry and a political ethic of prudence, or *phronēsis*. Isaiah's covenant theology is rooted in a revelation of the holy God, leading to a prophetic critique of political idolatry and a political ethic of covenant responsibility. This understanding of Plato and Isaiah better represents both the similarities between them—namely, a theologically grounded political critique of the illusory power politics of ideologues—and the differences in their views of human nature—for Plato, the contrast between ignorance and understanding, and for Isaiah, between sin and faith.

I

According to Buber, Plato's "doctrine" is "the most sublime instance of that spirit whose intercourse with reality proceeds from its own possession of truth."[4] Socrates and Plato both encountered obdurate resistance and ultimately failed in their attempts to establish the soul's vision of the good as the foundation of true justice in the real world of the polis. How did they understand this failure on their own terms? Buber's implied answer seems to be that while Socrates and Plato possessed spiritual insight and truth, they were unable to obtain possession of political power so as to realize their soul's vision of the good in the living form of a "just state." There are problems with this account of failure that arise from Buber's doctrinal reconstruction of Plato's *Republic* as the elaboration of a utopian ideal, a timeless truth, an eternal image of perfection. For Buber's Plato, the ideal will be historically realized when it is able to gain political power—a power that the

---

3. Voegelin, *Order and History*, vol. 1, *Israel and Revelation*, chap. 13; Voegelin, *Order and History*, vol. 4, *Ecumenic Age*, 26–27; Voegelin, *Order and History*, vol. 5, *Search for Order*, 33; and Voegelin, *Autobiographical Reflections*, 68.

4. Buber, "Demand of the Spirit," 185–86.

philosopher is not likely to gain without divine intervention, as book 9 of the *Republic* seems to suggest.

It is no wonder that Buber wants to claim that Isaiah's spiritual failure is of quite a different sort. Given the rather sublime portrait of Plato as the detached beautiful soul whose ideal republic was far too noble and pure for the wild beasts or hoi polloi that surrounded him, the rather more engaged, concrete, and sympathetic account of Isaiah's failure cannot fail to succeed in winning the reader's vote. After all, here we have the call of a prophet who acknowledges that he too is a man of unclean lips who lives among a people of unclean lips, not above them. He does not claim to possess a perfect soul; indeed, he does not claim to possess spirit or truth, either. Isaiah is just an ordinary man who is suddenly and dramatically confronted by the holy God whose spirit invades him and calls him to a concrete task. This prophet possesses no grand idea, no lofty vision of the ideal state to be established, and therefore "Isaiah does not believe that the spiritual man has the vocation to power. He knows himself to be a man of spirit and without power."[5]

This ordinary man claims nothing for himself, and yet he is confronted with an overwhelming theophany and entrusted with a message, an oracle of God that he is called to proclaim to the powerful and the common people alike. The message is not his, he is but the messenger, and it concerns not his own vision but rather the revealed will of the divine king (*ha-melekh*) who ultimately rules this people and to whom they have a *common* responsibility. And this message presents no utopian political pattern but a word of spiritual reality addressed to a particular people—this people that calls Yahweh its king—in their concrete historical situation. Isaiah's failure, then, is not the failure of utopian politics (à la Plato's *Republic*) but rather the failure of a metapolitical truth that is neither sublimely religious nor politically irrelevant—namely, the call to a people to be faithful and responsive to its divine king by imitating the divine way in this *topos*, that is, in this historical and political situation.

Isaiah is told from the very beginning that he and his message will fail—the message will be misunderstood and misinterpreted, it will confirm the people in their faithlessness and harden their hearts, except in the case of a small remnant. Yet this failure is integral to the message and to the way Isaiah must proceed, for it represents the divine purpose. Hence there will be no disappointment such as that experienced by Plato in his failures at Syracuse. Nor can Isaiah withdraw into the lofty silence of the noble spectator when surrounded by wild beasts, for he is called to carry on the dialogue between God and the people.

What is wrong with Buber's analysis? In my view, it can be summed up in the fact that his portrayal of Plato is more like the Glaucon than the Socrates of the *Republic*. Many of the stark contrasts drawn between Plato and Isaiah—the idealist versus the realist, the perfect soul versus the unclean yet responsive man, the possessor of truth versus the man before God, the seeker of power versus the powerless messenger of God—are based on a dogmatic, let us say undialectical and unerotic reading of the *Republic*. Concerning true philosophers, Socrates says at one point in the *Phaedo*: "Many bear the

---

5. Buber, "Plato and Isaiah," 156.

thyrsus [the Bacchic staff], but few are the bacchantes" (*Phaedo* 69c–d). In his reading of Plato, Buber must be counted among the many rather than as part of the small remnant.[6]

And it is precisely the true philosophical remnant—the very small group that keeps company with philosophy in a way that is worthy (496a–e)[7]—that Socrates is speaking about in the passage from book 6 of the *Republic* cited negatively by Buber, in which the true philosopher surrounded by "wild beasts" refuses to join them in their injustice or to tickle their ears with sophistic words (493a–c). But this refusal is not presented in the *Republic* as a sectarian escape to some privileged sanctum of personal purity by those who possess truth and goodness as a private commodity. Indeed, in opposition to Buber's misreading, I wish to make two important points concerning Plato's *Republic* that bring Isaiah and Plato much closer together.[8]

The first point concerns the religio-political vision of the philosopher. For Plato, truth (*alētheia*) and the good (*agathon*) are not possessions of the soul, nor is the good envisioned as an existing thing or being of any kind, since the good is "beyond being [*epekeina tēs ousias*], exceeding it in dignity and power" (509b). The good is that which illuminates both the soul and the things known by the soul, but which is itself beyond human knowledge and is experienced by the soul as its divine ground. True philosophy, therefore, is not a matter of doctrinal abstraction or the possession of an ideal—that is Glaucon's erroneous view. Rather, it is the experience of the divine presence through the soul's participatory response toward the good beyond being. This is represented as an ascent of the soul toward the truth, and it culminates in a theophanic event—the vision of the good itself (*to agathon auto*, 540a–b), which becomes the paradigm for ordering all of life (public and private, soul and polis).[9] This Platonic anthropology is similar to Buber's Hebraic one in that "spirit" is not a possession but the "in between" of the human and the divine that constitutes the human quest for meaning and order in history, the ongoing, open-ended dialogue of the spirit in the real world.[10]

It is, rather, the disordered sophist who seeks the immanent realization of a transcendent ideal by claiming the power of the good as *his own* possession and on that authority carries around false invented images in the darkened cave of conventional pseudoreality inhabited by perpetual prisoners, persuading people that the phantoms

---

6. That is to say, Buber's reading of Plato as putting forward a "doctrine of ideas" and a utopian political ideal (in contrast, e.g., to Aristotle's prudential realism) is widespread in modern philosophy and classical scholarship.

7. All references to Stephanus numbers in this chapter refer to the *Republic* unless otherwise noted.

8. My reading of the *Republic* and of Plato in general has been influenced by Voegelin, *Order and History*, vol. 3, *Plato and Aristotle*; Jaeger, *Paideia: The Ideals of Greek Culture*, vol. 2, *In Search of the Divine Centre*; Gadamer, *Dialogue and Dialectic*. I am especially indebted to my colleague Zdravko Planinc, *Plato's Political Philosophy*.

9. I recognize the controversial nature of this understanding of Plato's theological anthropology and the fact that the theology of Plato is a good deal more complicated than my very limited and necessarily compact discussion indicates. For more extensive discussion of this understanding see Jaeger, *Paideia*, 2:279–80 (also 2:285–86); Voegelin, *Order and History*, vol. 3, *Plato and Aristotle*, 55, 112–13, and Voegelin, *Order and History*, vol. 4, *Ecumenic Age*, 36–37, 232–33.

10. Voegelin makes much of the *metaxy* ("in between") in Plato's anthropology, the tension between the human and the divine that underlies the movements of the soul. For Buber's related but different discussion of the "between," see Buber, *I and Thou*, esp. pt. 3.

are reality (515c–d, 516c–17a). The true lie, the *to hos alēthos pseudos* (382a, 535d–e) of sophistic disorder is not the possession of false knowledge (*epistēmē*) but the incorrect relation to the transcendent, the invisible God. No less than for Isaiah, it is a spiritual problem, a disease in the soul (*psyche*) that can be cured only by a "turning around" (*periagoge*) of the whole soul toward the divine good (518c–d, 521c), so that the soul might have "eyes to see" and "ears to hear" and an understanding of reality (cf. Isa 6:10) insofar as it is attuned to the divine measure.

Only such a turned-around soul in correct relation to the good beyond being can exercise prudent judgment (*phronēsis*, 518e–19a, 530b–c) or "free vision" unfettered by the ties of false images and shadow realities, because it sees that which truly *is* (*ta onta*, 518d, 521c–d) in the light of its real *cause* (*aitia*, 517b–c). Such a prudent person is also best able to make political judgments, but not through the implementation of an ideal—that is the wrong turn of Glaucon's *kallipolis* (527c), ruled by the immanent measure of geometric thinking applied to practical matters (527a). Glaucon is apparently afraid that the many might suppose him to be recommending useless studies, and he therefore finds it hard to trust that it is with a certain instrument (*organon*) of the soul alone that the truth is seen (527d–e). Glaucon is the one who does not want to fail and therefore fails to stand firm in spirit and truth, his soul constantly turning downward to seek useless and indeed harmful victory in the factional conflict of sophistic men who fight over shadows. It is Glaucon and not Socrates who harbors the desire to rule over the sophists.

Socrates possesses neither wisdom nor a perfect soul but rather loves wisdom and the good—this is the meaning of true *philia-sophon*. Such a love impels one constantly to move beyond oneself and one's own possessions toward truth itself and the good. The soul must be ever purified by being drawn beyond itself and thus turned around from conventional wisdom to real insight. That is the true *paideia* (518b–d). The source of political injustice and disorder is that the *philia* is broken by discord, by eristic contention that sets human beings at variance with the divine and therefore with their own origin and end. This leads to the falsification of reality through counterfeit claims, and it results in the world of illusion built on the *to hos alēthos pseudos*, the true lie hated by both gods and human beings. The world of *paranomia* (537e) that fills the harmful practitioners of dialectic, whose maimed souls (535d) cause them to use the power of *phronēsis* for destructive and vicious purposes, is ultimately ruled by tyrannical madness (book 9). This world is in reality a prison in which all dreams come true, a nightmare ruled by the "worst man," the awakened dreamer (576b; cf. 476c). Such a city is full of fear, always craving the possession of more to satisfy the insatiable desires of falsely turned love in the diseased, discordant soul.

The second point to be made against Buber's reading of the *Republic* concerns the vocation of the true philosopher, who has undergone the turning around of the soul and has had a vision of the good itself. In contrast to Buber's portrayal of the sublime, detached spectator, Socrates does not envision an emigration "to a colony on the Isle of the Blessed while they are still alive" (519c). Rather, having experienced the ascent of the soul to a vision of the divine, the philosopher will be compelled to go down (*katabasis*, 539e) again into the cave, down to the "common dwelling of the others" (520b–c) in order to speak the revealed truth about fair, just, and good things that the philosopher now knows and understands.

The philosopher does not seek political office and certainly will not attempt to seize the good through public affairs (521a). However, should the opportunity arise the philosopher will drudge in politics out of necessity (*ananke*), not desire (540b), and will do so in a state of wakefulness to the truth, not in a dream (520b). Such a person is "ruled by what is divine and prudent" and is oriented within by this rule (590d). But it is the rule according to a paradigm laid up in heaven (*en ourano*, 592b) for the one "who wants to see" and whose life is founded on the basis of this vision.

Here we are once again brought back to the vision and vocation of Isaiah, and we are now perhaps in a better position to undertake a comparative analysis of the historical failure represented by Plato and by Isaiah.

II

It is only fair that having clarified Plato by correcting the distorted reading of the *Republic* by a philosopher sympathetic to Isaiah, we now clarify Isaiah by correcting the distorted reading by a philosopher sympathetic to Plato. As was the case in our interpretation of Plato, where Eric Voegelin's work proved illuminating, so here Martin Buber's reflections on the prophetic consciousness help us interpret Isaiah's theological politics more accurately.[11]

Voegelin portrays Isaiah as a purveyor of "metastatic faith," which is little more than a euphemism for "magician"—a euphemism coined as a concession to Gerhard von Rad, who was apparently horrified by Voegelin's proposal to use the term "magician" for Isaiah, according to Voegelin's own account.[12] Von Rad's response is not terribly surprising, since he (in his classic *Theology of the Old Testament*) had identified Isaiah as "the theological high water mark of the whole Old Testament."[13] After von Rad's death, Voegelin retracted his concession and explicitly stated what he really thought.[14] Isaiah is engaged in magic fantasy because he believes that the structures of reality can be changed through an act of faith. In contrast to Plato, who is fully aware of the obstacles present in human nature and pragmatic history to the establishment of rule according to the divine paradigm (500e, 592b), Isaiah's faith calls the kings of Judah (both Ahaz, Isa 7, and Hezekiah, Isa 36–37) to place their trust in a divine intervention that will miraculously avert military attacks. According to Voegelin, Isaiah understands the order of faith in Yahweh to stand in direct contradiction to the order of power in historical political existence, and this leads him to postulate the necessity of miraculous divine intervention to change the structure of reality if divine order and rule are to be reestablished in history.

Isaiah's failure is, in Voegelin's view, related to a misunderstanding of spirit—a failure to understand how the divine truth of existence is related to and realized within the historical order of political society. In volume 1 of *Order and History*, Voegelin

11. See especially Buber, *Prophetic Faith*.
12. Voegelin, *Autobiographical Reflections*, 68.
13. See von Rad, *Old Testament Theology*, 2:147.
14. See also Voegelin, *Order and History*, vol. 5, *Search for Order*, 33.

PART 1: APOCALYPTIC MESSIANISM AND POLITICAL THEOLOGY

devotes considerable attention to what he calls the "unresolved problem at the bottom of Yahwism," namely, the relationship between the life of the spirit and life in the world.[15] This leads to a confusion in Israelite theological politics between the universal spiritual demands of a transcendent God and the practical exigencies of the political existence of a small nation. The development of a true political philosophy in Hebrew religion is prevented by the lack of a theory of the soul or psyche, which is not clearly differentiated from the "compact collectivism" of the people's existence.[16] This is the problem illustrated by reference to Isaiah's counsel to King Ahaz to trust in the *ruach* of Yahweh rather than in armies and alliances. Such counsel represents an ontological confusion between the existential formation of the personal soul and the practices and institutions of political order. It represents a "sublime rebellion" against the nature of things ordained by God, presenting the divine plan for the salvation of the people as a knowable, pragmatic policy to be historically effected:

> Isaiah, we may say, has tried the impossible: to make the leap in being a leap out of existence into a divinely transfigured world beyond the laws of mundane existence. The cultic restoration of cosmic divine order becomes the transfiguration of the world in history when carried into the historical form of existence.[17]

In contrast to the disappointing failure of a utopian idealist (Buber's portrait of Plato), we have here the fantastic failure of an apocalyptic gnostic who claims to *possess* a revelation—that is, information about how God will produce an immanent result outside the natural relations of cause and effect. The reified symbol of God as a personal agent in history has taken over the prophetic consciousness, causing Isaiah to lose sight of the ultimate mystery of reality as the process of the divine cosmos that becomes present or luminous through the noetic participation of the soul in it. Isaiah takes his personal vision too literally and therefore misunderstands the encounter and the mission he thinks he has received—the myth is historicized falsely. Fortunately, adds Voegelin, the king (one presumes he means Ahaz) retains his political common sense and pays his tribute money to the Assyrian king, thus averting military disaster via realistic foreign policy rather than magic.

But who is guilty of false literalism here? When Isaiah's particular political advice to Ahaz and Hezekiah is ripped out of its religious and symbolic (as well as historical and political) context and measured by the noetic theophanies of cosmic order becoming luminous in the philosopher's soul, it should surely come as no surprise to us if it causes a disturbance. Under such circumstances it is a little too easy to offer up Isaiah as comic fare. This too is a somewhat undialectical reading of Isaiah as an ardent fundamentalist. It does not adequately portray the dialogical character of the Hebrew "word," the *dabar* that is always spoken in the form of an address. Buber places this at the heart of the Hebrew religious consciousness: "God is the Being . . . that may only be addressed, not expressed."[18] In the prophet, spirit (*ruach*) and word are not expressed as a thinker seek-

---

15. Voegelin, *Order and History*, vol. 1, *Israel and Revelation*, 183; cf. 369, 444–45.
16. Ibid., 439.
17. Ibid., 452.
18. Buber, *I and Thou*, 80. In his essay on Exodus 20, "The Words on the Tablets," Buber states that

The Theological Politics of Plato and Isaiah

ing the truth and the good—in this sense the prophetic oracle "before God" is different from the *logos* of Greek philosophy. The prophet gives voice to the holy will of the God who stands in covenant relation to a people that is elected to become a "holy" people ("you shall therefore be holy, for I am holy," Lev 11:44–45; cf. Exod 19:3–8) by walking in the way, by imitating Yahweh, and thereby mediating the divine purposes in history. As A.J. Heschel's study of the prophets so beautifully portrays it, the prophets participate in and give expression to the purposes and the *pathos* of God—they cry out, cajole, threaten, weep, groan, exult as they call the people back to the way of faith.[19]

While this might look quite graceless and ridiculous (perhaps like a kind of "daimonic hyperbole"[20]) to the uninitiated, it appears otherwise to those who understand the symbolism and remember their covenant relation to Yahweh—a relation that is anything but magical. Of course the prophetic word disrupts and disturbs the people of the covenant as well, but it is important to be clear about the cause of the disruption: not magic, but the call to faith. These are two different things. As Buber puts it in *I and Thou*, "Magic wants to be effective without entering into any relationship and performs its arts in the void, while sacrifice and prayer [and, we might add, prophecy] step 'before the countenance' into the perfection of the sacred basic word that signifies reciprocity. They say You and listen."[21] The "Coming One" of the prophets cannot be conjured up, nor does faith consist of mysterious, esoteric knowledge or powers.[22] Rather, it is a matter of being addressed by God and entrusted with a message or task, with a claim that calls the people to respond to the holy God in all the concrete particularities of their life, including political affairs. The focus of the Hebrew prophets is not on the power of faith but rather gives testimony to the purposes and actions of God in historical events, whose meaning is discerned by faith.[23]

What then are we to make of the dramatic confrontation between Isaiah and King Ahaz on the highway to the Fuller's Field (Isa 7), an encounter that is placed immediately after the account of Isaiah's temple vision and prophetic call (chap. 6)? Here we must go beyond the form to the content of the oracle,[24] because it is the message announced by the prophet that is shocking and hard to understand by those rooted in the secure tradition of divine election and the Davidic covenant. It is a declaration of "holy war" by God against God's own chosen people, a judgment of the people by the holy God symbolized by the "Day of Yahweh" (chap. 2), and this directly concerns the political fate of Judah.

---

the soul of the Ten Commandments is found in the word "thou," in being addressed by the divine Word that constitutes Israel as a people. See Buber, "Plato and Isaiah," 106–7.

19. See Heschel, *The Prophets*.

20. Glaucon's charge against Socrates, when he (Glaucon) fails to understand (509c). See also the discussion of the graceless and ridiculous appearance of the philosopher who returns to the cave after the experience of divine contemplation (517d–18b).

21. Buber, *I and Thou*, 131.

22. Buber makes this point against Heidegger's interpretation of the prophets (which is not unrelated to Voegelin's misreading of Isaiah). See Buber, *Eclipse of God*, 73–74.

23. See von Rad, *Old Testament Theology*, 1:111–12.

24. This is precisely the stumbling block for Voegelin—the "mortgage of the historical circumstances of revelation" is "made permanent" by incorporating the circumstances of revelation into its contents rather than differentiating them. Voegelin, *Order and History*, vol. 1, *Israel and Revelation*, 369.

PART 1: APOCALYPTIC MESSIANISM AND POLITICAL THEOLOGY

Isaiah's vision in the temple of Yahweh "high and lifted up" introduces a divine measure and thereby reveals the sin of the people "before God." The people and the king will be judged because of their persistent violation of the covenant with their divine king, a violation rooted not so much in specific vices or lack of virtue as in a prideful, self-sufficient arrogance that seeks its security in the pragmatic weapons and arts of power politics rather than in obedient response to God. The sin to be judged is not lack of virtue but lack of faith.

Hence the coming of Yahweh in judgment is presented by Isaiah (chap. 2) as the day of Yahweh against all human pride and arrogance, which has led the people of Judah to seek its security in idolatrous political alliances. The land is full of signs of economic and political prosperity—silver and gold, treasures, horses and chariots—but it is also full of idols (2:7–9). This kind of power politics goes hand in glove with religious idolatry: the prideful man will not bend the knee before the Creator, yet he bows down to silver and gold, chariots and military might, the illusory trappings of false greatness. Pragmatic political and historical success is pursued at the expense of the great *religious* failure, which Buber in his essay on "Biblical Leadership" identifies as "the refusal to enter the dialogue" with God;[25] that is, lack of faith in Yahweh's sovereignty. God's terrible judgment (as "holy war") will reveal the nothingness of this security, the lie entailed in such political practices of unholy alliances (Isa 28:15).

It is this that lies behind the ostensible political defeatism of Isaiah's counsel to Judah's kings and his confrontation with King Ahaz. He is entrusted with a message of judgment against false security based on sin. Yahweh, the God of the covenant, is not a tribal deity who guarantees the historical success of the chosen people but the holy God who rules over all of history and creation. Lack of faith is a willful failure to understand this—it fails to grasp the significance of life "before God" and therefore inhabits the sin of false autonomy and the pretentious attempt to control historical destiny. Isaiah has "seen" Yahweh, the true king, whose *kabhod* ("radiation," or "glory") seeks to "fill the earth" (Isa 6:3, 11:9, 40:5), to become present in the world by those who imitate the divine holiness in a "spirit of wisdom and understanding" (11:2) that enables them to make righteous judgments and actions (11:3–5). In this manner political justice is concretely mediated because it is oriented by the divine measure, attuned to the purposes of the Creator. This is the essential nature and meaning of the covenant relation to Yahweh.

Ahaz cannot see this. He sees only the great powers that occupy center stage in his particular political theater, and his heart (and the hearts of the people) shudders with fear (Isa 7:2) at the threatened invasion by Israel and Syria, who seek Judah's support in a coalition against the Assyrian empire. Isaiah's advice is "pay attention, stay calm, don't fear" (7:4; cf. 30:15). Pay attention to the *real* danger, namely, idolatry and placing one's trust in false things out of despair in spiritual truth. Stay calm—do not rush off rashly to powerful Assyria for protection. Do not fear the temporal power of nations that come and go and ultimately stand before the judgment of the invisible God of history with whom you have an ongoing dialogical relationship. Stand firm in the spirit, or you will not stand. To stand firm in the spirit is understood by Isaiah as a form of *imitatio Dei*. Stability is to be found not in unholy pragmatic alliances but in faithful adherence to the

---

25. Buber, "Biblical Leadership," 49–50.

divine will that radiates righteousness, that "knows how to refuse the evil and choose the good" (7:16). However, such a response entails a willingness to *wait* for Yahweh (8:16, 30:15) rather than manage the peoples' security, because it fears the holy God rather than temporal power (8:11–15; cf. 11:3). This becomes a "stone of offense and a rock of stumbling" for those who seek more tangible signs and guarantees. As Buber puts it, "The true believer does not wish to hasten God's work, the work of salvation, even if he could. Small politics is a monologue of man; great politics is a discourse with the God Who 'keeps still.'"[26]

Ahaz's answer is a clear refusal to enter the spiritual dialogue: "No. I will not put Yahweh to the test" (Isa 7:12). This is the willful despair of the spirit that is characteristic of sin[27]—it refuses to stand before God and be measured, because that would mean acknowledging one's uncleanness along with the infinite demands of a holy God, and this is too high altogether. This would require a purity of heart that gives up the need to control life through self-assertion and enters humbly into relation, surrendering the self to the divine will. This the sinful self cannot do. It would rather maintain its proud self-reliance by sinking still deeper into despair than risk a dialogical relation to an invisible Wholly Other God. Indeed, the aim of magic is to be effective without entering a relationship, whereas faith risks all in the relationship and dares to live "before God" in fear and trembling.

"I will not put God to the test" reveals the heart of Ahaz. It can only be said at a self-imposed distance from God that does not allow itself to be addressed and therefore will not respond to the divine Word. Ahaz will not live "before God," and so he goes off with his tribute money to the king of Assyria who, after all, has horses and chariots and deals in political reality, not sin and faith. This is much more dignified and pragmatically effective than trying to understand the stammering words of a prophetic messenger (see Isa 28:10–15 in the *Jerusalem Bible*). Ahaz will continue to practice the politics of idolatry, using religion only for his own purposes as sacral legitimation for his own regime.[28] Religion will stay in its own proper domain, and therewith Ahaz resists the universal demand of the holy God, who demands all and gives all.[29]

Here we will break off our brief look at the political history of Judah in Isaiah's time, since it is really beside the point to add that Isaiah (in contrast to Voegelin's judgment) was really right not only about the spiritual costs but also about the high political costs of Ahaz's alliance with Assyria and later Hezekiah's alliance with Egypt. After all, in the *content* of Isaiah's vision we have encountered the decisive difference between the Hebrew prophets and Plato—sin and faith, in contrast to ignorance and understanding. The "before God" of the Hebrews is not primarily a noetic relation but a personal spiritual

---

26. Buber, *Prophetic Faith*, 137.

27. See Kierkegaard, "Sickness unto Death," pt. 2.

28. In 2 Kings 16 we find a description of Ahaz's sixteen-year rule in Jerusalem. He burned his son as an offering (v. 3) to "Moloch," an act that makes Isaiah's vision of Yahweh as *ha-melekh* more striking. Ahaz does not know the true God, and his worship becomes an abomination, indicating his loss of the true measure of kingly rule. When Ahaz goes to Damascus to meet Tiglath-pileser, the king of Assyria, he sends Uriah the priest a model of the Assyrian altar and offers sacrifices on it in Yahweh's temple. The political alliance must be religiously legitimated through cultic ceremonies.

29. See Buber, *Prophetic Faith*, 152.

encounter, a historical dialogue between God and humans in which the content of revelation is more than the fact that it occurs,[30] more than a disclosure of the intelligibility of the cosmos. It is a revelation of the infinite measure or demand addressed by the holy God to humankind, which also reveals the violation of a personal bond requiring repentance, forgiveness, and return.

We have, it is true, barely scratched the surface with respect to the theological and political implications of the different symbolisms employed by the Greek philosopher and the Hebrew prophet. To elaborate the substantive meaning of the contrast more fully would immerse us in complexities far too daunting to tackle here. Suffice it to say that the noetic deficiency resulting in a lack of prudence is a spiritual problem of a different order than the willful refusal to relate oneself in trust to God that constitutes sin. Nevertheless, I have tried to show in what the contrast between the two does *not* consist, and this itself points up the complexity of the comparative task that still remains. It also demonstrates—and this has been the burden of the constructive argument I have tried to make here—the convergence of Plato and Isaiah in their articulation of political order rooted in a theological understanding and spiritual vision of reality that is neither idealistic nor ideological. In this manner they point to the possibility of a symbolic or religious realism relevant to the development of theological politics in our own time. I wish to conclude this essay with some brief remarks on this point.

III

The theological politics of Plato and Isaiah both seek to illuminate the religious foundations of political judgment and wisdom. The problem of order and the common good in society is a spiritual matter not discerned so long as one is oriented toward the external power struggle of ideologues whose only aim is to conquer and control. The true nature of political reality can only be discerned by those who look beyond their own interests and the immediacy of social forces to the invisible, divine order of creation, oriented by noetic prudence or the righteousness of faith. There is no external political substitute for the rightly ordered *psyche* or spirit. Politics is therefore not merely a matter of the pragmatic management of external forces (in a power struggle or "balance of power") but the practical mediation of transcendent wisdom that binds the world together in a meaningful order.

The conditions for true political community and good order must be established existentially—they cannot be forcibly imposed through external constraints. This ultimately entails the formation of character in the well-ordered soul or the responsive heart, both of which are formed in participatory relation to the transcendent God. Political philosophy or theology, therefore, is a matter of the proper symbolization of human nature and society in relation to the divine order of reality in creation. It is a matter of the human mediation of the divine measure within the concrete circumstances of social life by making prudent judgments, giving expression to particular demands of justice that make a well-ordered, righteous, and peaceful life possible. Those who achieve such

---

30. See Voegelin, *Order and History*, vol. 4, *Ecumenic Age*, 233.

"free vision" are able to discern the meaning of particular concrete political realities in relation to the larger purposes of the created order.

Such discernment, however, will always be resisted by those who insist on imposing their own selfish measures, who seek to manipulate even God and the gods for their own puny purposes, trying to recreate the world in their own disordered image. Such purveyors of illusory politics will measure "success" in terms of the extent of their coercive mastery over reality in the vain quest to establish their own security over against that which they cannot ultimately control. This has destructive, and ultimately self-destructive, consequences, founded on a blindness to the things that are. For Plato this is a matter of ignorance, to be overcome through the therapy of *paideia*, whereby the soul is turned around to the good beyond being and is noetically reoriented toward true reality through the love of wisdom. For Isaiah the failure is a matter of sin, the willful refusal to see rooted in the failure to relate oneself in trust to God, the refusal to respond to the divine revelation. This can only be overcome in humble repentance, turning from the proud self-assertion of the defiant will that *will* not trust in God for its strength, that *will* not live "before God" and be measured by God's infinite holiness.

Of course, it will always also be possible to read Plato as a Glaucon and Isaiah as a fundamentalist, treating their theological (symbolic) politics as pragmatic political principles to be technically applied and enforced so as to gain power over others for parochial purposes (which are identified with the divine for purposes of legitimation). Indeed, both Plato and Isaiah recognized the spiritual blindness of the many that made possible the destructive rule of ideological tyrants in their own time. They also understood that this spiritual blindness cannot be overcome by means of policies, techniques, and institutions. The divine measure rules in the soul, says Plato, and so the soul must be turned from the phenomenal world of becoming toward the divine *sophon* in which it participates in the true, transcendent order of being. The unity of justice and righteousness can be understood only in relation to the sovereign God, says Isaiah, and it can be attained only in the religious act of the heart turning entirely to God, repenting of the vain attempt to establish forcibly one's own regime on an unwilling reality.

3

Augustine's Messianic Political Theology

An Apocalyptic Critique of Political Augustinianism

THE THESIS OF CHARLES Taylor's influential tome *A Secular Age* might be summarized as follows: modern secularization, a socio-political creation of the West, has given rise to an anti-religious "exclusive humanism" in reaction to a Latin Christendom obsessed with "reform"—that is, to an externalized juridical-penal institutionalization of Christianity that has lost the personal and incarnational essence of the original "Gospel" of the Messiah Jesus. Taylor identifies the source of this perversion of Latin Christianity as "hyper-Augustinianism," which takes both Catholic and Protestant forms but is particularly reified and hardened in Calvinist Protestantism.[1] Like Augustine, hyper-Augustinians believe that only a small number of the human *massa damnata* will be saved from sin in order to dwell eternally with God; the majoritarian remainder will be condemned to eternal hell.[2] Theologically this position is rooted in a juridical-penal understanding of the atonement, in which divine wrath against human sin must be appeased and Christ's sacrifice pays the debt of original sin. There is present here, argues Taylor, a tension between a juridical metaphor (payment of debt) and a redemption metaphor (freeing the captive), a tension between divine anger/wrath and divine love/mercy, between hell and heaven, that gets resolved in a rigid doctrinal logic in which ecclesial authorities display the all-too-human tendency to colonize divine violence in the service of their own. This logic is tied to a pernicious interpretation of suffering and punishment as a part of a providentially governed "divine pedagogy," in a narrative of total human depravity and limited atonement. Politically this view entails the belief that the godly minority should exercise political control so as to restrain evil and promote civil order.

---

1. See Taylor's discussion of "hyper-Augustinianism" in Taylor, *Secular Age*, 105, 227, 231, 319, 511, 626, 651–54.

2. See Augustine, *City of God* 13.23, 14.21, 21.12. All references to this translation will appear in parentheses (abbreviated as *civ. Dei*) in the body of the chapter.

Hyper-Augustinians emphasize divine punishment, foster a seamless and puritanical connection between piety and social order, and emphasize the transformation of the will in which virtue requires the disciplined, institutional imposition of the ordering of the good. But for hyper-Augustinians there are also real limits to such institutional, socio-political (re)ordering and reform due to the pervasive, incorrigible fact of human sinfulness, which must simply be coercively restrained in the earthly city. Think of Nietzsche's harshest articulation of Christian *ressentiment* against the sinful strong that gives birth to the juridical-penal conscience, which creates the "responsible, sovereign moral self" through the internalization of the transcendent "evil eye," institutionally mediated through various disciplines of religio-moral self-surveillance.[3] Here you have a précis of Taylor's "hyper-Augustinianism," and while he shares elements of the Nietzschean critique, Taylor also seeks to articulate a Christian vision that is able to address the critique from within a more faithful liberal Catholic political theology, one heavily indebted (Taylor claims[4]) to the work of Ivan Illich—particularly on the radical implications of a Christian understanding of incarnation that entails new motivation (divine compassion rather than penal pedagogy) and a new community ("Communion of Saints" rather than institutional church) based on voluntary neighbor love that goes beyond external religious identitarian markers and institutional codes.

It is hard to know how Taylor himself would distinguish or reconcile his account of hyper-Augustinianism from or with his account of Augustine in *Sources of the Self* and the Augustinian turn to the inner, intimate self in which God is nearer to me than I am to myself.[5] One thing seems clear: neither account is articulated in highly theological or existential terms. In *Sources* the conceptual Augustinian doctrine of the soul is related to Plato on the one hand and Descartes on the other. In *A Secular Age* Taylor conceptually distinguishes hyper-Augustinian reform and political Augustinianism but nowhere clearly spells out the theological terms and existential consequences of the distinction. Hence it is difficult to agree with John Milbank that Taylor speaks in a theological voice. In fact, Milbank goes much further to suggest that Taylor is "almost a modern equivalent of Augustine" in providing "a kind of . . . theologized ecclesiastical history."[6] Indeed, says Milbank, "Taylor has, with *A Secular Age*, consummated his invention of a new intellectual genre—a kind of historicized existentialism."[7] That Taylor is an intellectual historian of the highest order no one could contest; that he is theological and existential in an Augustine-like way, however, is questionable. I shall argue that Illich comes much closer to Augustine's existential historically informed political theology, and he does so because he shares Augustine's apocalyptic biblically formed theological perspective.

---

3. See, for example, Nietzsche, *On the Genealogy of Morals*.

4. See *Secular Age*, 737–43. Taylor also writes a very appreciative foreword to Illich, *Rivers North of the Future*.

5. Taylor, *Sources of the Self*, chap. 7. Nevertheless, I will take Taylor's position to be compatible with the political Augustinianism developed by Robert A. Markus in *Christianity and the Secular*. Markus himself makes the suggestion in his programmatic third chapter on "Consensus in Augustine and the Liberal Tradition." I will return to this below.

6. Milbank, "Closer Walk on the Wild Side," 55.

7. Ibid., 78.

PART 1: APOCALYPTIC MESSIANISM AND POLITICAL THEOLOGY

Neither Milbank nor Taylor does so, and this has important political theological consequences, some of which I shall try to articulate in this chapter. What is missing from Taylor's appropriation of Illich and critique of hyper-Augustinianism is the centrality of apocalyptic messianism in both Illich and Augustine, which mediates the spiritual causality of divine providence within the personal and political terms of created embodied reality, in a manner that resists the abuses of hyper-Augustinianism.

One of the central critiques Milbank makes of Taylor is that Taylor favors the "disenchantment" of reality by Enlightenment cosmology, a cosmology that calls into question (1) the popular religious experience of natural reality as "acts of God," (2) the assumption that the political and the religious orders are inseparable, and (3) the belief that the world is full of invisible spiritual forces.[8] At stake here, among other things, is the question of what constitutes Christian "sacramental mediation." Milbank favors a "re-enchantment" of the world to go along with Taylor's affirmation of Illich's call for a "festive conviviality," corresponding (for Taylor) to a "Communion of Saints" in which there is no exclusionary hell or "double predestination" but only an inclusive universalism rooted in incarnational love. Milbank's "re-enchantment" (as a kind of intellectual cultural romanticism) appears to accept Taylor's worry about Christian apocalypticism as somehow tied to hyper-Augustinianism, and yet Milbank seeks to find a place for the "practical bent" of Latin Christianity[9] in which sacramental mediation also takes procedural and institutional forms. He settles upon "medieval corporatism," and it seems that he considers this form of Christendom culture to model a more promising kind of Augustinianism.

It is not my brief to analyze Milbank's critical and constructive interpretation of Taylor as variants of a new kind of political Augustinianism, though I will return to this general question below. My point here is that Augustine's and Illich's thoroughgoing Christian apocalyptic stances are neither modes of "(re-)enchantment" nor are they, as such stances are often represented, averse to a disciplined, critical consideration of the institutional and procedural contexts of embodied socio-political human existence. Taylor and Milbank, unlike Illich and Augustine, fail to plumb the depths of biblical apocalypticism, preferring instead to develop grand philosophico-historical narratives. Illich, by contrast, performs his messianic apocalyptic critique of modern Western culture with reference to "the old Latin phrase: *Corruptio optimi quae est pessima*—the historical progression in which God's Incarnation is turned topsy-turvy, inside out. I want to speak of the mysterious darkness that envelops our world, the demonic night paradoxically resulting from the world's equally mysterious vocation to glory. My subject is a mystery of faith, a mystery whose depth of evil could not have come to be without the greatness of the truth revealed to us."[10] The demonic perversion of truth is not simply a violation of the laws of reality but a personal turning away from an intimate revelation of divine reality in whose image human beings are created. Its correlative is a turning in worship toward a false substitute, the apostatic *mysterium iniquitatis* Paul

---

8. Ibid., 58.
9. Ibid., 80–82.
10. Illich, *Rivers North of the Future*, 29.

speaks about in 2 Thessalonians 2,[11] revealed as anti-Messiah in the apocalypse of Messiah and characterized by mendacious power and wicked deception. This is the personal, intimate character of sin that also has pervasive social and political consequences—the substitution of other-regarding personal love by self-securing institutional power. It may also be described as a turn away from the divine Spirit of love enfleshed in the person of Jesus toward a trust once again in the juridical, institutional constraints of external rules and codes of behavior—a shift from a community rooted in "con-spiratio" (personal faith, love, sin, forgiveness inspired by the divine Spirit) to one rooted in "con-juratio" (the juridical state structure).[12] The impersonal, instrumental, and juridical character of modern social and political ethics, related to risk assessment and technical requirements of security systems (be they legal, educational, or medical), are the shared consequences of this shift in spiritual vision. While I cannot attend here to the rich detail of Illich's account, it is clearly an apocalyptic account derived from the New Testament, and it bears many political theological similarities to Augustine's apocalyptic account of the contrast between the Roman empire of his day and the biblical revelation of messianic authority, peace, and justice that governs citizens of the heavenly city.

For Augustine as for Illich, political justice is a matter of the mimetic objects of love and worship: whether that is the earthly mediation of true justice in the servant form of the messianic king of the heavenly city, or the perverse mediation of false images of justice by demons led by the "father of lies," *diabolus*. The spiritual and political tension between the two cities represents an apocalyptic conflict between the heavenly Jerusalem and the earthly Babylon, presided over by conflicting authorities.[13] I shall argue, in keeping with Illich's account and using some of his central *topoi*, that Augustine shares the (especially Pauline) apocalyptic urgency of the New Testament in which the conflict between the flesh and the spirit, first Adam and second Adam, messianic sovereignty and anti-messianic rebellion, may not be reduced to institutional authorities (such as "church and state"). Rather, they belong to very different orientations of life that extend from the inner conscience of each human being (the con-spiratio of the messianic conscientia, we might say) to household relations, to cities and peoples, to the cosmic ordering of all things in keeping with the spiritual causality of divine causality apocalypsed in Christ—an apocalyptic sovereignty that may not be institutionalized in any authoritative human cultural form but that lives by faith, oriented toward the invisible Sovereign it worships not only in its ritual forms but in all acts of loving service in the world. The political-ethical corruption of the best by the worst is characterized by a reversal in "use and enjoyment" displayed in the messianic *ordo amoris* in which earthly things are to be

---

11. Ibid., chaps. 2, 14. Here is one of Illich's pithy formulations of what he means: "The Anti-Christ, or, let's say, the *mysterium iniquitatis*, the mystery of evil, is the conglomerate of a series of perversions by which we try to give security, survival ability, and independence from individual persons to the new possibilities that were opened through the Gospel by institutionalizing them" (169). Compare Augustine's reflection on 2 Thessalonians 2 and the possible meaning of the *Antichristo* as the "universal body" of the prince of apostasy, standing over against the messianic body as lie against truth (*civ. Dei* 20.19).

12. Illich, *Rivers North of the Future*, chaps. 5, 15, 16.

13. See the valuable study by van Oort, *Jerusalem and Babylon*. He points up the problems (pp. 151–55) in R. A. Markus's anti-apocalyptic depiction of a possible political "neutrality" between the two cities in the *saeculum*, an issue to which we shall return below.

PART 1: APOCALYPTIC MESSIANISM AND POLITICAL THEOLOGY

used with reference to the peace found in the heavenly city,[14] in which the true nature of things is ultimately revealed:

> For this peace is a perfectly ordered and perfectly harmonious fellowship in the enjoyment of God, and of one another in God. When we have reached that peace, our life will no longer be a mortal one; rather, we shall then be fully and certainly alive . . . . a spiritual body standing in need of nothing; a body subject in every part to the will. This peace the heavenly city possesses in faith while on its pilgrimage, and by this faith it lives righteously [*iuste*], directing towards the attainment of that peace every good act which it performs either for God, or—since the city's life is inevitably a social one—for neighbour. (*civ. Dei* 19.17)[15]

Providence/Contingency

One of the most important features of Christian apocalypticism, argues Illich, following Hans Blumenberg, is the idea of contingency.[16] Briefly put, "Contingency expresses the state of being of a world which has been created from nothing, is destined to disappear and is upheld in its existence by one thing, and one thing only: divine will."[17] This idea of apocalyptic contingency owes its conceptual existence to Augustine's providential understanding that creation is at every moment the sovereign act of God's completely gratuitous will, who brings reality into being *ex nihilo*.[18] This places a lot of weight on will, not only in terms of the divine will but also of the human will made in God's image. Gratuity or gift, "a realm that comes into being in response to a call, rather than a determinative cause," is in fact the primary form of causation in the Bible—the causation of

---

14. The reversal is that citizens of the earthly city, oriented toward their own self-pleasure, use the true peace of the heavenly city to enjoy earthly goods for themselves in the power game. See *civ. Dei* 14.1–4; 15.7; 19.17.

15. Van Oort points out the centrality of chap. 17 in the central book 19 of *civ. Dei*. Citizens of the heavenly city who live by faith "make use of earthly and temporal things like pilgrims: they are not captivated by them, nor are they deflected by them from their progress towards God." In this way do both kinds of citizens make *usus communis* of the necessities of life, in a "cooperation of wills" (*composition voluntatem*) that are nevertheless oriented toward different ends (the *finis utendi* is divergent). It should be noted that the use and enjoyment language in *civ. Dei* is introduced in 1.8f., alongside the language of *peregrinatio* to denote in apocalyptic fashion the diaspora existence of the City of God on earth. In *civ. Dei* 1.10 Augustine provides a Pauline *hōs mē* apocalyptic warrant for his language of "use" taken from 1 Corinthians 7:31: make use of the world "as if not using it," a making use of earthly goods (as Augustine puts it in 1.29) "like pilgrims, without grasping after them" (*bonisque terrenis tamquam peregrine utitur nec capitur*). In *civ. Dei* 10.6 this kind of "use" is related to the apocalyptic "sacrifice" of the messianic body whose service in the world imitates the form of the servant.

16. Illich, *Rivers North of the Future*, chaps. 3–4. (Blumenberg's article is in *Religion in Geschichte und Gegenwart*).

17. Illich, *Rivers North of the Future*, 65.

18. For Augustine's language of creation *ex nihilo* with regard to the logic of defection and "fall," see *civ. Dei* 12.6f., 14.11 and 13; see also *Confessions* 12.7.7, 12.28.38, 12.29.40, 13.33.48. Importantly, therefore, for Augustine the human soul is also created *ex nihilo* and thus relies on God alone for its being and life (*civ. Dei* 10.31).

divine Word that constantly speaks the world into being.[19] The willed human response to this call is also highly consequential, both in terms of freely obeying the creative divine will or falling away from it in disobedience, or sin. Sin is on this view less the violation of a law than an intimate and relational infidelity that has natural and political consequences. The apocalyptic claim of the New Testament is, to put it in Pauline terms, that the whole of this creation is pregnant with the Messiah and is now (with the coming of Christ) groaning in labor (Rom 8). The groaning consists in the messianic revelation of a new possibility, a neighbor love that crosses all social, political, and cultural-religious boundaries as a "free creation" in response to a divine call.[20] This call entails not only a disruption of conventional moral categories (male/female, jew/greek, slave/master, friend/enemy), and hence a social disruption of role and behavior definitions, but also an account of virtue as suffering love that comes always only as a divine gift in response to a divine call that may be refused. And of course part of the messianic groaning and suffering of creation is that this call is resisted and refused (sin), resulting in both internal existential conflicts in the human will (Rom 7) and socio-political and religious conflicts. This means that the "mood, or ground-tone" of this new messianic way of being is contrition, "a deep sorrow about my capacity to betray . . . relationships . . . and, at the same time, a deep confidence in the forgiveness and mercy of the other."[21] Needless to say, this raises the stakes for social and political ethics considerably in the messianic community that seeks to live according to this newly revealed form of life, and it will find itself confronting not only internal collisions but also collisions with forms of life that are constituted quite otherwise, in power relations under human juridical and institutional control in the earthly city. Illich's argument is that the messianic apocalypse requires a radical, contingent faith that is constantly itself in danger of being perverted by sin, that is, "the decision to make faith into something that is subject to the power of this world,"[22] namely the "anti-messianic." This is the constant temptation within Christendom and it has led to significant perversions in the modern West. I will return to this below, but wish now to turn to Augustine's important formulation of this providential contingency in what I call his vision of spiritual causality.

I begin with Augustine's discussion of causality in book 5 of *City of God*, which is crucial to Augustine's case for divine providence rather than fate as the principle of interpretation for political order, peace, and justice. Roman historiography and political theory lacks insight into the spiritual causes of human action—the quest for happiness

---

19. Illich, *Rivers North of the Future*, 49. See Augustine's language of divine causation in *civ. Dei* 11. 21–22, 12.26—all movement comes from God's hidden, intimate, yet pervasive power, so that "if God were to withdraw His creative power, so to speak, from things, they would no more exist that they did before they were created"(22.24). Cf. *civ. Dei* 10.15 and 9.22, where knowledge of the divine will, the most potent causality, is a matter of spiritual participation in the divine Word—i.e., love (*caritas*), not "knowledge" (*scientia*, which is what the demons worship), in keeping with Paul's account in 1 Corinthians.

20. Illich, *Rivers North of the Future*, 51–52.

21. Ibid., 53. No reader of Augustine's *Confessions* and *The City of God* can fail to notice his repeated emphasis on the centrality of *misericordia* (misery) and *penitentia* (penance and forgiveness) in his account of the pilgrim Christian journey.

22. Illich, *Rivers North of the Future*, 57.

PART 1: APOCALYPTIC MESSIANISM AND POLITICAL THEOLOGY

(*felicitas*) and the conditions of peace and justice that make it possible—because it lacks this theological principle. Augustine understands divine providence as the ordering of all reality according to the rational power of divine will—God's perfect free agency—over against the impersonal, external causality of *fatum* and *fortuna*. Only a providential account will overcome the problematic either-or distinction between the external mechanisms of nature (inanimate causality) and human free agency (moral causality) that seeks to establish a rational relation between them, a relation that cannot be accounted for via various earthly measures. Only a messianic measure will offer insight into the true ground of human liberation (freedom of the will) from bondage to perverse demonic affective and social orderings.

In *City of God* 5.9, Augustine develops his account by denying any contradiction between divine *praescientia* of all things that God has made, and *libera hominis voluntate*. But this requires the recognition that the *ordo causarum* in which all motion (and motive) finds its intelligible principles is established by the divine Word of creation, rooted in God's eternal will. The efficient causality of all that happens is tied to will, and ultimately to the divine will that gives life to everything; that is, there are "no efficient causes which are not voluntary causes: belonging, that is, to that nature which is the 'breath of life' (*spiritus vitae*)." All bodies, inanimate as well as rational, are subject to God, the uncreated, uncaused breath of life who alone gives the power to move and the power to act freely: "Thus the real cause which causes and is not caused, is God." God freely establishes the spiritual terms of movement and agency (power), including free human agency (will), and this means that all motion and power must be understood in relation to God and the causal order established by divine Word and Spirit.

Augustine spells this out in *City of God* 5.11, which I shall quote at length:

> Thus the supreme and true God, with his Word and the Holy Spirit, which three are one, is the one omnipotent God, creator and maker of every soul and every body; participation in whom brings happiness to all who are happy in the truth and not in illusion (*vanitas*). He has made man a rational animal; and when man sins he does not let him go unpunished, nor does he abandon him without mercy. He has given, to good and bad alike, the existence (*essentia*) they share with the stones, reproductive life (*vita seminale*) they share with the plants, sentient life they share with the animals, and intellectual life they share only with the angels. From him comes every mode of being, every species, every order, all measure, number, and weight. From him comes all that exists in nature, whatever its kind (*generis*), whatever its value (*aestimationis*), and the seeds of forms (*semina formarum*), and the forms of seeds, and the motions of seeds and forms. He has given to flesh its origin, beauty, health, fertility in propagation, the arrangement and healthful concord of its members. He has also given the irrational soul memory, sense, and appetite; and in addition has given the rational soul mind, intelligence and will. Neither heaven nor earth, neither angel nor man, not even the inner parts of the smallest and lowliest creatures, nor the feather of a bird, nor a tiny flower of a plant, nor the leaf on a tree, has God left without a harmony and, as it were, a peace among their parts. In no manner can it be believed, then,

that he should have willed the kingdoms of men, their dominations and their servitudes, to be outside the laws of his providence.[23] (Translation altered)

Clearly for Augustine nature is not a closed system but rather a dynamic, dramatic ordering animated by the living Spirit of the triune God. This principle is fully coherent with the further implication that human rational will images the divine will insofar as it moves freely toward the happiness it desires, and that it understands its motion and the entire order of causality only in relation to the God that created and continues to sustain them. The principles of political order and moral judgment concerning politics are therefore fundamentally tied to divine providence. Access to this moral order is to be found in the internal witness of conscience, says Augustine (5.12), by which he means a fully public and testable witness, not private consent to doctrine. Any conception of political power or measure of political order that does not attend to the love of justice therein attested (5.14) misses the mark, the true path of virtue.

While conscience is an inner spiritual measure, it is not autonomous—it finds its measure, however, not in an earthly city but in the heavenly one, the eternal City of God where true happiness is realized as a divine gift (5.16). This city is not directly present, nor does its Sovereign rule in any directly visible way on earth (which is why "the just shall live by faith," one of Augustine's, and Paul's, favorite biblical lines). It is accessible only in the worship and imitation of the true God, whose rule is mediated on the earth only in the form of the servant, a form whose authority is revealed not in the "power-game" but in the "justice-game" (*Trinity* 13.17; E. Hill's free but apt translation).[24] It is only in the inner spiritual and outer corporeal imitation of this form that one can make proper political judgments. Thus when Augustine begins his critique of the Roman empire in earnest in book 4 of *City of God*, he too (like Plato before him and Hobbes after him) will ground the act of political judgment in the "human writ large" (4.3). At issue is the standard of true happiness, a life lived in harmony with the highest eternal good, in which worship of the true, immortal God will overcome the false measure of "fear of death" rooted in excessive love of (or orientation toward) the temporal.

In contrast to those "gangs of criminals on a large scale" who cannot rule themselves except by "dividing the plunder" according to conventions of human justice, and arrogate to themselves political legitimacy by means of mortal power, the community of the just is displayed in another model—the martyrs who follow in the steps of the apostles, who imitate the crucified Christ. Ultimately Augustine, as the title of his famous work signifies, will develop this political contrast between types of human being with reference to the two cities of the apocalypse: one ruled by the slain Lamb, the other by its lying mortal parodies who imitate the devil. Is it not precisely here, in Augustine's apocalyptic interpretation of political judgment, that his account of spiritual causality will run afoul of political theorists who will reject it as too mythological and otherworldly to be of real practical or theoretical value? The burden of my argument will be to show that this is not the case, that it is precisely Augustine's apocalypticism that offers critical and

---

23. See also Augustine's account of seminal causality rooted in invisible divine agency in *civ. Dei* 12.26, a measure "deemed fabulous" by those oriented according to external and technological measures of the real (12.24).

24. See Augustine, *Trinity*, trans. Edmund Hill.

PART 1: APOCALYPTIC MESSIANISM AND POLITICAL THEOLOGY

constructive resources for political theology and ethics in our own time no less than in his, and further, that it is crucial to understand his influential language of conscience and "will" (also a central modern political category in the contractarian tradition) in the context of apocalyptic causality and not (as yet another recent interpreter has defined it[25]) as a disembodied inner selfhood.

The Messianic Mediation of Virtue and Sin

In keeping with this apocalyptic cosmology, for Augustine the Messiah, as both "Son" and "second Adam," reveals the meaning of the Fall and human sin in both personal and political terms. Augustine contrasts this new form of mediation that reveals God in human form as "servant" and the Trinitarian form of the human made in God's image to the deceptive mediations that characterize the imitation and worship of fallen spiritual powers. While some attention has been given to apocalypticism in Augustine's theology,[26] the overwhelming scholarly consensus—represented above all in the influential studies by Robert A. Markus—is that while eschatology is important for Augustine's political theology, it is in fact *anti*-apocalyptic.[27] Though political Augustinians such as Oliver O'Donovan and Robert Dodaro (among others) have developed criticisms of Markus's language of secular political "neutrality" in characterizing Augustine's position, they have generally avoided the characterization of Augustine's political theology as apocalyptic, preferring to develop a sharp institutional dualism between church and state in their differing spheres of authority, mediated above all by the political conscience of the "Christian statesman."[28]

Robert Dodaro has provided a lucid account of what is at issue here by outlining three different neo-Augustinian interpretations of Augustine's political thought, focusing especially on his understanding of the relationship between *ecclesia* (the role of

---

25. Cary, *Augustine's Invention of the Inner Self*. Of course what Cary (and others) locate in Augustine, others (like Daniel Boyarin) locate in Paul—namely, an otherworldly spiritualized conception of self and identity derived from disembodied Platonism.

26. See van Oort, *Jerusalem and Babylon*; and Vessey, Pollman, and Fitzgerald, *History, Apocalypse, and the Secular Imagination*.

27. Markus's basic claim in *Saeculum* is that like Tyconius, Augustine transposed the apocalyptic two-cities language (interpreted in earlier African theology in more empirical sociological categories of church and pagan society) into an eschatological key, locating the tension in the individual human heart rather than public institutional embodiment. This paves the way for a greater recognition of ambiguity in the *saeculum*, an openness toward both cities reconfigured typologically rather than sociologically, that ultimately precludes both triumphalist Christendom and apocalyptic sectarian forms of political theology (Markus, *Saeculum*, esp. 55f., 120f., and chap. 7). I agree with James Wetzel that Markus's basic claims remain fundamentally unaltered in *Christianity and the Secular*—see Wetzel's introduction to *Augustine's "City of God,"* 3n5. See also the essays (the second of which is dedicated to Markus) by Fredrickson, "Tyconius and the End of the World" and "Tyconius and Augustine on the Apocalypse."

28. For Oliver O'Donovan the church represents "mercy" while the state represents "judgment"—see *Desire of the Nations*, 259–60. On the political virtue and conscience of the Christian statesman, where classical political virtues are transformed by "true piety," see Dodaro, *Christ and the Just Society*; Dodaro, "Augustine and the Possibility of Political Conscience"; and Dodaro, "*Ecclesia* and *Res Publica*."

bishop) and *res publica* (the role of statesman).[29] For Dodaro, the key to a proper understanding of Augustine's political theology is Christology, since for Augustine Christ is the divine mediator of justice who alone mediates true virtue to the soul (and thus to the statesman). Dodaro points out that Augustine was not preoccupied with the relationship between church and *res publica*—that is a modern preoccupation, and thus stated it is a theoretical rather than spiritual question. (And yet Dodaro, like most political Augustinians, can't resist this framing for the sake of political relevance.) Dodaro argues that for Augustine, political justice is most crucially dependent upon freedom from the fear of death, which the humility of Christ and his vulnerability to death most fully mediates, in a manner that liberates human beings from the fallen desire for their own earthly glory. To explain this mediating capacity, Dodaro avers that Augustine brings together two christological doctrines: (1) the unity of human and divine natures in one person (*civ. Dei* 9.5–17)—a mystery of faith (not the *scientia* of our own *ratio*) that enables those who imitate Christ to participate in divine love, the true end and form of all virtues; and (2) the *totus Christus* teaching of Paul, whereby Christ as the head of the messianic body offers himself up sacrificially in the form of a servant in such a manner that the entire body participates liturgically in this sacrifice in which love of God and neighbor are realized (*civ. Dei* 10.6, 20; 17.18).

What Dodaro overlooks is the apocalyptic background of Augustine's Christology—the cosmic conflict between the divine and the demonic that structures Augustine's mediation language in *City of God*, so closely connected to the language of worship and sacrifice in political theology. Dodaro pays attention to Christ's mediation, but not so much to the false mediation that Christ combats.[30] Not only does Augustine provide an apocalyptic demythologization of Roman imperial ideology through what Gerard O'Daly calls a "demonic reading of Roman history"[31] (see *civ. Dei* 2.25–29, where Augustine identifies the problem as the libidinous imitation and worship of demonic exemplars who foster division, deceit, and conflict), he extends this demonic reading to the Platonic mediation of virtue in books 9 and 10, where he articulates the centrality of the above christological doctrines for a critique of political idolatry in the more spiritual and intellectual registers of Platonic political virtue.

The warrior ethic of glorying in power (*civ. Dei* 5.12–20) is rooted in a lie about divine glory and power, a lie perpetuated in the public media (theater and civil religion) that focus on the love of power rather than the power of love. The powerful motivational

29. See Dodaro, "*Ecclesia* and *Res Publica*." The three interpretations are (1) Peter Iver Kaufmann's "minimalist" approach, where no real Christian transformation of political institutions is possible, only modest dispositional effects upon politicians (which for Dodaro is too pessimistic about the real effects of Christ's mediation in the conscience and particular ethical judgments of Christian statesmen); (2) Robert Markus's "secularist" account, focusing on a reading of the consensus of wills rooted in common objects of love (*civ. Dei* 19.17) in a neutral secular pluralist state (which ignores the substantive implications of Augustine's *totus Christus* for the mediation of a Christian politics); and (3) Milbank, the triumphalist ecclesiology that challenges modern liberal secularism in an idealist, conversionist church (which ignores the limits of fallenness in Augustine's *ecclesia permixta* in which the pilgrim church remains fallen and limited in its transformational powers).

30. Here again, it might be useful to compare the importance of the *totus Christus* of *civ. Dei* 10.6 and 20, 17.18, with the "universal body" of the *Antichristo* in *civ. Dei* 20.19.

31. O'Daly, *Augustine's "City of God*," 84.

correlative of such love of power is the fear of death.[32] Such a focus cannot bring the happiness of peaceable harmony rooted in the true justice of God that orders the good. To develop good judgment in "seeing where true happiness (*felicitas*) lies, and where an empty show (*vanitas*) dwells" entails "the worship of the true God by true sacrifices and the service of good lives (*bonis moribus*)" (*civ. Dei* 4.3). This shifts the focus from the earthly stage show of battling libidinous deities (both human and humanly projected) to the cosmic stage of divine providence. It also shifts the focus of attention from the divinity of human *virtus* to God's gift of virtue, which comes by *fides*—represented in the biblical statement that "the just shall live by faith."[33] Happiness and virtue are the gifts of God, and to receive them requires a proper spiritual orientation, not toward the moribund glory (the false immortality) of the earthly city but the eternal glory of the heavenly city (5.14, 19). It is in this context that one must interpret Augustine's statement in *City of God* 6.9: "It is, strictly speaking, for the sake of eternal life alone that we are Christians"—it is here that human happiness is found, the life of the soul rooted in God, not on its own as an individual but in the community of worship, the messianic body of Christ.

Before elaborating his Christian apocalyptic interpretation of political judgment, however, Augustine develops a distinction between Roman civil theology and Platonic natural philosophy. In *City of God* 6.5 he introduces Varro's tripartite division of theology: mythical (based on the fables of the poets, which cater to pleasure), natural (based on philosophy, attuned to the eternal good that orders the world), and civil (the public cult of priests and citizens, focused on the city). While Varro praises the second, it is clear that he considers the third to be politically the most important and, furthermore, that the third and the first are really similar. The eternal order of divine good is abandoned for the human works of cities and theaters—which confirms Augustine's judgment that Varro really advocates the useful public worship of humanly fashioned gods, the gods of pleasure and coercive power, by turns flattering and threatening the citizens to behave. For this reason, the only natural theologian worthy of the name is Plato, who acknowledges the God who transcends the soul and gives blessedness (*beatitudo*, which goes beyond *felicitas*) to the rational soul through participation in God's unchanging and incorporeal light of wisdom (*civ. Dei* 8.1). Only such an orientation offers moral insight into the true ordering of reality, in contrast to the deceptive external measures of the extension and duration of imperial power, in the service of which the deceptive rhetoric

---

32. Augustine begins his lengthy deconstruction of Roman civil religion (which underlies its warrior domination model of political sovereignty and ethics, and which measures the strength of a regime by the extent of its empire), with the following remark (*civ. Dei* 4.3): "But I should like to preface the inquiry with a brief examination of the following question: Is it reasonable (*ratio*), is it sensible (*prudentia*), to glory in the extent and magnitude of empire, when you cannot show that men lived in happiness (*felicitas*), as they passed their lives in the midst of war, amid the shedding of men's blood—whether the blood of enemies or fellow-citizens—under the shadow of fear and amid the terror of ruthless passion (*cupiditas*)? The joy (*laetitia*) of such men may be compared to the fragile splendor of glass: they are horribly afraid that it may suddenly be shattered." For an excellent discussion of Augustine's insight regarding fear of death as the basis of Roman political deception and ideology, see Dodaro, "Eloquent Lies." How this pertains to the Pelagian controversy is also addressed in Dodaro, "'Christus Iustus' and Fear of Death."

33. Hab 2:4; Rom 1:17; Gal 3:11; Heb 10:38.

of Roman civil theology is marshaled. That is, only Plato's theology is truly theological, and therefore also effective in moving the political discussion from the rhetorical play of power to the love of wisdom. Socrates stands at the transition point of political philosophy from the study of external causality to spiritual causality: "He believed that the first and highest cause exists in nothing but the will of the one supreme God; hence that the causation of the universe could be grasped only by a purified mind (*mundata mente*)" (*civ. Dei* 8.3).

If Plato says that wisdom is found in the imitation, knowledge, and love of this God, in the participation in whom is found true happiness, then, says Augustine, "none come nearer to us than the Platonists" (8.5). Indeed Plato's trinitarian structure in his philosophical theology—in God is found the *causa subsistendi* (the *principium* of all life and all being, 8.6), *ratio intelligendi* (the *logos*, the light of the mind that enables wise discernment, 8.7), and *ordo vivendi* (the discovery of happiness in the *summum bonum* to which all moral action is referred, 8.8)—suggests to Augustine the purest example of the natural revealed wisdom described by Paul in Romans 1:19–20 (8.10). The reference to Paul, however, signals the beginning of critique. It is a critique paralleled in the *Confessions* (book 7)—Platonic pride in the reputation for wisdom earned in the heroic disciplines of dialectical *paideia* and the intellectual virtues. Lacking here are the penitential tears of confession that purify the vision of the heart in a manner quite unlike anything found in Plato's dialogues. This is due to a very different principle of mediation in Paul—the Word made flesh (mortal) in the "form of a servant," whose death makes possible participation in the divine life itself (insofar as he remains also "in the form of God").[34] Only this death makes possible the overcoming of the fear of death by faith in Christ as the one who is also raised up to God beyond death.

Equally important here is the model of imitation we are given to follow in Christ. Unlike a stage play, the model is not one of emotional catharsis in which one participates as an intellectually and emotionally engaged but inactive spectator. Unlike Plato's Socrates, the model is not an educative one of intellectual purification through the critical, dialectical expurgation of myths and conventional traditions. The key to spiritual causality is now to be found in an embodied model that nevertheless is claimed to be the very spiritual principle underlying all created reality, and this embodied model takes the form of a lowly servant, not an exalted ruler—political or philosophical or otherwise. It is an enactment in the most audacious terms of the principles of motion now brought into scandalous collision not only with political ideals but also intellectual and spiritual ones. It introduces a divine seriousness into the historical drama that compels recognition of God as not only the builder of the theater (which is "all the world") and the author of the script but also the primary actor in all agency as its personal, creative, and moving principle. We learn what it means to take part in this divine agency when we follow the path of humble love (which cures our blinding pride) taken by God in the world, the *via caritatis*, and imitate its spiritual motion. For it is the divine Truth itself (*ipsa Veritas* and *ipsa Sapientia*), "that Word through whom all things were made," that

---

34. See *civ. Dei* 9.15, 10.6, and 20. This logic of mediation, taken from the christological hymn in Philippians 2, is elaborated in extensive detail in *De Trinitate* as the basic rule of interpretation, and it is closely linked by Augustine to 1 Corinthians 15 (see *Trinity* 1).

was made flesh so that God may dwell with us. "Although he is our native country, he made himself also the way to that country."[35]

As Augustine makes clear (*Teaching Christianity* 1.12; *Trinity* 2.7) this divinely given spiritual motion by which God comes to dwell in God's own creation is not some form of space and time travel—God comes to where God already is. So also, therefore, the motion of our return to God is not a spatio-temporal tradition to be studied or preserved any more than it is simply the motions of our psyche, but rather the fulfillment of our created existence designed for eternal communion with God and our neighbors. The cosmic spiritual drama in which we participate has its terms in the very shared life of the divine trinity. This is not something that can be worked out by human reasoning.[36] It can only be accepted by faith as God's gift. So too the model of political authority, the rule of Christ that reigns not only in the heavenly city but also in the hearts of the citizens of the city of God on pilgrimage in the world. This is why Augustine introduces language of divine agency as the central interpretive *principium* of political judgment in *City of God*: one must understand human agency not in terms of stories of human beings or the gods or other narrative accounts (which must themselves be measured by a larger good), but in relation to God who has created human beings with the power to act (in God's image) and therefore alone can measure it. As Augustine makes clear in *City of God* 8.20ff., the key issue is mediation—the Platonic daemonic mediation (since "no god mingles with human beings"[37]) is contrasted to messianic mediation, as Augustine argues that only the God-man can liberate human beings from bondage to the lordship of demonic powers with the chains of their own disordered desires attached to false libidinous images (*simulacra*, 8.24). Similitude to the true God is possible only by conformity in worship to the fully divine yet fully human form of Christ. Only through the humility of Christ, the "good mediator, who reconciles enemies," can the human will be liberated from the "evil mediator, who separates loved ones" in the divisions of self-love (9.15). The universal path toward the liberation of the "whole human" (body, mind, and spirit, 10.27) from the diabolical dominion of injustice is the royal road (*via regalis*, 10.32) of the servant king. The apocalyptic terms of this spiritual and socio-political liberation are clearly spelled out in *City of God* 14: the earthly city lives wholly oriented according to the diabolical lie that the principle of mediation is found in my self, my own soul (the *similis diabolo* is a measure of possession rooted in pride and envy, 14.3), whereas the heavenly city lives on pilgrimage in the *saeculum*, wholly oriented by the sacrifice to God that is the messianic body mediated by Christ, a sacrifice that heals the defective will of its deluded desires and enables it to obey the divine will exemplified in the city's sovereign (14.13).

---

35. *Teaching Christianity* 1.12–13, 34.

36. This is Augustine's point in criticizing the cyclical process cosmologies in book 12 of *City of God*—the attempt to grasp immortality via human reason (cf. *Trinity* 13.12) leads one in circles (and indeed human attempts to "close the circle" through human substitutions for the divine gift of immortality that cannot be possessed). Such a rational disembodiment of the *logos* robs the *saeculum* of its significance, the beginnings and endings of which are in God's power and the revelation of which can only be accepted by faith, not rational sight.

37. "*Nullus Deus miscetur homini*" (*civ. Dei* 8.18, 20; 9.1, 16); the Platonic principle Augustine fastens upon from *Symposium* 203a is related to the principle of erotic mediation in *Symposium* 201e, where *eros* is described as neither divine nor human but "between" (*metaxu*).

Augustine's Messianic Political Theology

Thus is the messianic social body liberated from domination to Babylon, the diabolical/demonic order, to the properly ordered will and *ordo amoris* of the *rex optimus* (17.16).

Insofar as the church embodies the kenotic servant posture of Christ and a vision of justice that lives by faith, it adopts a martyrdom stance and not a heroic one. The *agon* (*certamen*) of faith, in which fear of death is conquered, is seen preeminently in the holy martyrs (*civ. Dei* 13.4). The justice that defeats sin in the death of Christ and brings with it participation in divine immortality (*Trinity* 13) overcomes the fear of death and enables the martyrs to die rather than to sin.[38] In *City of God* 14 Augustine develops this model of martyrdom further in terms of the will ordered *secundum spiritum*—a good will is good and at rest in its desires when ordered by love of God. Here Augustine makes reference to the apostle Paul, that *vir optimus et fortissimus* (political terminology[39]) who glories in his weakness. Again, the point is that fear of death is overcome not by the possession of virtue but by the gift of divine love given to the penitent heart. As Augustine puts it in *City of God* 19.27: "Our righteousness (*iustitia*) also, though true righteousness insofar as it is referred to the true ultimate good, is in this life only such as to consist in the forgiveness of sins rather than the perfection of virtues. This is borne out by the prayer of the whole City of God during its pilgrimage in the world, which cries out to God in the voice of all its members: 'Forgive us our debts, as we forgive our debtors.'" This is a political and not merely private or spiritual vision and practice.[40] It is engaged by the communal body that bears the mind of Christ, but only insofar as it worships the true God in humility. Such worship, as *City of God* 10 makes clear, is both a spiritual and a bodily sacrifice, communally offered and received in penitence.

History thus plays a role in Augustine's apocalyptic vision of spiritual causality and political order that it does not in Plato, but history is not primarily about human agency. The dramatic text that must be read in order for human beings to have their discernment formed is the text of God's providential trinitarian action into the creation, ultimately by sending the eternal form of divine wisdom itself into the temporal form humanly required to discern it, the humble servant. The story of this providential agency is to be found in Scripture, interpreted according to the rule of *caritas*. The second half of *City of God* develops its alternative account of political order through a figural reading of Scripture that, like the New Testament, ends with an apocalyptic vision of the two cities that structures the whole. This apocalypse represents the city on pilgrimage in the world as a community of penitent martyrs who relate the earthly peace to the heavenly

---

38. Indeed the martyrs, like all Christians, realize (like Antigone and Socrates) that mortal human life itself is a "race towards death" (*cursus ad mortem, civ. Dei* 13.10) and that the death to the fleshly desire to cling to mortal life as if it were immortal is in fact to be liberated from bondage to the body of decay that is fallen human nature. This, however, is not entirely an intellectual or moral matter—it is a gift of faith. For a good discussion of how the various levels of justice are related to the disposition of the will and addresses the fear of death, see Studer, "Le Christ, notre justice, selon saint Augustin."

39. Augustine calls Christ the *rex optimus* in *civ. Dei* 17.16; see Dodaro, "Eloquent Lies," 129n83.

40. See Williams, "Politics and the Soul." Williams offers a good critical rejoinder to Hannah Arendt's claim that Augustine subverts the public realm by focusing on the non-political and otherworldly virtue of *caritas*. What Augustine subverts is a vision of public virtue modeled on the warrior hero, but such a vision is itself based upon violence and disorder—it cannot produce civic peace, and it is not in fact public enough. See also Breidenthal, "Jesus Is My Neighbor."

peace—but as pilgrims in Babylonian exile (19.26). This pilgrim, diaspora vision of the church's political service, rooted in an apocalyptic understanding of political discernment, represents a different vision of social conscience than that depicted in Dodaro's statesman. In conclusion I wish to discuss this with reference to one of Augustine's most moving political images in *City of God* 19, that of the "wise judge."

Political Conscience and the Wise Judge of *City of God* 19[41]

It is important to note that the context of Augustine's discussion of the wise judge remains his debate with "the philosophers" about the virtues of the *sapientes* who take positions of political responsibility in the earthly city (*civ. Dei* 19.5–6; cf. 14.28). In 14.28, Augustine contrasts the fleshly imagination of human wisdom, rooted in various forms of idolatry (false worship), with the wisdom of true piety oriented in worship of the one God of the heavenly city that serves God and neighbor with true charity. I have argued that this is for Augustine an agonistic apocalyptic contrast that pertains at every level of created reality, from the conscience of every person to the household to the city to the world to the universe, and that the virtue in question is closely tied to the service of worship by which earthly peace is referred to the perfection of heavenly peace (19.17). This religious vision informs every act in which the pilgrims of the heavenly city "make use" of the peace of the earthly city. It is just here that language of "necessity" (so characteristic of political Augustinians) enters in for Augustine, the necessities of not only mortal existence in a fallen world but also the social conditions of sin in the earthly city. While citizens of the heavenly city are in the process of being liberated from these necessities, their ultimate liberation is a matter of hope. The pilgrim life must contend with the miseries and ills, trials and temptations of life in the *saeculum*. While Robert Dodaro rightly contends that Augustine cannot therefore be construed as giving us a picture of an ideal political order, I suggest that neither may he be construed as providing an ideal of a Christian statesman, as the latter is still too individually and institutionally defined. The broader apocalyptic context is required so that the wise judge not be idealized nor even rendered ethically or politically normative.

In *City of God* 19.6 Augustine gives us his vivid image of the anxious wise judge who is called upon to exercise public political responsibility to make juridical judgments with the full awareness that in a sinful world those judgments will be flawed. They will entail a matter of evil necessity, evident in such practices as judicial torture, rituals of pain designed to evoke confessions of truth. Augustine's image is both moving and deeply disturbing. It is moving not least for its uncompromising honesty (some call it "realism") about the presence of evil in the world and the dutiful necessity to act politically despite the necessary limitations on our capacities—for example, we cannot see into the souls of those we judge, and so have to do the best we can with the appearances of things (including bodily pain and interrogation). It is also moving because Augustine

---

41. I borrow here from an essay (see also chapter 14, below) in which I discuss the broader question of the difference between torture and punishment with particular reference to Nietzsche and Dostoevsky, the latter of whom I interpret as an apocalyptic thinker. See Kroeker, "On the Difference between Torture and Punishment."

will advert repeatedly to what he calls the rallying cry of the Christian church in the midst of such miserable necessities: "Forgive us our sins," and "Deliver me/us from my/our necessities," a penitential disposition of humility. Yet it is also disturbing in that it appears to authorize practices such as various forms of corporal (and capital) punishment and judicial torture that are not necessarily to be viewed as "necessary," but perhaps as strictly sinful and thus avoided, even on Augustine's own account of messianic politics.

While Augustine clearly envisions the ritual of judicial torture as rooted in a secular and civil, not ecclesial and religious, liturgy, his position as conventionally read is nevertheless problematic on several levels. The first is that it does not conform to Augustine's theological understanding of truth and lying—for him clearly not a bodily matter but a matter of the soul[42]—and this would pertain no less in the secular than in the ecclesial domain. In fact, Augustine's description of the "necessity" of judicial torture shows a clear awareness that innocents will often confess (untruthfully) to crimes they have not committed under pain of torture: "And when [the accused] has been condemned and put to death, the judge still does not know whether he has slain a guilty man or an innocent one, even after torturing him to avoid ignorantly slaying the innocent. In this case, he has tortured an innocent man in order to discover the truth, and has killed him while still not knowing it."[43] The second problem is that judicial torture stands in egregious contradiction to the defining liturgical drama of his apocalyptic political theology, namely, the Eucharist—itself a sacrificial meal in which the church receives and offers itself in humble and penitential service to God and to the neighbor in an act of dispossessive self-giving. This is done in memory of another criminal torture and punishment, indeed under the sign of crucifixion, that both puts on cosmic display the sinful pretension of falsely sovereign human judgment and reveals the martyr form of the servant (not domination and coercive control) to be the sovereign and liberating form of God in a world of evil necessity. Clearly the torments of Augustine's judge derive from this more primary liturgical enactment. It is hard to see how appeals to "necessity" make any moral sense, then, with regard to the practice of judicial torture. Indeed, it is possible to see in Augustine's conscience-plagued figure the origins of the despised priest of Nietzsche's genealogy—one who is able to move adroitly between juridical inquisitorial torture (and why not use rituals of pain to evoke confessions also in an ecclesial setting where, even more, the eternal soul's salvation/condemnation is at stake?) and the many possible pastoral uses of conscience-vivisection and tortuous self-surveillance to keep citizens and Christians in a state of moral conformity.[44]

42. For helpful discussions of Augustine's interpretation of truth and lying, see Rist, *Augustine*, 193–97, and Griffiths, *Lying*.

43 Augustine's reflections continue: "[The wise judge] does not consider it a wickedness [*nefas*] that innocent witnesses should be tortured in cases which are not their own, or that the accused are so often overcome by such great pain that they make false confessions and are punished in spite of their innocence. Nor does he think it wicked that, even if not condemned to die, they very often die under torture or as a result of torture. . . . Witnesses may lie in giving testimony; the defendant himself may be obdurate under torture and refuse to confess; and so the accusers may not be able to prove the truth of their accusations, no matter how true those accusations may be, and the judge, in his ignorance, may condemn them." The key point for Augustine is that the wise judge's *intention* is not to do harm.

44. Here one finds the narrow opening for William Connolly's Nietzschean-Foucauldian

PART 1: APOCALYPTIC MESSIANISM AND POLITICAL THEOLOGY

It is my view that Augustine cannot have it both ways. He cannot participate in the eucharistic liturgy and then advocate participation in the liturgy of judicial torture. If the former is true, the latter must be a lie—one cannot join the eucharistic cup of liberation with the demonic cup (*civ. Dei* 8.24; compare also the "whole body" of Antichrist in *civ. Dei* 20.19 and the *totus Christus*). This is indeed what Augustine himself would seem to be arguing in Letter 104 to Nectarius.[45] Furthermore, while I have not argued it here, I have assumed it is the case that the language of human dignity, rights, forgiveness, and the Right (I mean this as a synonym for the Good, not an ideological partisan political term) in the secular West is heavily indebted to Christian religious practices and ideas. It is therefore important to draw analogically and comparatively upon these interrelations in thinking through the question of torture and punishment, and not simply in institutional or doctrinal terms, since of course the *anti*-messianic may appear precisely where the messianic is revealed. Such analogical and agonistic thinking is characteristic of the apocalyptic messianism of Augustine's political theology. Above all, it would be dangerous to impose a strict institutional dualism (e.g., the church represents "mercy" while the state represents "judgment") upon these questions in a manner that precludes a fully critical analogical consideration.

Here book 19 of *City of God* may itself provide a helpful structure. Augustine is convinced that the same existential relations of human love and justice hold true from the most intimate levels of self and household to the civic and international domains, from the most visible bodily level to the cosmic spiritual context concerning the origin and end of all things. No false boundaries will enable us to sort this out more simply. This does not mean that divine justice or judgment is transparent in the world, but it does mean that those ordered by the liturgical practices of penitence and self-offering may not presume to mediate divine judgment in anything but the servant form enacted therein. To the extent to which judicial torture and indeed any retributive judicial practices are devoted to the possessive and dominating "order" of the security state that claims to mediate a non-penitential justice, such practices are rooted in evil necessity and contribute to the "lie" of a strictly human sovereignty. They are subject to the Nietzschean critique of a Christianity that seeks coercively to impose its humble and confessional truth through internal and external disciplinary mechanisms of sovereign control. On the other hand, Nietzsche's reading of conscience, crime, punishment, and torture is not the only possible reading—either of the Christian tradition or of the rise of the "sovereign" moral self in the modern (and postmodern) West. Augustine points to another possibility that is utterly pertinent to these questions, an apocalyptic political theology heavily influenced by Paul and the New Testament, that has also informed the work of Ivan Illich, whose work may be properly aligned with an apocalyptic neo-Augustinian

---

interpretation of Augustine's political theology in *The Augustinian Imperative*; see Dodaro's excellent critique of Connolly's too-narrow reading in "Augustine's Secular City."

45. In this letter, Augustine characterizes the disciplined practice of civic punishment in terms of a contrast between "Christian mercy" and "Stoic hardness" (which criticizes mercy as weak), and he makes this comment with regard to judicial torture: "I wished no action to be taken in the case of the instigators [pagans whose riotous celebrations resulted in the burning of Christian churches], because the matter perhaps could not be investigated without the use of physical torture, which is abhorrent to our [Christian] way of thinking" (Augustine, *Political Writings*, 21).

perspective. On this reading, the *sapientes* examples of the early chapters of *City of God* 19 would not be ethically normative in the ways that Christ, Paul, and the martyrs are throughout the *City of God* and Augustine's other writings. But this may only come into proper perspective if we take the apocalyptic context consistently and pervasively into account, as I have suggested Augustine himself does.

4

Messianic Ethics and Diaspora Communities

Upbuilding the Secular Theologically from Below

Liberalism and Religious Reasons

In a recent article on religion and secularity in American culture, *Communio* editor David Schindler elaborates the following credo: "I believe with the 'left' that American religiosity typically harbors an inadequate sense of and appreciation for the secular; and I believe with the 'right' that American secularity has wrongly emancipated itself from religion."[1] Schindler's thesis is that a defective American religiosity has largely set the terms for America's defective secularity (or secularism), and that the relation between these is mutual. Citing the American culture critic Wendell Berry, Schindler suggests that the religious disaster is the conceptual division of the Creator from the creation, leading to an untenable and reductive dualism—an extrinsic relation between God and the *saeculum* that warrants the abstraction of the religious realm of individual, voluntarist piety (the human will) from the secular realm of nature and the cognitive order of purely natural, scientistic reason. This, suggests the Roman Catholic Schindler, is not only a Protestant malady but a general characteristic of American religiosity. It is rooted in a moralized and voluntarized religion that is coincident with a mechanized, indifferent, or "neutral" ("disenchanted") secular cosmos. In short, the problem is one of cosmology.

Schindler cites the work of the late Canadian political philosopher George Grant to show further how the secular liberalism of the English-speaking world has become increasingly aligned with the development of technology as the site where the value-generating human will finds the value-neutral means for establishing control over an indifferent nature. In his essay "Thinking about Technology," Grant argues that "technology has become the ontology of our age" and that, far from being instrumentally "neutral,"

1. Schindler, "Religion and Secularity in a Culture of Abstraction."

technological mastery imposes upon us a structure of choices and public "goods" that threatens the very freedom it supposedly serves and undermines the disciplined cultural practices that sustain justice as a shared good.[2] As he argues in *English-Speaking Justice*, the "cup of poison" being raised to the lips of modern contractual liberalism (he has Rawls in mind) is its "unthought ontology."[3] This unthought ontology concerns what it means to be human in a technological liberal public order, and how this may relate to the enactment of public and political justice—as justice cannot remain value-neutral.

For Grant the computer serves as a symbol of this often-hidden determining power of technology in our culture, which belies its supposed neutrality:

> The phrase "the computer does not impose [on us the ways it should be used]" misleads, because it abstracts the computer from the destiny that was required for its making. Common sense may tell us that the computer is an instrument, but it is an instrument from within the destiny which *does* "impose" itself upon us, and therefore the computer *does* impose.[4]

What it imposes, among other things, are forms of community that make possible and that accommodate themselves to the representations and uses attached to computer technologies and their "progress." Such a socially mediated conception of human destiny, furthermore, hastens the global movement toward cultural homogeneity and the gradual loss of a genuinely pluralistic public life. On this point Grant's analysis is confirmed and deepened by the work of Albert Borgmann: "Liberal democracy is enacted as technology. It does not leave the question of the good life open but answers it along technological lines."[5] Such a political culture produces a rich diversity of commodities, argues Borgmann, "but underneath this superficial variety, there is a rigid and narrow pattern in which people take up with the world."[6] As the responses to Wendell Berry's controversial *Harper's* article "Why I Am Not Going to Buy a Computer" indicate, even gently calling into critical question the central icon of technological civilization will generate intensely emotional moralistic responses (after all, the article is not entitled "Why You Should Not Buy a Computer" or "Why the Computer Is Evil"). This leads Berry to tweak *Harper's* liberal-minded, cosmopolitan readers: "I can only conclude that I have scratched the skin of a technological fundamentalism that, like other fundamentalisms, wishes to monopolize a whole society and, therefore, cannot tolerate the smallest difference of opinion."[7]

---

2. See Grant, "Thinking about Technology."

3. Grant, *English-Speaking Justice*, 71. The particular context of Grant's claim here is Justice Blackmun's majority decision in Roe v. Wade, which begins from the principle that the allocation of constitutional rights cannot be decided on the basis of any knowledge of what is good. And yet the judgment presumes to make an ontological distinction between members of the same species—the mother is a person, the foetus is not. This raises the question of what the human species is: "What is it about any members of our species which makes the liberal rights of justice their due. The judge unwittingly looses the terrible question: has the long tradition of liberal right any support in what human beings in fact are?"

4. Grant, "Thinking about Technology," 23.

5. Borgmann, *Technology and the Character of Contemporary Life*, 92.

6. Ibid., 94.

7. Berry, *What Are People For?*, 175. This response has been confirmed repeatedly in my own

PART 1: APOCALYPTIC MESSIANISM AND POLITICAL THEOLOGY

Jeffrey Stout's *Democracy and Tradition* is a welcome contribution to the literature in liberal democratic public philosophy for several reasons. He offers an account of modern secular democracy that does not narrow-mindedly and dismissively rule out the public expression of religious premises but that seeks to bridge the divide described by Schindler from the non-religious secular side. In particular he rejects the Weberian secularization thesis accepted by so many liberal political theorists, and by Jürgen Habermas and John Rawls in particular, that assumes (and demands) intellectual conformity to the "disenchantment of the world" hypothesis as a condition for public political philosophy.[8] Rather, Stout suggests, Emersonian democrats such as himself find themselves in alliance with religious traditionalists such as Augustinian Christians in focusing political discourse upon matters of shared social concern (not salvation), to which people may bring their particular moral perspectives without privileging any one tradition as authoritative. In this sense liberal democracy is itself a tradition that fosters the disciplines necessary to sustain responsible, critical public conversation among people whose "expressive rationality" will differ. The assumption at its best of secular pluralism is precisely that open, critical discussion of the variety of spiritual and moral symbols, traditions, and experiences can enhance the understanding and experience of all. In this regard is Stout critical of the more restrictive secularist liberalisms of Rawls and Habermas.

In an open, pluralistic society it becomes all the more important to attend to the substantive meaning of particular symbols that are used by people to represent the meaning and purpose of life. Moral meaning is best discovered and communicated not in generic abstractions or formal codes that avoid discussion of the particular spiritual and moral commitments of real human beings, but in shared critical exploration that calls these commitments and symbols to public account in terms of their theoretical and applied implications. Stout argues against Rawls's contractarian quest for a "freestanding procedural justice" on epistemological grounds, suggesting that it excludes the consideration of principled political reasons, including religious reasons, from public debate.[9] To restrict public reason to juridical procedural discourse is too narrow a paradigm; it cannot facilitate reasonable political exchange in a pluralist democracy. Stout argues that true public respect for others entails a greater focus on the particularity of their reasons and a commitment to a more expressive conception of rationality and the disciplined practice of immanent critique.

Yet I confess that here is where I find Stout's book most disappointing. He states in his introduction: "The religious dimensions of our political culture are typically discussed at such a high level of abstraction that only two positions become visible: an authoritarian form of traditionalism and an antireligious form of liberalism."[10] And yet neither in

---

experience of teaching Berry's essay to undergraduates—they are invariably scandalized, offended, and outraged by his brief individual challenge to the shibboleth of "technological progress." The original *Harper's* article is also reprinted in *What Are People For?*

8. Stout, *Democracy and Tradition*, 175–76.

9. Stout's critique of Rawls is developed in ibid., 65–77. Stout calls himself a Hegelian pragmatist, but he is equally critical of the controlling and restrictive secularist pragmatism of Richard Rorty (85–91).

10. Ibid., 10.

part 2, where he engages in critical conversation with so-called Christian traditionalists, nor in part 3, where he elaborates his own case for an Emersonian democratic piety of self-reliance and pragmatic conversation, does Stout himself descend from theoretical abstraction to the kind of textured, nuanced consideration of contextual examples needed to show what practical difference different kinds of religious expressions might make to our public life. Indeed, while in chapter 7 he argues for a notion of democratic tradition that stands—like the modern essay, play, or novel—between example and doctrine so as to avoid authoritarian moralizing in order to explore moral complexity, Stout's vision of ethics as social practice tends to focus on sports (soccer in particular—better than computers, not virtual soccer, but still . . .), not politics or religion or art for its exemplars. This leads him to a moralistic kind of conclusion that I find troubling and wish to consider further.

The conclusion is this: "It seems to me that great urgency attaches to the general project of cultivating identifications that transcend ethnicity, race, and religion—at the local and national levels."[11] And further: "The kind of community that democrats should be promoting at the local, state, and national levels of politics is the kind that involves shared commitment to the Constitution and the culture of democracy. In America, this culture consists of a loose and ever-changing collection of social practices that includes such activities as quilting, baseball, and jazz. But its central and definitive component is the discursive practice of holding one another responsible for the actions we commit, the commitments we undertake, and the sorts of people we become."[12] Such a culture of democracy is not serious enough to address the spiritual crisis at the heart of technological globalizing culture—a cosmological matter, as I have suggested.

Stout is clear that to cultivate excellence in this discursive practice is a matter of inculcating habits of moral observation, moral witness, and moral imagination. These habits combine a contextualist account of justification with a non-relativist account of moral truth, and yet we are left again with a very abstract definition of moral truth as generalized "moral law" understood not in terms of metaphysical reality but of imaginative projection.[13] Why? It seems that because we will never find agreement on metaphysical reality, the best we can do is treat our various perspectives as imaginative projections. To cite Stout again: "The theologies of Antigone, Jefferson, and Martin Luther King [all important social critics] could hardly be further apart: pagan polytheism, Enlightenment, deism, and Trinitarian Christianity. When they [each] claim that there is a law higher and better than the artificial constructions of human society, they differ drastically over the source and substance of that law."[14] But what is this except another liberal reduction of religion and other "thick" identities to abstract rational norms that can be rendered publicly meaningful and contextual only on a playing field that keeps them expressively inarticulate, incapable of communicating with one another in their own particular witness to reality? What remains is a variant of Plato's cave, with public intellectuals as image-projecting sophisticates seeking political influence. Stout's public forbids us to

11. Ibid., 302.
12. Ibid., 303–4.
13. Ibid., 242–43.
14. Ibid., 241.

PART 1: APOCALYPTIC MESSIANISM AND POLITICAL THEOLOGY

raise and address the "unthought ontology" question, and in this regard I see him as closely allied with the juridical procedural liberalisms of Rawls and Habermas.

Take two appeals to divine moral law mentioned by Stout—those of Antigone and Martin Luther King—in which the invoking agents become political martyrs. There is no doubt whatsoever that neither of them understand themselves to be engaging in a conversation about moral projections, but rather in a life-and-death struggle over the moral truth of reality and what it commands religiously. Their actions—discourses and practices—are not comprehensible without paying attention to the particular content of their theological cosmologies. Both of them are indeed appealing to an agential force beyond the law (not their own moral projections) by which the laws of the land are judged unjust and faulty.

It is precisely at this point that Stout's "immanent criticism" of the religious traditions he interprets remains inadequate, abstracted behind a veil of ignorance. His accounts are by definition reductionist and non-theological. For this reason he cannot see the metaphysical danger in our current political context. Certainly he sees the moral dangers of various forms of oligarchy and plutocracy that threaten any so-called democracy that becomes corrupted by love of power and money above civic honor and love of justice. Certainly he sees the political danger of the American Religious Right, rooted in authoritarian conventional religion that believes in the divine right of its globalizing rule. Indeed he may even see what David Schindler, George Grant, and Wendell Berry see about the dangerous public and political idolatries entailed in the salvific claims of our globalizing technological culture—virtual reality as our *telos* where all our individual imaginative projections may equally come true, at the expense of truly shared reality. (A *cauchemar* if I ever imagined one!) He may see and wish to resist all of these dangers, but he cannot acknowledge a theological or religious account of them, and his inability to do so makes him unable to see how so-called religious traditionalists such as Wendell Berry, Alasdair MacIntyre, and Stanley Hauerwas are attempting to alert us to the true ontological and metaphysical extent of our public spiritual and cultural crisis. For example, Stout expresses appreciation for Berry as a great observational social critic and "environmental ethicist"—but Berry would certainly not understand himself in these terms nor consider his vision to be the "product of democratic culture," even though it is lived out, shaped by, and dedicated to some extent to the preservation of such a culture. For none of these witnesses could public piety be construed even analogically in terms of Emersonian "self-trust" and "self-reliance." Indeed for each of them such a piety is itself a dangerous self-delusion that leads quickly to self-righteous, self-assured, and self-centered judgment and action that ultimately lies behind all totalitarianisms—of the left and of the right, ancient and modern and postmodern.

One of the reasons Stout's "immanent criticism" of traditionalist Christians in *Democracy and Tradition* fails, in my judgment, is that he tends to concentrate on the "church-world" dualism without giving any attention to the apocalyptic cosmology that underlies it.[15] This is not surprising, because apocalyptic is a disruptive, anti-totalizing

---

15. That Stout chooses in his representation of the "new traditionalism" of Stanley Hauerwas (his primary interlocutor) to affiliate Hauerwas with philosophers of the grand narrative of modernity failure, such as Alasdair MacIntyre and John Milbank, rather than with more engaged theologians such as

logic that is not easily assimilated into the terms of conventional political theory. Messianic political theology and ethics in particular are often viewed as a dangerous threat by modern political theory, and not without reason. It worth noting, however, that the first theory of the *saeculum* in Western political thought was developed precisely within an apocalyptic messianic understanding of history and politics, Augustine's *City of God*. It is also the case, I suggest, that the notions of neutral technology and juridical state sovereignty that underlie current conceptions and embodiments of the secular are themselves dangerously totalitarian, exclusivist, and violent, even while hidden beneath the veneer of progressivist liberal assumptions.

Secular State Sovereignty and Moral Causality

This is the position articulated in the apocalyptic messianism of the secular Jewish critic of liberal culture, Walter Benjamin. The concept of political sovereignty at the heart of modern secular politics and political theory was given its classical formulation by Carl Schmitt.[16] Crucial for Schmitt is the recognition that there is a constituting political power behind the law that entails a decision about the relationship of nature to the law. "Sovereign is he who decides on the exception" says Schmitt in the famous opening line to his definition of sovereignty, which therefore requires that sovereignty be seen not in strictly juridical terms but as a limit concept in which there is a power who decides on the "state of emergency" that suspends the normal rule of law. In the power to decide the exception, the truly sovereign "power of real life breaks through the crust of a mechanism."[17] This founding notion of sovereignty must be read together with the founding definition of the political, namely, the distinction between friend and enemy.[18] For Schmitt the ultimate challenge to this basic political principle is found in the words of Jesus, "Love your enemies" (Matt 5:44)—words that Schmitt, in keeping with both conventional Christendom and individualist liberal political ethics, regards as *private*, a spiritual and not a public political ethic. Surely former President George W. Bush would agree. Ultra-liberal Canadian Prime Minister Pierre Trudeau would also have agreed as he invoked the War Measures Act in Canada during the Front de Libération du Québec (FLQ) crisis of 1970, thus deciding the exception—the emergency situation in face of the enemy that required the suspension of "normal law." Stout agrees with this as well in his chapter on "Democratic Norms in an Age of Terrorism," where with reference to the problem of "dirty hands" he states that "in situations of extreme emergency, the worst thing an official can do is to allow the people to perish at the hands of its enemies."[19]

John Howard Yoder and Oliver O'Donovan, can be interpreted as a deliberate avoidance of messianic political theology.

16. Schmitt, *Political Theology*, 33–53; 47–52.
17. Ibid., 15.
18. Schmitt, *Concept of the Political*, 26.
19. Stout, *Democracy and Tradition*, 192. Stout here frames the issue with reference to the just war argumentation of Michael Walzer, and it is not clear that he would side with Walzer's judgments regarding "supreme emergency" in all cases, but he sees the need to frame the issue in this manner. See my discussion in chapter 14, below.

PART 1: APOCALYPTIC MESSIANISM AND POLITICAL THEOLOGY

Walter Benjamin had this definition and practice of modern secular sovereignty in mind when he wrote his eighth thesis on the philosophy of history:

> The tradition of the oppressed teaches us that the "state of emergency" in which we live... is the rule. We must attain to a conception of history that is in keeping with this insight. Then we shall clearly realize that it is our task to bring about a real state of emergency, and this will improve our position in the struggle against Fascism. One reason why Fascism has a chance is that in the name of progress its opponents treat it as a historical norm. The current amazement that the things we are experiencing are "still" possible in the twentieth century is *not* philosophical. This amazement is not the beginning of knowledge.[20]

Benjamin clearly sets himself against this secular progressivist politics to which all seeming political options are conformed, and he does so in the name of a "*weak* Messianic power" in which each day is lived as the day of judgment on which the Messiah comes, "not only as the redeemer" but also "as the subduer of Antichrist."[21] Such a "Messianic time" may not be thought within the categories of historicism but only from the perspective of a *Jetztzeit* (Thesis 18), a *real* state of emergency that calls into fundamental question the "state of emergency"—that is, the politics of modern secular state sovereignty—in which we live. It will bring into view the violent and destructive foundation of this sovereignty with its homogeneous and totalitarian order by remembering another sovereignty: a messianic sovereignty that reorders the secular (the present time) on completely different terms. I shall return to this in my discussion of messianic political theology, but first it is necessary briefly to show how Hobbesian political theory seeks to eliminate the messianic from public view.

Thomas Hobbes fashioned himself as a Plato *redivivus* for modernity who believed he could succeed where ancient political philosophy had failed—to become the first to develop a true *science* of civil philosophy that could rationally guide political action.[22] In *Leviathan* he claimed to provide a definitive account of the motivations, constitutive principles, and practical requirements of political order and natural justice—founded, he asserted, on the "the only science that it hath pleased God hitherto to bestow on mankind," Euclidean geometry (4.12; cf. 46.11). The key to scientific order is correct speech, the accurate representational definition of real things and their causal connection in a rational deductive logic. This method is superior to classical philosophy because it assumes no "spiritual causality" by which the soul is somehow ordered toward a transcendent good beyond being—such a religious cosmology leads to false representation rooted in ignorance of true causes (12).

Hobbes's Euclidean reason makes two crucial assumptions (3.12): first, "a man can have no thought representing anything not subject to sense"—hence, all causality is related to what is externally visible and material; and second, God is by nature

---

20. Benjamin, "Theses on the Philosophy of History," 259.
21. Ibid., Theses 2 and 6. The progressivism Benjamin has in view here is identical with "technological development" (Thesis 11). For interesting further reflections along these lines see Agamben, "The Messiah and the Sovereign."
22. See Hobbes, *Leviathan*, 31.41. Further references will appear in parentheses in the text.

incomprehensible and therefore cannot be imaged or represented in rational human speech.[23] There is no spiritual teleology in nature, no *summum bonum* toward which human passions are oriented and by which they are ordered—happiness itself is but "a continual process of the desire, from one object to another" (11.1; cf. 6.58). Human reasoning is nothing but the reckoning by means of linguistic conventions that makes possible the better or worse acquisition and use of the objects we desire (5.2; 6.7), and this desire remains fundamentally private, passional, and amoral. Classical language of moral and political philosophy based on spiritual cosmology, therefore, is but a mask for private passions and the desire for temporal power (which alone are real).

Political order, therefore, is reduced to the external calculation of motion—for individuals, a calculation of self-interest: how to guarantee the greatest freedom of external motion in order to acquire the objects of desire, and to avoid the greatest threat to that motion, namely death. At issue here are the motivational conditions for consent to political authority by which such motion is regulated. Political sovereignty entails a procedural set of laws that defines and governs contractually represented relations between individuals, and has the power to enforce them ultimately under threat of death. It is important to note that individual passions are morally neutral (there is no justice in the state of nature) and may in fact be reduced to the desire for power (8.10, 15ff.). Morality, conscience, and justice are socially constituted conventions, tied fundamentally to external human power to enforce law, a state of social order or peace imposed forcibly upon the violent state of nature, "the war of every man against every man" (8.8).

It should come as no surprise, then, that when Hobbes follows Plato's lead in the *Republic*, where the polis and its justice are understood as "man writ large," Hobbes depicts the commonwealth (*civitas*) as a gigantic "artificial man," mechanistically construed: "For what is the *heart* but a *spring*; and the *nerves*, but so many *strings*; and the *joints*, but so many *wheels*, giving motion to the whole body."[24] This mechanistic animal (it is a "man" only by legal fiction) is imaged poetically by Hobbes by that most obscure yet fascinating of biblical figures, the "great Leviathan" of Job 41, whose symbolic meaning is obscure. One might consider this to be a strange choice of images by one so concerned about geometric precision in the definitions that ground a new political science.[25] Yet Hobbes had the image artistically engraved on the frontispiece of the first published edition of *Leviathan* (with his own face depicted on the head).[26] Leviathan stands in fact for the "artificial soul" that governs the artificial body politic, namely the "*sovereignty*" that gives "life and motion to the whole body."

---

23. See ibid., 11.25: there is no human idea of God "answerable to [God's] nature."

24. Hobbes, *Leviathan*, introduction.

25. Several recent studies have explored the importance of Hobbes's rhetoric: see especially Johnson, *Rhetoric of Leviathan*; Skinner, *Reason and Rhetoric*.

26. For an excellent, detailed description of the frontispiece, see Corbett and Lightbown, *Comely Frontispiece*, 219–30. That Hobbes had his own face portrayed on the head of Leviathan is his own stamp of conceptual authority and authorial pride in the work he so keenly hoped would "fall into the hands of a sovereign" and thus be converted "into the utility of practice" (31.41), thus also succeeding practically where Plato had failed (Syracuse), not only theoretically. Of course, on any account Hobbes's new theory of political representation is of decisive importance for modern political science and practice.

PART 1: APOCALYPTIC MESSIANISM AND POLITICAL THEOLOGY

"Leviathan" is the name Hobbes gives to the sovereign power worthy of worship that publicly represents the conventional order of the modern commonwealth and enforces its contractual justice upon threat of death. Yet, as the frontispiece also makes clear, this Leviathan is both beast and man. The Latin inscription superimposed above the image of the gigantic figure with a man's crowned head and a scaled body comprised of contractually joined individuals (and which rises imperiously beyond the artificially reduced natural landscape) reads as follows: "*Non est potestas Super Terram quae Comparetur ei Iob: 41:24.*" There are several ironies to be noted here. The inscribed reference appears in Job 41:24 in the Latin Vulgate, but in the verse sequence of most English translations, verse 24 reads as follows: "His heart is hard as stone, hard as the nether millstone." It is no less ironic that the dramatic setting in Job is God's answer to Job's theodicy question: How is divine justice present in the experienced suffering of the righteous? The divine response out of the whirlwind (Job 38–41) is to pose a series of counter-questions concerning the power of God in creation, a creation that ultimately bears witness to the divine purposes (not sheer power) in it. Those purposes are not subject to human judgment, for the goodness of creation is larger than can be discerned by any mortal part. The whole of created order is made and measured only by the Creator. In contrast to the proud self-assertion of hard-hearted fools who rely upon their own external measures, wise human beings find and fulfill their place in the moral order of creation. And here the fear of God, not fear of Leviathan; deference to the dictates of Lady Wisdom, not worship of the chaotic power of a monstrous mortal god; love of the Creator, not fear of losing one's possessions or the external power of motion, is the beginning of wisdom and good judgment.[27]

Despite Hobbes's assertion that the singular mark of New Testament prophecy is found in the doctrine "*That Jesus is the Christ*, that is, the king of the Jews, promised in the Old Testament" (36.20; cf. 48.11ff.), this can have no immediate political import. That is, the rule of God can only be construed in material terms as a direct sovereignty (as in ancient Israel before the monarchy), and which therefore has political purchase only upon the bodily return of Christ to rule the world literally at the second coming. In between, it has force only as a doctrinal teaching requiring the consent of faith, a

---

27. The contrast between a materialist or technological human knowledge and spiritual insight into divine wisdom is developed in Job 28. Here human knowledge of things and the technical ability to use them—"Man puts his hand to the flinty rock, and overturns mountains by the roots. He cuts out channels in the rocks, and his eye sees every precious thing. He binds up the streams so they do not trickle, and the thing that is hid he brings forth to light" (28:9–11)—is distinguished from wisdom, which is not an object of human knowledge under human control: "But where is wisdom to be found? And where is the place of understanding? Man does not know the way to it, and it is not found in the land of the living.... It cannot be gotten for gold, and silver cannot be weighed as its price" (28:12–15). Wisdom is linked to the divine purposes of the Creator in fashioning the creation, and it has a moral quality: "God understands the way to [wisdom], and he knows its place ... When he gave to the wind its weight, and meted out waters by measure ... then he saw it and declared it; he established it and searched it out. And he said to man, 'Behold, the fear of the Lord, that is wisdom; and to depart from evil is understanding'" (28:23–28). Wisdom, unlike knowledge, is not a human possession, nor is the measuring here best represented by Euclidean geometry—after all, wisdom is personified in the wisdom literature in terms of dramatic agency (not technical making) that stands in intimate, indeed erotic, relation to the divine purposes she mediates—purposes that can only be discerned by human beings also in erotic relation to them, themselves mediating or embodying their spiritual motion.

private matter that makes no reference to some imagined active spiritual agency or order with political significance here and now. In effect, Hobbes's Christian political theology purges Christianity of any spiritual meaning. All politics is temporal and material; as Hobbes puts it: "Temporal and spiritual government are but two words brought into the world to make men see double and mistake their lawful sovereign"—which sovereign in a Christian *civitas* is the "one chief pastor . . . according to the law of nature," namely the civil sovereign (39.5), namely Leviathan.

In my judgment, the following commentary by Carl Schmitt on Hobbes's project is not an exaggeration:

> The most important statement of Thomas Hobbes remains: Jesus is the Christ. Such a statement retains its power even when it is relegated to the margins of an intellectual construct, even when it appears to have been banished to the outer reaches of the conceptual system. This expulsion is analogous to the domestication of Christ undertaken by Dostoevsky's Grand Inquisitor. Hobbes gave voice to and provided a scientific reason for what the Grand Inquisitor is—to make Christ's impact harmless in the social and political spheres, to dispel the anarchistic nature of Christianity while leaving it a certain legitimating effect, if only in the background; at any rate, not to abandon it.[28]

What is missing in Schmitt's commentary is Dostoevsky's recognition that the Grand Inquisitor, who is indeed the prophetic political face of Leviathan in *The Brothers Karamazov*, can only adequately be understood with reference to the apocalyptic vision of God and immortality displayed in the New Testament Christ. That is, Dostoevsky's (or, to be poetically precise, Ivan Karamazov's) Inquisitor is not only a "domesticator" of Christ but a destructive distorter of the vision of divine rule and goodness that Christ represents, according to the image of a Euclidean earthly realism.[29] Dostoevsky's art is prophetically clear: the Euclidean political theory of the Inquisitor, including the conscription of religious authority in the service of purely temporal ends, stands in rebellion

---

28. Quoted by G. L. Ulmen in his introduction to Carl Schmitt, *Roman Catholicism and Political Form*, xv.

29. I provide an extensive interpretation of the theological, ethical, and political meaning of the apocalyptic poetics displayed in Ivan's Grand Inquisitor, and in *The Brothers Karamazov* more generally, in chapters 1, 4, and 6 of Kroeker and Ward, *Remembering the End*. Briefly, the base logic of Ivan's Euclidean realism can be discerned in propositions such as the following—which, though atheist, have distinctly Hobbesian echoes:

"There is no law of nature that man should love mankind"–the law of love is a religious proposition rooted in belief in God and immortality, without which "the moral law of nature ought to change immediately into the exact opposite of the former religious law," namely the egoism of "all is permitted" (Hobbes's state of nature).

Egoism must nevertheless be restrained if human happiness and political order are to be realized. Hence, religious and moral ideologies (including Christianity) must be used in the service of taming human nature, but they must be politically controlled and managed via extensive technological, economic, and military networks of external power.

When the idea of God has been eviscerated in human beings, a "new man" will arise, a nature-conquering man-god who will remake the world in the image of a virtual reality and "will thereby every hour experience such lofty delight as will replace for him all his former hopes of heavenly delight." Ivan's sidekick Rakitin, the socialist seminarian, is especially enamoured of the glorious possibilities for social and mental engineering this "new man" will facilitate.

against God and the providential display of divine governance revealed in the crucified Christ. We have here not only the reversal of Jesus's responses to the three temptations of the devil but also, in Dostoevsky's portrayal, the parodic reversal of Jesus's messianic mediation of divine justice, rule, and authority, poetically depicted in the dragon, beasts, and whore of Revelation 12–18. That is, the Leviathan/Grand Inquisitor mediates Anti-Christ—a scientific, political, and religious correction of the work of Christ, a solution to the problem of evil that eviscerates the transcendent dangers of the human spirit so as to make possible political security (I do not call it peace) on the earth.

Diaspora Messianic Ethics and Secular Reason

As chapter 30 of *Leviathan* makes clear, Hobbesian sovereignty represents the founding of the modern welfare state—sovereignty is expanded, extended, and "democratized" via consent and the willing transfer of power from individuals to the state for the sake of those goods that all desire: protection, security, and the "contentments of life" (cf. 13.9; 17.1). Michel Foucault distinguishes between the juridical-political theory of sovereignty derived from medieval royal ideology and the normalizing disciplines of bio-power and self-surveillance that increasingly extend a technology of power over human bodies and life itself.[30] In Hobbes's *Leviathan*, however, these are united in a theory of sovereignty that joins the language of right and justice (juridical discourse) with the language of normalization (scientific discourse). The meeting ground, as Hannah Arendt points out, is technology, with its promise of delivering human control over life in both natural and socio-historical processes.[31] This implies an ontology, a value-laden decision about the relation between nature and law that warrants an increasingly externalized, mechanistic notion of the secular as the public realm of technical means by which to achieve individual self-fulfillment defined in economic terms.

What has been lost in this process, as Wendell Berry argues, is that important mediating "third" between the private individual and the technological public realm, namely, community:

> By community, I mean the commonwealth and common interests, commonly understood, of people living together in a place and wishing to continue to do so. To put it another way, community is a locally understood interdependence of local people, local culture, local economy, and local nature. (Community, of course, is an idea that can extend itself beyond the local, but it only does so metaphorically. The idea of a national or global community is meaningless apart from the realization of local communities). Lacking the interest of or in such a community, private life becomes merely a sort of reserve in which individuals defend their "right" to act as they please and attempt to limit or destroy the rights of other individuals to act as they please.[32]

---

30. See Foucault, "Two Lectures"; and Foucault, "Right of Death and Power over Life."

31. See Arendt, "The Concept of History." The connection lies in the concept of developmental "process."

32. Berry, "Sex, Economy, Freedom, and Community," 120. I offer an account of Berry's thesis that "sexual love is the heart of community life" in Kroeker, "Sexuality and the Sacramental Imagination."

Communities require for their flourishing the "common virtues of trust, goodwill, forbearance, self-restraint, compassion, and forgiveness"—virtues that are evoked and maintained not by legal contract and coercion but by education, education not in technical expertise but in moral wisdom and the disciplines of community responsibility and the burdens of love and relationship. Here there is a continuing and important public role for religious communities that may shape the secular through a different moral imagination and ontology of the common good than is evident in the technological paradigm of statist sovereignty.

In the remainder of this essay I shall explore briefly the possibility of a messianic paradigm that addresses the problem of secular pluralism quite differently from the approach displayed in technological globalization. By calling the paradigm "messianic" I am of course being deliberately provocative, as it is precisely the messianic forms of religion that have been judged to be dangerously apocalyptic and politically totalitarian by modern liberal theories. There is no doubt that some have been.[33] The challenge here is to show how messianic religious communities can engage a secular public realm defined in terms of technological empire in constructive moral terms without accommodating themselves to its colonizing vision and monolithic ontology.

The paradigm of "weak messianic power" (Benjamin) here proposed is a "diaspora" vision, a sovereignty of servanthood that stands in contrast to technological globalization. The focus here is on particular, scattered forms of "local identity" rooted in historical memories, and their relationship to larger "host" powers.[34] Diaspora messianism is a language of identity and cross-cultural engagement critically related to the dominant political institutions and norms of a culture—and it relates itself to multiple attachments—rather than a language of either accommodation or resistance. Built into the diaspora paradigm, therefore, is a tension between on the one hand displacement or separation or otherness, and on the other hand entanglement or assimilation; and this tension attends to particular cultural issues through a dialogical imagination without privilege. This is not only a sociological paradigm but also a theological one, related originally to the Bible and with important sources in Judaism.[35] In the biblical myth of the Scattering of the Peoples in Genesis 11, the creation mandate to "be fruitful and multiply and fill the earth and subdue it" is restated polemically against an imperial sovereign, "tower of Babel" interpretation of its meaning. The reduction of meaning and cultural identity to a single language, a univocal "naming" of reality in order "to make a name for ourselves," is depicted as being against the Creator's intention in making human beings in the divine image. Contrary to what many dogmatists and religious imperialists have done with it, the Bible does not oppose but celebrates plurality and diversity as the gift of creation. The monolithic, monolinguistic structures of efficiency in communities that seek to

---

33. Norman Cohn discusses numerous examples in *Pursuit of the Millennium*.

34. A significant sociological literature has developed around the language of "diaspora," including the journal named *Diaspora*. See Cohen, *Global Diasporas*; Clifford, "Diasporas"; Boyarin and Boyarin, *Powers of Diaspora*.

35. The Christian theological formulation of this that most influences my account is that provided by John Howard Yoder, "See How They Go with Their Face to the Sun"; Yoder, "Meaning after Babble"; and Yoder, "On Not Being in Charge."

colonize global resources and cultures to enact a civic vision of world-historical greatness are depicted here as a parody of creation's play of radical diversity. Pieter Breughel's painting *Tower of Babel* displays the grotesque distortion with insight—like Hobbes's *Leviathan* his Romanesque tower dwarfs the natural landscape, with ant-like humans working like slaves on its completion, even as the tower itself is already crumbling. It is an aesthetic disaster and, above all, it is completely uninhabitable, an inhumane and unnatural political abstraction. As the political scene in the front corner of Breughel's painting demonstrates, he is making a critical observation about the model of secular sovereignty underlying the Holy Roman Empire of medieval Christendom.

In Genesis 11 the divine scattering through linguistic "confusion" (Hebrew, *balal*) is viewed as an act of mercy that restores the possibility of *shalom* through diverse, local communities of scale. But the Bible is not simply anti-urban or anti-technological, nor does it try to destroy or refuse to engage empire civilizations. A second significant biblical text pertaining to the diaspora paradigm is found in Jeremiah 29, where the prophet is giving divine advice to those being taken into Babylonian exile. Here again the scattering experienced by the people is interpreted as a good, so long as they can remain focused on the creation mandate: be fruitful and multiply, set down roots (build houses, plant gardens, intermarry) in a foreign land, build community amidst differences, and above all, seek the *shalom*—the shared common well-being and just flourishing—of the empire city into which you are being sent, for in its *shalom* you will find your *shalom*. This is neither advocacy for the empire ethos of Babylon (its political tyranny, economic expansionist exploitation, and monolithic colonization of other cultures) nor a call to create a separatist community of religio-cultural purity and isolation. Rather, the people are called to live out of their alternative vision of justice even where the homeland is alien, without being in control institutionally, numerically, or spiritually.

A diaspora ethic, then, is a public ethic that is neither isolationist separatism nor complacent accommodation to tyranny—Babylon and empire do not define the terms—and that lives out of a moral orientation toward shared *shalom*. It is an ethic of community dwelling that entails respect for local cultures and learns the languages of the other in order to communicate about the shared good, rather than imposing a single language or monolithic vision of the good upon all. Diaspora Jews in exile, tellingly, became expert translators, scribes, and cross-cultural communicators who were linguistically and culturally creative, not focused upon the conservative preservation of a single system or set of institutions or struggles for civil sovereignty. The vocation of this public ethics, furthermore, is one of cultural and social responsibility in the everyday—quotidian ethics—not a heroic quest for transcultural, globalizing idealism or the "end of history." Indeed, history itself (as the Bible displays) is viewed as collections of particular and diverse narratives in various languages with a variety of genres, approaches, and traditions that foster open engagement (intertextuality), the creative play of plurality, rather than a single overarching cultural linguistic system that homogenizes meaning and seeks to control its production and distribution (including that of a romanticized, formalized policy of "multiculturalism," as in the politically correct Canadian version).

Finally, as I have already suggested, this is a political ethic of *shalom*, community well-being, and public culture not limited to certain defining institutions and their codified procedures and norms (be it the temple, cathedral, monarchy, constitutional democracy, parliament, or law court). Rather, it is characterized by cultural flexibility and communication, bringing portable, shareable skills not tied to one context, focusing on the non-coercive and local engagement of shared problems and possibilities. Leadership is defined as serving the shared good rather than establishing sovereignty and control. It therefore requires the attitudes and disciplines of humility, openness, and listening rather than conquest, the imposition of solutions and professional authority.

These elements of the diaspora paradigm are also central to the New Testament vision of messianic community. It carries on this pattern of authority and of rebuilding the secular not through control of the dominant centers of social and political power but by modeling a different path of community building as cultural service from below. This is what Paul identifies in 1 Corinthians as the "calling" or "vocation" (*klēsis*) of the *ekklēsia* to be witnesses not to the power and wisdom of human beings but to the power of God, a foolish wisdom displayed in a servanthood that possesses nothing but acts as if all things are given to it as God's gift. The diasporic and political character of Pauline messianism has recently become the subject of several interesting studies by secular political philosophers who discern in it the radical disruption of certain modern conventions, political ontologies, and habits of mind, and in particular a challenge to the technological globalizing wisdom and rulers of this age.[36] Contrary to the "secularization thesis" of Max Weber, Hans Blumenberg, Jürgen Habermas, and others who interpret Paul's eschatological messianism as indifference toward worldly or secular conditions, Badiou, Taubes, and Agamben interpret Paul's messianism as radically political, a challenge to the politics of human sovereignty in any form. The Messiah is not indifferent to the worldly, nor does he merely interpret it; as Walter Benjamin puts it in his "Theologico-Political Fragment," the Messiah and only the Messiah transforms it:

> Only the Messiah himself consummates all history, in the sense that he alone redeems, completes, creates its relation to the Messianic. For this reason nothing historical can relate itself on its own account to anything Messianic. Therefore the Kingdom of God is not the *telos* of the historical dynamic; it cannot be set as a goal. From the standpoint of history it is not the goal, but the end. Therefore the order of the profane cannot be built up on the idea of the Divine Kingdom.[37]

This is because the realm of history and nature is the realm of what is "passing away," whereas the messianic is the realm of God's eternal wisdom and power. At the heart of the Pauline messianic ethic, for both Taubes and Agamben, is the *hōs mē* ("as if not") of 1 Corinthians 7:29–31:

> I mean . . . the time (*kairos*) has become contracted; in what remains let those who have wives live as if they did not (*hōs mē*) have them, and those who mourn as if not (*hōs mē*) mourning, and those who rejoice as if not (*hōs mē*) rejoicing, and those who buy as if not (*hōs mē*) possessing, and those who use the world as if not (*hōs mē*) fully using it. For the outward form of the world is passing away.

---

36. See Taubes, *Political Theology of Paul*; Badiou, *Saint Paul*; Agamben, *Time That Remains*. For my fuller analysis of these thinkers, among others, see Kroeker, "Whither Messianic Ethics?"; and chapters 1 and 9 of this book.

37. Benjamin, "Theologico-Political Fragment," 312.

PART 1: APOCALYPTIC MESSIANISM AND POLITICAL THEOLOGY

There is a particular kind of "making use" of the world that treats it in a manner appropriate to its ontology of "passing away"—a using that is not proprietary, not related to human sovereignty or juridical ownership, that dwells in the world ("remain in the calling in which you have been called," 1 Cor 7:20) in a manner that opens it up to being made new, to "being known by God" (8:3). The nullification of secular vocation is not abandoning it for somewhere else but dwelling within it as in exile, in dispossession. This dispossession allows the power of God to transform it in keeping with its true condition or figure, its "passing away" toward an "end" that lies beyond it. This transforming power is a messianic use of the world that stands in opposition to possessive control, whether juridical, noetic, or technological.

The identity of the Christian borne by the messianic community, in other words, is not a new universalism that somehow transcends or escapes particularity and difference. Indeed it is not to be related to a form of universal knowing or theory of any sort ("if anyone imagines that he knows something, he does not yet know as he ought to know"). It is rather an identity "in the Messiah" that seeks the perfection of love not in the domination or possession of any part, but in the dispossessive transformation of all partial things to their completion in divine love. This transformation occurs in the messianic body conformed to the "mind of Messiah" that willingly empties itself in order to serve the other, a pattern of radical humility and suffering servanthood. It is a pattern that can only be spiritually discerned, even though it is being enacted in the bodily realm that is "passing away," and therefore appears as failure—as Paul emphatically insists in 1 Corinthians 1, scandalously relating the calling of the *ekklēsia* to the foolish power of the cross, which is mysteriously related to divine power and wisdom depicted not as ontological plenitude but as emptiness: "God chose what is low and despised in the world, even things that are not in order to bring to nothing the things that are." In this way secular vocations and identities are never replaced by something new, but there is rather a making new that occurs within them that transfigures and opens them up to their true use. In effect this is a messianic slavery liberated from juridical bondage to worldly possession for free creaturely action that glorifies God in the earthly body.

This "as if not" messianic ethic is the opposite of Kant's "as if" moral universal that strives to possess an ideal, that seeks to make humans the sovereign masters of their own moral and political destinies. Paul's position, by contrast, is rooted in a kenotic movement of dispossession that cannot become yet another act of (self-)legislation. The "as if not" relinquishes its moral striving and its hold—whether of the technological means of progressive liberation from the decay and bondage of nature or the political means of liberating particular identities from the burdens of their oppressive traditions and conditions. The point is rather to open all worldly callings and conditions to the transfiguring passage of God, through slavery to the sovereign crucified Messiah. Here it is necessary to get beyond possessive identities and aspirations altogether via messianic healing, which is also a messianic suffering that chooses to pass through and not merely leave behind or replace the groaning weight of past cycles of victimization, violence, and retribution. With Karl Barth and Franz Kafka, the Pauline messianic subject knows that in messianic secular time, the saved world coincides exactly with the lost world, that is, there is no path to salvation and *shalom* except through self-losing service to what cannot be saved. This is why both Kafka and Barth emphasized the secular language of the parable as the proper discourse for ethics, since the parabolic reverses the conventional criteria by which we measure strength and weakness, success and failure. It does so by discerning the passing action of God not from above in a position of world-historical dominance but from below, in a manner that emphasizes failure and thus sees differently. In Kafka's parabolic formulation, "there is salvation, but not for us."[38] Only thus is the world emptied for its reconciliation with the divine passage through it. A messianic political ethic, then, is finally a pattern that can be described as sacramental or parabolic, in which the excess of the whole may be discerned within the particular part that is selflessly and in loving use of the world, bearing witness to its hidden and sustaining divine life. This would be to restore secularity to its truest meaning—its full but not self-sufficient significance as the site where God is becoming "in Messiah" "all in all."

Conclusion

In terms of the place of theology in public reason, then, I have tried to make a case for a messianic political theology that brings into bold relief the sovereignty question—who holds the authorizing power to judge in our public life? Such a perspective may not accede to the demands by Rawls, Habermas, and Stout that theology behave more modestly and restrainedly in the public *fora* of a pluralist society. This means not that messianic claims will seek coercively and heroically to win the sovereignty game, but will precisely call into question all human claims to benevolent sovereignty rooted in possessive measures of the good—be it mammon, political power, fame, moral purity, or technological efficacy. Messianic ethics will focus less upon the legitimating claims of defining institutions (law courts, parliaments, churches, etc.) than upon the embodied practices of communities that shape the public polis in the *saeculum*, the everyday of the present age—but always with witness-bearing reference to the parabolic passage of the divine through it. For messianic ethics the fact of modern pluralism is not a lamentable fragmentation of some monolithic ideal tradition but a providential opportunity to rediscover the multiplicity of peoples and cultures as a divinely given good that saves human beings from the idolatrous imposition of political and technological uniformity in order to attend to the particular relations of particular communities in particular relevant languages. It opens up the space for vulnerable encounters from below, as opposed to domination through coercive imposition from above. The *shalom* of such reconciling encounters, furthermore, will frequently be re-presented to the messianic body by "outsiders" such as Gandhi, whose practice is more compatible with Jesus's messianic vision than the practice of many "Christians" may be. Such dialogical diasporic practice is always full of surprises and paradoxical reversals in which public judgment takes time

---

38. Kafka's discussion of parables is itself parabolically mediated in his "On Parables," 158. For Benjamin's discussion of Kafka and especially of the beauty of failure in it, see *Illuminations*, 141–45. Barth, in the section of the *Epistle to the Romans* called "The Problem of Ethics," explicitly ties the language of parables to 1 Corinthians 7:31, "the form of the world passes away," and considers that the only ethical form that bears testimony to divine action is one that is "offered up" sacrificially in self-dissolution or worldly failure or brokenness. See Barth, *Epistle to the Romans*, 433–36, 445, 462–65.

and requires patience. Yet this patience is a "wild patience"[39] that can take the many particular forms needed for vulnerable secular engagement, discernment, and participation in the mysterious judgments and pathways of divine wisdom in the present age.

---

39. This is how the political theorist Romand Coles characterizes the messianic political ethic of John Howard Yoder, in "The Wild Patience of John Howard Yoder." See chapter 9, below.

PART 2

Political Theology and the Radical Reformation

5

Anabaptists and Existential Theology

Since first reading Robert Friedman's book on Anabaptist theology, I have taken his description as my own—theology is properly "existential theology."[1] Insofar as the Mennonite or Anabaptist approach to theology is above all existential (rather than dogmatic, creedal, doctrinal, systematic, fundamental, academic, ecclesial, or other such primary descriptors), I have happily continued to consider myself "Anabaptist" despite no longer being a formal member of the Mennonite church. Of course, so described, Anabaptist theology cannot be practiced in isolation from other approaches and traditions, nor can it avoid entering into conversation with alternative theological construals of human existence—Christian and otherwise. In this essay I reflect on what it means to practice existential theology and, in particular, Anabaptist existential theology, and I do so in conversation with other approaches and traditions as an embodiment of what I take such practice to entail.

Perhaps it is useful to begin at the beginning: Who coined the term "theology," and why? The origin of the word is neither Christian nor Jewish but Greek—it was introduced by Plato in *The Republic* (book 2). What types or models of speech about the god (*hoi typoi peri theologias*, 379a) best represent the truth about human existence and its formative experiences, its ordering, its "good"? Theology for Plato is existential theology. Not content simply to repeat uncritically the tales of the poets or conventional opinions and doctrines about human beings and the gods, he wants to know the truth: how do these tales and teachings illuminate and inform human life in the world? The model of theological education he develops in *The Republic* is devoted to the critical clarification of the assumptions, stories, ideas, and doctrines by which we live in order to find the true meaning of our existence.[2] Without such concern for truth, which is not only a cognitive matter but a moral matter of how to order desire—the quest for truth requires both a certain sort of person and a certain kind of *technē*, or method—we live in danger

---

1. Friedman, *Theology of Anabaptism*.
2. For further discussion of Plato's approach to theology, see Kroeker, "The Ironic Cage of Positivism."

of naming reality falsely, bound by fetters of our own making in the artificial light of conventional caves presided over by unenlightened, power-hungry image makers (and their media). For Plato this is a spiritual matter, for the truth of human existence seeks contact with the eternal good beyond all images and external appearances, the true invisible measure of all visible reality.[3]

Hence the central importance of theology. Misconceptions about the god are not ordinary falsehoods. They represent the "true lie" (*to hos alēthos pseudos*, 382a; cf. 535d–e), the lie in the soul about "the highest things" (*kyriotata*) to "what is highest" in oneself. The lie of disordered theology is therefore not merely the possession of distorted knowledge; it is a wrong relation to God—a spiritual problem affecting the whole of existence: personal, social, and cosmic. I believe this is no less true for Christians and for Mennonites than it was for the ancient Greeks, and there is good reason for us to have adopted Plato's word in developing our own accounts of the meaning of existence before God. Doctrine is tied to the drama of life, and this drama is not just a personal or communal story or tradition; it is a cosmic drama. Yet our only way toward understanding ourselves within it is the low road of particularity, exploring the narratives, symbols, and doctrines that shape us in order to recover the dramatic spiritual motion they represent.[4] In order to do that properly, we must seek the truth about the spiritual order of reality and our place within it.

Here it is wise to attend to the existential theology of Augustine, who shared the Platonists' concern for the truth and who, like Plato, understood the journey toward it to be a spiritual one toward God as our "homeland," traveled along the "road of the affections."[5] The desire of human existence is to find the true fulfillment of its earthly

---

3. I trust it will be evident, therefore, why and where I disagree with postmodern Mennonite voices calling for poetry to replace philosophy and theology. While I welcome Scott Holland's affirmation of "theopoetics," I cannot agree with his unerotic reading of Plato. Plato certainly did not fear poetry or the poets, just as he did not fear politics, politicians, intellectuals, and sophists. What he feared "more than anything" (in himself, in others, and in the city) was to lie "to the soul about the things that are" (*Republic* 382ab): the willful ignorance of truth, the manipulation of ideas, images, emotions, desires without regard for understanding their meaning and good ordering. See Holland, "Theology Is a Kind of Writing." For my alternative reading of Plato, see chapter 2. An insightful interpretation of Plato and the poets is Gadamer, "Plato and the Poets." An astute deconstruction of the dogmatic Derridian reading of Plato is Pickstock, *After Writing*, pt. 1.

4. Augustine refers to "intentional signs" (*signa data*) as "those which living creatures show to one another for the purpose of conveying, in so far as they are able, the motion of their spirits or something which they have sensed or understood" (*Teaching Christianity* 2.3). In order to understand and interpret those signs properly one must attend to and imitate their existential meaning. Hermeneutics is not only an intellectual exercise.

5. See Augustine, *Teaching Christianity*, bk. 1. One can only chuckle at Rudy Wiebe's depiction of "Augustine's Plato-influenced love of ethereal spirit and the literally untouchable soul," in Wiebe's "The Body Knows as Much as the Soul," 196. "Love" was not a word Augustine threw around casually—he knew the variety of ways embodied souls experience it, and he tried to understand the good ordering of that experience theologically. Ironically, what Wiebe modestly claims as his own daring insight, namely the wilful autonomy of the male sexual organ, is the subject of unstinting, illuminating analysis by Augustine in *City of God* (bk. 14). I suppose Wiebe will object that Augustine ties this too closely to THE FALL (how negative of him!), a story whose profound spiritual motion Wiebe reduces to a moralistic homily on Mennonite Brethren guilt; see Wiebe's dismissive treatment in the title essay of *River of Stone*, 298f.

loves, and this entails the purification of the eye of the heart or the soul so as to see and be guided by the truth, goodness, and beauty that ultimately moves us within the embodied particularity of our worldly experience. For Augustine, however, this path takes a form unexpected by the Platonists—not philosophical dialectic, but tears of confession as we turn to follow the "form of the servant," the path of humble love (which cures our blinding pride) taken by God in the world.[6] We learn what it means to partake of the divine nature when we follow that path, the *via caritatis*, and imitate its spiritual motion, for it is the divine Truth itself (*ipsa Veritas*), "that Word through whom all things were made," that was made flesh so that God may dwell with us.[7] "Although He is our native country, He made Himself also the Way to that country."[8] It is the bodily particularity, of course, that scandalizes the Greeks, and yet it is crucial to the Christian model of God to recognize the personal intimacy of God's spiritual relation to creation.

In the remainder of this essay I reflect on some representative stories that have helped me re-think in a broader existential context the particularity of the Mennonite Christian memory in which I dwell, one that is also shaped by other particular memories and motions. Two of the most fateful of these cultural signs in our own context are: (1) the Canadian and North American story, or "primal" (as George Grant puts it[9]), of the expanding domination of technological consumer culture, which has led to a growing cultural homogeneity in the service of the liberating promise of technology;[10] (2) the parallel story of religio-cultural diversity in a secular democratic society in which people from many traditions, backgrounds, and identities have had to wrestle with what it means to get along and relate to one another across *different* particularities. These two dramas stand in difficult tension with each other, and the temptation has been to flee or subvert the substantive challenge of the second by appealing to the hollowed-out, externalized, and increasingly generic identities (without meaningful memory) offered by the first, by a commodified consumer vision of "the good life."

---

6. Augustine says the following about the difference between his Platonism and the path of Christ: "I began to want to give myself airs as a wise person. I was full of my punishment, but I shed no tears of penitence. Worse still, I was puffed up with knowledge (1 Cor 8:1). Where was the charity which builds on the foundation of humility which is Christ Jesus? . . . None of this is in the Platonist books. Those pages do not contain the face of this devotion, tears of confession, your sacrifice, a contrite and humble spirit. . . . It is one thing from a wooded summit to catch a glimpse of the homeland of peace and not to find the way to it" (Augustine, *Confessions* 7.20–21).

7. See Augustine, *Teaching Christianity* 1.12–13, 38.

8. Ibid., 1.11. As Augustine makes clear (1.10–12), this divinely given spiritual motion by which God comes to dwell in God's own creation is not some form of space and time travel—God comes to where God already is. So also the motion of our return to God is not some spatio-temporal tradition but the fulfillment of our created existence, which was designed for eternal communion with God and our neighbors. The cosmic spiritual drama in which we participate has its terms (nature) given by the Creator God who does not abandon us to our distortions of that nature but seeks to cure our relation to the source and end of love. To quote Augustine: "One lives in justice and sanctity when one is an unimpaired appraiser of the intrinsic reality of things. Such a one has an ordered love, who neither loves what should not be loved, nor fails to love what is lovable" (1.28; my translation).

9. See Grant, "In Defence of North America."

10. I offer an interpretation of this story as one of "spiritual crisis" in *Christian Ethics and Political Economy in North America*, esp. chaps. 1 and 5.

In the face of this dangerous, soul-destroying idolatry the irony is that more than ever, we need the rich particular resources of lived religious traditions and their spiritual disciplines (principles of motion) in order to develop viable alternative forms of human existence. Mennonites, like the other existential traditions represented in the examples below, face the challenge of how to wrestle with this tension in seeking to serve the larger good of our culture. Our form of service seeks to embody the pattern imaged by Christ, taking the low road of kenotic particularity, the humble path of suffering love—recognizing this to be the worldly form of cosmic glory.

My representative stories are novels that I teach in a secular urban university. They have prompted me to reflect anew upon existential theology, the relationship of the spiritual motion given in Christ as exemplified in my Mennonite Christian memory to the time and place in which I live. I offer these reflections not as an expert Mennonite theologian nor from an academic or ecclesial ivory tower, but rather as someone struggling to give an account of what it means to be answerable for what I have been given to be and to do. These stories have enabled me to chart my own personal, but I trust not idiosyncratic, journey from rural Mennonite village to the city, concluding with the challenge of what it might mean to cultivate the spiritual disciplines of the penitential community of reconciling divine love in our own modern culture.

I

The first story is *Remembering*, a novel by the Kentuckian farmer Wendell Berry.[11] This story is close to home for North American Mennonites who began their sojourn here in rural farming communities, a time and place from which many of us are not far removed in memory, and a form of life whose passing Berry laments. Andy Catlett has devoted his life to such a rural community composed of small-scale family farms, but in the loss of his right hand to a corn-picking machine he finds he has "lost his hold" on his motivating vision.

The novel begins in a state of profound disorientation and disembodiment that represents Andy's spiritual condition as he awakes from a disturbing technological nightmare in the strange San Francisco hotel room to which he has fled. He will find no liberation from his past problems by reshaping his identity through the commodified procurements of urban anonymity. Only by remembering who he is, the defining moments of the life history of his soul, the tangled pattern of embodied memories—words, gestures, voices—will he recover his purpose, the true direction of his bodily and spiritual desire. Andy's movement of repentance and return is captured in evocative prose:

> He is held, though he does not hold. He is caught up again in the old pattern of entrances: of minds into minds, minds into place, places into minds. The pattern limits and complicates him, singling him out in his own flesh. Out of the multitude of possible lives that have surrounded and beckoned to him like a crowd around a star, he returns now to himself, a mere meteorite, scorched, small, and

---

11. Berry, *Remembering*. For my longer essay on this novel, see Kroeker, "Sexuality and the Sacramental Imagination."

> fallen . . . He will be partial, and he will die; he will live out the truth of that. Though he does not hold, he is held. (57–58)

In this complex particular pattern he meets his own life in freedom, significant within the embodied terms in which it is given and remembered, claimed by love experienced in body and soul in a manner connecting him to the cosmic drama itself:

> That he is who he is and no one else is the result of a long choosing, chosen and chosen again. He thinks of the long dance of men and women behind him, . . . who, choosing one another, chose him.
> He thinks of the choices, too, by which he chose himself as he now is. . . . Those choices have formed in time and place the pattern of a membership that chose him, yet left him free until he should choose it, which he did once, and now has done again. (60)

What Andy Catlett recovers is the memory of why he chose to resist the siren voices of technological and economic "progress" in order to cultivate another way of life on the land. This other way has been given him as a choice by his parents and the people of his community, who have fostered it through the disciplines of love. It is a radically traditional vision of rural existence in which fidelity to marriage, family, farmland, community, and God are richly woven together in a demanding pattern of skill and trust that our dominant urban technological culture views with either sentimentality or disdain. When Andy, as a young aspiring "professional" agriculturalist—the newly minted product of an agricultural college seeking to make a career in farming journalism, thereby trading on his rural experience to advance his way of life—dares to voice his preference for the Amish farm he visits over the technological farming of large-scale agribusiness, he realizes this is more than an argument about agricultural methods and techniques. It is a cultural battle,[12] a spiritual struggle over the meaning of the "highest things," over a good life and a bad one. Agribusiness, says Andy at an academic conference on "The Future of the American Food System," is an abstract "agriculture of the mind" (23) that cannot think humanly and spiritually about what it does, and therefore lacks good judgment. It produces death, not life.

This story holds relevance for existential Anabaptist identity and theology. I find it ironic that just when Mennonite theology as a formal academic discipline is growing—we are rapidly becoming more sophisticated in our understanding of methodology, systematics, and intellectual trends, and we measure our success partly by the number of prestigious professional theologians we can boast—there is less and less of significance distinguishing our way of life from the cultural mainstream. Is our newfound "Anabaptist theology" another abstract "theology of the mind" where no real people and communities dwell, rather than an existential theology cultivating a whole way of life in communion that keeps faith with one another, the land, and God—embracing and embodying, in disciplined skills of love and care, a life-giving vision of peaceable justice? In our rush to join a "progressive" mainstream culture, eager to cash in our hard-earned

---

12. Cultural in the twofold meaning of *cultus*: (1) what we worship, respect, venerate—the teachings, rituals, and practices that re-mind us who we are; (2) what we cultivate as worthy of attention, labor, and care so as to serve the good of a place, a community, and a time in all aspects.

countercultural identities for careerist success, have we become willing to lose our embodied Mennonite soul?

This is not to say that moving from the village to the city necessarily entails such a loss of soul, but neither is it true that to be *die Stillen im Lande* is somehow an abdication of human cultural, social, and spiritual responsibility. It may be, as Wendell Berry believes, that such a way of life preserves a crucial set of cultural, familial, social, and spiritual disciplines rooted in a vision of existence that our culture powerfully needs to bring it back from a headlong rush toward spiritual (and ecological, civil, economic) death. At the very least this should mean that in our eagerness to dialogue with modern and postmodern theorists and writers, Anabaptist theology dare not cut off dialogue with our past and with those "backward" and "conservative" traditional communities (the Amish, for example) who continue to give visible, embodied cultural testimony to a radically different way of life that judges our own simply by being what it is. I suggest that because of what we count as worthy models of theology, such a dialogue has become far more challenging and difficult than the conventional forms of academic and avant-garde theological reflection we cite in our footnotes.[13]

II

I turn now to a very different novel, representing a very different context of dialogue, urban and in some ways more recognizably theological—but perhaps only in a shock of recognition. Chaim Potok's *My Name Is Asher Lev* is set in the heart of New York, where a young Orthodox painter seeks to find the artistic forms by which to communicate the painful tensions of his experience as Hasidic Jew and painter, both to his own community and the wider culture. Thus it too deals with what Annie Dillard calls the "scandal of particularity."[14] As the painter of the *Brooklyn Crucifixion*, Asher Lev appropriates the central Christian symbol to express his personal pain and his vision of atonement, and creates scandalous offense on every side. The painting depicts his mother crucified between his father and himself, representing the riveting and poignant familial tension in the novel—an image inviting Freudian interpretations.

Yet the painting is not only a depiction of the painful, indeed violent, conflict of desire. To understand Asher's scandalous art we must go well beyond Freudian psychoanalysis, which reduces religious symbolism to the objectified drama of human feeling. For Asher's feelings (and the feelings he represents in the painting) are themselves organized in relation to religiously (not just aesthetically or culturally) interpreted existence. It is the mother who is crucified, after all, and not simply in the ritual slaughter of a victim in order to achieve the object of desire. The mother's sacrifice is a voluntary self-giving, an "awesome act of will," as Asher comes to see, in the service of a larger, nurturing

---

13. Two Mennonite theologians—Harry Huebner and David Schroeder—have conducted a fascinating dialogue with the Amish community, sharing their common struggles over how to cultivate the disciplines of visible Christian community in a seductive consumer culture. The dialogue has not, I take it, been conducted as "field research" for academic publication (the preservation of Mennonite "folklore") but with the aim of critically and constructively understanding what it might mean to be the church in late modern North America.

14. See Dillard, *Holy the Firm*, pt. 3.

reconciliation between father and son and the very different and yet related objects of their love, "ways of giving meaning to the world."[15] Her anguish, embodied in her own personal suffering, also represents and participates in the anguish of the universe and cries out for a form "of ultimate anguish and torment" (313). For this reason the observant Jew Asher Lev, who loves his parents, his Hasidic tradition and community, paints a crucifixion because "I would not be the whore to my own existence" (312).

This forceful language invites us to see how well Asher Lev understands the existential meaning of the Christian symbol he must employ—necessarily, he feels, in full shuddering recognition of the painful scandal it will create. The mother is crucified "between" the way of the father (strict, literal observance of the Torah—and therefore wary of the visual arts as potentially idolatrous—as the embodied path of atonement in the world) and the way of the son (the path of a gift divinely given that represents the world in a new form, one influenced by the Christian *goyim*, the tradition of Christian art). The borrowed form—the crucifix—and its content is itself profoundly Jewish, even while breaking scandalously with traditional Jewish forms.[16] In Asher's hands it also breaks with the traditional Christian forms which have themselves been used— idolatrously and violently—to oppress Jews.[17] Asher's *Brooklyn Crucifixion* is a scandal to both Jews and Christians. The larger question it raises is, What shall we do with these differing paths, images, embodiments of redemption? How shall we find "at-one-ment" in a suffering world in which fathers and sons and their warring ways destroy one another (313)?

The implied answer of Potok's novel is: not by denying the particularity and embodiment of one's existence (family, ancestral past, religious traditions), nor by denying what is truly and revealingly—indeed, redemptively—embodied in the "other." One might find in embodied forms not available in one's own tradition what is needed to express "at-one-ment" in the tangled particularity of created existence. Such a path of dialogue will always risk scandal in order to participate responsibly in the redemptive task of bringing "the Master of the Universe into the world." Such an existential theology as a way of life will not be afraid to break those idols (reified symbols, traditions, doctrines that have become detached from lived meaning in relation to the living God) that enclose, entomb, encapsulate the light of God's holy presence in the world.[18] It will

---

15. Potok, *My Name Is Asher Lev*, 309. Her act of will sharply contrasts to the aesthetic vision articulated in an art book Asher's mother gives him to read early in his formal education, Robert Henri's *The Art Spirit*, where the powerful artistic will is fostered by "freeing" oneself from all creeds and communities. Asher's mother's act of will is a religiously informed and inspired devotion of love toward (neither liberation from nor enslavement to) her family and her community.

16. For an interesting Jewish interpretation of Jesus's death as another particular form of the pattern of fraternal displacement and redemptive "chosenness" found in the Hebrew Bible, see Levenson, *Death and Resurrection of the Beloved Son*.

17. One reason Asher's family is so deeply offended by the crucifixion is that Asher's grandfather (after whom he is named) was killed on his way home from synagogue one Saturday night by a drunken Christian peasant—"somehow my grandfather had forgotten it was the night before Easter" (11).

18. Hasidic cosmology says the spiritual task of Jewish life in community is to liberate the light of God's glory (*shekinah*) hidden and imprisoned in the shells of hardened worldly forms. This is a messianic task in which, through human deeds of service (sparks of responsibility), the world is hallowed for God's presence. This requires engagement with the powers of darkness; God approaches us in the alien, the partial, the incomplete, and invites us to join in the work that transforms it "into the substance of true life," as Martin Buber puts it. See Buber, *Origin and Meaning of Hasidism*, 78; cf. 53ff.

therefore seek the very heart of God's purpose for the world rather than narrowly and self-righteously defend its own partial truth as the only path (which is to lust after false, more immediate gods). But such a theology will not break and destroy particularity in a gratuitous manner; it will seek to be faithful to the larger truth that has inspired the particular and that nurtures it through self-giving service.

Existential theology keeps faith with the particular gift of one's own life given by the God whose life and purpose transcends (and therefore breaks) all static images. As images, Torah and cross remain true only as embodied in lives that point in freedom toward the true inner-outer, dynamic meaning of those embodiments and their challenging, illuminating, and saving power. This power is tied to its particularity, and it can only be kept alive by cultivating its meaning in the disciplined lives of committed community members—through prayer, the shared reading and study of scripture, worship. Above all it is important, as the wise old Rebbe says, "to open our eyes wide" (271) to see what new thing God is revealing and doing in the world.

Few urban Mennonites have taken the Hasidic path of visible communal separation from the wider culture. Indeed, urban Mennonites have become quickly acculturated and are, for the most part, virtually indistinguishable from other traditions by way of life and community discipline. Given the virtual absence of liturgical form in Mennonite worship and the ready willingness to jettison those forms that may offend sophisticated urban tastes (e.g., community fasting, kneeling for prayer, community confession and discipline, and the ordinance of footwashing—all practiced in my own urban Mennonite church for less than a generation), little remains to distinguish the urban path of particular Mennonite witness from others in the low Protestant mainstream.

Indeed, the spectrum of doctrinal options now characterizing debates about Mennonite identity—are we a "peace church," an adult believers' baptism church, an evangelical or liberal church, a "voluntarist" tradition, "synergist" rather than predestinarian? etc.—can readily be found in other Protestant denominations. This does not mean the spectrum or the debates are meaningless or unimportant, or that the above-mentioned practices are unproblematic. However, the spectrum so defined does obscure certain scandalous oddities of traditional Anabaptist existential theology, oddities that might offer creative resources for cultivating needed forms of particular Christian witness in our wider culture.

III

The third and most explicitly Christian of the novels that I am bringing into dialogue here is a work that resonates richly with many theological aspects of the Anabaptist tradition (and not just those of the Russian Mennonites!), Dostoevsky's *Brothers Karamazov*. Its hero is Alexei (Alyosha) Karamazov, "a strange man, even an odd one" whose significance is related to his particularity precisely insofar as he "bears within himself the heart of the whole, while the other people of his epoch have all for some reason been torn away from it for a time by some kind of flooding wind."[19] Alyosha's strange path, as "an early lover of mankind" (18), is shaped by Christian monasticism and the commis-

---

19. Dostoevsky, *Brothers Karamazov*, 3.

sion given him by his unconventional spiritual father, elder Zosima, to "sojourn in the world like a monk" (285). Dostoevsky's hero comes to embody a form of Christian ascetic theology in imitation of the image of the suffering Christ, a form of life with many parallels to Anabaptist existential theology understood as "ascetic theology."[20] Kenneth Davis has compellingly argued that three influential characterizations of Anabaptist theology—Stauffer's "theology of martyrdom," Bender's "theology of discipleship," and Friedman's "doctrine of two worlds"—can be interpreted as complementary facets of an ascetic theology of holiness, tied to certain medieval and monastic movements of reform.[21] This points to a promising prophetic direction for existential Anabaptist theology, a direction I will explore below.

In book 6 of *The Brothers Karamazov*, entitled "The Russian Monk," Dostoevsky develops, in the voice of Alyosha, his poetic prophetic answer to Ivan Karamazov's powerfully articulate rejection of the meaning of God's creation as expressed by Christ. Dostoevsky wrote these pages in fear and trembling, concerned that in this "culminating point," for whose sake "the whole novel is being written," he would be able to communicate in persuasive artistic form the practical realism of "pure" Christian existence.[22] Not surprisingly, however, it is Ivan's legend of the Grand Inquisitor, not Alyosha's life of the elder Zosima, that has become the most famous of Dostoevsky's prophetic texts in the twentieth century. As Dostoevsky feared, the odd path of Christian asceticism—even in the form of "sojourn in the world"—would not capture the imagination and commitment of Russian culture. This too is foretold in the narrator's preface to the novel: modern critical realists will judge the hero to be "unrealistic," the representative of an isolated, otherworldly path that cannot be recommended as a model for our time. Yet the narrator insists that Alyosha was "even more of a realist than the rest of us" (25) and surely less isolated in the sense expressed by the words of Jesus that stand as the epigraph to the entire novel: "Verily, verily, I say unto you, Except a corn of wheat fall into the earth and die, it abideth alone; but if it die, it bringeth forth much fruit" (John 12:24).

How does the ascetic path lead us out of the darkness of falsehood and isolation to the light of truth, thus uniting us through death with "the heart of the whole"? For Dostoevsky this can only be understood in relation to Johannine cosmology, God's higher, "spiritual" truth that is nevertheless embodied in the world as the pattern of self-giving, suffering love. Unlike his compatriot Tolstoy, who translated the Gospel into a liberal pacifist moral vision, Dostoevsky sees the Christ of the Gospels as a cosmic apocalyptic figure who tears open the hidden meaning of everyday life and exposes it as spiritual crisis (*krisis*, in the literal sense of judgment or decision; in a metaphysical and theological, not just a sociopolitical or moral, manner). Entailed here is a radical reversal of meaning, cultivated in the ascetic spiritual disciplines, of conventional measures of meaning,

---

20. The term "ascetic" has been used in many ways. Etymologically it is tied to *askeo*, "to work," in the sense of giving artistic form (in the Homeric literature), and to *askesis*, the practice of or in something, especially a "mode of life" (in the religious and philosophical sense). See Liddell and Scott, *Greek-English Lexicon*; and Wimbush and Valantasis, *Asceticism*.

21. Davis, *Anabaptism and Asceticism*. On the dialogue with Eastern Orthodox theology, see the excellent comparative study by Finger, "Anabaptism and Eastern Orthodoxy."

22. See letters 784, 785, 791, and 807 in Dostoevsky, *Complete Letters*, vol. 5.

truth, and lie. To those captured by a slavishly materialist vision of human freedom and fulfillment, the "tyranny of things and habits" that truly isolates selves (as "rights-bearers") and kills community, the monastic way may seem isolating and constricted. The elder Zosima begs to differ:

> Obedience, fasting, and prayer are laughed at, yet they alone constitute the way to real and true freedom: I cut away my superfluous and unnecessary needs, through obedience I humble and chasten my vain and proud will, and thereby, with God's help, attain freedom of spirit and, with that, spiritual rejoicing! Which of the two is more capable of upholding and serving a great idea—the isolated rich man or one who is liberated from the tyranny of things and habits? (314)

Only one freed from the isolation of self-love can truly love others, and such freedom is made possible through spiritual rebirth in the image of Christ—that is, conformity to the "form of the servant" that builds up human community through deeds of humble love.

Thus in answer to the question raised earlier, it is not *ascesis* per se that "saves." After all, *The Brothers Karamazov* also gives us the cramped, judgmental asceticism of *ressentiment* in the character of Father Ferapont, who is captured by a crudely materialist religious cosmology (and the Grand Inquisitor too is a rigorous ascetic). Rather, it is ascesis in the service of the truth of Christ that saves, a sincere inner penitence where one becomes "also guilty before all people, on behalf of all and for all, for all human sins, the world's and each person's, only then will the goal of our unity be achieved. . . . This knowledge is the crown of the monk's path, and of every man's path on earth" (164). Only such a conscious solidarity with the world's sin and guilt can move human hearts to participate in the divine love that seeks to reconcile the world in a peaceable harmony. Such an asceticism seeks not "otherworldly" purity nor, as the elder reiterates, is it afraid of human sin; it rather "keeps close company" with the heart where the image of Christ presides, taking the penitential path of continual confession and suffering servanthood in which the re-creative mystery of divine love is powerfully enacted. "And what is the word of Christ without an example?" asks the elder. Alyosha's biography proceeds to recollect examples of the penitential life taken from the elder's memory. They follow a common pattern: an existential revelation of the "whole truth" of life, the confession of solidarity in human guilt, repentance, forgiveness, and a turn to the path of community brought about through active embodied love. To quote Father Zosima again:

> Every action has its law. This is a matter of the soul, a psychological matter. In order to make the world over anew, people themselves must turn onto a different path psychically. Until one has indeed become the brother of all, there will be no brotherhood.
>
> No science or self-interest will ever enable people to share their property and their rights among themselves without offense. Each will always think his share too small, and they will keep murmuring. (303)

Such a vision of "the truth alone," and "not earthly truth, but a higher one" (308), dies to the pursuit of retributive justice and its alienating, isolating claims (which underlie Ivan's and the Inquisitor's rebellion) in order to be reborn into the suffering solidarity of human-divine community, where God's presence is lovingly served in all its created likenesses on the earth.

Dostoevsky's artistic portrait of ascetic theology has interesting parallels in the Anabaptist tradition, not least in the ascetic theology of Menno Simons. As in Dostoevsky's portrait, Anabaptist asceticism seeks the restoration of true humanity in the image of Christ made possible in the "penitent existence," as Menno calls it.[23] For him, as in *The Brothers Karamazov*, the truth of this image and existence is discerned from within the apocalyptic framework of the "slain Lamb" who rules in the heavenly city, a rule mediated on earth in the suffering servant church. To awaken and to remain attentive to this truth requires rebirth and the existential practice of the disciplines of the penitential life—for it is a truth that is transparent neither in the fallen human soul nor in fallen human society. "All who are born of the truth hate the lie," says Menno, echoing John (and Plato): "Conversely, all who are born of falsehood hate the truth."[24] This cosmic struggle between divine truth and its false, parodic copies defines the terms of human existence; to serve the truth is an *agon* for which only the reborn are equipped.[25]

Yet this rebirth and awakening is neither simply an inner matter of the heart nor an individualistic experience. It is a being reborn into the true nature of divine love that becomes visible in the world through embodied expression, the mimesis of the spiritual motion of humble love incarnated by Christ. If the pattern is true, then its nature cannot be an abstract or formal or "otherworldly" ideal; it must hold in all aspects of existence. "If you are born of the pure seed of the holy Word, the nature of the seed must be in you,"[26] and all things will proceed according to that nature, as Menno's extensive discussion of examples of the penitent life in "True Christian Faith" makes clear. Such love, in the language of *The Brothers Karamazov*, is not a "miracle impossible on the earth," a kind of otherworldly dream "staged" by the Gospel stories and the Christian church for dramatic inspiring effect (237, 58). It is a demanding way of life, yet precisely one for which human beings have been made. That is the premise of existential Anabaptist theology—the Gospel is not an unattainable ideal of love presided over by the church as

---

23. Menno uses this language everywhere, but my interpretation focuses on Simons, "Foundation of Christian Doctrine," and Simons, "True Christian Faith." See also Voolstra, "True Penitence."

24. Simons, "True Christian Faith," 330.

25. Dostoevsky depicts this insight in his portrayal of Alyosha's conversion, following the death of his beloved elder which provokes a crisis of faith in Alyosha's "virgin heart." It is only when, in response to a sisterly act of love from an unexpected source (the seductive, "fallen" Grushenka), Alyosha experiences for himself the full inner-outer meaning of the elder's teachings that he becomes equipped for the ascetic "sojourn in the world" to which he has been called. It is a penitential rebirth characterized by weeping and ecstatic, erotic confession: "It was as if threads from all those innumerable worlds of God all came together in his soul, and it was trembling all over, 'touching other worlds.' He wanted to forgive everyone and for everything, and to ask forgiveness, oh, not for himself! but for all and for everything, 'as others are asking for me,' rang again in his soul. . . . He fell to the earth a weak youth and rose up a fighter, steadfast" (362–63).

26. Simons, "True Christian Faith," 394. Menno argues that the nature of divine love into which followers of Christ are reborn is of a piece with the "natural love" of parents for children and spouses for one another, where inner intention and external deed are not falsely divided but represent an inner-outer coherence within a larger natural and social ordering of love (338).

the custodian of proper doctrine and otherworldly hope, while the realities of worldly justice and social order are addressed by other more attainable means.[27]

Hence the sacraments and the body of Christ must be interpreted in a fully existential manner as well, as the real presence and embodiment of the penitential pattern.[28] The weeping of true repentance, says Menno, is not empty or formal display—it is the expression of a new mind, a new nature, which will become manifest in deeds.[29] Baptism represents the "true new birth with its fruits" of obedience to the inner Word; the Lord's Supper conforms the outer sign to its true meaning, the body of Christ in which those who partake become "flesh of his flesh and bone of his bone" and incarnate Christ's kenotic pattern of humble love in all of life.[30] At the motivating heart of this participatory ascesis is neither dazzling miracle nor forensic status—it is the transformation of holy erotic divine love. The culminating image here is the celebratory assembly of the marriage feast of the Lamb.[31] So too in *The Brothers Karamazov*, where Alyosha's rebirth is sacramentally and iconically depicted in another of Dostoevsky's "culminating" moments—a chapter entitled "Cana of Galilee," in which Alyosha is granted a vision of the heavenly wedding feast that ties together earthly joy and its heavenly completion. It is this unity of inner and outer, temporal and eternal, earthly and heavenly, personal and cosmic, that equips him for ascetic sojourn in the world, his ministry of reconciliation that helps transform the community of children from a pattern of strict, retributive justice to that of humble, restorative love.

IV

This brings me to my concluding point, and the one with which I began. Existential Anabaptist theology of the sort described above must be particular but it cannot be isolated.

---

27. The active involvement of the Mennonite church in establishing the practice of "restorative justice," for example, bears powerful continuing witness to this theological vision.

28. This existential interpretation of the sacrament of penance and confession is present also in the path of elder Zosima—for which he is criticized by opponents, who claim "that here the sacrament of confession was being arbitrarily and frivolously degraded," an ironic charge given the complete religious and moral seriousness of the elder, whose focus is on the power of the Gospel and the image of Christ to transform all of life.

29. See Grislis, "Menno Simons on Sanctification": "Menno's understanding of sanctification was remarkable both for its realism and its high expectations[his] concern was personal but remained in a distinctively ecclesial setting. The Christian love he celebrated was no mere ideal but a participatory reality" (246).

30. Note the elder's words as recorded by Alyosha: "One may stand perplexed before some thought, especially seeing men's sin, asking oneself: 'Shall I take it by force, or by humble love?' Always resolve to take it by humble love. If you so resolve once and for all, you will be able to overcome the whole world. A loving humility is a terrible power, the most powerful of all, nothing compares with it. Keep company with yourself and look to yourself every day and hour, every minute, that your image be ever gracious—Brothers, love is a teacher, but one must know how to acquire it, for it is difficult to acquire, it is dearly bought, by long work over a long time, for one ought to love not for a chance moment but for all time" (319).

31. Simons, "Foundation of Christian Doctrine," 148ff., and especially Menno's use of erotic language from the Song of Solomon to describe this vision of fulfillment, 221ff. See also Kreitzer, "Menno Simons and the Bride of Christ."

Just as Christ incarnated the creative power of divine love in the particular form of a humble servant, thus reversing expectations for how to understand the cosmic authority of divine rule and its worldly embodiment, so also the community of Christ's followers seeks to embody this pattern in our own time and place. This astonishing image is dramatically unveiled in Revelation 5, in John's vision of the sealed scroll that contains the hidden meaning and destiny of historical existence. No one is worthy to open the scroll and God will not break the seals—human destiny and with it the destiny of creation is mediated in the world by human freedom. God does not interfere magically. John begins to weep—how will God's purposes for this alienated creation be realized? Who is worthy to be the agent of redemptive justice and reconciling harmony in the world?

The answer is given in an amazing conjunction of images. The elder *says* to John, "The Lion of the tribe of Judah, the Root of David, has conquered, so that he can open the scroll and its seven seals"—an image of the messianic warrior king. What John *sees*, however, is "a Lamb, standing, as though it had been slain"—the messianic conquering of evil is accomplished by death. The messianic agency that draws all creation to its fulfilling completion is the power of suffering, serving love that exhausts the strength of evil by patient martyrdom. This calls for an alternative vision of the meaning and end of human existence (represented by a "new song" in Rev 5:9–14) founded on the model of worthiness of the slain Lamb.

And yet this ascetic vision of humble, serving love has as its final aim the inclusion of all reality in the joyful feast of the remembering people of God, the descent out of heaven of the holy Jerusalem lit up by the Lamb in whose light walk all the nations, each bringing their own particular gift of glory to it (Rev 21–22). It is no accident that Dostoevsky places this vision of the eschatological banquet in the New Jerusalem at the culminating points of existential "rebirth" in *The Brothers Karamazov*. Alyosha is directed by his dead elder to the focus of true worship, "our Sun," with the words "We are rejoicing . . . we are drinking new wine, the wine of a new and great joy. See how many guests there are? Here are the bridegroom and the bride."(361).[32] Mitya, having undergone the three spiritual torments by which he is brought to penitent confession (though not of the kind sought by his prosecutors), has a dream of "the wee one," an image in response to earthly suffering that enables him to love existence "as it is" and initiates a humble, loving (rather than retributive, accusatory) quest for understanding its meaning. It is an image related to John's vision in Revelation 21:3–4, in which suffering, tears, pain, and death are overcome as God comes to dwell with human beings. Mitya is increasingly sustained by the "new man" that has arisen in his soul,[33] who, in contrast to the tempting image of the "new man" of technological liberal progress, is capable of the suffering, reconciling love

---

32. In response to Alyosha's fear to look upon the glory of "our Sun" (a reference to Rev 1:16; 21:23–26) the elder says, "Do not be afraid of him. Awful is his greatness before us, terrible is his loftiness, yet he is boundlessly merciful, he became like us out of love, and he is rejoicing with us, transforming water into wine, that the joy of the guests may not end. He is waiting for new guests, he is ceaselessly calling new guests, now and unto ages of ages" (361–62).

33. Note also the role that Grushenka and her purified "worldly love" plays in the conversion of Mitya, who confesses: "Before it was just her infernal curves that fretted me, but now I've taken her whole soul into my soul, and through her I've become a man!" (594).

of God's dwelling because nurtured by God's gift of joy, "without which it's not possible for man to live" (592).

This is the hymn-singing "underground man" born anew, who knows the transcendent sun of the New Jerusalem—even "if I don't see the sun, still I know it *is*. And the whole of life is there—in knowing that the sun is" (592).[34] So also the very end of the novel, where Alyosha speaks to the boys at the "big stone" on the occasion of Ilyusha's funeral, about the truth of existence as revealed by the resurrected slain Lamb, that joins in a life-giving union what seems so opposed: unjust suffering and the joy of life, pain and yet praise of creation as it is. As the precocious Kolya puts it: "It's all so strange, Karamazov, such grief, and then pancakes [*bliny*] all of a sudden—how unnatural it all is in our religion!" (773).

Such penitential asceticism, and then *Tweeback* all of a sudden! That the tears of penitence and overwhelming joy mingle together to water the soil of our hearts and enable the seeds of our higher homeland to grow is something I learned as a child in a Mennonite household and church community. Here we are brought to the center of existential Anabaptist theology, in a conjunction of body and soul, penitence and joy, death and resurrection movingly depicted also in a well-known passage by Menno:

> Just as natural bread is made of many grains, pulverized by the mill, kneaded with water, and baked by the heat of the fire, so is the church of Christ made up of true believers, broken in their hearts with the mill of the divine Word, baptized with the water of the Holy Ghost, and with the fire of pure, unfeigned love made into one body.[35]

It is not accidental, I believe, that the Johannine and Pauline images of death and resurrection are agricultural—as "seed"—and not mechanical or abstract artistic or intellectual theories. The meaning of our embodied existence is of a piece with the order created by God, the dynamism of which is the continual self-giving gift of God's creative Spirit (not dead mechanism, not human contrivance) that enlivens the world through love. As participants in that cosmic drama we need not fear to be who we are, so long as we give ourselves to cultivating the divine seed given us in Christ that joins our particular partiality to the suffering, celebratory completion of the "all in all."

---

34. This redemptive knowledge of the loving source of human solidarity enables Mitya, finally, to speak of his hated sibling rival as "brother Ivan"; his last words in the conversation with Alyosha are "love Ivan" (597). By contrast, Ivan's parting words to Alyosha concerning his brother Dmitri are "I hate the monster! I don't want to save the monster, let him rot at hard labor! He's singing a hymn!" (654) These words occur at the end of his own "three torments" in the form of visits to the illegitimate brother Smerdyakov, but Ivan's journey represents a contrasting movement of "truth" regarding the parricide to Mitya's path. Mitya is publicly accused of a murder he did not commit, and yet recognizes his murderous heart and takes free responsibility for it in a full, life-changing confession. Ivan, who has reserved complete freedom for hatred in his "wishes," is confronted by Smerdyakov with his actual complicity in the parricide and cannot accept responsibility. At the end of his tormenting visits he too has a dream, not of a "wee one" or an eschatological wedding feast, but a "nightmare" of "the devil," who reminds him of yet another of his poetic creations, "The Geological Cataclysm," which elaborates the existential consequences of modern scientific cosmology—the appearance of a "new man" in whom the idea of God has been destroyed, making possible the emergence of a titanic, nature-conquering "man god." For more extensive discussion of the apocalyptic theopolitical vision of *The Brothers Karamazov*, see Kroeker and Ward, *Remembering the End*.

35. Menno Simons, "Foundation of Christian Doctrine," 145.

6

Eschatology and Ethics

Luther and the Radical Reformers

IT HAS BEEN A common prejudice in late modernity to assume that Christian doctrines of eschatology, resurrection, and immortality are world-denying and escapist, rooted in the desire for otherworldly consolation or, even worse, for divine vengeance upon non-Christian enemies. That is, Christian eschatology, especially in its apocalyptic forms, is questionable not only on scientific grounds but on moral and indeed theological grounds. Two prominent nineteenth-century philosophers bear powerful and influential witness to this view—Friedrich Nietzsche and Ludwig Feuerbach. In *On the Genealogy of Morals*, Nietzsche identified beliefs in God and immortality as the creations of human beings who could not tolerate a world in which there is suffering, who out of weakness invented a fictitious invisible reality corresponding to their desires for peace, comfort, and the elimination of suffering (attributed to "evil" causes).[1] The "impertinent" doctrine of personal immortality, says Nietzsche in *The Antichrist*,[2] is the most egregious form of egoistic wish fulfillment in Christianity. It is symptomatic of the anti-natural "hatred of reality" in a theology that lacks contact with reality and caters to personal vanity and *ressentiment* at the same time.

Ludwig Feuerbach, though more subtle than Nietzsche in his treatment of theology, was no less critical of religious doctrines that are believed uncritically in order to serve the human need for consolation. Feuerbach's primary example of doctrine in the service of egocentric anthropology is the belief in immortality held by Christians, which he believes is rooted "in the undoubting certainty that their personal, self-flattering wishes will be fulfilled."[3] Belief in personal immortality thus represents an infinite cos-

---

1. See Nietzsche, *On the Genealogy of Morals*, 1.14–16. In 1.16 he calls the Apocalypse of John (the book of Revelation) "the most wanton of all literary outbursts that vengeance has on its conscience," a book motivated by extreme *ressentiment* against the powerful Roman Empire.

2. Nietzsche, *Antichrist*, secs. 41 and 43.

3. Feuerbach, *Essence of Christianity*, 136.

mic egoism even though it pretends to bow down before God in humble self-surrender. It is therefore not only a religious but a moral delusion, and it alienates human beings from nature. The more Christians invest in the other world, the less value is given to life in this world, and Feuerbach suggests that doctrines of immortality and heavenly bliss are closely connected to the ascetic, monastic disparagement of sex.[4] We do not have the space to consider in detail the very similar judgments concerning Christian eschatology offered by Nietzsche and Feuerbach. I suggest, however, that these interpretations have come to represent the "common sense" of late modern, educated Westerners, for whom such beliefs have become not only an intellectual but a moral embarrassment. Interestingly, the belief in immortality that was traditionally so closely allied with moral judgment (not only for Christians and Jews but also in the Platonic tradition of moral theory) has now become suspect precisely on moral grounds.[5]

In this essay I want to examine Luther's understanding of the connections between ethics and eschatology in relation to certain approaches identified with the "radical Reformation," with a view to testing the claims of Nietzsche and Feuerbach. Are these forms of Christian eschatology world-denying and escapist, a form of vengeance upon enemies, an egoistic wish fulfillment rooted in an alienated and self-enclosed disparagement of bodily nature? Perhaps the best way to get at Luther's understanding of eschatology and ethics is to pay attention to his "apocalyptic" religious vision. Apocalyptic is, of course, a term with many meanings. It comes from the Greek word that means "revelation" or "unveiling" or "disclosure," and forms part of the title of the famous final book of the New Testament, the Apocalypse of John—a text often associated with the aforementioned prejudices about Christian eschatology and one that Luther himself found ambiguous. In his first preface to the book of Revelation in his *Deutsche Bibel* of 1522, he said frankly, "Meyn geyst kan sich ynn das buch nicht schicken" (or, in current informal speech, "My spirit cannot get into this book").[6] And yet that same edition of Luther's Bible carried the notorious woodcuts by Lucas Cranach depicting the papacy as the Antichrist and the Whore of Babylon in John's Apocalypse.[7] Of course, Luther's identification of the Roman papacy with the Antichrist was neither unique nor innova-

---

4. Feuerbach's opening words in his chapter on "The Christian Heaven, or Personal Immortality," are: "The unwedded and ascetic life is the direct way to the heavenly, immortal life, for heaven is nothing else than life liberated from the conditions of the species, supernatural, sexless, absolutely subjective life. The belief in personal immortality has at its foundation the belief that difference of sex is only an external adjunct of individuality, that in himself the individual is a sexless, independently complete, absolute being." *Essence of Christianity*, 170.

5. This is true not only for non-Christians; it is also increasingly common in Christian theology. James Gustafson, for example, has recently developed a theological ethics "from a theocentric perspective" in which God, not human being, is the measure of all things. For Gustafson this theocentrism warrants a strong theological and moral critique of belief in immortality or eternal life, precisely because he concurs with thinkers such as Nietzsche and Feuerbach that such doctrines are rooted in the inordinate human desire for self-fulfillment and egoistic consolation. Theocentric Christian theology is therefore prepared to jettison traditional eschatology not only on scientific grounds but also on theological and moral grounds. See Gustafson, *Ethics*, vol. 1, *Theology and Ethics*.

6. Quoted in Hofmann, *Luther und die Johannes-Apokalypse*, 253. See the discussion by Barnes, *Prophecy and Gnosis*, 36–53.

7. For a discussion of these illustrations, see Martin, *Martin Luther und die Bilder zur Apokalypse*.

tive. As Bernard McGinn shows, Luther was here following an earlier medieval tradition of Antichrist interpretation that identified the Antichrist's evil as hypocrisy and corruption in the church, and especially the papacy.[8] That is to say, despite Luther's initial reservations about the genre of Christian apocalyptic (a judgment he revised in his 1530 preface to the book of Revelation), and despite his rejection of the chiliastic prophets, such as Thomas Müntzer (as we shall see), Luther's vision of reality was most certainly apocalyptic in outlook. This is nicely captured in Heiko Oberman's title to his fine study: *Luther: Man between God and the Devil* (1989).

How is it that the form of rule depicted in John's Apocalypse as the evil parody of Christ's authority in the kingdom of God, the Antichrist, is identified in Luther's writings with the Roman papacy? We get our first clues in that famous early polemical address, "To the Christian Nobility of the German Nation" (1520). Here Luther calls for the reform of the "Christian estate" by tearing down each of three walls of the Romanists, the first of which is the unwarranted papal arrogation of secular power, a power that is also used to buttress unwarranted religious authority (the second wall is that the pope alone can properly interpret Scripture, the third that the pope alone can summon and sanction a council). Thus have the Romanists effectively hedged the church (and Christendom) against the reforming work of the Holy Spirit. This is the devil's work, says Luther—a religious authority that appeals to the sword and the dazzling corruptions of economic splendor in order to establish and defend a false gospel. Like the Antichrist in the Revelation of John, this is a form of authority that claims spiritual power but is really only interested in the temporal control of wealth and empire through violence and external display:

> The pope is not a vicar of Christ in heaven, but only of Christ as he walked the earth. Christ in heaven, in the form of a ruler, needs no vicar, but sits on his throne and sees everything, does everything, knows everything, and has all power. But Christ needs a vicar in the form of a servant, the form in which he went about on earth, working, preaching, suffering, and dying. Now the Romanists turn all that upside down. They take the heavenly and kingly form from Christ and give it to the pope, and leave the form of the servant to perish completely. He might almost be the Counter-Christ, whom the Scriptures call Antichrist, for all his nature, work, and pretensions run counter to Christ and only blot out Christ's nature and destroy his work.[9]

Such a confusion of spiritual and temporal authority, the kingdom of God and mere earthly kingdoms, the form of God and the form of the servant, are precisely characteristic of the perverse logic of the Antichrist, in Luther's view. As he had put it earlier in the "Theses for the Heidelberg Disputation" of 1518, the "theology of glory" calls the bad good and the good bad (Thesis 21), for it lacks insight into the invisible things of God. Only a "theology of the cross" founded, one might say, upon the divine authority of the slain Lamb will be able to see and thus bear witness to the truth about God in the world. It will see God's presence in the world "by beholding the sufferings and the cross" (Thesis 20), not in ostentatious displays of human works (Thesis 22). Therefore, while a

---

8. See McGinn, *Antichrist*, chaps. 7 and 8.
9. Luther, "To the Christian Nobility," 165.

puffed-up theology of glory presumptuously abuses the highest gifts of God to the world in order to aggrandize itself, a humble theology of the cross bears witness to the invisible God through a penitent faith active in the worldly form of a servant.[10]

Ethics thus entails an understanding of this eschatological vision, this apocalyptic unveiling of the true nature of worldly and spiritual reality *coram Deo*. Luther's ethics is essentially rooted in a penitential vision, even as the book of Revelation is written as a letter to the churches calling them to awaken, to remember what they have received from God, and to repent. This is truly a matter of life and death—not in some other world, a heavenly future of the sort depicted by Feuerbach as a "mausoleum" in which the Christian enshrines his own beloved soul.[11] It is a life-and-death struggle lived out in the common social and bodily world in which Christians and non-Christians dwell. The struggle between God and the devil, Christ and the Antichrist, is not for Luther some fictitious consoling abstraction. Quite the contrary, it is the battle of the incarnate Lord to restore a corrupted, death-destined creation to the life-giving rule of the kingdom of God. In order to participate discerningly in this apocalyptic conflict—that is, in a manner that bears faithful witness to God's hidden but very real rule—it is necessary to sort out the confusion between the kingdoms represented in the logic of the Antichrist, largely with reference to Augustine's model of the two cities (itself taken from the book of Revelation[12]).

Like Augustine, Luther divides human beings ("all the children of Adam"[13]) into two kingdoms: the kingdom of God (Augustine's *civitas Dei*), and the kingdom of the world (Augustine's *civitas terrena*). Christ's reign pertains to the first kingdom and is guided by the Word and the inner testimony of the Holy Spirit, not the secular sword or law. Were all the world composed of "true Christians, that is, true believers," Luther says, "no prince, king, lord, sword, or law would be needed." However, the "unrighteous" need the law and external rule to instruct, constrain, and compel them to do what is good. The worldly kingdom therefore has need of an established political order backed by the power of the sword. As does Augustine, Luther believes this kingdom of the world will pass away, to be replaced in the end by the kingdom of God. In the meantime, however, the external order of secular law and sword are required to avert chaos.

There should, therefore, be a clear distinction between the external peace and order of worldly politics and the perfect peace of Christ's spiritual rule, taught and represented by the church. However, and here too Luther resembles Augustine, this does not mean that Luther's theory of secular politics (if one may indeed call it a "theory"[14]) is "mod-

---

10. See Luther's appeal to Philippians 2:1–4 in "Freedom of a Christian," 74–75. Luther interprets the words of Paul concerning the "form of God" and "form of a servant" and "human form" not as referring to Christ's human and divine natures, but as a statement of the form God takes in the world, the exercise of divine power as service. For Luther this has implications for ethics.

11. Feuerbach, *Essence of Christianity*, 179.

12. For a good discussion of the roots of Augustine's eschatological "two cities" doctrine in Tyconius's *Commentary on the Apocalypse*, see Fredriksen, "Tyconius and Augustine on the Apocalypse."

13. Luther, "Secular Authority," 368.

14. David Steinmetz makes the following helpful observation: "A historian reading Luther's discussion of the two kingdoms for the first time might be tempted to remark that it all sounds more like pastoral advice than like political philosophy. And, of course, pastoral advice is exactly what it is. By linking the

ern." Luther certainly opposed any attempt by the church to seek political domination or temporal power, as in the case of the papal Antichrist. And yet the following comment by Heiko Oberman is potentially misleading: "For us Luther is 'modern' insofar as he promoted an ecumenical pluralism and warned against resolving spiritual questions by government pressure, let alone by armed force."[15] Luther did not consider the ordering of the earthly kingdom to imply a pluralistic, religiously neutral civil society. After all, it is God, says Luther, who has ordained two governments (*Regimente*) that order life in the world—the church, which presides over the spiritual, inner life of Christians (the order of redemption), and the secular political order, which presides over the material, outer realm (the orders of creation). The kingdom of Christ, therefore, which has no place for sword and law, rules in the hearts of true Christians. No human political government can do so, for it cannot see into the human heart; it sees only the outer and establishes a social order to regulate external matters of justice. Christians in their personal relations will follow the example of Christ in the nonresistant practice of loving service, adhering literally to the words of the Sermon on the Mount in turning the other cheek and not resisting evil (Matt 5:39). Luther avers that "a Christian should be so disposed that he will suffer every evil and injustice, not avenge himself nor bring suit in court, and in nothing make use of secular power and law for himself. For others, however, he may and should seek vengeance, justice, protection and help."[16] That is, in the sphere of political society that governs the external relations of people and states to one another, it is necessary to apply a different standard. This standard, however, is also related to the rule of God—it is not religiously neutral. When a governing authority declares a war, for example, certain criteria for a just war must be met. If they are, then "it is a Christian act and an act of love confidently to kill, rob, and pillage the enemy, and to do everything that can injure him until one has conquered him according to the methods of war."[17]

In combining Augustine's doctrine of the two kingdoms (*Reiche*) or cities with this added distinction between two governments (*Regimente*), some will say that Luther has not clarified Christian social ethics but further confused them. It is not my purpose here

---

two kingdoms tightly together, Luther is advising Christians on the nature and character of Christian existence. Only incidentally is he interested in advising statesmen on the discharge of their public office." Steinmetz, "Luther and the Two Kingdoms," 124.

15. Obermann, *Luther*, 49. Here it is relevant to point out a similar problem in the excellent study of Augustine's eschatological politics in Markus, *Saeculum*. Markus says, "Christian hope, just because it is eschatological, resists the investing of immediate projects, policies and even social ideals, with any absolute character.... Augustine's attack on the 'sacral' conception of the Empire liberated the Roman state, and by implication, all politics, from the direct hegemony of the sacred. Society became intrinsically 'secular' in the sense that it is not as such committed to any particular ultimate loyalty.... His 'secularisation' of the realm of politics implies a pluralistic, religiously neutral civil community" (173). For an excellent critique of Markus on this point, see O'Donovan, "Augustine's *City of God* XIX."

16. Luther, "Secular Authority," 379.

17. Ibid., 398. In his commentary "The Sermon on the Mount" (5:38-42), Luther elaborates the proper distinctions between the two kingdoms, secular and spiritual, kingdom of Christ and kingdom of the world. On a personal level, the Christian serves neighbor and enemy in a completely non-resistant love, but outwardly as "Christian-in-relation" in the secular sphere "it would be a mistake to teach: Turn the other cheek, and throw your cloak away with your coat.'"

to argue this point, for to do so properly would be a large undertaking.[18] Perhaps it is more accurate to say that for Luther there is no alleviation of the eschatological tension between the "already" of God's rule in the believer's heart and the "not yet" of Christ's rule in historical society. It is precisely when this tension is collapsed—either through the temporal political aspirations of the church (the Romanists) or through the attempt to set up an external order of spiritual perfection (the Anabaptists)—that Luther believes devilish confusion will arise, in both forms of government. Luther, furthermore, rejects the Augustinian division of morality into two classes of Christians—the religious (who adhere to the eschatological counsels of perfection found in the Sermon on the Mount and thus seek to escape the vocational tensions of worldly existence), and the lay (who take up the burdens of secular vocation but cannot be guided by Gospel ethics):

> For perfection and imperfection consist not in works and do not establish a distinct external order among Christians; but they exist in the heart, in faith and love, so that they who believe and love the most are the perfect ones, whether outwardly they be male or female, prince or peasant, monk or layman. For love and faith produce no sects or outward differences.[19]

There is no escape, therefore, from the tension of the struggle between God and the devil that rages both in the church and in society, and indeed in the conscience of every human being who of necessity lives under both governments. The difficult task of moral discernment cannot be evaded either through false double standards or the attempted escape from worldly responsibility. The eschatological vision of the Sermon on the Mount is equally binding upon all Christians, but Christians may not retreat from their worldly responsibilities and duties so as to follow Jesus's commands literally. Rather, there must be a frank recognition that human relationships differ and therefore the external duties (though not the inner dispositions) of love differ as well. To confuse these is to pervert the truth of the relations in which one stands. To treat one's children and family according to a literal application of the precepts of the Sermon on the Mount would bring murder and chaos no less than were one to attempt to run a state that way.

On this point, of course, Luther's more radically apocalyptic fellow reformers begged to differ. And, as Gerhard Ebeling points out, "Luther did not work out his real doctrine of the two kingdoms in direct confrontation with medieval Catholic social doctrine, but

---

18. For helpful discussions of Luther's teaching on the two kingdoms, I recommend Ebeling, *Luther*, chaps. 11 and 12; Althaus, *Ethics of Martin Luther*, chap 4; Thielicke, *Theological Ethics*, vol. 1, chap. 18; Pannenberg, *Ethics*, chap. 6. Thielicke helpfully identifies three related dangers in Luther's teaching on the two kingdoms: (1) The danger of the bifurcation of morality into personal (or private) versus official (or public) ethics—a dualism attributed to Luther by Troeltsch in *Social Teaching of the Christian Churches*, 506–11. This dualism can lead to an ethic of political quietism, precisely when sight is lost of the eschatological tension in Luther's vision; (2) The danger of secularization, in which religion is separated from public life, allowing the latter to become autonomous and overly dichotomizing the orders of creation (social and public) and redemption (individual and private); (3) The danger of harmonization, in which the New Testament language of two "aeons" and the eschatological dynamism of the coming kingdom of God is replaced by a static or timeless harmony of God's twofold rule in the temporal and spiritual orders. Clearly for Thielicke (and also for Ebeling and Pannenberg), there is a need to maintain the eschatological dynamism underlying Luther's view, which Luther himself did not always emphasize—perhaps in reaction to the apocalypticism of the radical reformers.

19. Luther, "Secular Authority," 368.

only when he was challenged by the radicalism of the enthusiastic sects"[20]—both pacifist and militant. If the Romanists failed to understand the difference between the eschatological kingdom of God (which appears on the earth in the form of a suffering servant) and temporal power, substituting the latter for the former, the apocalyptic radicals were too eager to realize the former in an external manner. Of course, the radicals, for their part, considered Luther's eschatological understanding of God's redemptive intention for the world expressed in the rule of Christ to be too detached from his conception for political life. Pannenberg puts this well when he suggests that for Luther, "political order does not belong to human destiny as such, to that which will find its fulfillment in the future Kingdom of God. Instead, that order is only an emergency measure which God has provided against sin, a divine interim that will disappear in the eschatological future, and of which the Christian in himself has now no need."[21]

To sort out the complexities of Luther's eschatological view of the two kingdoms in relation to the radical reformers is no less impossible here than to attempt to do so in relation to Augustine's two cities. I wish simply to point out some of the implications for ethics of these differing sixteenth-century forms of apocalyptic vision. The apocalyptic visions of the radical reformers—both nonviolent and violent forms—portrayed the rule of Christ and the kingdom of God in the world even now through the church in more overtly political terms. Some of the same tensions embedded in Luther's doctrine of two kingdoms reappear in remarkably different normative form in the writings of Thomas Müntzer, especially his "Sermon before the Princes" of (1524 just prior to the armed peasant revolt he helped organize) and of the Anabaptists, as expressed in the *Schleitheim Confession* of 1527.

Müntzer's "Sermon" was a revolutionary spiritualist rebuttal to Luther's understanding of the secular authority of princes, rejecting the sharp distinction between the outer realm ruled by law and sword, and the inner spiritual realm ruled by Christ and the Word. Luther applied a strict limiting principle on the authority of each—the Gospel of Christ rules only in the inner life and may not be imposed externally by force, and the secular ruler governs only in external, not spiritual, matters (though the Christian secular ruler's inner dispositions, of course, should be ordered no less than those of the priest or Christian housewife by Christ's form of the servant). Müntzer considered this division to be heretical, a public betrayal of "pure Christianity,"[22] which is founded not only upon the Word of God in Christ but upon the continuing revelation of the Inner Word of the Holy Spirit.[23] Müntzer says of the learned Lutheran divines, "Without any experience of the arrival of the Holy Spirit, the overcomer of the fear of God, they fail to separate (in their disdain for divine wisdom) the good from the bad which is camouflaged under the

---

20. Ebeling, *Luther*, 181.

21. Pannenberg, *Ethics*, 126. Pannenberg attributes this (in his view, too limited and negative) view of politics to the influence of Augustine upon Luther. While Luther's view offered a corrective against empire politics and the excesses of "fanatical enthusiasm," Pannenberg laments, "nowhere in Luther can we find any inspiration to transform political conditions by the powerful vision of the eschatological Lordship of God which already illumines the present world. This inspiration made its breakthrough elsewhere, in the so-called left wing of the seventeenth century" (130–31).

22. Müntzer, "Sermon," 50.

23. Ibid., 54, 56ff.

appearance of good."[24] Consequently Luther and his followers are themselves confused, calling the good bad and the bad good because of their lack of spiritual experience.[25]

Müntzer's sermon is "an exposition of the second chapter of Daniel,"[26] and Daniel is the apocalyptic exemplar of the prophetic experience of the Inner Word of the divine Spirit. The book of Daniel is a visionary depiction of the eschatological transformation of the world, and its meaning is revealed, claims Müntzer, to the elect of God such as himself—a meaning in the form of "a decisive, inevitable, imminent reformation [accompanied] by great anguish, and it must be carried out to completion."[27] The final kingdom in Daniel's vision is the present, the apostate Christendom of Romanists and Lutherans, and Müntzer appeals to the princes to take on the fight of God against the Antichrist. At this point the apocalyptic spiritualist's message takes a somewhat surprising outer turn. Though he appeals to the book of Revelation, he does not understand its sword to be the Word of Christ but a literal physical weapon. The inner spiritual order of pure Christianity must be externally established, according to Müntzer's interpretation:

> Now if you want to be true governors, you must begin government at the roots, and, as Christ commanded, drive his enemies from the elect. For you are the means to this end. Beloved, don't give us any old jokes about how the power of God should do it without your application of the sword. Otherwise it may rust away for you in its scabbard! . . . If you do away with the mask of the world, you will soon recognise it with a righteous judgment (John 7:24). Perform a righteous judgment at God's command! . . . For the godless person has no right to live when he is in the way of the pious.[28]

The only way to give visible expression to divine rule is to eliminate the evil opposition to it in the world (those who reduce politics to mere civil unity) and thus defeat the devil. Müntzer, despite his spiritualist hermeneutic, offers a highly literal interpretation of apocalyptic symbolism. His end was a literal enactment of Jesus's words, "Those who live by the sword will die by the sword." After the defeat of the Peasant Revolt of 1525, Müntzer was arrested and executed. He is not considered a martyr of the radical Reformation, but he did become a martyr for the communist movement of the past century.[29]

In stark contrast to this apocalyptic attempt to establish politically the inner rule of God via the sword of Christian princes was the Anabaptist attempt to establish the

---

24. Ibid., 56.

25. Müntzer states, "He [who has not the Spirit] does not know how to say anything deeply about God, even if he had eaten through a hundred Bibles!" (ibid., 58). Of course, Luther for his part said he wouldn't trust Müntzer even if he swallowed the Holy Ghost, feathers and all.

26. The full title of Müntzer's sermon is "Exposition of the Second Chapter of Daniel the Prophet Preached at the Castle of Allstedt before the Active and Amiable Dukes and Administrators of Saxony by Thomas Müntzer, Minister of the Word of God." The sermon was delivered in the presence of Duke John, brother of Frederick the Wise who was the protector of Luther, and in it he was calling for the princes to launch a militant political counter-reformation against Luther. For good accounts of Müntzer and his movement, see Gritsch, *Thomas Müntzer*; Friesen, *Thomas Muentzer*.

27. Müntzer, "Sermon," 62.

28. Ibid., 66.

29. I have in my possession a fünf-Mark bill of the Staatsbank of the now-defunct DDR (Deutsche Demokratische Republik), on which is displayed the face of Thomas Müntzer.

Reformation through the visible community of believers. The Anabaptists also broke with Luther and the "mainstream" reformers over the question of how to interpret in worldly ethics the eschatological conflict between the kingdom of God and the earthly kingdom of the devil. However, they clearly rejected Müntzer's advocacy of violence, accepting Luther's view that the kingdom of God cannot be externally established via the sword or by the authority of secular princes. Unlike Luther, however, they did not interpret the teachings and example of Christ in purely spiritual terms. The apocalyptic tension between the reign of Christ in the community of believers and the reign of human power via the sword (allied with the Antichrist) is a visible and sociopolitical struggle, not merely an invisible and spiritual one. The form of the suffering servant is addressed not only to the personal and dispositional aspects of Christian existence; it pertains equally to social and political life in the world. The *Schleitheim Confession* was drafted at a meeting of Anabaptist leaders in 1527 in order to establish a unifying statement on the Christian way of life, in the face of serious threats to the continued existence of the rather scattered and persecuted movement.

The cover letter of the confession emphasizes that the "obedient children of God" should stand united (*vereinigt*, a key word in the document), separated from a world characterized by the works of darkness by those who follow the devil, and instead follow Christ in the way of peace.[30] In contrast to Luther's two kingdoms doctrine, in which the "Christian-in-relation" lives in the secular realm according to the laws of external peace backed by the sword and the "Christian-qua-Christian" lives according to the self-denying rule of the Gospel, the Anabaptists viewed conversion as the transference of allegiance from the worldly kingdom of darkness and its sinful means to the kingdom of Christ. The baptism of repentance (article 1) entails a complete transformation of life through following Jesus as a literal example. In effect this requires the establishment of a new social and political order, the voluntary community of believers committed to the *Nachfolge Christi*. The language of union and separation therefore is explicitly tied to the sharp distinction between the two kingdoms: the kingdom of God ordered by the "perfection of Christ" and a literal following of Christ's teachings in the Sermon on the Mount (the "rule of Christ"), and the kingdom of the devil ordered by idolatry, abomination, and "the diabolical weapons of violence—such as sword, armor, and the like, and all of their use to protect friends or against enemies."[31] Union with Christ requires separation from the world (those not *vereinigt* with God in Christ) in a community that replaces the secular courts and the sword with the practice of binding and loosing (the ban) and nonviolent resistance to evil through spiritual weapons. Article 6 of the *Schleitheim Confession* most clearly displays the literal interpretation of the rule of Christ:

> VI. The sword is an ordering outside the perfection of Christ. . . . But within the perfection of Christ only the ban is used for the admonition and exclusion of the one who has sinned, without the death of the flesh, simply the warning and the command to sin no more. . . . Lastly . . . it does not befit a Christian to be a magistrate: the rule of the government is according to the flesh, that of the Christians according to the Spirit. Their houses and dwellings remain in this world,

---

30. *Schleitheim Confession*, 8–9.
31. Ibid., 13.

that of the Christians is in heaven. Their citizenship is in this world, that of the Christians is in heaven. The weapons of their battle and warfare are carnal and only against the flesh, but the weapons of the Christian are spiritual, against the fornication of the devil. . . . In sum: as Christ our Head is minded, so also must be minded the members of the body of Christ through Him, so that there be no division in the body, through which it would be destroyed. Since then Christ is as is written of Him, so must His members also be the same, so that His body may remain whole and unified for its own advancement and upbuilding.[32]

The teaching and example of Christ in these matters is the authority in all things—inner and outer, personal and political—and the community that follows Christ must do so in complete obedience.

Clearly, then, the Anabaptists would reject the apocalyptic politics of Müntzer no less than the two kingdoms ethic of Luther. Müntzer's spiritualized interpretation of Christ's teaching is a betrayal of its incarnate authority for Christian faith and life. In this sense Müntzer no less than Luther has spiritualized away the apocalyptic form of the servant embodied in Christ, replacing it in temporal matters with the third temptation of the devil, the domineering power of the sword. On the other hand (and here the Anabaptists would agree with Luther), Müntzer has literally misread the apocalyptic language of divine judgment and divine rule in a grossly externalized way as vengeance upon the enemies of "the elect." While the Anabaptists took literally the servant form of Christ, they interpreted the apocalyptic language of judgment, sword, and power in Daniel and Revelation as referring to divine, not human, action, and therefore to be interpreted spiritually, not externally.[33] The Lamb of Revelation who conquers the world remains the slain Lamb and rules by the sword of the Word dangling from the mouth, to which the church is called to bear witness—even as martyrdom—in the world.

The *Schleitheim Confession* was drafted largely by the pen of Michael Sattler, a former Benedictine who became an important Anabaptist leader. Immediately upon his return from the Schleitheim conference, Sattler was arrested, along with his wife and several other fellow Anabaptists, and interrogated and tortured. Various accounts of his subsequent "Trial and Martyrdom" were preserved by the Anabaptist community (the only South German martyrdom story taken into the Dutch Mennonite martyrologies and Hutterian *Chronicles*).[34] When given the opportunity to hire a lawyer to defend him, Sattler declined, saying this was not an issue for legal process but a matter of faith: "I have not been sent to defend the Word of God in court. We are sent to testify thereto."[35] Among the charges for which Sattler was executed were his rejection of infant baptism, refusing to swear to the government, refusing to wage war against the Turks, the "great-

---

32. Ibid., 15–16. Article 7 of the oath also takes literally Christ's prohibition of swearing in the Sermon on the Mount as expressing the "perfection of the law" (that is, the perfection of the new law of Christ). The oath is outside the perfect ordering of Christ, who rejected it as a usurpation of God's authority and implying a double standard of truth.

33. I am here making some rather large and perhaps unwarranted generalizations. The Anabaptist movement did not, of course, have only one interpretation of what I am here calling "apocalyptic." For a good discussion of the range, see Klaassen, *Living at the End of the Ages*.

34. See Yoder, *Legacy of Michael Sattler*, chap. 4.

35. Ibid., 74.

est enemy of our holy faith," and marrying a wife. These last two charges are of particular interest for this chapter. In his reply to the charge of pacifism, Sattler replied:

> If the Turk comes, he should not be resisted, for it stands written: thou shalt not kill. We should not defend ourselves against the Turks or our other persecutors, but with fervent prayer should implore God that He might be our defense and our resistance. As to me saying that if waging war were proper I would rather take the field against the so-called Christians who persecute, take captive, and kill true Christians, than against the Turks, this was for the following reason: the Turk is a genuine Turk and knows nothing of the Christian faith. He is a Turk according to the flesh. But you claim to be Christians, boast of Christ, and still persecute the faithful witnesses of Christ. Thus you are Turks according to the Spirit.[36]

With regard to his abandonment of the Benedictine order and marrying a wife, Sattler appealed to an eschatological text (1 Tim 4:3): "In the last days it shall come to pass that they will forbid marriage and food, which God has created that they might be enjoyed with thanksgiving."[37] Here, it should be noted, an eschatological appeal is made precisely contrary to Feuerbach's portrayal of ascetic monasticism and the "anti-natural" roots of Christian eschatology. On this last point the Anabaptists agreed with Luther's high view of marriage and of the good material gifts of creation (despite Luther's labeling of the Anabaptists as "the new monks"[38]). The commands of Christ concerning divorce, for example, are in no way a disparagement of natural sexuality. To the contrary, they imbue it with God-given spiritual significance.[39] As Oberman points out, Luther uses language of God and the devil so often in his discussion of marriage because of his apocalyptic vision of the crucial connection of the Word of God with corporeality. A purely otherworldly conception of spirituality thus plays into the hands of the disincarnate devil, who indeed hates God's life-giving power in all its healthy forms.[40]

It would seem clear, upon examination, that some of the prejudicial assumptions concerning Christian eschatology in the modern world do not apply to the views of Luther and the radical Reformation. There is nothing ethereal, egoistic, or escapist in their use of apocalyptic language to engage in moral discernment and action in the social and political context of their time. Yet we have also seen that questions of interpretation and

36. Ibid., 72–73.

37. Ibid.

38. See, for example, Luther, "Sermon on the Mount," 5, 14–15.

39. As Luther's interesting treatise on "The Estate of Marriage" indicates, this goes not only for the experience of sexual desire (which could be corrupted into an egoistic lust, at the root of so much fornication, also among the so-called religious) but precisely in its creative, shared, and faithful expression in marriage and family. This extends to such humble tasks as rocking babies and changing their dirty diapers. See "Estate of Marriage," 17–49. In case there is any doubt here about "roles," Luther adds: "Now you tell me, when a father goes ahead and washes diapers or performs some other mean task for his child, and someone ridicules him as an effeminate fool—though that father is acting in the spirit just described and in Christian faith—my dear fellow you tell me, which of the two is most keenly ridiculing the other? God, with all his angels and creatures, is smiling. . . . Those who sneer at him and see only the task but not the faith are ridiculing God with all his creatures, as the biggest fool on earth. Indeed, they are only ridiculing themselves; with all their cleverness they are nothing but devil's fools" (40–41).

40. See Oberman, *Luther*, chap. 10.

moral discernment are not straightforward. Unlike Nietzsche and Feuerbach, the Reformers we have considered did not view the eschatological symbols themselves as mere human inventions but as the revelation of God's active presence in the world—action in which Christians are invited to participate in the process of ethical discernment. Yet this does not in itself settle the question of how exactly the spiritual and material, church and world, the divine (and the demonic) and the human are related. The use that is made of apocalyptic language can take many different theological, ethical, and political forms. Furthermore, there is no position that can escape the difficult eschatological tensions that Luther recognized in the ethical demands of Christian existence. To label one as more or less worldly or sectarian or faithful, however, does not get us very far without specifying more clearly the criteria by which one is making such judgments. If this essay has contributed any insight into how these fascinating examples of Christian ethics have done so in relation to apocalyptic eschatology, then its modest purpose is served.

7

Why O'Donovan's Christendom Is Not Constantinian and Yoder's Voluntariety Is Not Hobbesian
A Debate in Theological Politics Redefined

Two of the most provocative recent proposals for Christian ethics and politics are those developed by John Howard Yoder and Oliver O'Donovan. There are many reasons to bring their proposals into dialogue and critical engagement with one another (and not only because it promises an entertaining cockfight between an "arch-Anglican" and a "morose Mennonite"[1]). Both may be called "narrative theologians," which means they do not believe there is some neutral philosophical ground or trans-historical rational foundation by which to validate public moral claims. Both Yoder and O'Donovan are therefore radical critics of liberal modernity and its moral and political assumptions. Most importantly, neither of them accepts the modern liberal separation of religion from politics, nor the view that there can be some universal, non-particular moral discourse to mediate between these two particular, historically contingent realms.

However, neither Yoder nor O'Donovan accepts the postmodern skepticism about the existence of truth, goodness, justice, and beauty across cultures and historical epochs. Precisely within our particularity we continue to seek better ways to understand, communicate, and live within the divinely created structures of reality. The way to do that is not to find some neutral (and therefore bland) formal language. It is rather to engage in thick description of the particular symbols, narratives, and community identities that shape our moral judgments and responses to political questions. And of course religion

---

1. In keeping here with O'Donovan's charge that the problem with Karl Barth is that he is "too sober" with regard to power politics and is not filled with enough evangelical faith and hope when it comes to matters such as war, see O'Donovan, "Karl Barth and Ramsey's 'Uses of Power,'" 14. This charge would apply much more so to Yoder, who remains critical of Barth on these points as not being "sober" enough! See Yoder, *Karl Barth and the Problem of War*. No doubt Yoder, for his part, would have considered O'Donovan far too sanguine about the abilities of "clear-sighted" individuals to see the temptations of power politics in a Christendom (or any other) setting—see O'Donovan's quick dismissal of Hauerwas's critique of Christendom on this point in *Desire of the Nations*, 216.

will be centrally important to such a task. What people worship as of ultimate meaning and importance will surely affect not only their political judgments on particular issues but also what political life in general is all about. Thus both Yoder and O'Donovan begin their constructive proposals from within the Christian church—the social community that lives out of a vision of life shaped by the biblical narrative and the liturgical forms of worship. Both seek thereby to redescribe the political meaning of the Christian narrative vision for the late modern West and to show how liberalism represents a false copy of the Christian vision. As might be expected, then, both carry out their proposals with extensive reference to biblical texts, to the ordering liturgical practices of the church, and to post-biblical historical developments concerning the church and political order. My comparative analysis will attend to their interpretations of these three shared points of reference.

Despite their commonalities, there are fundamental disagreements between O'Donovan's retrieval of Christendom political theology and Yoder's elaboration of the church as a voluntary political community of nonviolent believers. Unfortunately, the precise character of their disagreements tends to be obscured by caricatured descriptions of the other on both sides. Yoder, though he does not cite O'Donovan explicitly, tends to reduce all Christendom political theologies to a rather crude typological depiction of Constantinianism, the fall of the church from its calling as servant into the libidinous desire for historical mastery and political domination. Such a reduction cannot do justice to O'Donovan's position. For his part, O'Donovan is content to dismiss Yoder's emphasis on a "free" church and its voluntariety as a form of "neoliberalism" in which freedom is purchased at the expense of belief, a loss of confidence in truth claims that views all social doctrines as inherently coercive—thereby likening Yoder's position (at best) to a kind of Hobbesian political voluntarism. In this chapter I will try to show how and why each of these erroneous caricatures sabotages the possibility for constructive dialogue and debate on the more interesting disagreement between Yoder and O'Donovan, namely, their distinctive interpretations of biblical eschatology and models of political responsibility.

To frame the comparison I wish to develop, I have found it helpful to engage the political philosophy of a contemporary critic of modernity, Eric Voegelin.[2] The "genealogy" of modern political thought and ethics elaborated by the critics of modernity is an enterprise with which both O'Donovan and Yoder are in sympathy, compatible in their view with the task of Christian moral discernment.[3] Voegelin argues that the spe-

2. Neither Yoder nor O'Donovan makes reference to the writings of Voegelin, and this is especially surprising in the case of O'Donovan, since he makes considerable reference to the "modernity critics" (including such thinkers as Leo Strauss, George Grant, Jacques Ellul, and Hannah Arendt). See O'Donovan, *Desire of the Nations*, 227f.; 271f. This is surprising because Voegelin, of all these political thinkers, is most attentive to theological symbols and traditions. See his multivolume *Order and History*, especially vol. 1, *Israel and Revelation*, and vol. 4, *Ecumenic Age*; also Voegelin, *New Science of Politics*.

3. O'Donovan states: "The disciplines we need are those that good modernity-critics display: to see the marks of our time as the products of our past; to notice the danger civilization poses to itself, not only the danger of barbarian reaction; to attend especially not only to those features which strike our contemporaries as controversial, but to those which would have astonished an onlooker from the past but which seem to us too obvious to question." *Desire of the Nations*, 273. A good example of Yoder's theological modernity-criticism in action is his "Ethics and Eschatology." Elsewhere I have tried to show

cifically modern problems of political representation are connected with what he calls a "re-divinization" of society according to the apocalyptic symbolism of Christianity, especially as mediated in the chiliastic historicism of Joachim of Fiore, a twelfth-century apocalyptic mystic.[4] Joachite apocalyptic speculation represents the metastatic "immanentization of the eschaton" that lies at the heart of modern liberal and technological idolatries—the secularization of the Kingdom of God in an entirely this-worldly and humanly accomplished fulfillment. We have here, argues Voegelin, a reversal of Augustine's sensible theoretical reinterpretation of Christian apocalyptic symbolism in terms of the two cities, one temporal and one eternal, each represented in distinctive social forms, the state and the church. When the tension of this double representation of the human condition (as both temporal, an order that is "passing away," and eternal, the order of ultimate judgment) is lost in immanentist eschatologies such as followed from Joachim's theology of history, social and political order is violently disrupted—in both its religious and its secularist forms. It led, in the context of early modern Europe, to various religiously motivated disruptions of public civil order.

It was in this context that Thomas Hobbes articulated the modern problem of political order in his new theory of representation. Voegelin states the Hobbesian solution with admirable brevity:

> On the one hand, there is a political society that wants to maintain its established order in historical existence; on the other hand, there are private individuals within the society who want to change the public order, if necessary by force, in the name of a new truth. Hobbes solved the conflict by deciding that there was no public truth except the law of peace and concord in a society; any opinion or doctrine conducive to discord was thereby proved untrue.[5]

Fundamental to Hobbes's conditions of political peace was his use of Christianity as a civil theology that, ironically, eviscerated the human soul or spirit of any meaningful content beyond the passions[6]—there is for Hobbes no *summum bonum* that orders the life of the spirit. Such ideas are the inventions of power-hungry private individuals who seek to rule others (indeed, it was precisely the passional lust for power of the religious revolutionaries in Hobbes's own time that, he believed, was corrupting the public order and its peace). The solution for Hobbes—by which to construct a new form of political representation that gathered isolated individuals into a commonwealth whose corporate will (and therefore authorized power) is represented by the sovereign—was to appeal to

---

that Yoder's approach also has parallels with Nietzschean postmodern modernity criticism. See chapter 8, below; also published separately as Kroeker, "War of the Lamb."

4. See Voegelin, *New Science of Politics*, chap. 4. Voegelin writes, "Joachim broke with the Augustinian conception of a Christian society when he applied the symbol of the Trinity to the course of history.... In his trinitarian eschatology Joachim created the aggregate of symbols which govern the self-interpretation of modern political society to this day" (111). These symbols include the three ages of history (culminating in the Age of the Spirit), the prophetic political leader of the "new man" in the "new age," and the brotherhood of autonomous persons all equally inspired and gifted in a spiritually perfect society. For another fascinating modernity critic's account of Joachim's theology of history and its modern historicist forms, see Lowith, *Meaning in History*, chap. 8.

5. Voegelin, *New Science of Politics*, 153.

6. See Hobbes, *Leviathan*, 34.

a passion stronger than these desires for power, namely, fear of death. Again, to quote Voegelin:

> The style of the construction is magnificent. If human nature is assumed to be nothing but passionate existence, devoid of ordering resources of the soul, the horror of annihilation will, indeed, be the overriding passion that compels submission to order. If pride cannot bow to Dike, or be redeemed through grace, it must be broken by the Leviathan who "is king of all the children of pride." . . . The "King of the Proud" must break the *amor sui* that cannot be relieved by the *amor Dei*.[7]

In Hobbes's political theology, then, the problems of eschatological activism and apocalyptic violence are resolved by constructing a politics that bans from public speech and civil representation all references to "ghostly authority" and an invisible spiritual kingdom beyond the corporeal world of external motion—"as it were a kingdom of fairies, in the dark."[8] Politics, in contrast to Augustine's formulation, will work with only one volitional center—the *amor sui*. This understanding of Hobbesian psychology should be kept in mind when we consider O'Donovan's reading of Yoder's language of voluntariety, which I suggest is rooted in a quite different psychology and cosmology.

For now I simply want to observe that neither O'Donovan nor Yoder can accept the non-eschatological political theology of Hobbes. Indeed both of them appeal saliently to the apocalyptic language of the biblical texts in developing their theological visions of politics as rooted in the language of two kingdoms. Neither of them, however, historicizes this language in the manner of a Joachim of Fiore, or literally identifies apocalyptic symbols with specific political regimes or movements. Yet neither of them will be content with Voegelin simply to interpret apocalyptic symbols in terms of the inner life of the soul or a mode of consciousness, and not include also a social and political reality.[9] The "human carrier" of this eschatological vision of reality is the church, and its mission has very definite political consequences in history—although it is precisely at this point that we will encounter their major disagreement: over the status of the story of Christendom and the political responsibility of the church in a still-unredeemed world.

Yoder

What is often overlooked by those who conveniently caricature Yoder's work as "sectarian," in order to dismiss it as politically irrelevant, is that although Yoder emphasizes the

---

7. Voegelin, *New Science of Politics*, 184.

8. Hobbes, *Leviathan*, 29.15.

9. See, for example, Voegelin's chapter on "The Pauline Vision of the Resurrected," which criticizes Paul's apocalyptic assumption that Christ's resurrection has already begun the process of transfiguring reality itself under divine rule—Paul takes the myth too literally. States Voegelin: "Transfiguring incarnation, in particular, does not begin with Christ, as Paul assumed, but becomes conscious through Christ and Paul's vision as the eschatological *telos* of the transfiguring process that goes on in history before and after Christ and constitutes its meaning" (*Order of History*, vol. 4, *Ecumenic Age*, 270). Of course, for both Yoder and O'Donovan, the carrier of this vision is not a nation or a historical epoch or civilization—it is the church, an ecumenical *ekklesia*.

particularity of the church's identity, he consistently ties this to a cosmic vision of God's sovereign rule in creation. The controversial claim that founds Christianity is that this divine cosmic rule made its definitive appearance in the first century CE in the form of a humble servant with a very short career during which he rejected virtually every available political option, only to be killed nevertheless as a political figure. For Yoder this means that the form of God's rule is here publicly revealed in the world for all to see, and this rule is neither coercive nor externally triumphal—it is visibly characterized by the story of the cross. It is as the slain Lamb that Christ is worshipped as king also by the church in the heavenly court described so vividly in the Apocalypse of John, and this symbolism is laden with sociopolitical meaning and consequence. Indeed, says Yoder, this is the "good news" that constitutes the witness and mission of the Christian church, but it is a message that cannot be communicated or lived without belief in both its particular historical and its cosmic, indeed apocalyptic, claims.[10]

The Jeremian Shift

I do not have the space here to represent the richness of Yoder's exegetical interpretations of biblical texts in fleshing out this political vision. I will have to be selective and choose only a few representative texts, and I have chosen texts that are also important for O'Donovan in order to compare these two thinkers. Given his emphasis on historical particularity, it is not surprising that Yoder closely relates the meaning of Jesus's life and his "Messianic ethic" (as he calls it) to his Jewish background and the biblical history of the people of Israel. Those familiar with *The Politics of Jesus* will recall Yoder's extensive treatment of Jesus's proclamation of the rule of God in relation to the Jubilee year and the Old Testament tradition of holy war. In his later work Yoder makes more extensive reference to the prophetic tradition, and especially to what he calls the "Jeremian shift,"[11] to show that the political pattern taught and practiced by Jesus was a renewal and extension of "Hebrew hope" expressed from Moses through the prophets as the constitution of a shalom community under the rule of God, a hope that by Jeremiah's time had been fatally betrayed by Israel's failed kingship experiment.[12] Yoder clearly advocates the "antiroyal" account of the Deuteronomic historian, which retells Israel's story from within the paradigm shift to diaspora ethics clearly expressed in the book of Jeremiah—most pithily in Jeremiah's letter to the exiles in Babylon where he says: "Seek the peace of the city where I have scattered you . . . for in its peace you will find your peace" (Jer 29:7).

In his final book, *For the Nations*, Yoder makes extensive reference to Stephan Zweig's *Jeremias*, a poetic retrieval of the diaspora paradigm of Jewish social life and identity, written during World War I. Like diaspora Jews, Christians are called to live out their identity in a condition of "cosmopolitan homelessness."[13] The Jeremian approach,

---

10. See Yoder, *For the Nations*, 23ff.; Yoder, "To Serve Our God" (this was Yoder's 1988 Presidential Address to the Society of Christian Ethics).

11. See, for example, Yoder, *For the Nations*, chaps. 2 and 3; and Yoder, *Royal Priesthood*, 133.

12. Yoder, *For the Nations*, 141–42.

13. Ibid., 51. States Yoder, "The dramatic poem *Jeremiah* affirmed the vision of *galuth* or diapora identity which accepted as normative God's negative judgment on the Davidic project, after the failures

which sees the scattering of the people and especially their exile to Babylon (the center of religious and political idolatry) as "mission," prefigures Christ's attitude to the Gentile world. The mission of the church is precisely to witness to the flaws in Babel-like unity, rooted in coercive, centralized, sacral authority, the idolatrous politics of empire that substitutes human for divine kingship and that tries to take charge of human history by imposing a univocal, totalizing regime through territorial and economic conquest. The rule of divine love and harmony represents a very different pattern of ecumenicity: a pattern of creative diversity, dialogue, a community that welcomes outsiders and that understands leadership as servanthood. In the Jeremian shift this is represented by cultural linguistic plurality (diaspora culture is polyglot and on the move, not univocal and sovereign) and the creation of a synagogue rather than a temple culture (the focus is now the interpretation of story in ever-new situations, not an altar in cultic support of a sacral regime); it is the building of God's city and God's rule "from below."

The significance of this Jeremian shift toward diaspora political ethics is also emphasized in the writings of Eric Voegelin and Oliver O'Donovan (and before them, of course, in the "two cities" political vision of Augustine—see *City of God* 19.26). In his first volume of *Order and History*, entitled *Israel and Revelation*, Voegelin argues that Jeremiah marks the high point of Israel's exodus from a politics of "cosmological empire" (sacral kingship) into the recognition that existence under God's rule can take different sociopolitical forms.[14] The people's existence is not to be identified with a particular regime or political entity, and its "compact collectivism" is replaced by an understanding that divine rule entails the "existential participation" of the human heart for its realization in the world. The Jeremian shift represents not only a movement away from pragmatic kingship as the model of how shalom community is built, but also a movement toward the prophetic-eschatological recognition of a new covenant of the heart, in which God's rule is universally or ecumenically established. Oliver O'Donovan is in agreement with these readings of Jeremiah's paradigmatic role for prophetic political theology. His interpretation concurs with Yoder and Voegelin on this point—not only Jeremiah's words but also his representative experience of suffering *between* God and the people signals an important turn in theological political understanding: "The prophet has, in effect, taken over the mediatorial role, a sign that the monarchy, which was to mediate Yhwh's rule to his people, has been set aside."[15] Henceforth, asserts O'Donovan, "an element of

---

of four centuries" (52). In "To Serve Our God," Yoder says, "The age of Jeremiah, and his message, precipitated the definition of diaspora as not merely a chastisement but also a calling. To 'seek the peace of that city where YHWH has sent you' meant for Jewry all the way from Jeremiah to Rosenzweig and Buber the acceptance of a non-sovereign, non-territorial self definition" (133).

14. Voegelin, *Order and History*, vol. 1, *Israel and Revelation*, chap. 13 (especially 482f.). For Voegelin's discussion of the difference between cosmological and ecumenical empires, see *Order and History*, vol. 4, *Ecumenic Age*, especially chap. 1. In this latter work Voegelin locates the shift not so much in Jeremiah as in the Deuteronomic historian: "The exodus from cosmological civilization and the entrance into freedom under God were historical events in the eminent sense whose memory had been preserved through liturgies and prayers. As they contained the meaning of Israel's existence, they could not be eliminated like the predynastic rulers of Egypt without destroying the people; once they were understood in the fullness of their meaning, they had to take spiritual precedence over any foundation of an empire, even an Israelite one" (98).

15. O'Donovan, *Desire of the Nations*, 77.

confessional voluntarism enters into Israel's sense of itself."[16] The emphases not only on diaspora and the mediating role of the suffering servant but also—surprisingly in view of O'Donovan's critique of Yoder on this point—on voluntarism are shared features of these political readings of the Jeremian shift.

The Diaspora Church and Prophetic Politics

We will return to O'Donovan's interpretation and its divergence from Yoder's below, but I want to make one further point here about Voegelin's analysis that marks a sharp divergence from Yoder on the question of political ethics and, in particular, on the church's role as social carrier of this theological vision of divine rule. "The representative thinkers of Israel and Hellas," writes Voegelin, "were well aware that the pragmatic order of history did not go the way of their spiritual order."[17] This represents a challenge for political theory and ethics; namely, how are visions of transcendent spiritual order to be mediated politically or pragmatically within particular societies? How is the temporal related to the eternal? For Voegelin the great temptation and heresy is the attempt to identify the pragmatic structure of sociopolitical existence with the spiritual ecumenicity and "supraethnic" consciousness of spiritual order under God. It is the attempt to realize the eschaton within historical society.[18] The "great issue of the Ecumenic Age," says Voegelin, is "the relation between the concupiscential and the spiritual exodus"[19]—that is, the relation between the concupiscent attempt to establish an ecumenical empire by conquering territory through the exercise of pragmatic power, and the recognition of a spiritual ecumenicity understood as personal response to the divine ordering of the soul (the latter of which represents a breakthrough in consciousness, not a conventional social field). Only the spiritual exodus can give one insight into the relations between types of soul and types of society in historical experience. When human beings seek to realize the order of spiritual universality via pragmatic politics, one has by definition a concupiscential exodus or empire—symbolized in the book of Revelation as the Antichrist. It is not possible for human beings to transfigure the worldly structures of political existence in the light of a realizable transcendent "end." There can be no pragmatic political "carrier" of the eschatological vision, which represents the struggle for spiritual order, not its salvific resolution.[20]

16. Ibid., 79.
17. Voegelin, *Order and History*, vol. 4, *Ecumenic Age*, 115.
18. Ibid., 134ff., 196ff.
19. Ibid., 196–97.
20. To cite Voegelin once again on the Pauline imbalance, which paves the way for concupiscential interpretations of the spiritual ecumenicity of eschatological symbolism, and of Christ's resurrection in particular: "The cause of the discrepancy in Paul's interpretation can now be more exactly determined as an inclination to abolish the tension between the eschatological *telos* of reality and the mystery of the transfiguration that is actually going on within historical reality. The Pauline myth of the struggle among the cosmic forces validly expresses the *telos* of the movement that is experienced in reality, but it becomes invalid when it is used to anticipate the concrete process of transfiguration within history" (*Order and History*, vol. 4, *Ecumenic Age*, 270). Voegelin will not countenance language of the spiritual "principalities and powers" within the realm of pragmatic politics—that would be to introduce a

PART 2: POLITICAL THEOLOGY AND THE RADICAL REFORMATION

With this point, of course, Yoder is in fundamental disagreement. For Christians the social forms of worship of God as sovereign will take a similar form to the prophetic model displayed in Israel's diaspora, but with particular reference to the imitation of Jesus Christ and the pattern of the cross. The key to proper political discernment will be to live out the vision for community articulated in the New Testament witness. The focus here is not a structure of hierarchical authority or institutional establishment or a doctrinal creed but rather the sociological (i.e., visible, embodied) and liturgical (i.e., dramatic, particular, community-based) "marks" of the community that believes Christ embodies the cosmic rule of God and lives out that story. Thus for Yoder there is no separation between the church and politics, as if these were somehow two separate realms—what is precisely at stake is the pattern of human community and relatedness that best defines our lives. For Christians, the "body of Christ" *is* a social body, the social carrier of the mind of Christ, a polis that represents the rule of God for the nations. What then are the marks of this body politic? Yoder spells them out most clearly in his little book *Body Politics*: binding and loosing (the "rule of Christ"), Eucharist, baptism, the fullness of Christ's body, and the "rule of Paul" practiced in the open meeting.[21]

Once again we do not have the space here to examine in detail the fivefold ecclesial and political pattern elaborated by Yoder. What is most important for Yoder's proposal is to recognize that each mark or pattern is rooted in what he calls the "doxological" vision, which is "to describe the cosmos in terms dictated by the knowledge that a once slaughtered Lamb is now living," as depicted in the Apocalypse of John.[22] This vision is not simply a conceptual structure, a mythos, nor is it a set of moral rules or institutional policies. Although it is a cosmic vision rooted in the worship of God as unveiled in Christ, it is also embodied in social practices that shape the identity and discernment of Christians in the world. Not only Christians, however, but all peoples are invited to join the Christian polis and to understand the meaning of their own lives in terms of its distinctive patterns. Hence Yoder can also trace analogies of the marks of Christian community in the world: for example, binding and loosing, which in the Christian community is linked to the practice of reconciling dialogue and forgiveness, is displayed in a non-confessional society as conflict resolution and mediation; the Eucharist, enacted in Christian community as table fellowship and covenant celebration in a new community

---

distorting confusion between religious myth and political analysis. By contrast, Yoder elaborates the political significance of Paul's language, not literally but analogically. O'Donovan tends to ignore the political significance of this language and would agree with Voegelin's basic point about pragmatic politics—that the *esse* of politics is human power, including coercive power, which cannot however mediate the cosmic judgments of God; the *bene esse* of Christian politics cannot transform the pragmatic structure of temporal human politics (we will return to this point below). See O'Donovan, "Karl Barth and Ramsey's 'Uses of Power.'"

21. Yoder, *Body Politics*; cf. Yoder, *Priestly Kingdom*, chap. 1; *For the Nations*, chap. 2; and *Royal Priesthood*, pt. 4. Yoder writes this about his fivefold christological pattern: "Stated very formally, the pattern we shall discover is that the will of God for human socialness as a whole is prefigured by the shape to which the Body of Christ is called. Church and world are not two compartments under separate legislation or two institutions with contradictory assignments, but two levels of pertinence of the same Lordship. The people of God is called to be today what the world is called to be ultimately" (*Body Politics*, ix).

22. See Yoder, "To Serve Our God," 128.

of consumption and production, is displayed in the wider world as the sharing of goods and reinterpretation of power and rank. Clearly, then, for Yoder the rule of God is not described in terms of the orders of creation or of juridical authority but in terms of the pattern of life displayed in the slain Lamb. This apocalyptic christological paradigm entails three overlapping political "scandal factors"[23]: the renunciation of domination in favor of servanthood, the love of enemies which breaks down ethnocentric identities, and the practice of forgiveness rather than retributive justice as the path to social harmony.

Critique of Christendom

This alternative account of Christian politics brings us to our third focus, the post-biblical history of Christianity and politics—in particular, Yoder's interpretation of Christendom politics and of modern liberalism.[24] Yoder's eschatological political proposal obviously rejects what he would judge to be the "concupiscential exodus" entailed in both Christian ecumenical empire politics and Joachitic chiliastic politics from Müntzer to Marx. For the purposes of this essay, it is the first alternative—ecumenical Christendom politics—that is of greatest interest. However, it should be said in passing that any account of modern liberalism that ignores the influence of Christian apocalypticism (as O'Donovan's does) is missing an important part of the picture.[25] I am aware of no one who has developed a more trenchant, sustained, and unrelenting critique of Christendom political theology than Yoder. If ancient Israel's experiment in kingship, especially in its post-Solomonic form, represents the idolatrous compromise of Israel's religio-political vision centered upon the worship of God as sovereign, so does Christendom for Yoder in the history of Christianity in the West. I can only sketch the bare outline of Yoder's critique, focusing on those aspects of what he calls "Constantinianism"[26] that contradict the politics of Jesus and the early church. The flawed assumptions of Christendom may be described as follows:

1. Constantinian Christian empire is rooted in a falsely realized eschatology. No longer is God's sovereignty a matter of faith, tied to the slain Lamb as the one who has conquered kenotically and who appears on earth as the suffering servant crucified by violent powers. After Constantine, God's governance becomes visible through the

23. See Yoder, *For the Nations*, 47–48.

24. Yoder considers the political ethics of modern liberalism to be another variant of the Christendom dualism in ethics between private and public, visible and invisible, individual and social. See his account of various "neo-Constantinian" positions in "The Constantinian Sources of Western Social Ethics," *Priestly Kingdom*, chap. 7.

25. It is worth noting that O'Donovan completely neglects the tradition of apocalyptic politics in his *Desire of the Nations* and almost completely excludes it in the wide-ranging new anthology *From Irenaeus to Grotius*, which includes only a brief selection from Hans Hergot, an obscure spiritualist influenced by Joachim and Müntzer. O'Donovan's neglect of this tradition perhaps also partly explains why he ignores the most theological of the modernity critics, Eric Voegelin, whose project attributes considerable importance to this non-mainstream tradition of Christian political reflection.

26. Yoder's discussion of various historical forms of Constantinian and "neo-Constantinian" politics can be found in Yoder, *Priestly Kingdom*, chaps. 4 and 7; *Royal Priesthood*, 56ff., 115ff., 195ff., 243ff.; and *For the Nations*, chap. 5. The Constantinian caricature lies behind almost everything he writes.

agency of the Christian emperor, and through an established church presided over by an official ruling clergy that functions politically as "chaplain" to governing authority. Sociopolitical ethics now becomes tied to the power structure of the empire and its ruling representatives, not to the body politics of the Christian community.

2. Ironically enough, as the institutional church now becomes more visible and powerful (in the conventional political sense of the word), the scandalous christological "marks" of the church become increasingly *invisible*, interpreted as inner dispositional traits and pertaining only to private, interpersonal ethical relations. Of course, since everyone is now officially Christian, the "real Christian" or "true church" is now invisible as well, as the official church must create ethical standards that apply to everyone. This also leads to a duality of ethics: on the one hand, the "ordinary ethics" of those who live everyday lives in the world, of whom perfection cannot be expected, including a general secular political ethic that is "more realistic" in its demands and expectations and that is more concerned with pragmatic calculations in conventional power politics (for which there is little practical advice in the New Testament; hence the need to develop an autonomous tradition of political reflection). On the other hand, for those willing to take them on in what will now be called a "religious life," there are the "evangelical counsels" of perfection for those who live separate from the world. Here the ethics of absolute nonviolence, chastity, poverty, and so on become the norm—not now for the church community but as an individual calling.

For Yoder this shift can only be understood as the fall of the church from its true religious, ethical, and political calling. No longer imitating the *kenosis* of the sovereign lord into the form of a suffering servant, Christians rather seek control of the levers of historical mastery and political domination. Yoder will refuse the various kinds of metaphysical and moral dualisms that divide up the world into a "visible" pragmatic realm of conventional "responsibility," where the power of violence and the external calculi of retributive justice prevail, and an "invisible" spiritual realm where Christ's love and self-denial rule. The spiritual "mind of Christ" and the material "body of Christ" cannot be so divided.

O'Donovan

Of course, from the point of view of Oliver O'Donovan, Yoder's reduction of the Christendom political vision to this crude caricature of Constantinianism is not only historically naive (as when Augustine's *City of God* is lumped together with Eusebian caesaropapism[27])—it is theologically, ethically, and politically suspect. O'Donovan offers no Eusebian brief for Constantinianism.[28] Rather, his project is to recover the biblical

---

27. Note, for example, Yoder's description of the "fall of the church," located "at the point of that fusion of church and society of which Constantine was the architect, Eusebius the priest, Augustine the apologete, and the Crusades and Inquisition the culmination." *Royal Priesthood*, 89, cf. 154; and Yoder, *For the Nations*, 82. The responsible historian can only cringe in the face of such crudities.

28. O'Donovan's discussion of Eusebius and Constantinianism is critical (*Desire of the Nations*,

roots of the political theology that informed the history of Christendom both for good and for ill. Only such an interpretive exercise will enable Christians to make judgments about their own narrative past in the light of Christ's disclosure of the meaning of divine rule. That is, O'Donovan will not proceed in the manner of Yoder's Christendom caricature by asking what is the ideal set of political institutions, structures, and offices.[29] Rather, he will focus dramatically on the meaning of the political "act"—a narrative category, which will be modeled (as in Yoder's approach) ultimately on divine action and on the cry that echoes throughout the whole of the biblical literature: "YHWH rules." Such an approach will be thoroughly historical, not totalizing or coercively foundationalist, according to O'Donovan.

The Prophetic Tradition

The first point O'Donovan makes about the claim "YHWH reigns" is that it evokes free human action and renders such free action intelligible. The rule of God in biblical texts is focused neither on coercive force nor on the power of persuasion (rhetorical force); rather, it sets out the terms for the meaning and fulfillment of human agency.[30] And it does so liturgically, in the expression of human worship of God as divine ruler, not in terms of particular political institutions and forms. Here too it is impossible to explicate the richness and complexity of O'Donovan's exegetical and historical work. I can only select a few representative samples for comparative attention.

First of all, as I've already mentioned, O'Donovan agrees with Yoder about the priority of prophets over kings in Israel's political history as recounted in biblical texts.[31] However, unlike Yoder, O'Donovan ties this to the central importance of *law* and the authority of law in the biblical community. This law, according to the prophets, extends beyond Israel since YHWH is king over the whole earth. Israel's political vision therefore does not call for the monolithic unity of a religious empire; to the contrary, it affirms international and political pluralism, but this is possible only in relation to the divine law that justly orders the whole of reality in a juridical ecumenicity. Thus, while Jeremiah is the representative prophet,[32] he is representative in a revealingly different capacity. As the prophet of the new covenant of the heart, he mediates a new understanding of the relationship between God and the people that focuses on an internalization of divine law and divine justice. This newly individual conscience can now be scattered anywhere and

---

197–98) but also appreciative. Unlike Yoder, he does not interpret it as the "fall of the church" but rather as a theologically flawed form of "realized eschatology"—it loses the tension of the already and the not yet—that nonetheless bears witness to the key insight of Christendom political theology: the victory of God displayed in the obedience of worldly rulers. "It was not the conversion of the empire that occupied Eusebius's thoughts, but the overthrow of its tutelary deities" (198). Constantine, for Eusebius, is "God's champion, not the heir of the Caesars," and in this his discernment was properly ordered, says O'Donovan.

29. Ibid., 20–21. Yoder states, "To ask, 'What is the best form of government?' is itself a Constantinian question" (*Priestly Kingdom*, 154).

30. O'Donovan, *Desire of the Nations*, 32.

31. Ibid., 65.

32. Ibid., 76ff., 83.

speak out of this internalized, though not individualized, awareness of the social moral understanding represented in Israel's experience of the divine rule:

> To generalize . . . we may say that *the conscience of the individual members of a community is the moral repository of the moral understanding which shaped it, and may serve to perpetuate it in a crisis of collapsing morale or institution.* It is not as bearer of his own primitive pre-social or pre-political rights that the individual demands the respect of the community, but as the bearer of a social understanding which recalls the formative self-understanding of the community itself. The conscientious individual speaks with society's own forgotten voice.[33]

This provides the opening for O'Donovan's critical appropriation of Augustine's political theology which, O'Donovan argues, is a form of Christendom but not Constantinianism. Augustine also appeals to Jeremiah's letter to the exiles in Babylon as "the archetype for the duality of this-worldly and divine rule,"[34] and hence it becomes the model for Augustine's own "two cities" political ethics (*City of God* 19.26).[35] Unlike Yoder's characterization of Augustine's "Constantinian" position as the beginning of the loss of eschatology,[36] O'Donovan's retrieval of Augustine's position is thoroughly christological and eschatological. No human political regime is independent of divine judgment and rule, which ultimately has reference to the representative mediating act of Christ, whose life and death points toward the deeper meaning and fulfillment of human life—not only in heaven but also on the earth (and therefore politically).[37] Thus, while Christendom refers to a *secular* political order, it is not morally neutral but is obedient to the rule of Christ in the moral content of its political principles.[38]

33. Ibid., 80.

34. Ibid., 83.

35. It is perhaps worth noting that O'Donovan will translate the Hebrew *shalom* of Jer 29:7 differently than Yoder does—not "peace" but "welfare" (Augustine's Latin is, of course, *pax*). O'Donovan will sternly oppose a pacifist interpretation of Christian politics.

36. See Yoder, *Royal Priesthood*, 154.

37. O'Donovan's appropriation of Augustine is critical precisely on the question of eschatology and its public, historical reference. More precisely, he criticizes Augustine's allegorical identification of Israel and the church, which tends to spiritualize the important social and political content of the Christ event (*Desire of the Nations*, 162–63). This can lead precisely to the kind of Erastian dualism that characterizes Hobbes's modern civil society, in which the church "has become the ecclesiastical system within a community that is primarily structured otherwise, as a civil kingdom"; here "the key element which made sense of the Christendom idea is missing: the eschatology which founded dual institutions in the confrontation of the victorious Christ with the defeated world-rulers and protected them against a loss of tension" (165). This requires the church to pay closer attention to the public historical (and political) tradition of Israel, and to how the church relates to it under the rule of Christ (132). Having said that, however, O'Donovan goes on immediately to qualify this: "We assert that the political character of the church, its essential nature as a governed society, is hidden, to be discerned by faith as the ascended Christ who governs it is to be discerned by faith" (166). We will explore this tension further below.

38. For a helpful elaboration of this retrieval of Augustine (over against Robert Markus's modern interpretation of "secular" politics as a "pluralistic, religiously neutral civil community"), see O'Donovan's "Augustine's *City of God* XIX ." Justice, for Augustine and for O'Donovan, is filled with thoroughly Christian theological content—which limits its enactment by human beings in the temporal conditions of worldly experience (no one can see into the hidden recesses of the human heart) and requires the constant reference of all limited enactments to the *summum bonum* of divine goodness via the rallying cry of the City of God on pilgrimage in the *saeculum*: "Forgive us our sins . . ." (*City of God* 19.27).

Why O'Donovan Is Not Constantinian and Yoder Is Not Hobbesian

Marks of the Church and Secular Order

Again like Yoder, O'Donovan develops the representative political meaning of Jesus with reference to the sacramental marks of the worshipping church. The church *is* a kind of political community marked by allegiance to the authority of Christ in mediating and representing God's rule on earth.[39] This is not only an inner event but a fully public one tied to the narrative moments of Christ's representative "act." Note also that for O'Donovan the church's identity and social form is not derived (*pace* Yoder's characterization of Christendom) from a hierarchical institutional "order of ministry" but from Christ's representative act.[40] Hence just as secular forms of government are not the starting point for normative political ethics, so also forms of church government and institutional order or hierarchical authority are not politically normative. The representative act for O'Donovan, as for Yoder, is a kenotic act; God's rule in the world which is the church's mission takes the form of a servant.[41] But the servant can only properly function within a social space presided over by secular authority, suggests O'Donovan: "If the mission of the church needs a certain social space, for men and women of every nation to be drawn into the governed community of God's Kingdom, then secular authority is authorised to provide and ensure that space."[42]

It is at this point that the disagreement between Yoder and O'Donovan begins to open up. It is clear that secular judicial order possesses a sanctified status for O'Donovan that it does not have for Yoder.[43] For Yoder, the church as servant is in no way dependent for its "social space" upon a secular judicial order; the "marks" of the church indeed delimit the church's own alternative social space in which mercy does away with the coercive and alienating claims of conventional judicial processes. This becomes very evident in Yoder's and O'Donovan's divergent interpretations of Matthew 18:15–20 on "binding and loosing."[44] For Yoder the practice of binding and loosing is tied to a community process of discernment and reconciliation—it can only work in voluntary community where people are prepared to engage one another in dialogue over conflicts and disagreements, in a spirit of mutual forgiveness, responsibility, and trust. This is a process and an authority that Jesus extends to all, not only official rabbis, and it is a process that applies in all cases of disagreement and conflict, no matter what the issue. By contrast, O'Donovan develops a rather more formal point from Matthew 18 about God's judgment in community:

> The only judgement with which the church has to reckon is the final judgement, dividing between belief and unbelief. The secular authorities, on the other hand,

39. O'Donovan, *Desire of the Nations*, chap. 4.
40. Ibid., 166ff.
41. Ibid., 133–36.
42. Ibid., 146.
43. Hunsinger, "Karl Barth and the Politics of Sectarian Protestantism," notes a similar divergence between Yoder and Barth—namely that for Barth the state has an independent positive relation of its own to the order of redemption that is not mediated by the church. Hence, argues Hunsinger, Barth is not (*pace* Yoder) a free church theologian.
44. For Yoder's treatment, see Yoder, *Body Politics*, chap. 1; Yoder, *Royal Priesthood*, 265ff., 328ff.; and Yoder, *Priestly Kingdom*, 26ff. For O'Donovan's, see his *Desire of the Nations*, 150–52.

deal only in provisional and penultimate judgements. By embracing the final judgement of God Christians have accepted that they have no need for penultimate judgements to defend their rights. The continued presence of such judgements in the world, however, is an important witness to those to whom the word of final judgement has yet to come.⁴⁵

This formal reading becomes practically significant in O'Donovan's argument concerning Christendom, in which secular authorities officially recognize the authority of Christ in carrying out their limited acts of judicial authority.⁴⁶ That is, secular authorities are "no longer in the fullest sense mediators of the rule of God . . .. There remains simply the rump of political authority which cannot be dispensed with yet, the exercise of judgement."⁴⁷ I consider this to be a significant yet confusing passage in *The Desire of the Nations*. What exactly does it mean to say that secular authorities mediate "only" God's judgments, and not God's rule? Can anyone mediate these without also what O'Donovan calls the "possession" of divine rule—which is truly represented in Christ and mediated in the political identity known as the body of Christ?⁴⁸ O'Donovan's focus on God's "rump" in the secular sphere is analogous to Moses's vision of the "backside" of divine glory (Exod 33, just before the mediation of the tables of the Law), prior to the Jeremian shift (cf. Jer 31:31f., the law written upon the heart) and its (for Christians) visible embodiment in the messianic incarnation (described by Paul in 2 Cor 3, linking the glory and likeness of God to the freedom of the heart⁴⁹). This is evident in the privatized meaning that O'Donovan gives to the practice of "binding and loosing": "a Christian who believes himself ill-treated by a fellow-Christian must try to reach an understanding privately first, . . . the aim of the whole process being to keep the issue confined and to bring to bear the least weight of public pressure capable of doing the job."⁵⁰

---

45. O'Donovan, *Desire of the Nations*, 150–51.

46. "Antichrist" governments, of course, are another matter (*Desire of the Nations*, 217)—one of O'Donovan's criticisms of Yoder is that he considers *all* governments to be demonic by nature (*Desire of the Nations*, 151–52). Yoder might agree insofar as his argument is that any and all violence goes hand in glove with idolatry (Yoder, *Royal Priesthood*, 209–17; Yoder, *For the Nations*, 76), including technological and economic violence, all of which are rooted in desire for *control* as domination.

47. O'Donovan, *Desire of the Nations*, 151.

48. Ibid., 148.

49. This is recognized by O'Donovan himself, who quotes 2 Corinthians 3:18 in connection with the centrality of freedom for the narrative of liberal society (O'Donovan, *Desire of the Nations*, 252). O'Donovan makes some very fine observations on this, also in connection with 1 Corinthians 14:24ff., on church order (which Yoder identifies as the "rule of Paul," his fifth mark of the church, whose analogue in the secular world is free speech and the open meeting): "It is a paradigm for the birth of free society, grounded in the recognition of a superior authority which renders all authorities beneath it relative and provisional. We discover we are free when we are commanded by that authority which commands us according to the law of our being, disclosing the secrets of the heart. There is no freedom except when what we are, and do, corresponds to what has been given to us to be and to do. 'Given to us,' because the law of our being does not assert itself spontaneously merely by virtue of our existing. We must receive ourselves from outside ourselves, addressed by a summons which evokes that correspondence of existence to being." (ibid., 252) What Yoder holds together here, however, O'Donovan seems to thinks should be separated—though exactly how is not quite clear.

50. Ibid., 150.

At this point, it might be suggested, O'Donovan opens himself to the very charge he makes against Yoder concerning voluntariety (to which we shall return)—allowing Christian symbols to be conscripted by the reductionist politics of liberalism. In this case, it seems to entail the privatization of the practice of "binding and loosing," which overlooks the complex interpersonal but also communal and political process of human conflict resolution and reconciliation. The process (on Yoder's account) is indeed a public and politically normative one—even if it remains interpersonal—that emphasizes responsible engagement with the other rather than adversarial claim and counterclaim, and personal mediation rather than mechanical or procedural justice. The appeal is to conscience with reference to divine judgment, but this is not merely "final judgment" that "divides between belief and unbelief" (as O'Donovan represents it[51]). It is, I think, tendentious to divide judicial form from eschatological substance here. Is it really the case, as O'Donovan asserts, that Christians for their part "have no need for penultimate judgements"?[52] This claim, I think, is no less questionable than the claim that the rump can function without the whole body in secular rule. What are the acts of discernment and interpersonal engagement in Christian community if not provisional and penultimate, having to do in most cases not with doctrinal issues of belief and unbelief, but with practical questions of worldly ethics and temporal relationships? That such matters cannot be reduced simply to "defend[ing] their rights"[53] is precisely part of the point about worldly justice made in Matthew 18—the context of which, lest it be forgotten, is how to deal with social forms of offense and the sinful cycle of violence and retaliation. There is a formalism here in O'Donovan's analysis that does not clarify.

That O'Donovan's interpretations of both biblical texts and the marks of the church are more formal than Yoder's should come as no surprise. O'Donovan explicitly states that his project in *The Desire of the Nations* is to develop the conceptual categories of a political *theology* ("a *theoretic* discipline," he calls it[54]), which must precede political *ethics* (presumably a "practical" discipline). Yet this hermeneutical distinction (nicely challenged by Hauerwas and Fodor[55]) entails precisely the sort of separation rejected by Yoder—conceptual theory must be entailed in embodied practice and vice versa. Hence where Yoder sees political meaning and implications in the concrete detail of biblical narrative, detail that can be drawn upon analogically to address the current political life and witness of the church,[56] O'Donovan draws out formal concepts and applies them as an "architectonic" to engage critically the history of Christian political thought. And on this point concerning "binding and loosing" and the relation of judgment and mercy or forgiveness, the implications move in quite a different direction from Yoder's understanding.

51. Ibid.
52. Ibid., 151.
53. Ibid.
54. Ibid., 15.
55. Hauerwas and Fodor, "Remaining in Babylon," 209ff.
56. For Yoder, the Jesus narrative as paradigm is not reducible to general principles. This is for him a central hermeneutical point and it is tied to his reflections on the practice of binding and loosing. See, for example, Yoder, *Priestly Kingdom*, chap. 1, and also p. 117; Yoder, *Politics of Jesus*, 76

PART 2: POLITICAL THEOLOGY AND THE RADICAL REFORMATION

Christendom, the "Free Church," and Liberalism

The distinction between the ultimate judgment of God recognized in the church and the provisional judgments required by God in secular political order entails for O'Donovan the theoretical legitimation of different roles of church (mercy) and state (judgment), though the aim of both complementary roles in their "mutual service"[57] is the same: reconciliation. O'Donovan contrasts this mutual complementarity to the "unhappy tension which tormented the classical world, between the philosopher with his truth and the ruler with his power." Yet this conceptual Christian complementarity becomes highly (but "happily"?) dialectical in his treatment of the outworking of mercy and judgment in liberal society.[58] Secular politics constitutes the realm of judgment regarding provisional temporal questions of justice; the church constitutes the realm of ultimate divine judgment in which the mercy of the cross reconciles the guilty.

Yoder's view will certainly dissent from O'Donovan's narrative interpretation of biblical political theology on this point. For Yoder the church cannot be understood as one limited social institution, somehow balanced by the different political and ethical roles of the state and other "public" institutions. Yoder would argue, I think, that O'Donovan has yet again compromised an eschatological two kingdoms/two ages vision by dividing it into two conflicting (in terms of roles and methods) institutional authorities. For Yoder, Jesus's life is not only descriptive of how God's ultimate judgment reconciles sinful humanity in a heavenly peace; it also describes how that ultimate judgment of divine love is *implemented provisionally* in various forms of earthly peace. That is, Jesus's identity as cosmic ruler entails the very worldly enactment of the "Jeremiah shift"—the acceptance of a non-sovereign, non-territorial self-definition.[59] Conventional royal ideology of whatever kind, insofar as it is linked to coercive judicial rule, has been eschatologically declared a failure even when it appears powerful and "successful" in the world.

This divergence in interpretation of the biblical narrative also shows up prominently in O'Donovan's and Yoder's respective readings of political developments and Christianity in the modern period. For Yoder the church is a voluntary community of shared discernment in which all are free to speak because all (in their differences) are gifted and joined together in a new human identity—open in its entire life to creative divine agency. Such a community that practices forgiveness, love even of enemies, and leadership as servanthood (not dominion) models what *all* human communities are called to. It can *only* be sustained by the church's "doxological" identity shaped by its worship of the God revealed in Christ[60]; it is not sustained by any established or conventional judicial power. Such a church must therefore by definition be "free" and not established by any state, since the "responsibility" it practices presupposes voluntary commitment (inner and outer, visible and invisible) to living out its kenotic vision of divine rule, which is ultimately nonviolent.[61] It is not difficult to see how Yoder's vision stands in critical

---

57. O'Donovan, *Desire of the Nations*, 217.
58. Ibid., 256ff.
59. See Yoder, *Royal Priesthood*, 133ff.
60. Ibid., 109ff., 128ff.
61. Ibid., 245f., 265ff.; and Yoder, *Priestly Kingdom*, 22ff.

distinction from Christendom ethics. It should also be clear that Yoder's view of human freedom and responsibility in community under God's rule is quite different from the political voluntarism of social contract theory. And yet, according to O'Donovan, Yoder's emphasis on voluntariety and the "free church" is purchased at the expense of *belief*; that is, it is rooted in an intellectually flabby liberalism that has lost confidence in truth claims and views all social doctrines as inherently coercive.

> A voluntary society is one that I could leave without incurring grave or irremediable loss, which might seem a strange thing for a Christian to think about the church. Finally, does the concept of the church as a voluntary society not commend itself chiefly because it fits late-modern expectations of how civil society will be organised? Is Yoder, in the name of non-conformity, not championing a great conformism, lining the church up with the sports clubs, friendly societies, colleges, symphony subscription-guilds, political parties and so on, just to prove that the church offers late-modern order no serious threat?[62]

This caricature[63] of Yoder's clearly stated and argued theological belief in the principle of voluntariety (which is anything but in support of a "take it or leave it" membership to a politically non-threatening social club[64]) should be ignored in order to focus on the difference in theological stance that divides them. After all, O'Donovan no less than Yoder wants to celebrate the liberal principle of *freedom*,[65] not its parodic mimic "free choice" as depicted in modern individualistic liber*alism*.[66] The law of our being and hence our freedom is the law of love, which is rooted in the free self-giving love of God (as enacted in Christ). This view of human freedom in community under the rule of God is quite different from the abstract naked will of modern individualism and the voluntarism in the political myth of social contract, argues O'Donovan[67]—here in agreement with political critics of modernity. Yet it is precisely here, in their mutual criticism of liberal individualism and their understanding of what social forms the freedom of Christ should take in the world, that O'Donovan and Yoder disagree. It is indeed disingenuous of O'Donovan to suggest that Yoder follows the liberal principle that "social doctrine of any kind is coercive."[68] For Yoder, the social body politic of the church is

---

62. O'Donovan, *Desire of the Nations*, 223–24.

63. Indeed, the pages on Yoder (see especially *Desire of the Nations*, 151–52) have to qualify as leading candidates for the crankiest pages of O'Donovan's generally restrained and judicious work. This makes it too easy for O'Donovan to dismiss Yoder's careful and extensive biblical, theological, and historical arguments for an alternative to mainstream Christendom ecclesiology and political ethics.

64. For a helpful historical and theological study on Anabaptist voluntariety (in dialogue with concerns expressed about voluntarism by Joan Lockwood O'Donovan), see Reimer, "Adequacy of a Voluntaristic Theology."

65. O'Donovan, *Desire of the Nations*, 252–53.

66. Ibid., 275–67.

67. Ibid., 278–81.

68. Ibid., 223, 221. It is true that Yoder assumes the coercive character of civil politics, as expressed in the following statement: "It remains the nature of the civil order itself that its coercive control is prior to any justifications or qualifications thereof," a view that Yoder attributes to "biblical realism" about political power. See Yoder, *Priestly Kingdom*, 159. But then O'Donovan also argues that this (power entails coercion) is an important assumption about politics, "because the survival of a human community depends *in the first place* on its capacity to use force if required." O'Donovan, "Karl Barth and Ramsey's 'Uses of Power,'" 10; cf. 21.

precisely not so, and precisely because it is not in the business of enacting and enforcing judicial authority—it proceeds on a different paradigm of divine rule and justice. It will therefore not alter its process of and criteria for moral discernment when rulers join the church,[69] nor "employ" instrumentalities of power foreign to its own identity and calling.

And yet, there is something to O'Donovan's criticism of Yoder, although it should be otherwise formulated. Yoder has not adequately attended to or clarified the complex relations between soul and society and, in particular, the difficult question of how the eternal, spiritually discerned *invisible* wisdom and judgment of God is related to pragmatic political history—including particular *visible* social communities such as the church. In his concern to distance himself from forms of unworldly or subjectivist "pietism" that neglect the political claims of the Gospel,[70] Yoder has occasionally resorted to unnecessarily extreme formulations, such as the following: "The challenge to which the proclamation of Christ's rule over the rebellious world speaks a word of grace is not a problem within the self but a split within the cosmos."[71] No less than pietism is such a formulation a distortion of the New Testament witness, where the fault line of sin runs through the cosmos, but also through the human self. The mind of Christ, though embodied in a social community, is not externally visible in a direct sense—its discernment makes judgments about the whole range of temporal bodily life but is oriented by a mysterious divine wisdom that does remain invisible, that is not rendered fully transparent by the difficult discipleship of those who imitate Christ. Without the inner purification of the mind, without the proper orientation of the soul, the "rule of Christ" and the "rule of Paul" (as Yoder calls marks one and five of "body politics") are subject to the same distortions as any other political forms in the world. No visible form of any kind can guarantee the proper bodily enactment of the mind of Christ, since the wisdom it represents is hidden (1 Cor 2).[72] Hence, for example, when Yoder says as he does in various places that society exists for the sake of the church,[73] he ironically leaves himself open to another kind of Christendom triumphalism. The church, from my reading of the New Testament, exists rather (as did Christ) for the sake of God's service in the world. How this point is *formulated* is crucial, and a proper formulation will of necessity be more attentive to the tension between visible and invisible wisdom of God than Yoder is. Otherwise it may easily fall into a new form of "compact collectivism" that is nonecumenical and dogmatically closed.

Conclusion

I conclude, then, with some reflections on O'Donovan's and Yoder's divergent understandings of Christian eschatology and political responsibility. It is clear that while both reject an apocalyptic politics that seeks to immanentize the eschaton—the rule

---

69. Yoder, *Priestly Kingdom*, 82ff.
70. See Yoder, *For the Nations*, 143–44; and *Royal Priesthood*, 131.
71. Yoder, *Politics of Jesus*, 161.
72. I discuss this problem in greater detail in chapter 8, below, "The War of the Lamb."
73. See Yoder, *Christian Witness to the State*, 12ff.

of God—coercively, neither of them accepts the religious neutrality of secularist liberal politics or the withdrawal of Christians from the public political order. Both believe that the Christian church is called upon to develop a prophetic or even apocalyptic witness to the rule of God revealed in Christ, a revelation that cannot (à la Voegelin) be reduced to yet another symbol of the tensive structure of human consciousness. With Paul and the New Testament witness, they wish to affirm that Christ's death and resurrection has defeated the cosmic powers of sin, and this victory is proclaimed in the ongoing historical witness of the *ekklēsia*—those called to imitate Christ in the building up of a true social ecumenicity. This vision is not to transfigure worldly structures through human eschatological agency in a politics of conquest (a project that so worried Hobbes and that continues to afflict modern politics); indeed it rather issues a humbling challenge to self-aggrandizing human agency in the public political realm with reference to the authority of Christ's very different rule.

O'Donovan asserts: "The political doctrine that emerged from Christendom is characterised by a notion that government is responsible."[74] This assertion means, first, a new form of political authority as "state"—an invention of Christendom unknown in antiquity (cf. *politeia, civitas, res publica*, all of which refer to "political community"). In terms of political theory, this claim entails a limited governing authority that coexists with other structures so that people are not defined solely by their "political" roles. Such a "responsible state is therefore minimally coercive and minimally representative."[75] Its judgment is always under law, understood ultimately as divine law which is truly international, and it must always be legally constituted as representative in which the political act of ruling is responsible to the divine law. And as this divine law is divided into secular provisional judgment and the prophetic law of the Spirit of Christ,[76] responsible government will make a place for the church and defer to its law—that is, to the moral *society* (ethos, shared moral purposes) that it represents (which is never simply an agglomeration of individuals, and certainly not abstract individual, rights-bearing wills). Responsible government, therefore, will be neither the triumphalist service of a Christian empire nor secularist political neutrality. O'Donovan uses his understanding of responsible government to develop a Christian understanding of the limited liberal state and its anti-Christian parodies.

From Yoder's perspective O'Donovan's characterization of the church would no doubt be judged to be more a form of chaplaincy than a prophetic understanding of "responsibility." Too much is baptized in this Anglican vision of Incarnation;[77] the continuities between the old aeon and the new concede too much to untransformed secularity. At the same time, perhaps somewhat ironically, O'Donovan too narrowly construes the political in terms of the secular state or judicial authority. Political responsibility for the Christian church, says Yoder, is to discharge a "modeling mission. The church is called to be now what the world is called to be ultimately. . . . The church is thus not chaplain or priest to the powers running the world: she is called to be a microcosm of the

---

74. O'Donovan, *Desire of the Nations*, 231.
75. Ibid., 232.
76. Ibid., 233–34, 241.
77. See, for example, Yoder, *Royal Priesthood*, 172ff.

PART 2: POLITICAL THEOLOGY AND THE RADICAL REFORMATION

wider society, not only as idea, but also in her [social] function."[78] The responsible use of power is found in the kenotic servanthood of the church, not in ruling acts of political judgment from on high in dominant positions of power. The landscape of responsibility looks different "from below." The words of the seer of Patmos may not be forgotten: "The Lamb that was slain is worthy to receive power"—Christ renounced the claim to govern history and so must his followers, but this is surely not to renounce the political.[79] That is, in contrast to the charge by Hauerwas and Fodor that O'Donovan's eschatology is too "realized," it might rather be said that here the political consequences of O'Donovan's eschatology are not "realized" enough.[80] No less than Yoder does O'Donovan link the mission of the church to its eschatological vision, which precludes any form of religious coercion and can only be understood as humble service and the spiritual *discernment* of the rule of Christ as opposed to Antichrist—the false "immanentization of the eschaton" in earthly political rule.[81] And yet when O'Donovan elaborates this idea politically in his model of limited government and "balance of roles" between church and state,[82] the eschatological language mysteriously drops out, to be replaced by a functional dialectic between institutional roles. The politics of the state will have no real eschatological substance and will exercise only a limited public juridical role. Correspondingly, the church will have no visible political character—"its essential nature as a governed society, is hidden, to be discerned by faith as the ascended Christ who governs it is to be discerned by faith."[83] Its public witness has no direct political substance, and its identity is not yet clear as its meaning is tied to the ascended Christ.

78. Yoder, *Priestly Kingdom*, 92.

79. See Yoder, *Politics of Jesus*, chap. 12. Yoder states, "Perhaps Christians in our age are being made ready for a new awareness of the continuing relevance of the message of the Apocalypse. There is a widespread recognition that Western society is moving toward the collapse of the mentality that has been identified with Christendom. Christians must recognise that they are not only a minority on the globe but also at home in the midst of the followers of non-Christian and post-Christian faiths. Perhaps this will prepare us to see how inappropriate and preposterous was the prevailing assumption, from the time of Constantine until yesterday, that the fundamental responsibility of the church for society is to manage it" (240).

80. See especially Hauerwas and Fodor "Remaining in Babylon," 206, 208, 221n7. On this point I suspect they are influenced by Yoder's Constantinianism caricature, which interprets Christendom ethics as a form of "realized eschatology" of the sort displayed in the Eusebian panegyric to Constantine, aptly characterized by O'Donovan as follows: "The divine rule, with all its attributes, had become luminously present in the royal man. It is as though the eschatological horizon of all political theology has, in the moment of astonishment, come to be spoken of as present" (*Desire of the Nations*, 198). This is not a vision to which O'Donovan is remotely susceptible, and once again shows the limitations of the Yoderian caricature for interpreting Christendom political theory.

81. "Mission is not merely an urge to expand the scope and sway of the church's influence. It is to be at the disposal of the Holy Spirit in making Christ's victory known. It requires, therefore, a discernment of the working of the Spirit and of the Antichrist. These two discernments must accompany each other: to trace the outline of Christ's dawning reign on earth requires that one trace the false pretension too. . . . Yet there is a single theme which connects the varied warnings of Antichrist in different ages: the convergence in one subject of claims to earthly political rule and heavenly soteriological mediation. . . . The rejection of Antichrist is the rejection of a unified political and theological authority other than that which is vested in Christ's own person" (O'Donovan, *Desire of the Nations*, 214–15).

82. Ibid., 217.

83. Ibid., 166.

Why O'Donovan Is Not Constantinian and Yoder Is Not Hobbesian

Here important further work remains to be done, if I am correct in suggesting that neither Yoder nor O'Donovan has adequately articulated an eschatological vision of the relation between the visible and invisible rule of God. Yoder, for his part, seems not to allow for the distinction at all, causing him to focus excessively on the social embodiment of Christ's rule in the political community that is the church, without paying enough attention to the inner formation of the wills and minds of Christian witnesses who must exercise political discernment in all manner of contexts. There is an ironic lack of attention to the complex character and (trans)formation of the human *voluntas* in Yoder's voluntariety.[84] O'Donovan refuses to allow that the church constitutes a new political order or alternative society, since it serves a hidden Lord whose rule cannot yet be made visibly public. This refusal causes him to limit formally the meaning of Christian political witness to addressing the judicial acts and authority of the secular state, even while suggesting that the visible practical form of the church offers substantive prophetic content to political society through obedience to the divinely authorized rule of Christ. Yet I have also tried to show that both Yoder and O'Donovan offer important elements to such an undertaking, and that their approaches share more than is evident in their own depictions of the other. If that is so, then it is not unreasonable to hope for the further development of a more ecumenical approach to theological politics, an apocalyptic political discernment and ecclesial practice that restores the connections between various human communities and cultures in a reconciling, life-giving mutuality, over against the violent destructiveness of various forms of empire homogeneity and domination.

---

84. Here Augustine's account of *voluntas* remains the most important resource, one that Yoder generally ignores and otherwise misconstrues as being overly individualist and otherworldly (see Yoder, *For the Nations*, 82). Augustine's account of the will cannot be understood without reference to *sacramentum*, God's revealed mystery in which Christians participate (not only individually but communally) for the proper formation and ordering of our loves and our lives. Yoder's inattention to the rich sacramental meaning of the marks of the church is lamentably characteristic of the "free church" tradition.

8

The War of the Lamb

Postmodernity and Yoder's Eschatological Genealogy of Morals

POSTMODERNITY IS AN INHERITANCE bequeathed by Nietzsche, who attempted to think through to their nihilistic conclusions the assumptions of modern Western culture. The foundational assumption of modernity, Nietzsche asserts, is the death of God[1]—that is, the death of a transcendent suprasensory reality that grounds and measures the visible world of appearances. The death of God is the cultural deed of the modern West; it entails the disempowerment of a divinely ordained or sovereign good to bestow life, truth, and moral order. The God of Judaism and Christianity, the transcendent Good of Platonic philosophy no longer offer hope and consolation, no longer orient modern thought and action. Nietzsche's prophetic word calls us to take responsibility for this deed and to overcome the destructive vestiges of dead traditional idolatries, especially in the realm of morality and cultural creation.

Here lies the agenda of postmodernity. Morality, like truth and reason, is historically contingent and without final purpose. All moral meaning is the creative expression of particular, culturally and historically situated human wills. We postmoderns will act in the full recognition that human beings must shape their own meaning by cultural self-creation without appealing to some higher *hinterweltlich* power for support. Indeed such appeals are disloyal to the human spirit; they devalue this world and worldly responsibility. The only real question for postmodern culture, in Nietzsche's judgment, is: Will we become the shrunken-souled "last men" who remain sick with nihilistic despair and *ressentiment*, and who seek to inoculate themselves against a harsh chaotic reality by indulging in cheap, homogeneous bourgeois pleasures?[2] Or will we be able to overcome this modern lassitude of the spirit in order to become culturally creative once again without consoling illusions and false hopes? Will it be possible to reverse the spiritual

---

1. See Friedrich Nietzsche's parable "The Madman," in *The Gay Science*, sec. 125; and cf. Martin Heidegger's illuminating reflection, "The Word of Nietzsche: 'God is Dead.'"
2. See Nietzsche, *Thus Spoke Zarathustra*, 129–30.

dissolution of modernity by founding a higher, healthier order of values? Can we give birth to the *Übermensch*? Nietzsche's project is to offer a diagnosis and a cure for the spiritual illness of modernity so that a postmodern culture of spiritual health can be born.

Key to this project is the critique of conventional morality, for at the heart of the human and cultural illness is the spirit of self-deception and revenge, the unwillingness to take full responsibility for who and what we are. Conventional morality not only masks our spiritual illness, it aids and abets it.

Anabaptists may celebrate Nietzsche's (and the Nietzschean) critiques of modern idolatries—especially the pretensions of modern scientific reason to ground and measure all true knowledge of reality and moral order[3]—and welcome his call for a dramatic, historical understanding of morality that overtly recognizes that it is engaged in an agonistic spiritual and cultural struggle. However, they will have to wrestle seriously with Nietzsche's critique of Christianity, for a central presumption of his postmodern hypothesis is that the Christian drama and narrative is a major cause of the spiritual sickness, a workshop of idols that stinks of many lies.[4] And while Anabaptists may agree with Nietzsche about many aspects of conventional cultural Christianity, there is no easy way to get around Nietzsche's damning assessment of the perspective expressed in Menno Simons's favorite epigraphical verse from 1 Corinthians 3:11: "For other foundation can no one lay than is laid . . . Jesus Christ." This foundation is indeed historical and dramatic but it is also eschatological, and it entails a cosmic authority that judges and measures all reality—with reference to an image that Nietzsche despises: the slain Lamb and therefore a wisdom that celebrates weakness, foolishness, lowliness, meekness.

Anabaptists proclaim a transcendent and cosmic moral measure, but it is evident only to those who take the faithful path of discipleship, following in the way of the crucified Messiah. Such an eschatological genealogy of morals, engaged in a polemic against the pretensions of modernity—but also of Nietzschean postmodernity—is evident in the work of John Howard Yoder. I wish to offer a few reflections on this battle and the weapons and strategies of each side.

Nietzsche and Yoder on Genealogy: Rome versus Judea

Nietzsche's genealogy of morals is designed as a counterpractice to modern moralism, which pretends a kind of detached objective scholarship (morality "in general") that

---

3. Nietzsche comments on the prejudicial "faith" of modern materialistic natural scientists, which assumes reality can be measured objectively by human reason if only the correct methods are applied: "What? Do we really want to permit existence to be degraded for us like this—reduced to a mere exercise for a calculator and an indoor diversion for mathematicians? Above all, one should not wish to divest existence of its *rich ambiguity*: that is a dictate of good taste, gentlemen, the taste of reverence for everything that lies beyond your horizon. That the only justifiable interpretation of the world should be one in which *you* are justified because one can continue to work and do research scientifically in *your* sense (you really mean, mechanistically?)—an interpretation that permits counting, calculating, weighing, seeing, and touching, and nothing more—that is a crudity and naivete, assuming that it is not a mental illness [*Geisteskrankheit*], an idiocy" (*Gay Science*, sec. 373).

4. See Nietzsche, *On the Genealogy of Morals*, 1.14.

is nevertheless particular and historical. Conventional moralists remain deliberately blind to the historical evolution of moral ideas as rooted in particular dramatic enactments and embodiments of human agency and valuing. Hence Nietzsche's approach is philological (rather than abstractly conceptual) and physiological (rather than strictly psychological). It is designed to show that morality is always tied to embodied human judgments—ways of seeing and naming what is valued in the world within the changing circumstances and bodily conditions of experience (preface; essay 1, sections 2 and 17).[5] Nietzsche asks not, "What is morality?," but "Which morality" are we talking about, where does it come from (who invented it, how, and under what conditions)? In doing so he keeps in view the polemical (the subtitle of *On the Genealogy of Morals* is "*Eine Streitschrift*") character of the enterprise: doing ethics always entails the enactment and rank ordering of moral judgment; it is never neutral spectation.[6] *On the Genealogy of Morals*, then, is Nietzsche's polemical presentation of his ideas on the origin (*Herkunft*) of our moral prejudices (*Vorurteile*) in the attempt to understand who we are, under what conditions our moral language and judgments were created, and what life or vitality or "value" they possess.

John Howard Yoder shares this approach to ethics as dramatic, historical, embodied and polemical, and is especially on the lookout for taken-for-granted moral assumptions that represent a danger to real life and human, cultural health.[7] Yet the drama Yoder engages is not Nietzsche's "Dionysian drama of 'The Destiny of the Soul'" (preface, 7), the *Untergang* of the heroic soul exploring and doing battle with its own spiritual sickness in order to rise to higher cultural heights. The rebirth Yoder envisions is found in the apocalyptic drama of the war of the Lamb depicted in the words of the seer of Patmos—the author and text most closely identified with spiritual sickness by Nietzsche, who calls it "the most wanton of all literary outbursts that vengefulness has on its conscience" (1.16). We might note the context of Nietzsche's polemical judgment is his description of the battle between Judea and Rome, a battle in which Yoder would seem to take precisely the opposite side—Judea against Rome. Obviously, then, Yoder does not interpret the battle in the same terms as does Nietzsche, and it is here that Yoder makes an important Anabaptist contribution to understanding healthy Christianity over against its sick moral and cultural forms. The diagnostic criteria for interpreting sickness and health are developed with reference to different dramas, differing visions of life and its meaning.

Nietzsche understands the spiritual sickness of nihilistic modernity to be rooted in the victory of Judea over ancient Roman virtue—"consider to whom one bows down in Rome itself today" (1.16). But this representation of the "priestly type" is for Yoder no spiritual victory; indeed such a victor can only be so identified by Roman criteria. The

---

5. Subsequent references to Nietzsche's *On the Genealogy of Morals* will appear in parentheses in the text, citing essay and section number.

6. In this regard Nietzsche's Calliclean frankness is much to be preferred over the Polus-like pretence of modesty exhibited by certain postmodern followers of Nietzsche such as Michel Foucault or Jacques Derrida, who appear at times to "stand nowhere."

7. I take Yoder's incisive critique of the typological method employed by H. Richard Niebuhr's *Christ and Culture* to expose precisely this set of issues. See Yoder, "How H. Richard Niebuhr Reasoned."

desire of the Christian church to rule the world by the sword of Caesar is an idolatrous temptation. When successfully enacted, it becomes tremendously destructive of the human spirit and of human community and culture. Nietzsche's portrayal of the battle is not historical enough or subtle enough in pursuing the problem "value for what" (1.17, note) of the Christian Gospel. If we are to understand the battle of postmodernity more objectively—that is, with a greater variety of perspectives in the service of understanding (3.12)—we will do well to consider Yoder's alternative genealogical account of morals.[8]

Yoder's task can be interpreted as taking a closer look at the evolution of Jewish and Christian moral conceptions in history. Who is the opponent in Yoder's polemical genealogy? Not altogether unlike Nietzsche's opponent—conventional modern moralism, indeed conventional mainstream *Christian* moralism, blind to its own poisonous assumptions. Especially its assumptions about power, responsibility, and the origin of good and evil. Like Nietzsche, Yoder will examine this history with new questions and new eyes so as to articulate a new "saving tale" (or at least a novel retelling and possibly a reenactment of an old story—not of Dionysius, but the crucified Christ) within the modern-postmodern context. And Yoder will do so in a manner that exposes the motives of conventional Christian moralists: pretending to be neutral and pious, they have really stacked the ethics deck by reading their distorted priestly concepts back into the Christian origins of morality.

The sickness here is a desire for worldly power that in the name of general concepts of "responsibility" and "justice" willfully blinds itself to the true spiritual source of power. Like Nietzsche, then, Yoder seeks a cure for modern (and postmodern) nihilism in which human beings have become mere passive *spectators* of their own inner life rather than vital and willing *actors* in the multivalent, polyglot, pluralistic historical drama of existence.[9] Modern moralism, the vision of the mainstream priestly types, is "shrunken"—lacking creative love and imagination, stuck in reactive rancor and the casuistry of retributive justice, focused on false divided worlds rather than attuned to the true power of life itself.

Yes, with all this Yoder could agree. And yet, he takes the opposite side in Nietzsche's "Rome versus Judea" and offers a very different narrative reading of the battle,

---

8. I realize that to use the term "genealogy" in regard to Yoder's work is potentially misleading, especially in light of the further development of Nietzsche's concept by postmodern "new Nietzscheans" such as Gilles Deleuze and Michel Foucault. See especially Deleuze, *Nietzsche and Philosophy*; and Foucault, "Nietzsche, Genealogy, History." Foucault's work in particular is taken as the genealogical model of moral inquiry by Alasdair MacIntyre in his published version of the Gifford Lectures, *Three Rival Versions of Moral Enquiry*. Of course, Foucault's reading of genealogy is greatly indebted to Nietzsche, but it is possible I think to argue that it is less serious, that its cheerfulness is less a "Dionysian drama" than a Menippean carnival (the parodic and farcical use of history is the primary mark of the genealogist in Foucault's treatment; see pp. 160ff. of Foucault, "Nietzsche, Genealogy, History"). In any case, the meaning of the genealogical approach to morals as I am using it is broader than is suggested in MacIntyre's typology and need not exclude the marks of tradition or the conditions for "answerability" in speech and action in community. Thus it is also possible, I think, to use genealogy *against* Nietzsche even while affirming aspects of his genealogical strategy.

9. See especially Yoder's critical reflections on "establishment" epistemology (rooted in the "Christendom assumption" that there is some "single publicly accessible system of validation and rationality") and his own proposal of what could be called "missionary perspectivism" in Yoder, "On Not Being Ashamed of the Gospel."

the illness, and the cure—with reference to a very different representative life, namely (to quote Nietzsche), "This Jesus of Nazareth, the incarnate gospel of love, this 'Redeemer' who brought blessedness and victory to the poor, the sick, and the sinners." (1.8). Of course, for Nietzsche this is precisely the sickness itself and can only be understood by him as yet another (deeper) form of *ressentiment* fueled by divine retributive justice. Here is an unreal and yet universal moralism that "de-natures" the strong and inverts the active, value-positing eye (1.10–11); it is a story that leads to world-weariness, hatred of humanity, *contemptus mundi*. Why? I believe John Milbank is correct when he suggests that it is because Nietzsche ultimately accepts the Roman story of heroic virtue[10] (evident in the aphorism from *Zarathustra* interpreted in essay 3 of *Genealogy of Morals*: "Unconcerned, mocking, violent—thus wisdom wants *us*: she is a woman and always loves only a warrior"). Here the *libido dominandi*, the violent will to power constitutes the essence (*wesen*, 2.12) of healthy human nature. Hence for Nietzsche, vengeful justice that destroys the noble soul and culture can only be self-overcome (*Selbstaufhebung*, 2.10; 3.27) by going beyond the dividing, paralyzing demands of the (reactive, moral) law. One must by sheer willpower struggle for clearer vision by warring against reactive feelings, training the eye to look outward creatively once again.

For Yoder, the way beyond the Law—by which the Law is fulfilled beyond the divided moralistic knowledge of good and evil, friend and enemy—is through the imitation of Christ, the wisdom of God and the power of God. The self-emptying motion of Christ (the *kenosis* of Phil 2) makes possible the life-enhancing expression of the overflowing fullness of divine love, which seeks not to escape embodied, worldly existence but to redeem it in all its diverse goodness. Hence the transcendent power of God does its work "from below" in embodied, particular, self-giving love.

Yoder's Counter-Narrative: Slave-Revolt in Morals?

The importance of apocalyptic symbolism and the slain Lamb in Yoder's work is well known.[11] The particularity of the church's identity is consistently tied by Yoder to this

---

10. See Milbank, *Theology and Social Theory*, chap. 10. While agreeing with Milbank's interpretation of the narrative source of Nietzshe's ethic as heroic virtue, I also agree with David Toole's insightful argument that (*pace* Milbank) Nietzsche is not a nihilist, but rather a philosopher of tragedy who seeks to overcome nihilism. See Toole, *Waiting for Godot in Sarajevo*, chaps. 3–4. Nevertheless, the kind of tragedy Nietzsche comes to affirm is precisely identified by Deleuze as the *heroic* expression of Dionysius "in which existence *justifies* all that it affirms, including suffering, instead of being itself justified by suffering" (*Nietzsche and Philosophy*, 18), i.e., one heroically and innocently affirms the chaotic, conflictual play of life forces without seeking some cosmic reconciliation or harmony that will redeem the suffering entailed in the violent clash of wills. See Deleuze, *Nietzsche and Philosophy*, chap. 1. This helps clarify the centrality of Nietzsche's statement of opposition—"Dionysius versus the crucified"—which Toole helpfully elaborates in his book as the decision "between the tragic affirmation of chance and the apocalyptic affirmation that what looks like chance is in fact the work of God." Toole, *Waiting for Godot in Sarajevo*, 206.

11. See, for example, Yoder's concluding chapter in *Politics of Jesus*, entitled "The War of the Lamb"; and Yoder, "To Serve Our God." See also Yoder's reflections on apocalypse in "Ethics and Eschatology"; and the illuminating discussion by Toole, *Waiting for Godot in Sarajevo*, chaps. 7 and 8, which draw upon Yoder to develop a metaphysics of apocalypse and an apocalyptic politics.

cosmic vision of God's sovereign rule in creation. The controversial claim that founds Christianity is that this divine cosmic rule made its definitive appearance on earth two millennia ago in the form of a humble servant with a very short public career during which he rejected virtually every available political option, only to be killed nevertheless as a political figure, and to found a new political community—the church—as the social carrier of that form of cosmic power and authority. For Yoder this means that the form of God's rule is here publicly revealed in the world for all to see, a form that is neither coercive nor juridical, neither externally imposed nor visibly triumphal—it is visibly characterized by the cross. It is as the slain Lamb that Christ is worshipped as king by the church in that vivid worship scene of the heavenly court described by John of Patmos, and this symbolism is laden with sociopolitical meaning and consequence.

The slain Lamb who alone is worthy to receive power is therefore the key to discerning the meaning of history and its ultimate direction. Indeed, this is the "good news" that constitutes the witness and mission of the Christian church on the earth. I cannot here represent the richness of Yoder's exegetical and historical ruminations in fleshing out his interpretation of this vision. I will focus on two significant foci in his work in order to link them critically to the Nietzschean postmodern problematic as I have sketched it above. The first is his more recent reference to the prophetic tradition as depicted in what he calls the "Jeremian shift"[12] to show that the political pattern practiced by Jesus was "no new beginning from scratch" but a renewal and extension of a "Hebrew hope" expressed from Moses through the Old Testament prophets.[13] The second is Yoder's critique of Christendom political ethics (whose heir is liberal Christian modernity), the various forms of which he habitually labels "Constantinianism." In these two representative symbols we will be able to trace Yoder's alternative to both modern and postmodern narrative visions.

The messianic Hebrew hope represented by Jesus is the constitution of a shalom community under the rule of God, a hope that by Jeremiah's time had been fatally betrayed by Israel's failed kingship experiment. Yoder clearly advocates the "antiroyal" account of the Deuteronomic historian, which retells Israel's story from within the paradigm shift to diaspora ethics clearly expressed in the book of Jeremiah—most pithily in Jeremiah's letter to the exiles in Babylon in Jeremiah 29:7, where he says, "Seek the peace of the city where I have scattered you . . . for in its peace you will find your peace." In his last book Yoder makes extensive reference to Stephan Zweig's *Jeremias*, a poetic retrieval of the diaspora paradigm of Jewish social life and identity, written during World War I. Like diaspora Jews, Christians are called to live out their identity in a condition of "cosmopolitan homelessness."[14] The Jeremian approach, which sees the scattering of the people and indeed their exile to Babylon (the paradigm of pagan political idolatry) as "mission," prefigures Christ's attitude to the Gentile world.

The mission of the church, argues Yoder, is precisely to witness to the flaws in Babel-like unity, rooted in coercive, centralized, sacral authority, the idolatrous politics of empire that substitutes human for divine kingship and that tries to take charge of

---

12. See especially Yoder, *For the Nations*, chaps. 2 and 3; Yoder, *Royal Priesthood*, 133.

13. Yoder, *For the Nations*, 141.

14. Ibid., 51.

human history via external conquest. The rule of divine love and harmony represents a very different pattern of ecumenicity: a pattern of creative diversity and dialogue, a community that welcomes outsiders and that understands leadership as servanthood. In the Jeremian shift this is represented by cultural linguistic plurality (diaspora culture is polyglot and on the move, not univocal and sovereign) and the creation of a synagogue rather than a temple culture (the focus is now on the interpretation of the story in ever-new cultural situations, not an altar that stands in cultic support of a sacral regime); it is the building of God's city and God's rule "from below."

This exilic movement takes Israel's exodus from "cosmological empire"[15] into the further recognition that spiritual existence under God can take different sociopolitical forms and is not to be identified with a particular spatio-temporal regime. What is at stake here is an understanding of how God's agency is experienced and at work to transform the world. The Jeremian shift represents a movement not only away from pragmatic kingship as the model of how shalom community is built; it is a movement toward the prophetic-eschatological recognition of a new covenant of the heart in which God's rule is universally established.[16] Diaspora ethics signal an end to "compact collectivism" toward a new understanding of participation in God's active rule, and this direction is definitively proclaimed by Christ who is the agent and embodiment of that rule.

And yet, says Yoder, this rule—while focused on the ultimate transformation of all things by divine action (the eschatological completion of history)—is active in embodied community here and now. For Christians the social forms of worship of God as sovereign will take a similar form to diaspora Judaism, but with particular reference to the imitation of the crucified Jesus as Messiah. The key to moral discernment will be to live out of the New Testament vision for community life established by Jesus. The focus here is not a structure of hierarchical authority or institutional establishment or doctrinal creed, but rather the sociological (i.e., visible, embodied) and liturgical (i.e., dramatic, particular, communally focused) "marks" of the community that believes Christ represents the cosmic rule of God.[17] For Christians the "body of Christ" is the social carrier of the mind of Christ, a polis that represents the rule of God for the nations.

Thus understood, God's action is decidedly not *hinterweltlich*, nor is God's rule ultimately construed in terms of juridical authority. Nor is its agent in the world represented as an "ascetic priest" filled with a reactive desire to rule over the unruly strong or to control history by moving it in the right direction. As Yoder's discussion of causality in the "War of the Lamb" chapter of *The Politics of Jesus* argues, the direction of history is precisely *not* under human control and the eschatological *telos* does not give us a managerial moral measure in a closed causal nexus. The cosmic causality revealed in the slain Lamb does not divide this world from some future or otherworldly ideal, however. Rather, it reveals the dramatic nature of causality in all reality to be the drama of divine

---

15. I borrow the term from Voegelin, *Order and History*, vol. 4, *The Ecumenic Age*.

16. Oliver O'Donovan develops this interpretation of the significance of the "Jeremian shift" in *Desire of the Nations*, 73–81. He states, "From that point on an element of confessional voluntarism enters into Israel's sense of itself" (79). I will return to this point below.

17. The marks of this body politic are spelled out by Yoder most clearly in his little book *Body Politics*. See also Yoder, *For the Nations*, chaps. 2 and 12; Yoder, *Priestly Kingdom*, chap. 1.

and human active, not reactive, love. This is the true natural life force that reveals the aristocratic warrior model to be the poison of life, fixated on power and using the gift of life to deny life. The slain Lamb exposes Nietzsche's strong, noble man to be the one engaged in "no-saying," in a "slave revolt" against the dramatic terms of worldly existence.

This becomes evident in Yoder's alternative account of "responsibility," where suffering love is not a strategy for success or an effective technique or tactic for getting one's way in an *essentially* violent or conflictual reality;[18] it is rather a matter of participation in life itself, the character of divine love. This character is embodied in the authority of Christ's *kenosis* and in the kenotic posture and "marks" of the body of Christ, in which differences are not obliterated in some stifling social straitjacket of homogeneous moral conventions. Rather, differences can be welcomed and given voice as community is built freely and creatively "from below." The kenotic posture of "consdescension" shows divine power taking the form of serving love. Such "slavery" can only be understood as liberation from the compulsive constraints of egoistic power.

Here Yoder's critique of Constantinian Christianity, modern liberalism, and postmodern pluralism begins to come into view.[19] Yoder will refuse the various kinds of metaphysical and moral dualisms that divide up the cosmos into a "visible" pragmatic realm of conventional "responsibility" where the power of violence and external calculi of justice prevail, and an "invisible" spiritual realm where "religious" love and self-denial rule. The spiritual "mind of Christ" and the material "body of Christ" cannot be so divided. The church cannot be understood as one limited social institution, somehow balanced by the different political and ethical roles of the state and other social institutions. For Yoder, Jesus's life is not only descriptive of how God's ultimate judgment reconciles sinful humanity in a heavenly peace; it is also descriptive of how that ultimate judgment is implemented provisionally in the earthly peace.[20] That is, Jesus's identity as cosmic ruler entails the very worldly enactment of the "Jeremian shift"—a non-sovereign, non-territorial self-definition.[21] Traditional or conventional royal ideology of whatever kind, insofar as it is linked to coercive external rule, has been eschatologically declared a failure even when it appears powerful and successful in the world.

For Yoder, then, the body of Christ is a voluntary community of shared discernment in which all are free to speak and act because all (in all their differences) are gifted and joined together in a new human identity—open in its life to creative divine agency. Such a community that practices forgiveness, love even (indeed especially) of enemies, and servant leadership models what *all* human communities are called to. It can *only* be sustained by the church's doxological identity, shaped by its worship of the God revealed in Christ;[22] it is not sustained by any established or conventional juridical power. Such

---

18. This is Nietzsche's claim in *On the Genealogy of Morals*: "*In itself*, of course, no injury, assault, exploitation, destruction can be 'unjust,' since life operates *essentially* . . . through injury, assault, exploitation, destruction and simply cannot be thought of at all without this character" (2.11; cf. 12).

19. See Yoder's account and critique of Constantinian and various "neo-Constantinian" positions in *Priestly Kingdom*, chap. 7.

20. See Yoder, *For the Nations*, 210ff.

21. Yoder, *Royal Priesthood*, 133ff.

22. See ibid., 109ff., 128ff.

a church must therefore by definition be "free" and not authorized or established by any state, since the "responsibility" it practices presupposes voluntary (inner and outer, visible and invisible) commitment to living out of its vision of divine kenotic, self-giving rule.[23]

It is not difficult to see how this vision stands in critical distinction from Constantinian or Christendom ethics. It should also be clear that this view of human freedom and responsibility in community under the rule of God is quite different from the abstract naked will of modern individualism and the political voluntarism of social contract theory. And yet Yoder's emphasis on voluntareity and the "free church" has recently been criticized in an important book on political theology by Oliver O'Donovan as being "neo-liberal," a freedom purchased at the expense of belief.[24] That is, Yoder's voluntareity is rooted in an intellectually flabby liberalism—or perhaps "postmodern liberalism"—that has lost confidence in truth claims and views all social doctrines as inherently coercive. However for Yoder, the social body politic is precisely not so, and precisely because of its believing vision. It is not in the business of enacting and enforcing judicial authority—it proceeds on a different paradigm of divine rule and justice. It will therefore not alter its processes of and criteria for moral discernment when rulers join the church,[25] nor "employ" instrumentalities of power foreign to its own identity and calling.

And yet, there is something to O'Donovan's charge, though it should be otherwise formulated. Yoder has not adequately attended to or clarified the complex relationships between soul and society, the action of God to transform the will and vision of Christians and the action of God to redeem all of creation. To understand the role of the church, the embodied mind of Christ, requires such noetic clarification. The great question here concerns how the eternal, spiritual, *invisible* wisdom of God is related to pragmatic political history and particular *visible* social communities (including the church). In Yoder's insistent and consistent desire to separate "cross" language from personal moral and "psychic" questions,[26] in order to focus on more general social issues (such as war

23. See ibid., 245ff., 265ff.; Yoder, *Priestly Kingdom*, 22ff.
24. See O'Donovan, *Desire of the Nations*, 221–24.
25. See Yoder, *Priestly Kingdom*, 82ff.
26. In his concern to distance himself from forms of unworldly or subjectivist "pietism" that neglect the worldly political claims of the Gospel (Yoder, *For the Nations*, 143, and *Royal Priesthood*, 131), Yoder has occasionally resorted to unnecessarily extreme formulations, such as the following: "The challenge to which the proclamation of Christ's rule over the rebellious world speaks a word of grace is not a problem within the self but a split within the cosmos" (Yoder, *Politics of Jesus*, 161). No less than "pietism" is such a formulation a distortion of the New Testament witness, where the faultline of sin runs through the cosmos, but also through the human self. A more adequate formulation is the following: "Let us posit as at least thinkable the alternate hypothesis that for Paul righteousness, either in God or in human beings, might more appropriately be conceived of as having cosmic or social dimensions. Such larger dimensions would not negate the personal character of the righteousness God imputes to those who believe; but by englobing the personal salvation in a fuller reality they would negate the individualism with which we understand such reconciliation" (*Politics of Jesus*, 215). The problem that remains here, I believe, is Yoder's (ironically liberal individualist) assumption that there is a "fuller reality" than the "personal" one. The point is rather to redefine what is personal in relation to its social and cosmic reality, in which our individual lives receive their fullest meaning and purpose. For my own attempt to do this in the context of Anabaptist theology, see chapter 5, above.

and peace) and political forms (the church meeting, patterns of conflict resolution, etc.), I believe he has lost sight of certain aspects of moral discernment that would allow for a better account of idolatrous "Roman" (or Constantinian) politics and how such temptations might be agonistically engaged also in the church and the academy.[27]

THE PLATONIC DIASPORA: ATHENS AND JERUSALEM

So far we have been discussing mostly politics and the church. Yet Yoder spent most of his career in the academy, and it also bears noting that "postmodernity" is largely an academic or at least intellectualist preoccupation. This is relevant because I think the academy, like the church, is an institution devoted to practices not to be identified with any particular earthly political regime or social or cultural community. It too was the creation of a diaspora movement, an exodus from the compact collectivism of the Greek city state prompted by an experience of revelation—a "noetic theophany" (as Eric Voegelin calls it[28]) in the Socratic soul. It is not accidental that Christians, like the Hellenistic Jews of antiquity, have appropriated the diaspora form of the academy—its language, practices, and disciplines. Platonic philosophy can help to clarify the problem of soul and society, the tension between the visible and invisible, in our attempt to formulate an adequate genealogy of Christian morality.

Here the Christian story will more explicitly engage Nietzsche's "Dionysian drama of the soul," but in terms that Nietzsche himself would reject. Plato is an enemy of postmodernism, even as Nietzsche viewed Socrates and Plato as the enemy, and for much the same reason that he so viewed Christ and the church. That is, Plato too understands the moral drama of soul and society in terms of a theocentric cosmology where the "Good beyond being" orders all reality toward its transcendent, harmonious, but also mysterious end. This is for Nietzsche the pernicious creation of the "inner man," the "soul" in which human beings declare war upon their instincts and thus their power—a creative act, says Nietzsche, that required the creation of divine spectators (*Genealogy of Morals*, 2.16). Such an act of self-violation, when carried too far (as in the case of Plato and Christianity, where the invisible divine world becomes the true reality that orders apparent reality) leads to a paralyzing denial of this-worldly power and reality—hostility to life and "ideals that slander the world" (2.24), of the sort depicted in John's Apocalypse. One's moral "answerability" (*Verantwortlichkeit*) becomes focused exclusively toward what is invisible and unreal.

---

27. For example, when Yoder says as he does in various places that society exists for the sake of the church—see especially his *Christian Witness to the State*, 12ff.—he leaves himself open to the most pernicious of Christendom triumphalist ideologies. The church, from my reading of the New Testament, rather exists (as did Christ) for the sake of God's service in the world. How we *formulate* this point is crucial, and a proper formulation will of necessity be more attentive to the tension between visible and invisible church than Yoder is. Otherwise it will fall into a new form of "compact collectivism" which is non-ecumenical and dogmatically closed. *Any* worldly institutional form is limited and partial, not the whole and not the fulfillment of human existence—even the most faithful of churches remains a partial and sinful witness.

28. See Voegelin, *Order and History*, vol. 4, *Ecumenic Age*, chap. 4.

That Nietzsche and many postmoderns object to here is the notion that there is a cosmic, all-embracing, reconciling truth beyond rhetorical particularity and worldly perspectivism. In regard to Plato's distinction between sophists (rhetoricians with no commitment to truth, only to the power of persuasion exercised in the power struggle of individual wills) and philosophers (who love divine wisdom and do not claim it as their own possession, but seek it through the education of desire, speech, and deed), Nietzschean postmoderns are self-confessed sophists. They reject the intellectual ordering of psyche and polis with reference to some transcendent Good known through the contemplative soul. Joyful Dionysian paganism rooted in orgiastic instinct and uninhibited aesthetic play must be recovered from the totalizing *Republic*-an rationality of sober Socrates.

For certain Jewish and Christian intellectuals this postmodern battle against (old, authoritarian, rationalist) Athens has paved the way for a return to liberating Jerusalem as the new philosophical city without foundations. Yoder has in certain ways aided and abetted such thinking, to the detriment of theological ethics. As Gillian Rose has argued, this postmodern move undermines the possibility for a critical, clarifying discussion of the ordered relationships between city, soul, and the sacred.[29] Yoder has tended to lump together the Platonic Christianity of classical theologians such as Augustine with Constantinian political theology in some unfortunate ways.[30] To call Augustine's city of God "otherworldly," representative of a personal pietistic Christianity that is content to leave the earthly city under the rule of empire politics,[31] can only be read as a deliberate distortion. Yoder is, after all, an historian seeking to overcome the historical blindness of moralists to the root causes of our cultural malaise. Is this perhaps an Anabaptist suspicion of intellectual power tied to establishment authorities? If so, I suppose one should be encouraged to see it so evident in an internationally eminent University of Notre Dame professor, as indeed it was evident also in that great Latin philosopher, Saint Augustine.

Unlike Yoder, however, Augustine did not allow that to prevent him from appropriating what he considered to be the great gifts and treasures of classical philosophy and employing them in the service of the peace of Christ. Here Augustine remains a powerful resource for a Christian ethics that seeks the whole truth of what it means to worship the cosmic Christ and so to realize peace. Christians, argued Augustine, have much in common with and much to learn from Platonic philosophy. Plato coined the term theology (*Republic*, bk. 2), and he transformed philosophy from a science of physical causality to the study of moral wisdom through the revelation of an invisible spiritual causality.[32] Of course Augustine also points out what he thinks is missing in the Platonists, a revela-

---

29. See Rose, *Judaism and Modernity*; and Rose, *Mourning Becomes the Law*.

30. Note, for example, Yoder's Anabaptist description of the "fall of the church" as located "at the point of that fusion of church and society of which Constantine was the architect, Eusebius the priest, Augustine the apologete, and the Crusades and Inquisition the culmination" (Yoder, *Royal Priesthood*, 89; cf. 154).

31. Yoder, *For the Nations*, 82.

32. Augustine, *City of God* 8.3; for the Socratic account of his experience in the search for a genealogy of morals, a more adequate account of spiritual causality and motivation, see the *Phaedo* 95–102.

tion of the perfect image of the invisible God, an image that would have surprised them by the form it took—a humble servant (though it is more complex than this). Insofar as Christians worship God through the image of the suffering servant, their moral logic will reflect this. The "royal road" of spiritual liberation in the world is humble service, and this road is given to all peoples as a mystery not conceived in any human soul or culture (Augustine, *City of God* 10.32). Augustine is helpful in clarifying the relations between the Jewish and Greek diasporas with reference to Christ.

Rather than pursue that discussion here, however, I will turn to a New Testament writer whose letters were foundational for Augustine, Menno Simons, and Yoder—Paul the Apostle.[33] In 1 Corinthians the Hellenistically educated rabbi Paul ties the noetic concerns of the Greeks and the messianic hopes of the Jews to the eschatological revelation of the wisdom and power of God in the crucified Jesus.

It is clear from reading Paul's letters that he does not consider himself to be a systematic theologian, the custodian of a timeless deposit of doctrine; nor is he a systematic philosopher. Rather, he is called to bear witness to a dramatic historical event: the incursion of divine wisdom and power into the world in order to cure it and restore it to health. This is what all Christians are called to be and do; Paul's first letter to the Corinthians is occasioned by their confusion over what this calling entails. They have been swayed by the eloquent and persuasive rhetoric of gnostic teachers, and this has divided them into ideological or intellectual camps headed by particular teachers. The quarrel concerns, precisely, who is the greatest *sophos*? Paul's message in 1 Corinthians is to deflate human pretensions with reference to the cross, the hidden wisdom and power "of God," which is contrasted to the human possession of wisdom and noetic power throughout chapter 1. God is the subject, not the object of Paul's teaching, and the cross of Christ as the visible embodiment of God's wisdom makes a fool of worldly human wisdom. When it is turned into but another form of worldly wisdom, then it makes God and God's wisdom but another human ideology, a self-justifying image, an idol—"*I* belong to Paul," or "*I* belong to Augustine," or "*I* belong to Yoder," or "*I* belong to Christ." At this point the worship of God has become the worship of a creature, a blinding and destructive form of life.

This is not, however (says Paul in chapter 2), to disparage wisdom. It is rather to suggest that divine wisdom is hidden and not to be found in rhetorical eloquence or persuasive speech. Among the mature (*hoi teleioi*) we can speak of this eschatological wisdom beyond visible human sight. The agent of this hidden power that reveals the hidden meaning of the cross is the divine Spirit "of God" and "from God." And it is here that Paul delineates and "rank orders" various types of human being, spiritually discerned. The created human being is a *psychikos*, a living, willing, feeling, thinking being who is nevertheless fallen into the divided state of the knowledge of good and evil, a self-sufficient and thoroughly blind egoist. Unredeemed *psychikoi* then are really better described as *sarkikoi*, people of flesh, insofar as they are pulled toward the immediate,

---

33. Let us not forget what Nietzsche said of him: "Paul was the greatest of all apostles of vengeance," the "dysangelist" whose lying invention of God and spiritual causality is rooted in resentful rebellion against reality, and masks Paul's real desire which is to rule the world. See *Antichrist*, sec. 42ff. Such a view of Paul is *au courant* in the fashionable Pauline scholarship of the postmodern liberal academy.

mortal, transitory realm of visible creation, the realm over which the human self has a measure of god-like knowledge, control, and power. Such human beings live according to the flesh by trying to construct their own meaning in the world, make their own mark, take their own measure independent of the divine and invisible source of life. Such a life is sinful not because it is embodied but because it cannot see and embrace the spiritual meaning of bodily life—it ends up in strife (political, intellectual, ecclesial, and indeed with itself, as Romans 7 shows), a strife that by its very nature *negates* what is good, the power to affirm and celebrate life. No innocence is possible here without complete self-deception.

By contrast Paul identifies the *pneumatikos*, the spiritually mature person who is oriented by the divine Spirit toward the invisible (hidden and mysterious) divine wisdom. Indeed the Spirit not only enables the inner apprehension of divine truth but provides the very language that makes conversation about it possible (1 Cor 2:13). Once again, this spiritual condition is not disembodied, just as the life of the flesh is not non-spiritual. But there is present a different kind of discernment about the meaning of bodily life, a different mind (*nous*), the *nous* of Christ. This inner mind makes judgments about the whole range of bodily life; the hidden wisdom of the cross of Christ relates as much to personal intimate questions of sexuality as to the questions about law courts and civil religion. Without the inner purification of the heart and mind, without proper spiritual orientation of mature *pneumatikoi*, the rule of Christ or the rule of Paul (as Yoder calls "binding and loosing" and the "open meeting," respectively) are subject to the same distortions as any other earthly, fleshly forms of rule. No visible form of any kind can guarantee the proper bodily enactment of the mind of Christ, since God's wisdom remains precisely hidden.

Furthermore, as Paul also argues in 1 Corinthians, no single person or group or perspective or charism can claim to *possess* knowledge of God's wisdom—it always remains a complete gift (8:2–3). In contrast to the "puffing up" of noetic insight, divine love "builds up" by taking the focus away from doctrine and rhetorical brilliance or dialectical ability and placing it on real other human beings. Love, which is the freedom to serve God and neighbor "from below," brings the other into my field of vision not as economic or intellectual competitor, not as ethnic or cultural or gendered "other," but as my sister or brother who represents Christ (8:12). To participate in this renewed field of vision requires a spiritual death, death to the idolatrous, falsely externalized symbols, creeds, and authorities that *prevent* communication and block the transforming work of the divine Spirit. This is the way out of the illness of *ressentiment*, petty quarreling, the paralysis of self-obsessed *gnosis*, the juridical model of righteousness. It is the way of serving love rooted in the gift of life itself, the power of cosmic love. This also represents the rebirth of dialogical community where consciousness or soul, the *inner* or *hidden* life of human beings, is not hermetically sealed within the individual skull of a "subject" but is found above all in the shared "mind of Christ." Here all perspectives are nurtured to build up the conscience of each and of all in *mutual* responsibility and service. This process is also abundantly *personal*—as one should expect in a cosmos created and sustained by a personal God whose rule is embodied in person: the slain servant.

With this, I trust, Yoder could finally agree—although, it seems, perhaps he did not.[34] We do not need a rhetorically brilliant postmodern theology or postmodern Christianity that "out-narrates" all rivals, which is, after all, another form of the Constantinian temptation. What we need are disciples of the slain Lamb who are prepared to follow in obedience in their daily lives—in their thoughts, speech, and deeds, without pretension, without boasting, without rancor. Such an ethic of conscience walks not by the external juridical sight of guilt and punishment but by faith, a faith that all created reality will be drawn up through death into eschatological completion, the "all in all" of divine love.

---

34. See the introduction.

9

Is a Messianic Political Ethic Possible?

Yoder Critically Considered

IN 1972, WRITING ON assignment from his position as associate director of the Institute of Mennonite Studies and president of the Associated Mennonite Biblical Seminaries in Goshen, Indiana, John Howard Yoder published his landmark monograph, *The Politics of Jesus*, posing the question, "Is a messianic sociopolitical ethic possible?" By doing so, and by providing an affirmative programmatic answer as one that is binding upon all who call themselves Christian (and, in effect, only upon those who do so), Yoder quite self-consciously placed himself into a provocative and radical dissenting position vis-à-vis the prevailing consensus of mainstream liberal and postliberal (Christian realist) Protestant social ethics. It was a challenge that did not go unnoticed. In a sentence that he might retrospectively have come to regret, James Gustafson, in the first volume of his *Ethics from a Theocentric Perspective*, stated his conviction "that all constructive theology in the Christian tradition needs to be defined to some extent in relation to this radical option"—by which Gustafson meant the challenging option of the "traditional radical Protestant view."[1] Gustafson himself devoted only a page and a half to this engagement, even though, as the "one most dramatically different from the option I shall pursue," it represented the "sharpest challenge" to his own position. For much of his career, Yoder served as a foil—representing a type of christomonistic sectarianism or politically naive pacifism or neoliberal free church voluntarism—rather than as a serious interlocutor warranting extensive engagement. To some extent Yoder himself bears responsibility for this, as much of his writing was occasional, prompted by the invitations of others to represent a radical dissenting opinion.[2]

This is, however, by no means the only or indeed the dominant story. When the second edition of Yoder's *Politics* came out in 1994 (by which time Yoder had for almost two decades been a professor at the University of Notre Dame), Stanley Hauerwas

---

1. Gustafson, *Ethics from a Theocentric Perspective*, 1:75.
2. See Yoder, *Priestly Kingdom*, introduction.

proclaimed, "I am convinced that when Christians look back on this century of theology in America, *The Politics of Jesus* will be seen as a new beginning"—a judgment recently seconded by Craig Carter in a fine systematic study of Yoder's theological social ethics, *The Politics of the Cross* (2001). Carter's book offers a sustained argument for the view that Yoder's work is best read not as an apologia for Mennonite pacifism or Anabaptist particularism but as the compelling normative articulation of the social-ethical implications of classical trinitarian and christological doctrine for the Christian church's witness in the postliberal, post-Christendom era that is now upon us. At the heart of Carter's argument is his thesis that Yoder's project unites important aspects of his Anabaptist heritage with the theological method (and "biblical realism") of Karl Barth to provide the most coherent, cogent, and classically orthodox alternative to Christian realism, liberation theology, and evangelicalism in current Christian social ethics. Hence the importance also of the posthumous publication of Yoder's *Preface to Theology: Christology and Theological Method* (2002), in which Yoder offers an account of the development of classical theology and his own brand of theological method.

There is yet another facet to the challenge unleashed in Yoder's project, and this has to do with his retrieval of Jewish messianism, not simply as a historical exploration of the apocalyptic setting of New Testament ethics but as a normative paradigm for understanding the social and political form of the church as the creation of a new community, made up of both Jews and Gentiles (and all manner of "others"). In the chapter of *The Politics of Jesus* entitled "Justification by Grace through Faith," Yoder cites Krister Stendahl and Markus Barth in arguing that Pauline language of "justification" has to do not only (or even primarily) with God's remission of guilt for the anguished conscience but primarily with the constitution of a new humanity "in Christ"—a new humanity in which hostility between peoples is also politically addressed and overcome through love of enemy. This early reference to a renewed Jewish-Christian dialogue about Christian origins signals a direction that Yoder pursued intensely in the final years of his life, the results of which are published in two volumes—*For the Nations* (1997), and the posthumous volume (with commentaries by Peter Ochs and Michael Cartwright) *The Jewish-Christian Schism Revisited* (2003). This direction has also been taken up critically in a number of recent publications.[3]

Barth and Biblical Realism

In *To Hear the Word* (2001), another of the growing number of posthumously published collections—this one having been collected by Yoder himself, before his death, under the title "How to Be Read by the Bible"—Yoder suggests that the most striking thing he noticed about critical responses to *Politics of Jesus* was the slight attention given to basic questions of textual interpretation. That is, criticisms of Yoder's book were seldom addressed to his literary or historical readings of the biblical texts—especially where his close readings of the texts called into question deeply believed axioms of Western

---

3. Hauerwas et al., *Wisdom of the Cross*; Harink, *Paul among the Postliberals*; Ollenburger and Koontz, *A Mind Patient and Untamed*.

Protestant culture.[4] The resulting irony is that Yoder was often the one characterized as having a "programmatic" reading of the Bible, when what he saw himself doing was simply allowing the political meaning of the New Testament claim that "Jesus as the Messiah is Lord" to be brought into focus for social ethics. It was the programmatic exclusion of this meaning from Christian ethics by, for example, Reinhold Niebuhr and Paul Ramsey, who set aside the authority of Jesus in favor of other sources and criteria of moral guidance for political thought, that Yoder sought to question. To assert the political authority of Christ, suggested Yoder, is by no means "sectarian." To the contrary, it is to raise and test the truth question implicit in New Testament christological claims that the crucified and resurrected Jesus is the cosmic Lord over all creation, whose lordship is expressed in the world by followers who imitate his kenotic "revolutionary subordination"—not only individually or "in their hearts," but visibly and socially as well. If this claim is true, it must be true not only for first-century Christians but also for twentieth- and twenty-first-century Christians, and it will be as communicable and as scandalous today as it was to the Jewish and Gentile communities of Jesus's day.

Yoder's messianic biblical realism, in other words, sets off the same apocalyptic charge detonated by Barth in the context of twentieth-century German cultural Protestantism and by Paul in what Jacob Taubes has provocatively called the "*nomos* consensus" of first-century Hellenistic Judaism.[5] Paul's apostolic calling as a prophet of the crucified Jewish Messiah to the Gentile nations required him to articulate a political sovereignty that radically called into question the sovereignty of Rome (and of ethnic Israel) and proclaimed the founding of a new people who would not recognize traditional boundaries of insiders and outsiders, friends and enemies, pure and impure. So also, claims Yoder in his 1988 Presidential Address to the Society of Christian Ethics,[6] the calling of the messianic ethicist is to be vigilant in upholding the authoritative speech and logic of the slain Lamb. This crucified Messiah even now exercises real, living cosmic sovereignty, a rule displayed not in the exercise of juridical authority or state power but in the pattern of life displayed in the slain Lamb and imitated in the community of disciples that follow him, identified by Paul as the "messianic body" or "body of Christ."

This apocalyptic christological paradigm has a number of characteristic social marks: binding and loosing as the messianic pattern of discernment, forgiveness, and reconciliation; the eucharistic pattern of table fellowship and economic sharing, rooted in the liturgical and celebratory receiving of life as divine gift; baptism as the initiation into a new humanity of inter-ethnic ecumenicity; the fullness of the messianic body in which no "I" stands alone but all are gifted and require the full participation of each gift; and the open meeting in which the freedom of speech is found through the shared discernment of what the divine spirit may be saying.[7] While this fivefold pattern of the messianic body politic should be explicitly displayed in the *ekklēsia*, the community called out in obedience to messianic authority, it is not limited to Christians. All people are to be invited into the messianic polis and to understand the meaning of their shared life

4. Yoder, *To Hear the Word*, 9.
5. Taubes, *Political Theology of Paul*, 23–24.
6. Yoder, "To Serve Our God."
7. Yoder, *Body Politics*.

in terms of its distinctive patterns, since the calling of the people of God is no different from the calling of all humanity. Hence Yoder can also trace analogies of the marks of the Christian community in the wider, non-confessional world.[8] For example, binding and loosing may be displayed in a non-confessional society as conflict resolution and mediation, eucharistic community as the sharing of goods and reinterpretation of power and rank, and so on. This is a lesson, Yoder indicates, that he learned from Barth.[9] Indeed this precisely is the mission of the messianic community:

> The challenge to the faith community should not be to dilute or filter or translate its witness, so that the "public" community can handle it without believing [in Jesus's cosmic sovereignty], but so to purify and clarify and exemplify it that the world can perceive it to be good news without having to learn a foreign language.[10]

The scandal of the messianic paradigm, therefore, is not its closed "insider" information or special privileged status, but precisely those visible authoritative characteristics of the crucified Messiah's sovereignty that always have and will continue to scandalize wise and responsible humanists, both inside and outside the church, who appeal to other models of responsibility. These scandal markers include the renunciation of domination in favor of servanthood, the pacifist love of enemies which breaks down closed identities, and the practice of forgiveness rather than retributive justice as the path to social reconciliation and harmony.[11]

These comments support Carter's argument, in *The Politics of the Cross*, that Yoder's biblical realism is Barthian but not "Yale school." That is, it is not tied to an epistemological or methodological theory about the Bible and Christian doctrine as a sociolinguistic "grammar." Rather, Yoder proceeds exegetically, seeking to expound the social ethical implications that follow if the biblical account of the sovereign agency of God revealed in the Messiah Jesus is true and indeed authoritative. In an interesting essay, Scott Davis (himself a non-believing Aristotelian) defends Yoder's messianic realism (against other putative Christian realisms), making the important observation that Yoder's biblical realism "is tied closely to what we might call the logic of lordship."[12] He points out that while one may think about lordship in terms of the law, and therefore about divine sovereignty in juridical terms of retributive justice, such notions of lordship and sovereignty are broken in Herbert Fingarette's reading of Job and Yoder's reading of Paul.

---

8. Sometimes Yoder also calls these "middle axioms": "These concepts will translate into meaningful and concrete terms the general relevance of the lordship of Christ for a given social ethical issue. They mediate between the general principles of Christological ethics and the concrete problems of political application. . . . Social-ethical thought has in the past tended to sway between a relativism that challenges the existence of any standards beyond the good intention of the person making a decision and a natural law concept which supposes that we can know clearly a pattern of ideal order which it is our assignment to impose on our society. The conception of middle axioms avoids these alternatives. It permits meaningful communication of a significant Christian social critique without involving extended speculation about the metaphysical value of the principles appealed to" (Yoder, *Christian Witness*, 32–33).

9. Yoder, *For the Nations*, 23–24.

10. Ibid., 24.

11. Ibid., 47–48.

12. Davis, "Tradition and Truth in Christian Ethics," 299.

PART 2: POLITICAL THEOLOGY AND THE RADICAL REFORMATION

The penitential, messianic logic of lordship evident in Yoder's biblical realism challenges other moral and political realisms. Davis helpfully enucleates the important relationship between lordship and realism for Yoder that also sets the agenda for this review essay. The binding nature of Jesus's call to discipleship is related not to the power of his moral example or teaching, nor to his "God-consciousness," but rather to the claim that in him the character of divine sovereignty is decisively disclosed as a sovereignty that dispossesses all other claims to power, wisdom, and goodness. There is here no appeal to a "public reason" or a "comprehensive doctrine" or theory of justice that grounds an ethic. Indeed there is here an active unveiling that dispossesses such human appeals of their prideful and often violent claims to universality and dominion—not by outdoing them, or even out-narrating them, but by refusing to exercise rule on those terms. This reading is in keeping with the kenotic posture of Jesus's messianic lordship in which the world is reconciled one particular, embodied act of serving, suffering love at a time.

If this is so, however, then it also calls into question Carter's description of Yoder's work as an "application" of Barth's theology to social ethics. Carter's point is to counter critics such as James Reimer, who argues that Yoder's historicist approach is incompatible with the theological orthodoxy of patristic Christianity, which grounds ethics in metaphysical-ontological affirmations about Christ. Carter's close reading of Yoder's relation to creedal orthodoxy, facilitated through the posthumous publication of Yoder's *Preface to Theology*, advances the discussion, particularly in the context of current debates about historical narrative and natural theology. Yoder, like Barth, is historicist but not relativist when it comes to Christology. He clearly affirms Nicene and Chalcedonian formulations. And Yoder, like Barth, rejects all appeals to a natural theology not in keeping with christological authority. While not himself a systematic theologian à la Barth, Yoder was, Carter argues, applying Barth's theology to social ethics in a coherent but necessarily occasional manner—through contextual ecumenical dialogue about particular ethical questions and issues rather than by developing an architectonic account.

However, it could be argued that the very success of Carter's systematic portrayal of Yoder's thought is a betrayal of Yoder's christological vision of diaspora ethics—a vision that in this regard may stand in contrast to Barth's systematic *Church Dogmatics* and therefore can hardly be depicted as an application of Barth's theology to social ethics.[13] Carter's criticism that Yoder, like Anabaptists in general, never wrote a systematics and therefore left himself open to misunderstanding and caricature, is finally a Constantinian criticism. It seeks to establish conceptual control within the theological domain. Insofar as systematic theology may be depicted as a "blood sport" of sorts, Yoder preferred to suffer harm in occasional contextual dialogue rather than to cause it. In this regard, it may be that Yoder is more of an Anabaptist than a Barthian, and this is a crucial point theologically, methodologically, ethically, and politically. The theological enactment of

---

13. Though here one would have to contend with the Yale school, and most recently the important account offered by Hauerwas in *With the Grain of the Universe*, chap. 7, insisting that Barth did not understand himself as a "systematic theologian" but rather as a "narrative theologian," retelling the Christian story in contemporary speech as an ongoing act of conceptual redescription of reality in the language of the church. If this is true, then Yoder could be (as indeed Hauerwas argues) simply doing what Barth was doing in his *Church Dogmatics* in a more occasional manner. Even this, however, could not simply be described as an "application" of Barth's theology.

the incarnation for Yoder is an ecclesial, dialogical, kenotic practice that lets go of the desire to control the reception and critical success of one's ideas (though it must be noted that Yoder did not always practice such "letting go" himself). This is not to say that it is anti-intellectual or incoherent. To the contrary, it proceeds on the conviction that understanding, like faith, hope, and love, is a matter of non-coercive servanthood that is built up in the ongoing historical drama, not doctrine, of God's sovereign governance—which is why the interpretation of Scripture and history in order to enact this governance, and not the building up of systems, is the central theological task of the church. Divine governance is best displayed not in architectonic systems or narrative "savanthood" but in the cross-bearing, fine-grained diaspora servanthood of the messianic body.

Yoder and Post-Constantinian, Augustinian Theology

In order to assess Yoder's contribution and its future directions, it is important to consider the two major posthumous publications of Yoder's work, *Preface to Theology* and *The Jewish-Christian Schism Revisited*, and critical responses to them. These books are helpfully examined together, in that in both of them Yoder develops his constructive theological account of the political and ethical implications of Jesus's messianic lordship with constant reference to the contrast between historical-Hebraic and philosophical-Hellenistic thinking. Within this broader context, Yoder builds up his heuristic contrast between the biblical trajectory of diaspora messianism (culminating in the politics of Jesus) and various forms of the "Constantinian temptation." It is not always clear how these at times descriptive, at other times normative, contrasts map onto one another in Yoder's own accounts. James Reimer argues that Yoder's suspicion of metaphysical-ontological thought in favor of historical-ethical categories is itself the product of post-Enlightenment historicism and therefore tends to reduce theology to ethics, indeed, to political ethics.[14] Yoder too uncritically reads modern ethical historicism as being in harmony with the "Hebraic view" of biblical Christianity, while the reputedly static, hierarchical metaphysics of Hellenistic and creedal Christianity are depicted as compatible with the trend toward the Christian empire politics of Constantinianism—where divine sovereignty becomes visible in an established church supporting the power structure of a dominant empire. Not only is such a reading tendentiously modern, argues Reimer; Yoder's preference for the prophetic-apocalyptic trajectory of the Jewish-Christian tradition that authorizes diaspora messianism over the priestly sacramental trajectory is too selective.[15] It compromises the "biblical realism" of Yoder's political theology in its ability to appreciate or appropriate important resources (a) in the Old Testament, especially Torah and legal covenant traditions; and (b) in the post-Constantinian church and Hellenistic Christianity, which Yoder tends to demonize. To put Reimer's critique another way, Yoder in these regards is not living up to his own vision of the Christian ethicist (articulated in his Society for Christian Ethics Presidential Address) as the scribal agent of communal memory, "selecting from a too-full treasury what just happens to fit the

---

14. Reimer, *Mennonites and Classical Theology*, 253–54, 168–69.
15. Reimer, "'I came not to abolish the law.'"

next question."¹⁶ He is rather rendering normative one limited historical ethical strand within the Jewish and Christian narratives that authorizes free-church pacifism but that cannot envision other important and necessary types of civic engagement and institutional forms.

There is a certain irony in the fact that Reimer's critique of Yoder comes not from the Protestant mainstream but in this case from a fellow Mennonite theologian who is interested in retrieving the classical ontological tradition for contemporary theological ethics so as to preclude the reduction of theological reflection to ecclesial moralizing. Reimer argues for a more honest Anabaptist theology of law and civil institutions that is both more attentive to the classical Christian tradition and more attuned to the range of social and political ethics in the Jewish story, both biblical and extra-biblical.¹⁷ A related criticism of Yoder's Anabaptist tendency to define Constantinianism as the most basic problem for Christian social ethics comes from another Anabaptist interpreter, Gerald Schlabach. Yoder's heuristic construal of the problem not only misrepresents the complexities of this period in church history.¹⁸ More importantly, it tends "to concentrate our ethical reflection on the effort to avoid evil and unfaithfulness—rather than the challenge of embracing the good in a faithful manner," and it was the good, after all, that provided the occasion of temptation in the first place.¹⁹ The more basic problem, Schlabach argues, is defined by the Deuteronomist's challenge as "the problem of how to receive and celebrate the blessing, the *shalom*, the good, or the land that God desires to give, yet to do so without defensively and violently hoarding God's blessing."²⁰ Defining the problem this way enables one to discern that the Christendom vision is itself a vision of *shalom* in which the right ordering of relationships in relation to God is the aim, thus providing an even stronger challenge than Yoder can to those aspects of historic Christendom that grasp prematurely, through faithless violence, the gift that God offers fully only eschatologically.²¹

This enables Schlabach to develop in his most recent essay the claim that Yoder may be read as an interlocutor in the Augustinian tradition, providing a pacifist ecclesial social ethic in answer to Augustine's definitive question: How are we to seek the peace of the earthly city without eroding loyalty to the heavenly one?²² Schlabach's argument is that Augustine and Yoder share a common eschatological realism—not a static ontology, but a messianic ethic rooted in a providential ordering of history and a theology of creation that is discerned christologically. While Yoder's elaboration of an ecclesial social ethic specifies more clearly the normative material implications of Augustine's own messianic realism in a creative politics for the pilgrim city that "uses" well the peace

---

16. Yoder, *Royal Priesthood*, 139–40.

17. Reimer, "'I came not to abolish the law,'" 252.

18. See also the following essays in Ollenburger and Koontz, *A Mind Patient and Untamed*: Thomas Heilke, "Yoder's Idea of Constantinianism," 89–125; and J. Alexander Sider, "Constantinianism before and after Nicea," 126–44.

19. Schlabach, "Deuteronomic or Constantinian?," 450.

20. Ibid. 451, cf. 454.

21. Ibid., 456.

22. See Schlabach, "Christian Witness in the Earthly City."

of the earthly city, Augustine's more robust theology of creation prevents Yoder's useful "mediating axioms" from devolving into liberal pragmatic compromises of the voluntarist sort. That is, in Augustine's view, "mediating axioms" that truly reflect the divine ordering of love, and therefore contribute to the *ordinata concordia* of peaceable earthly communities, must have some kind of "metaphysical" status beyond the value projections of human wills. Otherwise they would not be "useful." I will return to this dialogue between Yoder and Augustine opened up by Schlabach's unconventional and provocative essay below. First, with the above critical considerations in mind, let us consider Yoder's account of the relations between biblical and classical theology in the Christian tradition more carefully.

As we have seen, the heart of Christian theology according to Yoder is Christology, and its task—and the test of its development—is messianic discipleship. *Preface to Theology: Christology and Theological Method* was published first in 2002, though the mimeographed lectures on which it is based date back to the early 1960s and were regularly updated through 1981, when Yoder was teaching the course for Mennonite seminarians. The introduction, penned in 1981, suggests that the usefulness of these lectures lies "in the inductive portrayal of how theological discourse proceeds within the life of the church."[23] By inductive Yoder means "historically descriptive" of the development of central christological claims in early Christian communities, as the church sought to interpret and communicate that to which it was called to bear embodied witness. Since Christology is intelligible only in the context of Israel and the wider biblical narrative, Yoder begins neither with contemporary nor with classical theology but with the New Testament texts and their appeals to the Hebrew scriptures and the "received tradition" in order to account for the meaning of the messianic event.

Especially important for the New Testament witness, argues Yoder, is the "logic of solidarity" depicted by the early hymn in Philippians 2 (utterly central in Yoder's Christology) as the *kenosis* of Christ. This is to be interpreted not in terms of metaphysical humiliation (though Yoder will speak of divine condescension) but primarily in terms of the reversal of prideful Adamic grasping after godlikeness. It is this reversal—taking the form of the servant in humble obedience to death on a cross—that leads to the Messiah Jesus being exalted to cosmic lordship. Yoder thus points to the unity of condescension (as the mode of God's being in loving self-emptying) and exaltation (of the humble and obedient, crucified servant) as the pattern—the logic of solidarity—between God and humankind. The pattern reveals both the divine disposition of loving sovereignty and the proper human disposition as the sharing in and imitation of Jesus's humble obedience. At the center of this logic is the cross—the stance in the world that most truly participates in the messianic divine-human pattern of reconciliation that liberates human beings from bondage to the fallen "powers" (ordered by domination) so as to participate in God's new creation (ordered by "revolutionary subordination").[24] This new creation is

---

23. Yoder, *Preface to Theology*, 33.

24. See ibid., 105. This cruciform logic, so central to Yoder's political theology, is most clearly spelled out in chap. 8 ("Christ and Power") and chap. 9 ("Revolutionary Subordination") of *The Politics of Jesus*. Yoder's position (heavily indebted to a little book by Hendrik Berkhof, *Christ and the Powers*, which Yoder first translated into English in 1962) is that Jesus breaks the sovereignty of the fallen "principalities and powers" that bind human existence in slavery to self-glorifying and pretentious codes, customs,

pivotal for Yoder—not as a figure of speech but as a cosmic claim that must hold true on every level. It cannot be delimited by appeals to causal "necessity" that contradict this transformative messianic logic.

From the Pauline texts, Yoder moves to further intensifications of the logic of solidarity in the Christologies of Hebrews and John. The early church sought to express the meaning of the messianic event not only for themselves but also for others, and not only to other Jews already formed by the Hebrew scriptures and its categories of intelligibility (such as the priestly and sacrificial tradition) but also to the Gentiles of the pagan world. The traditions and language of the pagans are centered in "ontology,"[25] speculatively concerned about the origins of things, related ultimately to the reality underlying the appearances. In Yoder's view, New Testament christological affirmations regarding pre-existence and creation are not designed to deliver new speculative information; they are rather ways of expressing messianic priority over all cosmologies, including that found in the biblical narratives.

The process of theological growth and revision takes place in early Christianity through discriminating discernment. Not just a matter of translation or deductive elaboration, it is shaped by critical and creative responses to religious and sociopolitical challenges in the wider culture. Furthermore, "high Christology" expressing the cosmic lordship of Jesus as Messiah is present from the beginning (it is not a Hellenistic innovation). And it expresses, above all, the normativity of Jesus. The movement in the earliest stages is also toward, not away from, historicity, as the gospels seek to clarify and represent "the concrete human content of the faith in Jesus of whom the most exalted things were already being said."[26] In considering the development of postapostolic theology, the same sort of process is at work. Dealing with challenges as they arose, the apostolic fathers did not try to represent everything,[27] and again Christology was at the center of reflection. The burden of Yoder's interpretation of developments leading to Nicea and Chalcedon is to show that a high Christology entails a strong emphasis on the normativity of the historical Jesus, while lower Christologies (such as the Arians formulated) tended toward cultural and political alliances with the Roman empire/emperor in order to gain greater sociopolitical respectability and "influence."[28]

---

institutions, values, and theories that govern by the threat and fear of death. Jesus lives in a manner that is free from this threat, which leads to his crucifixion. By freely accepting this death, he exposes the destructive dominion of these powers, and his resurrection reveals that these powers are not ultimate—they are thus disarmed. The church is to herald this same freedom: "What can be called the 'otherness of the church' is an attitude rooted in strength and not in weakness. It consists in being a herald of liberation and not a community of slaves. It is not a detour or a waiting period, looking forward to better days which one hopes might come a few centuries later; it was rather a victory when the church rejected the temptations of Zealot and Maccabean patriotism and Herodian collaboration. The church accepted as a gift being the 'new humanity' created by the cross and not by the sword." Yoder, *Politics of Jesus*, 148–49. This new humanity exhibits the pattern of freedom for service in the world, the creative transformation of social relations by living according to an alternative structure of sovereignty.

25. Yoder, *Preface to Theology*, 130.

26. Ibid., 140.

27. Ibid., 153.

28. Ibid., 199. Yoder further states, "If you lower your concept of Christ, then you can raise your vision of the emperor because the *Logos* was in both Jesus and the emperor. . . . If Jesus is a little smaller, the

Despite these hermeneutical efforts, it must be said that Yoder's account of the Hellenistic traditions—Platonic and neo-Platonic Christianity in particular—is generally superficial and unsympathetic. This leads him to make rather sweeping statements about the contrast between the "Hebraic historic" and the "Greek onto-philosophic," and to represent the latter generally in negative terms. While he allows that Nicean trinitarian language of Father, Son, and Spirit is the way to communicate that God is "love" in the language of ontology,[29] he believes the form moves us further away from Gospel narrative and its dynamic eschatological realism. So also the subject matter moves away from focusing on the resurrection and exaltation of the *crucified* Jesus to debate about the eternal status of the resurrected and exalted one. Chalcedon for its part sought to affirm the full humanity of Jesus in the face of Monophysite deification and the theological challenges unleashed in the Nicean affirmations. As in the case of Nicea, the Chalcedonian creed was not a work of exegetical theology trying to understand the way different statements about Jesus might cohere. Rather, it was trying to define and address a problem arising from the encounter between different linguistic and cultural worlds. Yoder takes the Anabaptist position on the creeds, then—accepting them as part of the tradition and history of the church but not as having any final authority.[30] That is, Yoder will not allow that the ontological and metaphysical categories of the creedal tradition have the kind of definitional authority possessed by the biblical narratives.

The creeds of classical Christianity may not set the dogmatic terms for systematic theology in our own time, for two reasons. One is that the intellectual challenges and questions faced by Christians of another time and culture may well take different forms, and that to appeal to dogmatic formulations of the Greco-Roman world as the solution is to fall into a kind of Gnosticism (ironically, since Gnosticism was the primary adversary of early Christianity), which makes a speculative cosmology with its insider language and systematic structure the measure of "belonging" or orthodoxy.[31] High Christology, which affirms the priority of Jesus as Lord over all systems of speculation, is an anti-gnostic approach. It also requires Christians to articulate the normative meaning of Christ within the terms of the challenges, questions, and languages of the cultures and times in which they live—a normative meaning displayed above all in the biblical texts. The second reason for not granting the creedal tradition definitional authority, then, is that it tends to turn attention away from the embodied historical narrative context in which the normative meaning of Christ is both displayed and worked out. This normative meaning is above all an ecclesial process and practice that ignores the historical character of revelation and its implications for imitative discipleship to its peril.

---

king will be a little higher, and that is just what Constantine and his advisors wanted." On the other hand, Yoder suggests that the practical political realities were not so clear (which would seem to contradict the above claim): "But it must mean something to us that the Arians and the Nestorians—each in their own age—were less nationalistic, less politically bound to the Roman Empire, more capable of criticizing the emperor, more vital in missionary growth, more ethical, and more biblicist than the so-called orthodox churches of the Empire. At the most, these creeds fruitfully define the nature of the problem with which we are struggling. They are helpful as a fence, but not as a faith" (223).

29. Ibid., 202.
30. Ibid., 222–23.
31. Ibid., 258; cf. 275.

PART 2: POLITICAL THEOLOGY AND THE RADICAL REFORMATION

Yet this historical hermeneutic is precisely what Yoder himself neither practices nor recognizes with regard to Augustine and the post-Constantinian Christendom era of Western Christianity. Augustine's theological corpus is nothing if not exegetical and historical, though of course, it is also true that Augustine freely appropriates the "gold and silver and clothing" of the pagan philosophers (and especially the Platonists) in order to put to use those resources in the service of the *caritas* of the messianic body.[32] In doing so, however, Augustine simply practices the hermeneutical approach advocated also by Yoder in his depiction of "diaspora ethics," namely that like exilic and diaspora Jews, Christians are called to live out their identity in a condition of "cosmopolitan homelessness."[33] Like Yoder, Augustine in *City of God* articulates the mission of the "people of God" as a pilgrim people with an appeal to the prophetic word of Jeremiah 29:7 to the people being taken into exile: "He bade them, by divine command, to go obediently into Babylon, thereby serving God even by their patient endurance; and he himself admonished them to pray for Babylon, because 'in its peace is your peace,' the temporal peace shared for the time being by good and wicked alike."[34] Such an appeal does not hold up the virtues of the Babylonians or the Romans for their own sake or ascribe to them some independent religious or moral status, but rather uses them in the service of another end (the end of true peace) by referring them to the ultimate messianic peace of God. Insofar as the virtues (or any other useful conceptual or cultural categories) are treated as being self-sufficient possessions without reference to the ultimate Good who bestows them as gifts, they become vices that undermine temporal peace. This is no less true for people in the church than it is for people in the pagan world. It is for this reason that the "prayer of the whole City of God during its pilgrimage on earth . . . cries out to God with the voice of all its members: 'Forgive us our trespasses, as we forgive those who trespass against us'" (19.27; cf. 22.23).

This penitential vision of the people of God as humble servants rather than self-sufficient dominators certainly seems compatible with Yoder's ecclesial and political vision as well. Yet the context of Augustine's discussion in *City of God* begins to point up certain differences between himself and Yoder. That is, Augustine is clear in 19.27 that "true righteousness [*iustitia*] insofar as it is directed towards a good end, consists in this life more [or 'rather,' *potius*] in the remission of sin than in the perfection of virtue." The reason for this, Augustine goes on to explain, is that true peace or full peace [*plena pax*] is unattainable in this life—it is a peace anticipated by faith that provides a "solace for our wretchedness" rather than [*potius*] the "joy of blessedness." Until our fallen mortal nature is healed in that final eschatological peace by the divine gift of immortality and incorruption, "peace" in the earthly sense will continue to be mocked by the highly ambiguous "necessities" essential to governing and restraining the vices. Augustine adverts to a favored text in Job 7:1 (Septuagint), "Is not human life upon earth a temptation?" This mortal life, in other words, is a penal life full of anxiety and the agonistic struggle between virtue and vice (cf. 21.14–15).

---

32. Augustine, *Teaching Christianity* 2.40–42.

33. Yoder, *Jewish-Christian Schism*, 183–84; *For the Nations*, 51–52; *Royal Priesthood*, 133.

34. Augustine, *City of God* 19.26. Subsequent references to *City of God* will be will appear in parentheses in the text.

We see here a moral tone quite different from Yoder's emphasis on the "new creation" initiated by the messianic event. Yoder shares with Augustine a seminal cosmology in which divine providence, active in the humble causality of *caritas*, ultimately vanquishes the violent and punitive necessities of fate—leading both Yoder and Augustine to appeal to the exemplars of martyrdom rather than warrior heroes as most in keeping with divine causality. (Augustine too asserts that the blood of the martyrs works as seed with the messianic grain of the cosmos; 22.7.) And yet in Augustine's account of the social life, these tragic necessities continue to necessitate corporal household punishment, judicial torture, war, and other tragic duties that befall the Christian *sapientes* seeking to use responsibly the peace of the earthly city (19.5–6).

Gerald Schlabach valiantly argues that Augustine's purpose in these passages is about descriptive indictment, not normative guidance: "It is one of Augustine's many and characteristic endeavors to drive his readers to despair precisely in order that they like he will look elsewhere for hope, recognize their need for God and cry out for deliverance."[35] This is true, and yet it seems no less true that for Augustine, the ordered *concordia* of the earthly city requires evil necessities (especially of the corporeal and punitive sort) even of those whose leadership is motivated by loving duty rather than a lust for mastery (19.14–15). This is part of the punitive servitude of the fallen order to which even pilgrim Christians, "alien citizens" of the earthly city, belong and whose peace they must "of necessity" use (19.17). Yoder will refuse precisely such "necessity" language in his depiction of messianic ethics.

At the end of his life, Yoder was also working on the question of punishment (another of his numerous desktop publications of unfinished fragments is entitled "You Have It Coming: Good Punishment. The Legitimate Social Function of Punitive Behavior").[36] As in other places where he discusses this question, he acknowledges with New Testament authors (in Rom 13 and 1 Pet 2, for example) that modes of retributive justice have their place both politically and domestically. Christians therefore ought to be willingly subordinate to such disciplinary structures—not out of fear or spiritual subservience, but out of obedience to an even higher and precedent order rooted in divine gift, or grace. Thus Christians will not revolt against authority even when they are unjustly punished, or indeed punished for doing what is right. The point is that Christians will not return evil for evil, and while they are voluntarily subordinate to structures of retributive justice, they do not themselves live by such necessities. They live rather by reconciling forgiveness, the measure of justice revealed in Christ, which breaks the reciprocal cycle of offense, violence, and counterviolence. To do otherwise is to fail to "refer" earthly peace properly to its ultimate origin and end in God.

Here, of course, it is precisely an exegetical and theological engagement that may open up fruitfully between Yoder and Augustine, rather than the terse caricatured dismissals of Augustine—his Platonism and his "Constantinianism"—that one tends to get in Yoder. Were we to follow this exegetical engagement further in terms of messianic political theology, we might discover many shared *topoi* with mutually illuminating points of contrast. For example, Augustine understands the diversity of languages in the Babel

---

35. Schlabach, "Christian Witness in the Earthly City," 225.
36. Now published as pt. 5 of Yoder, *End of Sacrifice*.

story of Genesis 11 to be the result of God's punishment imposed upon human pride that seeks to build up a monolithic city against God's sovereignty (16.4).[37] The confusion of communication that results is precisely characteristic of Babylon itself, the epitome of hubristic human empire that stands against God's purposes. The punishment, claims Augustine, fits the crime: "Because the power of a ruler lies in his tongue, it was there that Nimrod's pride was condemned, so that he who refused to understand and obey God's bidding was himself not understood when he gave his bidding to men." To scatter the proud in the imagination of their hearts is the punitive but pleasing consequence of divine judgment, and it shows precisely that punishment need not be separated from what is good—which is how Yoder construes the "punishment" interpretation of Babel.[38]

Yet the punitive aspects of diversity, laments Augustine, remain with us, as the diversity of tongues continues to divide people from one another. Our differences divide and render human association and communication perilously difficult (19.7). Such punishing differences lead to ever-new imperial political impositions of one language "as a bond of peace and society" and of social cooperation for the sake of shared goods that nevertheless come at tremendous human cost of violence and bloodshed. Such imposed unities are necessary, claims Augustine, but also miserable. Of course citizens of the heavenly city on pilgrimage as exiles in the earthly city subordinate themselves to such necessities, but they do not themselves impose them. So ten chapters later in *City of God*, Augustine has this to say:

> Therefore, for as long as this Heavenly City is a pilgrim on earth, she calls out citizens of all nations and all languages, and brings together a society of pilgrims without concern for differences in the customs, laws, and institutions by which earthly peace is achieved or maintained. She does not rescind or destroy these things, however. For whatever differences there are among the various nations, these all tend towards the same end of earthly peace. Thus, she preserves and follows them, provided only that they do not impede the religion by which we are taught that the one supreme and true god is to be worshipped. (19.17)

---

37. So also does Oliver O'Donovan follow this Augustinian reading of the Tower of Babel: "The story of the Tower of Babel saw plurality as a necessary restraint, a curb on evil to which unity had given free reign" (O'Donovan, *Common Objects of Love*, 40). For O'Donovan and Augustine, then, plurality is a social problem to be solved ("redeemed") through disciplined self-restraint (since the real problem is the sin of idolatry, not the created fact of difference). It is not itself "good news" (as Yoder has it). Therefore, it is interesting that O'Donovan's christological grounding for "self-restraint, a patience that is prepared not to grasp" after social redemption prematurely (ibid., 41) is Christ's creedal status—very God and very man—as the "double representative" around whom the universal society (without particular identity) comes into being, in a negative, ascetic sense (44). For Yoder, of course, it is quite otherwise: "The ordinariness of the humanness of Jesus is the warrant for the generalizability of his reconciliation. The non-territorial particularity of his Jewishness defends us against selling out to *any* wider world's claim to be really wider, or to be self-validating. . . . The particularity of incarnation *is* the universality of the good. There is no road but the low road. The truth has come to our side of the ditch. . . . The real issue is not whether Jesus can make sense in a world far from Galilee, but whether—when he meets us in our world, as he does in fact—we want to follow him (Yoder, *Priestly Kingdom*, 62). Thus different normative meanings regarding the relations between particularity/plurality and universality/reconciliation flow from different (christologically informed) interpretations of the Babel story.

38. Yoder, *For the Nations*, 61–62; Yoder, *Jewish-Christian Schism*, 188–89.

Is a Messianic Political Ethic Possible?

While Augustine does not advocate externally imposed unities as a solution to the punitive aspects of diversity—indeed he believes such impositions often contribute to greater misery and punishment—he does not minimize the challenges of multiplicity and difference for earthly peace. The secular is precisely this ambiguous context in which earthly peace is in the process of being judged as well as transformed through referral to the ultimate peace of the heavenly city. This ambiguity is present in non-Christians and Christians alike, though Christians are to deal with it through penitential prayer and humble serving love, not the imposition of unambiguous monolinguistic regimes of political conformism so characteristic of human empires. The city of God on pilgrimage, says Augustine, speaks the truth of God by humble penitents in all languages (18.49); the kingdom militant is the church governed by martyrs who witness to the truth through death, not killing (20.9–10; 22.6–7).

While Yoder agrees with Augustine about this, and indeed offers a more extensive account of how the church witnesses to a different ethical vision of peace in the messianic "form of the servant," he seems less willing to concede the ambiguity and the punitive character of diversity and the continuing struggle for earthly peace for Christians. That is, he displays greater confidence in the agency of the church to maintain a visible messianic witness in the earthly city without attention to those internal conflicts generated by temptations of visibility (visible virtue, visible goodness, visible "results") that so plagued Augustine's ecclesial awareness. For Augustine, the fact that the net of the visible church comprises both the elect and the reprobate, who swim together without separation (18.49), would be true whether or not that church baptizes infants in a "state church" or baptizes adults in a "believers' church." Yoder's principle of voluntariety has too sanguine a vision of the human will and its ongoing conflicts with fallen desires. This debate between sinful necessity and the freedom of the will and its implications for messianic political ethics is important, not only for secular politics but also for the understanding of Christian moral agency and the penitential self-understanding of the church.

A second *topos* of exegetical engagement between Yoder and Augustine concerns their respective accounts of biblical political theology, and here too the similarities and the differences are important. In *Preface to Theology*, Yoder organizes his "systematic treatment of christological themes" (the second, constructive half of the book) around the Protestant "threefold office" of Christ as prophet, priest, and king—the marks of Israel's sociopolitical life in the Old Testament, all of which are related to the Messiah. Yoder relates each of these offices to classical theological *topoi*: king to eschatology, priest to atonement, and prophet to revelation. Not surprisingly, and in Barthian fashion, he begins with eschatology and the most explicit claim to Christ's royal sovereignty. In the Hebrew scripture, the king is the ambivalent expression and personification of Israel's identity—ambivalent because true kingship is reserved for YHWH alone.

In other writings, notably in *For the Nations* and *The Jewish-Christian Schism Revisited*, Yoder subordinates the kingship tradition to the Jeremian prophetic and diaspora tradition. This latter tradition becomes normative in the face of the "failed kingship experiment" of ancient Israel.[39] What Yoder argues here is not that the Davidic project

---

39. Yoder, *Jewish-Christian Schism*, 70–71, 187–88.

is restored in Jesus, but that Jesus "renewed the definition of kingship to fit with the priesthood and prophecy. He saw that the suffering servant is king as much as he is priest and prophet. The cross is neither foolish nor weak, but natural."[40] Eschatological kingship represents God's people in the suffering servant, as the one who will restore Israel to her true identity. And not only Israel but also the whole created order, insofar as the suffering messianic king fulfills the original creative intent of God and thus expresses the nature of divine sovereignty in the world.[41]

If this is so, then obedience is possible for those who live according to the "new creation" made present in the kingship of Christ. These exalted axioms lead Yoder to the following claim: "The fact that God extends Christ's reign in a hidden way through the powers [who in their violent rebellion reveal their defeat] and in a visible way through the servant church is the reason for history. This is why time goes on."[42] That is, the church moves history by the servanthood that participates in the divine messianic sovereignty, which transforms the world toward *shalom* through suffering love. From this it follows, argues Yoder, that eschatology cannot be understood in Platonic terms of immortality or timeless fulfillment, as Augustine envisioned it.[43] The biblical God is not atemporal but "hypertemporal," whose temporal dynamism is in radical excess of our own mortal historicity. Creation and providence require this and cannot be interpreted from within the framework of an ontological contrast between temporal bodies and eternal souls. It is the apocalyptic claim that a crucified criminal is cosmic lord, that the cross represents the causal movement of creation toward God's peace that ought to scandalize human beings, not the rupture of certain metaphysical or ontological categories.

Here again we see Yoder setting up a normative political, theological, and ethical contrast between biblical eschatology and Platonic ontology, with Augustine serving as the representative (without extensive analysis) of the Hellenist deformations of post-Constantinian Christianity. This is evident also in *The Jewish-Christian Schism Revisited*, where the "Augustinian" is portrayed as follows:

> In the Augustinian framework, finitude and sin tend to coincide. Faithfulness or "perfection" is an "ideal." The visible, the historical, participates by definition in the fallen state of all creation. Full obedience is by definition impossible, on grounds not of a wrong decision or rebellion but of ontology. No human being, no visible community, can be faithful to the will of God within a fallen history.[44]

Furthermore, claims Yoder, Augustine's contrast between the two cities is not a biblical eschatological contrast between the just and peaceable rule of God and the idolatrous rule of human sovereignty, but rather a neo-Platonic ontological one between the ideal heavenly realm of transcendent eternity and the finite sinful realm of temporal social life.[45] This shift from the Jewishness of early Christianity to the Hellenism of the Ro-

---

40. Yoder, *For the Nations*, 212; cf. Yoder, *Preface to Theology*, 243–44.
41. Yoder, *Preface to Theology*, 246.
42. Ibid., 248.
43. Ibid., 249, 266, 276.
44. Yoder, *Jewish-Christian Schism*, 122.
45. Ibid., 160.

Is a Messianic Political Ethic Possible?

man empire leads to a metaphysical and moral dualism between eternal messianic ideals impossible to realize on earth and earthly necessities imposed by the responsibilities of temporal power.

Augustine's biblical political theology of the two cities in the second half of *City of God*, however, diverges significantly from Yoder's caricatured account. His account of the two cities in books 15–18 in their historical development is, in fact, rooted in the apocalyptic Pauline anthropology of flesh and spirit and the two Adams typology, related to the two covenants represented allegorically/typologically by Sarah and Hagar. It is a complex, structured exegetical paradigm that is best understood not Platonically but eschatologically.[46] This means that the allegorical types may not be "spiritualized" as ciphers for speculation but ought rather to be "analogized" in a logic of spiritual-corporeal participation in the ordering of loves, delineated in book 14, that are worked out in history—in the *saeculum* "in which the dying accede to the newly-born who succeed them" (15.1). It is here that Israel's political theology becomes significant for Augustine. It is an alternative history to that of *pax Romana*, founded as it was on the fratricide of Remus by Romulus in a power struggle over temporal goods, a characteristic of the violent self-division (*adversus se ipsam*, 15.4–5; cf. 18.2) of desire in the earthly city. Israel's history may be interpreted with reference to another fratricide that symbolizes a different kind of struggle—the murder of Abel by Cain, rooted in "diabolical envy," in the desire to possess privately and selfishly the good that may only be enjoyed when shared with others in the concord of love.[47]

This is a struggle between the city of God and the earthly city over the true (spiritual and political) meaning of justice and peace. The humble referral of all loves to the shared goodness given by God is characteristic of those who imitate their *rex optimus*, Christ (17.16). This messianic kingship is prophetically revealed as the preeminent priest king according to the order of Melchizedek (17.17), whose name literally means "my king is righteous," the first priest king of Salem, the city of peace that becomes Jerusalem (Gen 14:17–18; Ps 110; Heb 5). The other city, of course, presided over by the "father of lies," is symbolized by Babylon, meaning "confusion," rooted in the self-division and warfare introduced by pride and envy. If the exemplars of the earthly city that orders its loves according to the flesh are warriors, the exemplars of the city of God on pilgrimage in the world are martyrs, in imitation of Abel-Christ. The martyrs become intelligible as exemplars only prophetically, by faith—as in the case of that *vir optimus et fortissimus* Saint Paul, who gloried in his weakness, was crucified with Christ, was made a spectacle (*City of God* 14.9), and yet as an exemplary embodiment of the messianic form of the servant shows us the standard of human justice (*Trinity* 8.9–10). It is a standard that is discerned only through the eye of the soul formed already by the imitation of divine love; it cannot be reduced to an external moral exemplarism. This is why, when Augustine reflects on the exemplarity of Davidic kingship in *City of God* 18.20, it is not to note David's great warrior exploits or nation-building but rather his penitential

---

46. See van Oort, *Jerusalem and Babylon*; Kamlah, *Christentum und Geschichtlichkeit*. See also chapter 3, above.

47. *Superbia* and *invidia* go together in *diabolus*, the exemplar of the vices of pride and envy; see *City of God* 14.3, 15.5; *Trinity* 12.15.

humility in seeking the forgiveness of sins. Indeed the Davidic kingship is not central to Augustine's exegetical political theology except insofar as it discloses (through the Psalms especially) the messianic hope, symbolized in the figure behind the city David renamed Jerusalem (the possession of no tribe) after making it the capital—namely the priest-king Melchizedek. Davidic kingship is prophetic insofar as it points penitentially beyond itself toward apocalyptic royal messianism. This is not a process of transhistorical idealism to be spiritually realized only in transcendent eternity; it is a process that is worked out historically via those who imitate the embodied form of the servant that radically refers all virtue to God's goodness. In all of these ways, then, it may be fruitful to explore further the suggestive intersections between the biblical political messianisms of Augustine and Yoder.

Jewish and Christian Political Messianism

In his final years, Yoder's exploration of the social embodiment of Jesus's messianic vision and practice led him to a critical reconception of the standard account of the Jewish-Christian schism.[48] The standard account, Yoder claims, is too reified and cannot adequately represent the true reality, either historiographically or theologically.[49] It is rooted in conceptions of normative Judaism and normative Christianity that render them mutually exclusive religions, but only by overlooking the actual historical and theological diversity in both traditions and in their interactions. Revisiting the standard account critically and recovering the diversity, Yoder believes, might open up a more engaging dialogue regarding Jewish and Christian identities and ethics in a post-Christendom, post-Holocaust context.

The assumption that there was a homogeneous rabbinic Judaism centered in Palestine from which Paul decisively broke away in order to found a new normative religion, patterned after Jesus's rejection of normative Judaism, is questionable on several accounts. Yoder argues that Paul did not found another religion but rather defined one more stream within Jewry that could only be intelligible within the background

---

48. Yoder, *Jewish-Christian Schism*.

49. It is beyond the scope of this essay and my competence to evaluate the historiographic account. However, recent scholarship seems to support Yoder's critical assessment of the "standard account" or "master narrative" of Jewish-Christian schism—see now especially Becker and Reed, *Ways That Never Parted*, 2–3: "Contrary to the 'Parting' model, our sources suggest that developments in both traditions continued to be shaped by contacts between Jews and Christians, as well as by their shared cultural contexts. Even after the second century, the boundaries between 'Jewish' and 'Christian' identities often remained less than clear, consistent with the ambiguities in the definition of both 'Jew' and 'Christian.' . . . Accordingly, a growing number of scholars have begun to challenge the 'Parting' model, citing its methodological paucity, its inadequacy as a historical account, and its inability to explain much of our primary evidence. Spurning the simplicity of the notion of a single, early, and decisive separation between the two religions, many have turned to explore now approaches for understanding the relationship(s) between Jews and Christians in the centuries after their purported 'Parting.' . . . Rather than approaching Judaism and Christianity as monolithic entities that partook in a single act of separation, we here attempt to illuminate the broad range of regional and cultural variation in the encounters between different biblically based religious groups—including Jews and Christians, but also those so-called 'Jewish Christians' and 'Judaizers' who so strain the dichotomous definitions of modern scholarship."

of Jewish messianism and defined in relation to Jewish mission to the Gentiles. The Pauline understanding of messianic mission, furthermore, was not new, nor was it "founded" by Jesus. The notion of diaspora (*galuth*) as mission is present in Jeremiah and in Babylonian Jewry long before Paul, and is itself rooted in an interpretation of the Jewish Scriptures and the meaning of Abrahamic identity and peoplehood to which Jesus's messianism is closely tied. What changed in Paul, then, was not his "religion" but his belief that in Jesus the messianic age and the eschatological ingathering of the Gentiles had begun. The exclusivist lines between early Christian messianism and rabbinic Judaism were not rigidly drawn until the Gentile cultural political establishment designated "Christendom" defined itself over against Judaism from the fourth century on.[50] In Yoder's view, this entailed as much a distorted reification of Jesus and Pauline messianism as it did of Judaism. Judaism as such never rejected Jesus or Paul—there could be disagreement about messianic claims and biblical interpretation within the tradition itself—and Christian messianism need not have become anti-Jewish. Given the breakdown of the Christendom establishment, Yoder is interested in revisiting the question of the messianic once again as an open question to be taken up by Jews and Christians together in dialogue: "The spectrum of differences *within* each of the faith communities is now broader than the distance between their centers; the terrain of their overlap may again become substantial."[51]

Yoder of course brings his own normative agenda to this dialogue, arguing that the essential trajectory of Jeremian "diaspora Judaism" leads directly to the missionary messianism of Jesus the Jewish pacifist and Paul his great Judaizing apostle to the Gentiles. This calls into question the "standard account" of the Jewish-Christian schism at the level of ethics, which Yoder characterizes as follows: "the Jews" rejected Jesus's messianic claims because they sought an earthly kingdom whereas Jesus offered a spiritual kingdom; Jesus's pacifism is not only a rejection of Old Testament holy war and violent retributive justice but also represents an interiorized dispositional ethic of love in contrast to an external legal covenant. According to Yoder, however, the Judaism of Jesus's time was shaped by the Jeremian notion of peoplehood identity that had abandoned kingship and nationalist sovereignty for diaspora community, military action for trust in divine providence, and a purely external legal covenant for a voluntarist covenant of the heart. This prepares the way for Yoder's characterization of both the "mental structure" and the sociological markers of Jewish pacifism and diaspora ethics,[52] a depiction that highlights the parallels not only with Yoder's description of early Christianity but also with radical "free church" Protestantism and the "peace churches."[53] In effect, then, the

50. In this regard, too, Yoder's account is confirmed in recent historical scholarship. See Becker and Reed, *Ways That Never Parted*, 22–23: "Even with regard to the Roman Empire, a strong case has been made that the fourth century CE is a far more plausible candidate for a decisive turning point than any date in the earlier period. It is, however, perhaps less profitable to debate the exact date of the 'Parting' than to question our adherence to a model that prompts us to search for a single turning point that ushered in a global change for all varieties of Judaism and Christianity, in all communities and locales." For Yoder, Constantinianism is precisely such a global model—setting the religious terms so as to establish generalized ethical and political control over the relevant categories.

51. Yoder, *Jewish-Christian Schism*, 62.

52. Ibid., 82–83, and 170–71, 187.

53. See ibid., chaps. 4–6. Yoder's claim is stated concisely as follows: "Judaism within Christendom

PART 2: POLITICAL THEOLOGY AND THE RADICAL REFORMATION

ethics and theo-politics of Jesus and of pacifist diaspora Judaism are much more closely related to one another than to the ethics and theo-politics either of the Davidic kingship or of post-Constantinian Christendom. It was in the process of becoming non-Jewish that Christianity also became non-pacifist, and correlatively, modern forms of statist Zionism are indebted more to Christendom than to Jewish theo-politics.[54]

Yoder's account of Christian-Jewish messianism is intended as a provocation to further dialogue. It is therefore appropriate that the posthumously published *Jewish-Christian Schism Revisited* contains helpful commentaries by the coeditors: postliberal Jewish scholar Peter Ochs, and one of Yoder's foremost Christian interpreters, Michael Cartwright. Both are critical of what they consider to be residual supersessionist tendencies in Yoder's work. While deeply appreciative of Yoder's alternative to the "standard account," Ochs argues that Yoder's diaspora pacifist portrayal of exilic Judaism is an overstatement or reification in the service of a "doctrinaire pacifism" that excludes other normative possibilities and features of diaspora and rabbinic Judaism. Hence Yoder is not only overly restrictive in his dualistic depiction of theo-political options within Judaism, but he unfairly dismisses other options as not essentially or authentically Jewish insofar as they fail to conform to the pacifist messianism of early Christianity—or indeed of the Anabaptist restitutionist vision of such an ethic. In his response to Yoder's compelling reading of Stephan Zweig's *Jeremias* (composed during World War I), Ochs suggests:

> The sad, tragic prophet Jeremiah dominates Yoder's book in the end. . . . For both Zweig and Yoder, chapter 29 of Jeremiah's prophecy offers a scriptural warrant for their desires to join the fate of the people Israel directly to the universal goal of redeeming humanity and, thereby, to avoid the embarrassment, burden, and unreasonable complexity of Israel's landedness. For both Zweig and Yoder, there is no middle between Israel's exilic separation from the land and the Maccabean strategy for remaining in it: that is, between an ancient foreshadowing of modern nationalist sovereignty in that land and Israel's forced separation from it in this world.[55]

Such a dichotomous modern and tragic logic may have defined Jewish life in late-modern Europe, but its unmediated tension does not fit post-Shoah Judaism, which must bring together both exilic and landed life into an emerging new theo-political relation. Here, argues Ochs, Yoder's paradigm remains unhelpful and burdensome.

Michael Cartwright further calls into question Yoder's binary logic, in which his master narrative of Jeremian-messianic *galuth* becomes normative as the model of Jewish-Christian faithfulness, and landed monarchial Israel, narrated in terms of pagan kingship and Constantinian establishment, the model of unfaithfulness. Not only does

---

since Constantine has the *shape* which historians later call 'radical reformation' or 'peace church.' Jews expect and accept minority status. They deny ultimate loyalty to any local nation or regime, which is what war presupposes, while they provisionally accept its administration. They look on past and present righteous violence and religious nationalism, including that of their own ancient history, as mistaken. . . . In sum: for over a millennium the Jews of the diaspora were the closest thing to the ethic of Jesus existing on any significant scale anywhere in Christendom" (81–82).

54. Ibid., 72, and 106–7.

55. Ochs, in Yoder, *Jewish-Christian Schism*, 203.

this overlook the "pluriform character" of covenant peoplehood both in the Hebrew Bible and in postexilic and postbiblical Judaism more generally, it also constructs a moral history of peoplehood that privileges Christian messianism as the normative essence of the Jewish-Christian dialogue.[56] Furthermore, it is a moral narrative centered upon the reductionist hermeneutics of obedience articulated in the pacifist vision of the Anabaptist tradition. The result, ironically, is a non-dialogical and ultimately non-peaceable narrative that "*erases* the covenantal basis of Jewish peoplehood even as it attempts to *redescribe* Jewish identity within the framework of the 'new covenant' of Jesus."[57] At the heart of this covenantal basis of peoplehood lies the vexed question of the "election" of Israel—an issue taken up centrally if controversially by Paul in Romans 9–11 but ignored by Yoder in favor of a moral history more attuned to the question of human faithfulness than to divine agency. Here Cartwright is indebted to the critique of Yoder developed in Douglas Harink's book *Paul among the Postliberals*,[58] which argues that Yoder loses sight of Paul's Jewish apocalypticism by focusing on the moral and voluntary character of diaspora Judaism as a way of life, rather than on a people that receives its covenant identity as a divinely given gift, even in exile.

Harink's argument is not that Yoder's messianic ethics is not Pauline. To the contrary, Harink argues that Yoder's *Politics of Jesus*, more than half of which is devoted to interpreting Paul, incorporated and anticipated some of the most important developments in recent Pauline scholarship, especially as concerns the political and the ethical implications of Paul's apocalyptic messianism.[59] This is extended, Harink suggests, in Yoder's Pauline articulation of the *ekklēsia* as a "body politics,"[60] the social form that "justification by faith" takes in the world, characterized above all by a reconciliation between Jews and Gentiles in the messianic community. In these ways, Yoder's work has provided a compelling and coherent rendition of Paul's political theology and its implications for contemporary ethics.

The problem with Yoder's account of Judaism, argues Harink, is that it is not Pauline enough. That is, unlike Paul in his letters, Yoder seeks to provide a moral history of Judaism that focuses more on the question on Jewish faithfulness or unfaithfulness than on God's action.[61] Paul's position is clear that a messianic theology and an "adequate ecclesiology must give priority to election over ethics, the faithfulness of God over the faithfulness of Jews and Gentiles."[62] By contrast, Yoder tends to focus on Jewishness as a "way of life," a chosen set of ideas and practices. Harink's critique of Yoder returns us to the question of voluntarism. Paul's insistence that "God's election of a specific, non-substitutable, fleshly historical people"[63] is replaced in Yoder by a notion of Abrahamic peoplehood that relativizes the historical and ethnic embodiment of the people of Israel

---

56. Cartwright, in Yoder, *Jewish-Christian Schism*, 228.
57. Ibid., 229.
58. Harink, *Paul among the Postliberals*, chap. 4.
59. Ibid., 106; cf. Hays, *Moral Vision of the New Testament*, 245–46.
60. Yoder, *Body Politics*.
61. Harink, *Paul among the Postliberals*, 201–2; and Harink, "The Anabaptist and the Apostle."
62. Harink, *Paul among the Postliberals*, 203.
63. Ibid., 202.

for a messianic diaspora identity rooted in a faith and a path of faithfulness that must be freely chosen. Cartwright expands on this same critical point, suggesting that Yoder redescribes the covenant with Israel in supersessionist terms:

> The notion of fulfillment that he puts forward . . . which he imaged as a *"permanently open border between what came before and what came next,"* conveys the strong sense of "voluntariness" that he ascribes to Jews and Christians alike. At the same time, *the way Yoder deploys the term* "fulfilment" (in opposition to abolition of the law) also functions to delimit the identity of authentic or "true" Judaism. Simultaneously, then, Yoder is opening "the border" between Christianity and Judaism even as he *relocates* the center of identity for Jews (in effect redescribing membership in synagogues as "voluntary") in a way that frames the conversation as "messianic" by definition.[64]

Whatever else one might want to say critically about Yoder's depiction of Paul as "Judaizer" of the Gentiles (or about his "binary logic" of hermeneutical judgment regarding the measure of obedience-disobedience or faithfulness-unfaithfulness), surely it is passing strange to suggest that in "framing" the conversation in terms of the messianic he is himself being unfaithful to Paul! And yet it would seem that Yoder himself paved the way for precisely this kind of interpretation.

In *The Politics of Jesus*, Yoder argues that Paul's messianic theology has to do not with a contrast between justification by faith and justification by law, but (here following Markus Barth) with the more basic question of the social form of the covenant people of God—was it to include the Gentiles or not, and would the Gentiles first have to become Torah-keeping Jews or not? Yoder answers: "What was at stake in the 'proclamation of the righteousness of God to both Jew and Gentile' was precisely that it was to be proclaimed to both and that both were to become parts of the new believing community, *some having come by way of the law and some not*."[65] The primary meaning of Paul's language of justification and reconciliation, then, has to do with the extension of neighbor love to enemies, breaking down the hostilities that divide through the renunciation of violence, and the enactment of a new messianic covenant, the "new law" of Jesus's Sermon on the Mount which is indeed nothing but an interpretation concerning the fulfillment of the Jewish law itself in its *halakhic* and *aggadic* unity.[66]

Without entering into the debate about the "new perspective" on Paul and the "Lutheran" Paul that pertains to these matters,[67] let me instead conclude with reference to another posthumously published work, the very interesting *Political Theology of Paul* (2004) by the Jewish philosopher Jacob Taubes. Like Cartwright and Harink, Taubes—whose study revolves around an interpretation of Romans 8–11—argues that for Paul, God's founding election of a people is of central importance to his political theology, which is fundamentally Jewish even while being messianic. Like Yoder, Taubes suggests that Paul understands himself to be called as a Jeremian prophet to the nations. This

---

64. Cartwright, in Yoder, *Jewish-Christian Schism*, 228.
65. Yoder, *Politics of Jesus*, 217; my emphasis.
66. Yoder, *Jewish-Christian Schism*, 140.

67. For the landmark account of this debate in Pauline scholarship, which is in many ways pertinent to this discussion, see now Westerholm, *Perspectives Old and New*.

Is a Messianic Political Ethic Possible?

calling is rooted in the revelation of Jesus enthroned as Messiah, who therefore poses a political challenge both to the empire sovereignty of Rome and to the "*nomos* consensus" of Hellenistic Judaism. However, and this is for Taubes a point of key importance, what is at stake in this messianic revelation is nothing less than *pas/pan*: "all, every, the whole," including the election of "all Israel."[68] It is here that Paul's messianic transvaluation of values carries its most intense political charge, as it calls into question any and all reliance upon *nomos*, whether Mosaic or Roman, Jewish or Greek:

> It isn't *nomos* but rather the one who was nailed to the cross by *nomos* who is the imperator! . . . This transvaluation turns Jewish-Roman-Hellenistic upper-class theology on its head, the whole mishmash of Hellenism. Sure, Paul is also universal, but by virtue of the "eye of the needle" of the crucified one. . . . So it's a universalism, but one that signifies the election of Israel. Only that Israel is now being transfigured, and then in the end it says *pas Israel*.[69]

For Paul, the messianic establishment of the people of God cannot be understood in terms of blood kinship, but in terms of the kinship of promise—a promise now revealed in the Messiah whom the people have rejected, condemned according to the law.

A new founding of the people of God is occurring here and Taubes shows, through a comparative reading of Romans 8–9, Exodus 32–34, and Berakhot 32a, that the central issue is the peoples' redemption from sin, atonement. Here the Paul-Moses typology comes into view. Paul, argues Taubes, is "outbidding Moses" by suggesting that in Messiah the inner meaning of the Law is realized in a manner that establishes a new people of God made up of both Jews and Gentiles. This is done, of course, not via ethics (a new ethics) but via "spirit"—"*pneuma* as a force that transforms a people and that transforms the text."[70] This is why Paul in Romans 9–11 proceeds with constant reference to the Torah and focuses above all on the question of election, with particular reference to the Abrahamic covenant of promise that precedes circumcision. The Gentiles, who are not Israel according to the flesh, may be elected to the peoplehood of Israel via the spirit and by faith in Messiah who hangs condemned on the cross. This does not mean, however, that for Paul there are two valid paths—the Law for Jews and Messiah for Gentiles. No, according to Taubes's Paul, the Messianic covenant enacts atonement for all—but only by way of a remnant, the remnant of faith. That is, justification by faith in Messiah is indeed the central question.

It is precisely at this point, states Taubes, that the central importance of enemy-love for Paul's political theology comes into view. "As regards the gospel," Paul says in Romans, "they [non-Messianic Jews] are enemies [of God; not in the Greek text], *for your sake*" (Rom 11:28). There is nothing moralistic here. The point is that enemy-love is not only characteristic of God (in every direction breaking enmity down), but must be characteristic also of human political community. The sovereign Messiah, by suffering death, bears witness to the breakdown of every human claim to self-sufficient autonomy. It is God who elects a people for the purpose of redeeming all. There is no ground in Messiah for anyone, Jew or Gentile, slave or free, to make a claim to represent divine election and

---

68. Taubes, *Political Theology of Paul*, 1, 10, 25, 47, passim.
69. Ibid., 24–25.
70. Ibid., 45.

purpose in anything other than the martyrdom and powerless "I" of faith that lives in the world as the sacrificial messianic body.[71] Unveiled here is a radical challenge to human political sovereignty that takes its stand on a completely different political theological ground—*pace* Carl Schmitt and his Christian authorization of state sovereignty. In a letter to Schmitt, Taubes writes:

> Perhaps there will still come a moment at which we can speak about what is to me the most significant Jewish as well as Christian political theology, Romans 9–11. The word "enemy" also appears there, in the absolute sense, but—and this seems to me to be the most decisive of decisive points— connected with "loved."[72]

What is significant here, of course, is that for Carl Schmitt the founding concept of political sovereignty is the constituting political power behind the law that entails a decision about the relationship of nature to law. "Sovereign is he who decides on the exception" says Schmitt in the famous opening line to his definition of sovereignty.[73] This requires that sovereignty be seen not in strictly juridical terms, but as a limit concept in which there is an agential power who decides on the "state of emergency" that suspends the normal rule of law. For Schmitt, this founding notion of sovereignty must be read together with the founding "definition of the political"—namely, the distinction between friend and enemy.[74]

The ultimate challenge to this basic political principle, as Schmitt recognizes, is articulated in the words of Jesus, "Love your enemies" (Matt 5:44; Luke 6:27)—words that Schmitt, in keeping with conventional Christendom political ethics, regards in terms of a private, spiritual, and ultimately depoliticizing ethic. Schmitt comments:

> Never in the thousand-year struggle between Christians and Moslems did it occur to a Christian to surrender rather than defend Europe out of love toward the Saracens or Turks. The enemy in the political sense need not be hated personally, and in the private sphere only does it make sense to love one's enemy, i.e. one's adversary.[75]

Precisely on this point Jacob Taubes disagrees, and so also John Yoder, in recognizing that for the messianic vision of the New Testament, "enemy" is not a private concept relating to private feuds. It is no less a public and political concept for being related to salvation and how God is related to friends and enemies.

For the record, we might note that Schmitt is also in error historically. The *Schleitheim Confession* (1527), which renounces the weapons of violence to protect friends and ward off enemies, was largely drafted by the hand of Michael Sattler, a former Benedictine who became an important early Anabaptist leader. Upon his return from the Schleitheim conference, Sattler and other Anabaptists were arrested, interrogated, and tortured before being condemned to death for (among other charges) refusing to wage

---

71. Ibid., 87.
72. Ibid., 112–13.
73. Schmitt, *Political Theology*, 5.
74. Schmitt, *Concept of the Political*, 26.
75. Ibid., 29.

war against the Turks, the great enemy of Christendom.[76] The reason Sattler gives for this refusal is no less agonistic and political than is the injunction by Christendom political authorities to wage war: there are enemies, and they are to be loved, not killed, in obedience to the messianic teachings of the kingdom of God ordered by the "perfection of Christ." These enemies, states Sattler, include not only the Turks:

> If the Turk comes, he should not be resisted, for it stands written: thou shalt not kill. We should not defend ourselves against the Turks or our other persecutors, but with fervent prayer should implore God that He might be our defense and our resistance. As to me saying that if waging war were proper I would rather take the field against the so-called Christians who persecute, take captive, and kill true Christians, than against the Turks, this was for the following reason: the Turk is a genuine Turk and knows nothing of the Christian faith. He is a Turk according to the flesh. But you claim to be Christians, boast of Christ, and still persecute the faithful witnesses of Christ. Thus you are Turks according to the Spirit.[77]

This messianic pacifism is therefore no liberal strategy of depoliticization through the individualization and privatization of the public realm. It is nothing less than a declaration of war, a war of messianic sovereignty over against all other political sovereignties (whether ancient or modern, religio-cosmological or secularist) that order human relations on non-messianic terms. But it is a war waged by martyrs who do not resist their enemies through violence but witness to another way, the messianic path of enemy-love. Such a politics, of course, will have no moral grounds for boasting in its own strength or virtue or purity. Messianic sovereignty dispossesses the faithful, as is indicated in the *hōs mē* logic of 1 Corinthians 7:29–31:

> I mean . . . the time (*kairos*) has become contracted; in what remains (*to loipon*) let those who have wives live as if they did not (*hōs mē*) have them, and those who mourn as if not (*hōs mē*) mourning, and those who rejoice as if not (*hōs mē*) rejoicing, and those who buy as if not (*hōs mē*) possessing, and those who use the world as if not (*hōs mē*) fully using it. For the outward form of the world (*to schēma tou kosmou*) is passing away.

There is a particular kind of "making use" of the world that treats it in a manner appropriate to its ontology of "passing away"—a using that is not proprietary, not related to human sovereignty or juridical ownership, that dwells in the world ("remain in the calling in which you have been called," 1 Cor 7:20) in a manner that opens it up to being made new, to "being known by God" (1 Cor 8:3).

The identity of the "Christian" born by the messianic community, in other words, is not a new universalism that somehow transcends or escapes particularity and difference. Indeed it is not to be related to a form of universal knowing of any sort ("if anyone imagines that he knows something, he does not yet know as he ought to know"). It is rather an identity "in Messiah" that seeks the perfection of love not in the domination or possession of any part, but in the apocalyptic transformation of all partial things to their

---

76. See the account of Sattler's trial in Yoder, *Legacy of Michael Sattler*.
77. Ibid., 72–73.

completion in divine love. This transformation occurs in the messianic body conformed to the "mind of Messiah" that willingly empties itself in order to serve the other, a pattern of radical humility and suffering servanthood. It is a pattern that can only be spiritually discerned, even though it is being enacted in the bodily realm that is "passing away" and therefore appears as failure. Paul emphatically insists on this in 1 Corinthians 1, scandalously relating the calling of the *ekklēsia* to the foolish power of the cross, which is mysteriously related to divine power and wisdom depicted not as ontological plenitude but as emptiness: "God chose what is low and despised in the world, even things that are not (*ta mē onta*) in order to bring to nothing *ta onta* (the things that are)." It is, finally, a pattern that can be described as sacramental or parabolic in which the excess of the whole (the "all") may be discerned within the particular part that is, selflessly and in loving use of the world, bearing witness to its hidden and sustaining divine life. This would be to restore the created, secular world order to its truest meaning—its full but not self-sufficient significance as the site where God is becoming "in Messiah" *ta panta en pasin* ("all in all").

It may be fitting to conclude, then, with reference to a recent article by the political theorist Romand Coles, "The Wild Patience of John Howard Yoder: 'Outsiders' and the 'Otherness of the Church.'" "As a member of no church," but rather as a participant in "radical democratic coalition politics," Coles finds Yoder's ecclesiology of "vulnerable receptivity" to others—both within the church and outside it—to be a compelling vision for "pursuing justice and political engagements in heterogeneous societies."[78] Differences are engaged not through strategies of universalizing claims, either religious or secular, but through reconciling practices bound to messianic lordship interpreted as "the opening of dialogical relations between the church and the world in which giving and receiving is possible, nay probable, in both directions."[79] Appealing to Yoder's image of tradition not as a tree but rather as a vine—"a story of constant interruption of organic growth in favor of a pruning and a new chance for the roots"[80]—Coles represents Yoder's account of messianic politics as the ecclesial enactment of vulnerable dialogue with others, looping back to Scripture precisely through the engagement of difference and diversity that the scriptural narrative itself enjoins. Coles puts it this way:

> In the presence of outsiders, the looping *back* of discerning ethical practice *cannot itself happen* in absence of a vulnerable and expectant looping *through* engagements with those of other dispositions, faiths and reasons. While the church has a certain precedence both epistemologically and axiologically as the body of focused dialogical discernment and action in light of Jesus' practices and pregnant wisdom . . . (and thus there can be no "politics of Jesus" that could be coercive, selfish, nondialogical, invulnerable, or cease to loop back to Scripture), it is . . . even the case that the church has often learned *about these most basic practices* from "outsiders."[81]

---

78. Coles, "Wild Patience of John Howard Yoder," 306.
79. Ibid., 307.
80. Yoder *Priestly Kingdom*, 69.
81. Coles, "Wild Patience of John Howard Yoder," 314.

Is a Messianic Political Ethic Possible?

For example, for Yoder the fact of modern pluralism is not a lamentable fragmentation of tradition (as Alasdair MacIntyre has it) but a providential opportunity to rediscover the multiplicity of cultures as a divinely willed good that saves human beings from the idolatrous imposition of political and cultural uniformity, in order to attend to the particular relations of particular communities in the relevant particular languages. It opens up a politics of vulnerable encounter "from below" as opposed to domination through coercive imposition "from above." Similarly, the nonviolence of such reconciling encounters may be represented to the messianic body by "outsiders" such as Gandhi, whose practice is more compatible with Jesus's vision than the practice of many "Christians" may be. Such dialogical practice and multidirectional witness, always full of surprises and paradoxical reversals as in the parables of the Gospel, takes time and therefore requires patience. For it is not the case that all traditions and cultural engagements are "good"; messianic traditioning is a complex and conflictual process of discernment that must keep faith with its messianic Lord. This is a delicate matter.

Coles nicely picks up on a phrase used in Yoder's characterization of such radical fidelity as "fidelity to the jealousy of Christ as Lord."[82] It is found in Yoder's description of the radical reformers' protest against all forms of "establishment" Christianity, which compromise messianic lordship with reference to some other measure of the good—power, mammon, fame, efficacy—that calls into question the fundamental cruciformity of the cosmos and the remnant character of the messianic community. This phrase intersects in a significant way with the foregoing discussion of Pauline political theology and the relations between Jews and Gentiles. At the height of Paul's discussion of the paradoxical mystery of divine election in Romans 9–11, he quotes the Moses song (*Ha'azinu*) of Deuteronomy 32:21–22, in which the relationship between God and the people is characterized as a "drama of jealousy."[83] Because the people have stirred God to jealousy with abominable practices of fidelity to what is no god, declares Moses, God will now stir the faithless people to jealousy with those who are no people. This too is how Paul understands the messianic drama between the people of Israel and the Gentiles, with the aim being the reconciliation and salvific inclusion of "all." Yet as we know, gifts given in jealousy can be both paralyzing and poisonously exclusive rather than liberating and redemptive. Paul is aware of this and tells his Roman audience, "So do not become proud, but stand in awe" (11:20). Coles is less certain than is Yoder that the jealousy of Jesus as Lord (not only as an idea, but as narrative, dispositions, habits, and practices—as Yoder always insists) can avoid the various pulls toward closure of the church or "people of God" to the generous and vulnerable engagement with others.[84]

The divine election to peoplehood is finally a mysterious drama of love that may not be possessed nor coercively imposed, and this, Coles points out, has implications for Yoder's elaboration of the church's discernment of fidelity in its "body politics."[85]

---

82. Ibid., 321; quoting Yoder, *Priestly Kingdom*, 86.

83. Cf. Taubes, *Political Theology of Paul*, 50.

84. Coles "Wild Patience of John Howard Yoder," 326–27.

85. Hence the importance of another of Yoder's comments on the jealousy of God, here in the context of his treatment of the Jeremian vision of diaspora community as the missionary form of the people of God: "This enormous flexibility and creativity force us to return to the question, Is there anything

PART 2: POLITICAL THEOLOGY AND THE RADICAL REFORMATION

> On Yoder's list of what and how fidelity is *not*: "polytheism." *For the church*, the path to reformation with the unanticipatable manifoldness of His gift must pass through the jealousy of the One. But, then, add this qualification: this paradox is too big for any *one* (individual, group, time) to handle or claim to possess entirely. Then add: that "the prophetic denunciation of paganism" will always be "ad hoc," "vulnerable," and "fragmentary." The sum, for Yoder, is that which is beyond a "sum."[86]

The non-summing practice that is central for Yoder's understanding of Christian ethics is found in his "Patience as Method in Moral Reasoning."[87] Messianic patience is not simply a matter of "self-restraint" or "moderation." It is, as Coles characterizes it, a "wild patience" that can take the many particular forms needed for vulnerable witnessing, discernment, and participation in the mysterious judgments and ways, the "unanticipatable breaking-forth," of divine wisdom. There is an excess in this radical, apocalyptic patience that has the courage to act from the modest stance of "infinality" just because in the cross of the resurrected Messiah is revealed the power of the sovereign God. This frees the church from the "compulsiveness of purpose" that understands political ethics as "moving history in the right direction." Here we may best conclude with Yoder's conclusion in his 1972 essay on *The Politics of Jesus*:

> Christians must realize that they are not only a minority on the globe but also at home in the midst of the followers of non-Christian and post-Christian faiths. Perhaps this will prepare us to see how inappropriate and preposterous was the prevailing assumption, from the time of Constantine until yesterday, that the fundamental responsibility of the church for society is to manage it. And might it be, if we could be freed from the compulsiveness of the vision of ourselves as the guardians of history, that we could receive again the gift of being able to see ourselves as participants in the loving nature of God as revealed in Christ? . . . A church once freed from compulsiveness and from the urge to manage the world might then find ways and words to suggest as well to those outside its bounds the invitation to a servant stance in society.[88]

---

nonnegotiable in the dispersed minority's witness? Anything untranslatable? Of course there is; it is that there is no other God. The rejection not only of the pagan cult but also of every way of putting their own YHWH/LORD in the same frame of reference with pagan deities, even while not speaking the divine NAME as others would, was tied for the Jews in Babylon with the proclamation of his sovereignty over creation and history. There is no setting into which that deconstructing, disenchanting proclamation cannot be translated, none which can encompass it. That anti-idolatry message is not bad but good news. It can free its hearers from slavery to the powers that crush their lives" (Yoder, *For the Nations*, 76–77). What Yoder here judges "good news" (in keeping with his account of God's jealousy and of the scattering at Babel) Derrida judges more ambiguously in "Des Tours de Babel." For Derrida, the scattering that results from God's jealousy, in which God imposes his untranslatable name over against all human namings, the act of divine deconstruction eventuates in irreducible confusion, "the necessary and impossible task of translation, its necessity *as* impossibility" ("Des Tours de Babel," 171). In effect, for Derrida there can be no clear line between a "colonial violence" (the universalization of an idiom) and a "peaceful transparency of the human community" (rational transparency). Coles worries in this same direction, suspicious that Yoder's language of messianic triumph can too easily be translated into the self-confident universalizing "good news" of particular insider communities.

86. Coles, "Wild Patience of John Howard Yoder," 322.
87. In Hauerwas et al., *Wisdom of the Cross*, 24–44.
88. Yoder, *Politics of Jesus*, 240–41.

PART 3

Messianism and Diaspora Ethics

10

Messianic Freedom and the Secular Academy

Educating the Affections in a Technological Culture

IN A RECENT ARTICLE on religion and secularity in American culture, *Communio* editor David Schindler elaborates the following credo: "I believe with the 'left' that American religiosity typically harbors an inadequate sense of and appreciation for the secular; and I believe with the 'right' that American secularity has wrongly emancipated itself from religion."[1] Schindler's thesis is that a defective American religiosity has largely set the terms for America's defective secularity (or secularism), and that the relation between these is mutual. The defective religiosity is the conceptual division of the Creator from the creation, leading to an untenable and reductive dualism—an extrinsic relation between God and the *saeculum* that warrants the abstraction of the religious realm of individual piety (the human will) from the secular realm of nature and a purely scientific reason.

This is, of course, not only an American malady. Schindler cites the work of George Grant to further show how the secular liberalism of the English-speaking world has become increasingly aligned with the development of technology as the site where the value-generating human will find the value-neutral means for establishing control over an indifferent nature. In his essay "Thinking about Technology," Grant argues that "technology has become the unthought ontology of our age" and that far from being instrumentally "neutral," technological mastery imposes upon us a structure of choices and public "goods" that threatens the very freedom it supposedly serves and undermines the disciplined cultural practices that sustain justice as a shared good.[2] For Grant the computer serves as a symbol of this often-hidden determining power of technology in our culture, which belies its supposed neutrality:

> The phrase "the computer does not impose [on us the ways it should be used]" misleads, because it abstracts the computer from the destiny that was required for its making. Common sense may tell us that the computer is an instrument,

---

1. Schindler, "Religion and Secularity in a Culture of Abstraction."
2. See Grant, "Thinking about Technology."

but it is an instrument from within the destiny which *does* "impose" itself upon us, and therefore the computer *does* impose.[3]

What it imposes, among other things, are forms of community that accommodate themselves to computer technologies and their "progress." Such a socially mediated conception of human destiny, furthermore, hastens the global movement toward cultural homogeneity and the gradual loss of a genuine pluralistic public life. On this point Grant's analysis is confirmed and deepened by the work of Albert Borgmann: "Liberal democracy is enacted as technology. It does not leave the question of the good life open but answers it along technological lines."[4] As the responses to Wendell Berry's controversial *Harper's Magazine* article, "Why I Am Not Going to Buy a Computer," indicate, even gently calling into critical question the central icon of technological civilization will generate intensely emotional moralistic responses (after all, the article is not entitled "Why You Should Not Buy a Computer" or "Why the Computer Is Evil"). This leads Berry to tweak *Harper's* liberal-minded, cosmopolitan readers: "I can only conclude that I have scratched the skin of a technological fundamentalism that, like other fundamentalisms, wishes to monopolize a whole society and, therefore, cannot tolerate the smallest difference of opinion."[5]

George Grant, in *Technology and Empire*, considers the implications of this in "The University Curriculum"—a curriculum increasingly focused upon the technological vision of rational mastery. The unity of the sciences, he suggests, is increasingly realized around this ideal of mastery—a subordination of the motive of wonder to the motive of power. Augustine, in his famous manual for the Christian liberal arts, *De doctrina christiana*, has taught us to attend above all to the question of motive in education. His rule for interpreting ambiguous signs is to pay attention to "the motive in using them and the way in which they are desired."[6] And to subordinate the power of love to the love of power is for Augustine the clearest indication of Faustian idolatry; it imitates the motives modeled by the father of lies.

To this bleak vision of the secular academy I wish to counterpose another vision, a vision not based upon any current slogan for university reform. I wish rather to consider a messianic paradigm rooted in the humility of Jesus, as it was for Augustine. Only such a radical spiritual re-visioning of the meaning of human life as made to desire God's life itself as its end will enable us again to reconceive (as Grant intended) our judgments about the essence of the university—its curriculum. This I will try to begin to do in the second part of this essay on "messianic freedom" in the academy, the mission of which is to educate the human affections according to another model of the human than technological mastery, namely, an ontology of mystery. This model of the human will be guided by an understanding of "messianic faith" as expressed in the following two definitions:

---

3. Ibid., 23.
4. Borgmann, *Technology and the Character of Contemporary Life*, 42.
5. Berry, *What Are People For?*, 175.
6. Augustine, *Teaching Christianity* 3.12.19.

1. A modern Augustinian definition, from Simone Weil: "We know by means of our intelligence that what intelligence does not comprehend is more real than what it does comprehend. Faith is the experience that intelligence is enlightened by love."[7]

2. A biblical definition, in Hebrews 11: "By faith we understand that the world was created by the word of God, so that what is seen was made out of things which do not appear." Hebrews goes on to talk about people of faith as sojourners, strangers, and exiles on the way toward a homeland that is hoped for but not seen. The pathway to that homeland, says Augustine in *De doctrina*, is the purification of understanding by love, or *caritas*, that travels along the "road of the affections."[8] Only those whose intelligence is enlightened by love will be capable of exercising good judgment in understanding and using well the things of the created world in which we live.

Learning has to do with the mind and the heart as well as the body, and therefore with the shape that human lives, communities, and cultures will take. We dare not take this on as a process of narrowing down but rather as a liberating, expanding, and integrative process according to what Augustine calls the "divinely instituted rule of *caritas*":

> "Thou shalt love thy neighbour as thyself," He said, and "thou shalt love God with thy whole heart, and with thy whole soul, and with thy whole mind." Thus all your thoughts and all your life and all your understanding should be turned toward Him from whom you receive these powers . . . [i.e.] that love of God which suffers no stream to be led away from it by which it might be diminished.[9]

What is required for this is a process of purgation of the eye of the mind/heart so that its motives will be guided not by pride, fear, and error, but by humility, wisdom, and truth. Only so will souls and societies be able to dwell in peace and well-being.[10]

The University of Secular Cybernetics

What happens educationally when the basic metaphors of nature, including human nature, are reduced to mechanistic process and technical information? I begin with a quotation from the well-known biologist Richard Dawkins, in *The Selfish Gene*: "We are survival machines—robot vehicles blindly programmed to preserve the selfish molecules known as genes. This is a truth which still fills me with astonishment," he gushes.[11] In case there were any doubt that this is no Socratic philosophical wonder, Dawkins clarifies his remark in his philosophical apologia: "But that was no metaphor. I believe it is the literal truth, provided key words are defined in the particular way favored by biologists."[12] This of course makes a humanist curious about the favored linguistic preferences of biologists—as it stands the statement is an astonishing reductionism. Not only

7. Weil, *Gravity and Grace*, 116.
8. Augustine, *Teaching Christianity* 1.17.16.
9. Ibid., 1.22.21.
10. Ibid., 2.7.9–11.
11. Dawkins, *Selfish Gene*, ix.
12. Dawkins, "In Defence of Selfish Genes," 572.

does it attribute a single moral intentionality (selfishness) to the whole of life, when it could equally be defined in terms of mutuality or reciprocity—it also uncritically names us "survival machines" or "robot vehicles," which one should have thought would be strange metaphors for a biologist to choose. And yet it is not uncommon. For biologists, human nature has become revealed as techno-genetic standing reserves.

Machines, of course, are humanly made, artificial, engineered, usually not as a display of beauty or spiritual identity but as instruments—usually of control or procurement. Is it surprising that our culture is increasingly taking on machine-like attributes when our primary metaphors are mechanistic and instrumental? Increasingly not only our industrial economy but also our politics and our aesthetics take on the features of our primary linguistic metaphors. Why else would people spend all that time and energy to make themselves look like the very muscle-building machinery they use to get them there? Why else are our lucrative fashion industries successfully marketing the hairless, well-oiled body except that we literally are coming to see ourselves not as animal creatures but increasingly as biomechanical machines? And of course who wouldn't be willing to become a machine if it means avoiding a human death? The future markets in the cosmetic, therapeutic, and functional enhancement of the human machine (indeed the "nature machine") are vast indeed—and a great deal of research is being funded to exploit these opportunities as central values in our public culture. To what extent is our technoscience guided by a morally laden metaphysic of nature that denies its own moral judgments and assumptions as such (by assuming the mechanistic metaphor is objective rational description)? Of course, machines are not moral agents; hence if we are machines, are we moral agents? Is the effort to enhance our machine-like efficiency a moral enterprise, and if so, what is the good it seeks and how will we speak about it?

In order to explore these questions, the good of technological research and development, we do well to examine the cultural-linguistic history of modern science and its intimate connections with technology and the mechanistic paradigm. The modern vision of science has been closely tied to certain Baconian moral assumptions, most notably the commitment to relieve and benefit the human condition by liberating human beings from the constraints of nature and deliver control of nature, including human nature, into human hands. "Knowledge is power," said Bacon, and by this he meant the power to *generate*, a power closely linking scientific research and technical development. "Nature shall be put to the rack to compel her to answer our questions," the rack being humanly fashioned scientific instruments that will crack the code of nature so as better to exploit its natural resources for technological advancement. Bacon scoffed at the wisdom of the classical moral traditions and their language of the good, comparing it to prepubescent boyhood: "It can talk, but it cannot generate."[13] It is worth paying some attention to this language of "generating," since etymologically it is linked to an important family of words in our public culture: *genius, engine/engineer, gene/genetic*—all linked to the Latin *gigno/gignere*, to beget, and the Greek *gignomai*, to be born/come into being, language closely linked to motives in our current academy (though we cannot explore this in detail here).

---

13. Bacon, *Instauratio magna*, preface.

Rather than focus here on particular ethical issues that are raised by this language and the action it generates—patenting of genetic information as intellectual property, various forms of genetic testing, cloning, and the new benevolent eugenics entailed in the biotech revolution—I want to consider the moral consequences of the shifts in language toward technological begetting. What happens when basic biological nature comes to be seen as information, and organisms as information-processing machines whose capacities can be progressively upgraded into increasingly efficient cybernetic survival systems? If nature is merely an information code to be cracked so that its various data might be reconfigured in endless different patterns, how might we distinguish true from false, benevolent from malevolent, healthy from harmful experiments, innovations, and developments? If there is no "good" in nature, including no moral goodness that can be commonly discerned, why even bother with ethics in scientific research and technological innovation?

Let us briefly consider a recent "posthuman" vision of technological empire that has in effect eliminated ethics, Ray Kurzweil's *Age of Spiritual Machines*. Ray Kurzweil is no flake; his work in artificial intelligence and pattern recognition technologies has led to the successful establishment of four high-tech companies (devoted, among other things, to pattern recognition technologies that aid the blind and the deaf), a number of influential books, and a host of academic and other awards. He is in many ways an icon of our culture's commercial and research aspirations. What is Kurzweil's vision? In a nutshell it is this: "Computation is the essence of order."[14] The evolutionary process that has begotten human intelligence is effectively generating an increasingly efficient information-processing machine. Kurzweil is convinced that human beings are the intermediate organic stage toward a new, cybernetic stage of evolutionary development in which machine technology will eventually "take full control of its own progression."[15] This is indeed what human intelligence and consciousness really is once we get past "hard-to-define questions such as human dignity."[16] While the Human Genome Project is important as a scanning operation of DNA codes, it will ultimately be superseded by machine intelligence, according to what Kurzweil calls the "Law of Accelerating Returns," which interprets all reality on the model of increasingly complex information processing. For intelligent organisms to adapt themselves to a changing natural—read "machine"—environment, in order to keep up with and maintain their evolutionary advantage, human beings will of necessity turn themselves into machines, gradually at first through genetic therapies, bioenhancement, and porting our brains to computer intelligence. But we will come to realize that "DNA-based evolution will eventually have to be abandoned" because "organisms created through DNA-based evolution are stuck with an extremely plodding type of circuitry."[17] Kurzweil's vision ends with the claim that "extremely little of the stuff on Earth is devoted to useful computation. This is even more true when we consider all of the dumb matter in the Earth's midst."[18] The aim of all life is

14. Kurzweil, *Age of Spiritual Machines*, 33.
15. Ibid., 32.
16. Ibid., 57.
17. Ibid., 101.
18. Ibid., 259.

PART 3: MESSIANISM AND DIASPORA ETHICS

to exploit nature for its computational intelligence (Kurzweil's "spirituality"), which will transform life into a shared machine consciousness, a posthuman virtual reality.

Kurzweil's book is filled with examples of what may be achieved through this biotechnological revolution, this "road paved with gold . . . full of benefits that we're never going to resist."[19] He is fond of speculating on the sexual possibilities that will open up when freed from the constraints of biological generation and conventional social norms. Sexual and spiritual activities can be reduced to information processing, not complex personal relations sustained through time or in nature, not educated through disciplined commitments between persons. Sex is merely the episodic manipulation of electronic data. Kurzweil finds it in him to celebrate the technological possibilities of virtual sex of every kind, which will no longer require moral censure because now safely detached from embodied nature. He imagines his fourth-grade son's ability to undress his fourth-grade teacher—and manipulate her in any way he desires—without affecting *her*; he imagines the ability to indulge many lovers at once, pleasuring himself by clicking on innumerable sites and partners at the same time (though I suppose no real clicking will eventually be required). So too the spiritual arts (music, poetry, painting) will easily be replicated by computer technology, and unfortunately Kurzweil cannot restrain himself from giving examples of his own design. The commodities on offer are at about the same level of moral wisdom and emotional intelligence as the fourth-grade sexual fantasies. We are now literally generating sex for prepubescent boys, who no longer need either to talk or to generate.

How is it that our human quest for liberation and happiness ends up in such a tawdry and dehumanizing vision of disembodiment—that is nevertheless celebrated as the benevolent salvation of the future? I suggest it has something to do with the idea that we will magically crack the code of life through the collection of data. This is a Faustian bargain. Data lacks sanctity and goodness; to be sure, it takes attention away from our moral and spiritual sensibilities, which are developed and communicated through a different sort of language—the language of symbol, narrative, and the ordering of love, justice, beauty, and goodness. This classical moral language is attuned to a different kind of knowing than is the instrumental procurement and processing of data, and it is important to recognize this philosophically if we are to preserve any moral notion of secular education as a shared rational language that discloses to us spiritually and culturally who we are.

What we need in the first place, then, is an account of spiritual causality rooted in the language of poetic, dramatic experience. This too is an academic and public science that considers generation, as Plato envisioned it more than two millennia ago, but not so much a biological or technological begetting as spiritual generation, an account of why things come into being and exist as they do. In his dialogue the *Phaedo*, Plato has Socrates give an account of why one must move beyond physical, mechanical, and formal causality in order to account for human motivation and judgment.[20] In order to do this it is necessary to consider the ordering power of the good, "which must embrace

---

19. Ibid., 130.
20. Plato, *Phaedo* 95–102.

and hold together all things."[21] And the good, as Socrates puts it in the *Republic*, is "beyond being, exceeding it in dignity and power," a transcendent measure that cannot be humanly manipulated, that can be discerned only by the properly ordered *organon* of the soul.[22] An account of that proper ordering is what ethics is. For this we need another kind of generative language and education, one that examines moral character and spiritual meaning in a non-instrumentalist but nevertheless rational manner. The science of spiritual generation will be different from the science of biological generation or technological begetting, though not unrelated to it.

However, which moral language, tradition, and symbolism will we use in a secular pluralistic society to adjudicate the disputes? As in the other rational sciences, there is no shortcut that gets around the particularity and diversity of what we encounter. Spiritual and moral symbols are not private or individual constructions, but nor are they universal abstractions—they are found in particular texts and traditions that can be studied seriously as representations of shared cultural and human experiences. When we examine them closely we will find some striking points of communication within the diversity. Without the resources and insights provided by such disciplined inquiry and serious public conversation, we will be ill-equipped to answer the Ray Kurzweils of the world, who tar any opposition with the same brush: anti-scientific, anti-technological *Luddism*. Of course, on the classical moral principle that it is better to suffer harm than to cause it, I am quite ready to champion the Luddites over Kurzweil. But it is a sign of the dangerously uncritical totalitarianism of Kurzweil and his ilk that *any* resistance is considered intolerant and intolerable, and dismissed with an epithet.[23]

It is clear to me that our public conversation about ethics, both in the university and in the wider society, is not adequate, and this leaves us ill-equipped to understand, never mind address, the moral quandaries that are raised by our growing technological capacities and their commercial applications (which are being pursued at full speed). This represents an opportunity in our culture and within the academy in particular, not for the imposition of new religious or moral orthodoxies in place of prevailing secularist and technicist ones, but for the serious conversation between the cultural sciences and religious moral traditions about the range of assumptions concerning nature and human nature that orient our thought and action. At its liberal best, "secular" has not meant the anti-religious privatization of religious and moral discourse, but rather that no one

---

21. Ibid., 99c.
22. Plato, *Republic* 509b, 518.
23. Few people who use the epithet "Luddite" know or care about its historical derivation—those wool-workers in early nineteenth-century England, as Wendell Berry tells it, "who dared to assert that there were needs and values that justly took precedence over industrialization; they were people who rejected the determinism of technological innovation and economic exploitation." While they destroyed machinery that had replaced them, they did not engage in violence against living beings until a band of them was shot down by soldiers in 1812—at which time their movement was obliterated. Berry comments: "The victory of industrialism over Luddism was . . . overwhelming and unconditional; it was undoubtedly the most complete, significant, and lasting victory of modern times. And so one must wonder at the intensity with which any suggestion of Luddism still is feared and hated." For Berry it is a sign of the triumphalistic technological determinism of the times that cannot tolerate any resistance to the inevitable, progressivist "destiny" of technological development. See the title essay in Berry, *Sex, Economy, Freedom, and Community*, 130ff.

PART 3: MESSIANISM AND DIASPORA ETHICS

religious tradition or moral position will be uncritically privileged as the only one (just as in natural science, neither theoretical nor commercial agendas should be so privileged). The assumption at its best of secular pluralism is precisely that open, critical discussion of the variety of spiritual symbols and traditions can enhance the understanding and experience of all. This is indeed what the liberal secular academy needs to relearn from its own founding "faith" traditions.

Why? Not least because openness and plurality, respect for difference and the shared exploration of the meaning of reality, are themselves particular spiritual qualities and disciplines that can be lost when they are no longer understood and cultivated. These qualities, rooted in a sense of the spiritual and moral dignity not only of human beings but of the natural world in general, embody the trust that truth about our shared reality can be discovered through humble exploration that will also respect the limits of our different forms of knowing. Such disciplined exploration and shared dialogue, not commercial utility or self-interested intellectual conquest, is the moral heart of the university as a public institution. Moral meaning is best discovered and communicated not in generic abstractions or formal codes that avoid discussion of the particular spiritual and moral commitments of real human beings, but when it calls these commitments and symbols to public account in terms of their theoretical and applied implications.

Messianic Freedom and the Affections

In the remainder of this essay I shall explore briefly the possibility of a messianic paradigm that addresses the question of education in the secular pluralist academy quite differently from the approach displayed in technological globalization. By calling the paradigm "messianic" I am of course being deliberately provocative, as it is precisely the messianic forms of religion that have been judged to be dangerously apocalyptic by modern liberal theories. No doubt so some have been.[24] However, it is also the case that the first theory of the *saeculum* in Western political thought, Augustine's *City of God*, was developed precisely within an apocalyptic messianic understanding of history and politics.[25] I have also suggested that the notions of neutral technology and rational mastery that underlie current conceptions and embodiments of the secular are themselves dangerously totalitarian, exclusivist, and violent, even while hidden beneath the veneer of progressivist liberal assumptions. The challenge is how messianic faith might engage a secular public realm of technological empire in constructively critical terms without accommodating itself to its colonizing and monolithic moral ontology.

We may begin by recalling some of the biblical images related to the "people of faith": strangers, exiles, sojourners—a people in "diaspora." These images help envision how messianic faith enables people to face the challenges of a pluralistic, multicultural world—not as established or privileged rulers of the domain, but as itinerant servants on pilgrimage who need certain portable skills that enable them, as Jeremiah exhorts the people as they are being exiled to the enemy empire of Babylon, to "seek the shalom

---

24. Norman Cohn discusses numerous examples in his book *The Pursuit of the Millennium*.
25. The classical study remains Markus, *Saeculum*.

of the people to whom you are being sent, for in its shalom you will find your shalom" (Jer 29). Such a way of life requires the building up of certain virtues: humility above all, as exemplified in Jesus, whom Hebrews 12 calls the "pioneer and perfecter of faith." It will also require openness to new and different experiences and paradigms, welcoming strangers, seeing leadership as servanthood, being willing to engage the difficult, polyglot disciplines of interpreting one's identity and story in new cultural forms and contexts. This is true not only in faith communities; it is also true in the university as a "diaspora institution" devoted to practices not to be identified with any particular earthly political regime. The academy too was the creation of a diaspora movement from the Greek polis, prompted by the revelation of something new in Socrates, who emphasized the importance of educating our desires theologically so as to be liberated from the lie in the soul about the things that are.

In terms of an understanding of education in our own time, this means first of all a liberation from the idolatry of literalism entailed in the "unthought ontology" of technological culture. John Henry Newman, following Augustine and Plato, states: "University teaching without theology is simply unphilosophical."[26] At issue here is the question of truth in its relatedness, where wholeness is more than the sum of its factual parts. A truly philosophical habit of mind that gets us beyond the "viewiness" of undisciplined opining and the passive reception of images[27] must bring human agency and judgment back into the scientific process. Otherwise we will end up in the superstitious literalism that now threatens to overwhelm the modern university (as Newman already anticipated), where only external causes are allowed to count in rational explanation. Newman points out that in such a university it would not be the sciences which were untrue, but the so-called knowledges deemed literally "unreal"—deciding on facts by means of narrow methods and theories. Such a university is no longer teaching liberal knowledge but only a narrow-minded bigotry.[28] A true university will require at its center a science that seeks

26. Newman, *Idea of a University*, 40.

27. Newman gives us an exquisite portrait of such unenquiring curiosity seekers (reminiscent of those described also by Augustine in *Confessions* 10.8.15, and 10.35.55—"in themselves they are uninterested," but they are fascinated by spectacles, the more outrageous the better) that now depicts not only "seafaring men" but university researchers at every level: "Perhaps they have been much in foreign countries, and they receive, in a passive, otiose, unfruitful way, the various facts which are forced upon them there. Seafaring men, for example, range from one end of the earth to the other; but the multiplicity of external objects, which they have encountered, forms no symmetrical and consistent picture upon their imagination; they see the tapestry of human life, as it were on the wrong side, and it tells no story. They sleep, and they rise up, and they find themselves, now in Europe, now in Asia; they see visions of great cities and wild regions; they are in the marts of commerce, or amid the islands of the South; they gaze on Pompey's Pillar, or on the Andes; and nothing which meets them carries them forward or backward, to any idea beyond itself. Nothing has a drift or relation; nothing has a history or a promise. Every thing stands by itself, and comes and goes in its turn, like the shifting scenes of a show, which leave the spectator where he was. Perhaps you are near such a man on a particular occasion, and expect him to be shocked or perplexed at something which occurs; but one thing is much the same to him as another, or, if he is perplexed, it is as not knowing what to say, whether it is right to admire, or to ridicule, or to disapprove, while conscious that some expression of opinion is expected from him; for in fact he has no standard of judgment at all, and no landmarks to guide him to a conclusion. Such is mere acquisition, and, I repeat, no one would dream of calling it philosophy" (Newman, *Idea of a University*, 99).

28. Ibid., 50.

a true account of the soul and its principles of motion in a spiritually ordered cosmos. It is not accidental that Plato coined the term "theology" in book 2 of the *Republic* in considering why education is required to liberate enslaved citizens from civic lies that bind them in ugly, violent caves. The theological question is entailed in the central question of a liberal, philosophical education: How should we speak the truth about the good so as to distinguish between a good life and a bad one (and to avoid the lie in the soul about the things that are)?

Such a process of liberation is articulated in Augustine's *De doctrina christiana*, where interpretation is most properly founded upon the rule of faith, none other than the principle of *caritas* that spiritually orients the human understanding to the "good beyond being." Here is what Augustine says about the state of enslavement: "There is a miserable servitude of the soul in this habit of taking signs for things, so that one is not able to raise the eye of the mind above things that are corporal and created to drink in eternal light."[29] The process of being liberated from such a servitude is no easy thing, but it is a process, a "turning" or "conversion" motivating every university worthy of the name: *universitas*, literally *turned* toward wholeness. It is ultimately, as Augustine put it, a return to the wisdom that one loves in the love of any particular thing that one therefore tries to understand, to know. But it is also a process characterized by imitation—we humans are creatures of imitation, we learn by imitating examples that move us. This of course is the whole meaning and power of "authority." We humans do not invent ourselves *de novo*—we are born into the world only to enter through speech "more deeply into the stormy society of human life," and in this society we learn our motives, we have our desires shaped.[30]

Augustine has some telling things to say about his teachers as models of imitation in the academic game: above all they focused on the appearance of loquacity and the glory of winning in verbal competition. In this regard, they were experts in the cultivation of affectation and style, not nurturing the affections on truth and substantive wisdom. Indeed they were masters of hypocrisy, attuned only to the visible and external, punishing the boys for their vanity and pleasure-seeking even while their disciplines and adult conventions were dedicated to the very same ends. Not only were these educational authorities corrupt, but so also the literary examples they taught—the Greek and Latin classics whose heroes displayed deception, violence, and fornication as models of success. While Scripture carries a much different authority than do Homer and Virgil, Augustine does not dismiss the study of literary classics but submits them to the scrutiny of a higher authority—divine wisdom. So also, then, does the messianic teaching authority of Jesus present us with a challenging model that turns the techniques and methods of rhetoric and intellectual inquiry to fundamentally different purposes. Augustine characterizes the distinctiveness of this authority in terms of what was lacking in the pagan philosophers: humility and tears of confession. For Augustine, to profess means to confess before others and thus to offer a model of imitation founded on humility.

Mark's gospel clearly ties Jesus's messianic authority—a public and political as well as religious and moral authority—to John the Baptist. The first word of this earliest of

---

29. Augustine, *Teaching Christianity* 3.5.9.
30. Augustine, *Confessions* 1.8.13.

the four gospels is *archē*, "the beginning" of the good news of Jesus the Messiah, a new beginning signaled as a new creation tied to the appearance of the Messiah, but Mark immediately sets another tone ringing from the prophet Isaiah. Like Isaiah, Mark sees the new beginning as taking place not in the political center of Jerusalem but rather in the wilderness, where the people learn to walk the unconventional ways of justice and mercy. Hence the prophetic importance of John the Baptist. John has no school, no sophisticated organization, no institutional location or authorization or credentials—yet he will prepare the messianic way. To begin to prepare this way means letting go, "repenting" of closed conventional markers about insiders and outsiders, the elite and the rabble, the respectable and the vulgar. John preaches renunciation of all closed claims and his rite of baptism is intended to open up the possibility of a completely new beginning. This baptism is not a special ritual code related to a creed and an insider community; it is a radical leveling and calls only for a complete turnaround of one's life.

Like Elijah, the prophetic judge of king and court who was continually viewed as a political danger, John the Baptist is no lapdog to power. Despite the fact that "all the people of Jerusalem" go out to see him and be baptized in the river Jordan, he remains a threat especially to the religious and political establishment, and is eventually arrested by King Herod (Mark 6). Clearly, then, when John says, "After me comes one who is mightier than I, the thong of whose sandals I am not worthy to stoop down and untie," he does not mean Herod, though Herod would no doubt think so. Rather, he is referring to an unknown man from hinterland Nazareth whose career will be very like his own and with whom he will intersect at strategic moments in Mark's gospel. That John and Jesus are no power rivals, however, is made evident when, far from requiring John to stoop before him, Jesus invites John to baptize him in the river Jordan. Does the Messiah need to be baptized? Perhaps it is best to reason not the need, but the answer appears to be yes—this paradigm entails the complete dispossession of privilege. After this Jesus too is "driven out into the wilderness" by the Spirit and wrestles with temptations concerning power and authority.

It is here that the parallels and intersections between Jesus and the Baptist begin. Jesus's public ministry begins, Mark tells us, when John is arrested by Herod, and he begins to preach the same message as John: "The kingdom of God is at hand; repent and believe in the good news." Later (Mark 11), when Jesus goes to Jerusalem and is questioned about his authority by the religious leaders, he ties his authority to John's baptism, which traps these leaders. Jesus asks them, "'Was the baptism of John from heaven or of human origin?' And they argued with one another, If we say 'From heaven,' he will say, 'Why then did you not believe him?' But shall we say 'Of human origin?'—they were afraid of the people, for all held that John was a real prophet." By responding in this way these leaders prove themselves characteristic of all conventional authority, which takes its cues from human beings, whose desires are shaped by the power games that accord status and respect through rivalry and domination. This is not the power that authorizes and motivates either John or Jesus, and this is at the heart of the good news that reshapes desire and establishes a very different line of authority, the way of the Messiah.

The messianic religious community displayed in the New Testament establishes this pattern of authority and of rebuilding the secular not through control of the dominant centers of social and intellectual power but by modeling a different path of community building as cultural service from below. The faith identity borne by the messianic community is not a new noetic universalism that somehow transcends or escapes particularity and difference. Indeed, it is not to be related to a form of universal "knowing" of any sort ("if anyone imagines that he knows something, he does not yet know as he ought to know"). It is rather an identity "in Messiah" that seeks the perfection of love, not in the domination or possession of any part but in the apocalyptic transformation of all partial things to their mutual completion in divine love. This transformation occurs in the messianic body conformed through baptism to the messianic mind that willingly empties itself in order to serve the other, a pattern of radical humility. It is a pattern that can only be spiritually discerned, even though it is being enacted in the bodily realm that is "passing away" and therefore may appear as failure—as Paul emphatically insists in 1 Corinthians 1, scandalously relating the messianic calling to the foolish power of the cross that is mysteriously related to divine power and wisdom, depicted not as ontological plenitude but as emptiness: "God chose what is low and despised in the world, even things that are not (*ta mē onta*) in order to bring to nothing the things that are (*ta onta*)." It is, finally, a pattern that can be described as sacramental or parabolic, in which the excess of the whole may be discerned within the particular part that is selflessly and in loving use of the world bearing witness to its hidden and sustaining divine life. To live in this way would be to restore secularity, including the secular university, to its truest ontological meaning—its full but not self-sufficient significance as the site where God is becoming "in Messiah" *ta panta en pasin* (all in all).

11

Gulag Ethics: Russian and Mennonite Prison Memoirs from Siberia

(with Bruce Ward)

THIS ESSAY FOCUSES ON Siberian prison memoirs penned by very different authors, culturally and religiously. Fyodor Dostoevsky and Aleksandr Solzhenitsyn are renowned Russian novelists whose prison camp and gulag experiences provoked their conversion from secular ideologies to radical (even if unconventional) Christianity that is identifiably Russian Orthodox. Bruce Ward argues in part 1 that for both writers, their Siberian exile transformed their understanding of human nature from vague humanism to a powerful conviction that the suffering Christ reveals the true *imago Dei*, which defines and redeems the human condition even in its sinful extremities. Their struggles to bear witness to the experience of the Siberian camps transformed them as writers and as people, and left its religious and ethical mark on their entire literary corpus. The Mennonite experience of the gulag, by contrast, involved an ethnic and religious minority who already inhabited a diaspora identity and a martyrdom theological and ethical tradition focused on following the nonviolent, suffering Christ. Yet the fictional prison memoir by Hans Harder and the Siberian diary of Aron Toews display a similar attunement to the transforming power of the suffering Christ experienced in the gulag and draw lessons from it for the Mennonite people. Above all, they suggest that the only truly human identity is not one rooted in ethnicity or in the achievements of a people, but rather one rooted in the self-emptying humility of Christ who took the form of the servant even unto death.

I: RUSSIAN PRISON MEMOIRS IN SIBERIA (BRUCE WARD)

Two of the most illustrious writers in Russian and indeed global literature, Fyodor Dostoevsky and Aleksandr Solzhenitsyn, each authored prison memoirs, and both of them spent time in prison in Omsk—one when it was a hard labor camp under the tsarist regime of Nicholas I in the nineteenth century (Dostoevsky), and the other when

PART 3: MESSIANISM AND DIASPORA ETHICS

it was a transit prison within the Stalinist gulag system of the mid-twentieth century (Solzhenitsyn).

Dostoevsky was arrested by the tsarist secret police in April 1849 for his involvement in the Petrashevsky group of radical liberals and socialists; after months of incarceration and interrogation in the Peter and Paul Fortress in Saint Petersburg, he was subjected to a mock execution and then sentenced to eight years of hard labor in Siberia. On January 23, 1850, he entered the prison fortress at Omsk, where he was to remain for four years (because of a reduction in his sentence), followed by four more years of Siberian exile as a soldier in a convict battalion stationed in the town of Semipalatinsk (now called Semey, located in Kazakhstan, further south down the Irtysh River from Omsk). He was finally to return to European Russia and resume his career as a writer in 1859, ten years after his arrest.[1]

Solzhenitsyn was arrested in 1944 while an artillery officer on active duty on the Russo-German front, because of correspondence with a friend that included criticisms of Stalin. After a period of incarceration and interrogation in the notorious Lubyanka prison in Moscow, he too was sentenced to eight years of hard labor in Siberia. During his three-month journey to the camp where he was to serve most of his sentence, in Ekibastuz (also in what is now Kazakhstan), he stayed for a time in Omsk, not in exactly the same barracks as Dostoevsky did but in a dungeon of the former military fortress built under Catherine the Great.[2] His description of this dungeon demonstrates his consciousness of following in the path of Dostoevsky:

> The prison at Omsk, which had known Dostoevsky, was not like any old Gulag transit prison.... It was a formidable jail ... and its dungeons were particularly terrible. You could never imagine a better film set than one of its underground cells.... The cell has no ceiling, but massive, menacing vaults converge overhead. One wall is wet—water seeps through from the soil and leaks onto the floor. In the morning and in the evening it is dark, on the brightest afternoon half-dark. There are no rats but you fancy that you can smell them.[3]

After his release from hard labor in 1953, Solzhenitsyn was to spend another four years in Siberian exile, until his "rehabilitation" in 1957 under Khrushchev. He would win the Nobel Prize for literature in 1970.

Such, in brief outline, is the connection between Omsk and two of the most significant voices of Russian—and indeed world—literature. My concern in what follows is with how this Siberian prison experience proved to be decisively transformative for Dostoevsky and Solzhenitsyn, both as individuals and as writers (though neither would acknowledge such a separation). The focus will be on their struggle to remain writers within an environment hostile (to say the least) to this activity, and on how this struggle proved spiritually transformative for both. It is our expectation that placing the world-famous Russian writers side by side with the "humbler" Mennonite literature in part 2 of this essay will yield some instructive parallels and contrasts.

---

1. For an excellent account of this period of Dostoevsky's life, see Frank, *Dostoevsky: The Years of Ordeal*.
2. See Labedz, *Solzhenitsyn*, 13–14.
3. Solzhenitsyn, *Gulag Archipelago*, 3:49–50.

Gulag Ethics: Russian and Mennonite Prison Memoirs from Siberia

Fyodor Dostoevsky

There are two primary sources for Dostoevsky's experience in Omsk: his rare letters from Siberia and his memoir, *The House of the Dead*. Because the latter is a work of literary art, it has to be considered as much poetry as fact, and therefore not as an innocently realistic reproduction of his day-to-day existence in prison—for instance, he clearly takes great liberties with time, ordering and compressing incidents into a time frame that serves his artistic goals. Nevertheless, the consensus among Dostoevsky's best scholarly biographers is that if *The House of the Dead* cannot be regarded as accurate in *form*, it can be taken as accurate in regard to *substance*, and hence a reliable source of biographical material. This is corroborated by other memoirs we have from people whose prison terms in Omsk overlapped with Dostoevsky's.[4]

It is Dostoevsky's long letter to his brother, written just a week after his release from the prison camp in Omsk, that furnishes the most unvarnished description of the actual physical conditions he encountered, because the letter was not subject to the tsarist censorship. It is worth quoting at some length:

> Things were very bad for us. A military prison is much worse than a civilian one. I spent the whole four years in the prison behind walls and never went out except to work. The work they found for us was heavy . . . and I was sometimes completely exhausted in foul weather, in damp and rain and sleet, and in the unendurable cold of winter. Once . . . the mercury froze and there was perhaps about 40 degrees of frost. My foot became frostbitten. . . . We lived on top of each other, all together in one barrack. Imagine an old, dilapidated, wooden construction, which was supposed to have been pulled down long ago, and which was no longer fit for use. In summer, intolerable closeness; in winter, unendurable cold. . . . Filth on the floors an inch thick; one could slip and fall. The little windows were so covered with frost that it was almost impossible to read at any time of the day. An inch of ice on the panes. Drips from the ceiling, draughts everywhere. We were packed like herrings in a barrel. . . . We slept on bare boards and were allowed only a pillow. We spread our sheepskin coats over us, and our feet were always uncovered all night. We shivered all night. Fleas, lice and black beetles by the bushel. . . . The food they gave us was bread and cabbage soup with a quarter of a pound of beef in it; but the meat was minced up and I never saw any of it. On holidays, thin porridge almost without fat. On fast days, boiled cabbage and hardly anything else. . . . I often lay in the hospital. Disordered nerves have given me epilepsy, but the fits occur only rarely. . . . Add to all these amenities the almost complete impossibility of possessing a book . . . the eternal hostility and quarreling around one, the wrangling, shouting, uproar, din, always under escort, never alone, and all this for four years without change. . . . Besides all this, the eternal threat of punishment hanging over one, shackles, the total stifling of the soul, there you have an image of my existence.[5]

---

4. See Martanyov, "V Perelome Veka"; and Lednicki, *Russia, Poland, and the West*, which contains a translation of the chapter devoted to Dostoevsky in the memoir of a fellow political prisoner, the Pole Szymon Tokarzewski.

5. Dostoevsky, *Pisma I*, 135–37.

PART 3: MESSIANISM AND DIASPORA ETHICS

The worst aspect of Dostoevsky's situation was that he was not able to write. By the time of his arrest, at the age of twenty-seven, he was already a writer celebrity in Russia, hailed by the leading critics as the new Gogol, and now this immensely promising vocation as a writer had been catastrophically interrupted. As he said in a later letter to a friend, "I cannot find the expressions to tell you what torture I suffered because I was not able to write."[6] Indeed, he was not able even to read; the only book allowed him in the prison camp was the copy of the New Testament given him by a widow of one of the Decembrists while he was in transit to Omsk. Yet Dostoevsky was utterly determined to remain a literary artist and to resume his writing career in the future. In the same letter to his brother I quoted earlier, he signaled this determination to make the most of his Siberian experience for his writing: "What a store of types and characters from the people I have carried out of the prison camp! I have lived closely with them, and so I think I know them thoroughly. How many stories of tramps and bandits, and in general of the entire dark and miserable milieu! Enough for whole volumes!"[7]

Dostoevsky read his New Testament, over and over again (also recording, in a charming vignette from *House of the Dead*, how he taught a young Chechen Muslim, Aley, to read Russian from this same New Testament, and how enthralled Aley was with the figure of Jesus);[8] and he reflected through long hours on his bunk in the evenings, when pretending to be asleep so as to not be disturbed by the other convicts with whom he lived in constant close quarters.[9] He was very observant, endlessly gathering material in his head. And not only in his head; he also managed to keep an improvised notebook which he made for himself by carefully sewing together pages on which he jotted down impressions, turns of phrase, stories, proverbs, even songs he heard from the convicts around him. If he had kept the notebook on his person or among his possessions, it would have been stolen by one of the other convicts or confiscated if found by the authorities, and he would very likely also have been flogged. So he kept it hidden in the prison hospital, confiding it to the care of a medical assistant there whom he trusted; Dostoevsky would add to it from memory during his hospital stays, which were fairly frequent because of his epilepsy. These *Siberian Notebooks* became a major source for *The House of the Dead* (it might also be noted that they have served as a source for later students of ethnology and Russian folklore).[10]

The House of the Dead offers a fascinating series of vividly drawn impressions of Omsk camp life, covering subjects such as food, shelter, work, the smuggling of vodka, escape attempts, punishment, various extraordinary characters among the convicts, the convict theatricals, and even camp animals. Yet underlying the documentary detail there is another level of concern, which we might call religious-ethical and which links this book to the metaphysical questioning of Dostoevsky's later major novels. At first glance, *The House of the Dead* can seem a fairly randomly organized series of impressions and

6. Ibid., 166.
7. Ibid., 135–37.
8. Dostoevsky, *House of the Dead*, 88–89.
9. This detail is found in Dostoevsky's retrospective account of a particular episode in the camp, written several years later; see the February 1876 section of Dostoevsky, *Writer's Diary*.
10. See Frank, *Dostoevsky: The Years of Ordeal*, 83–84.

episodes but on closer examination reveals a carefully organized aesthetic, especially in regard to the deployment of time, which serves the underlying religious-ethical theme. The theme I have in mind is that of the transformative effect of suffering. This transformation, which could even be called, more strongly, "conversion," has to do with the profound change of convictions wrought in the heart and mind of Dostoevsky himself by his experience in Omsk.

The popular literature on Dostoevsky often describes this change as an abrupt conversion from atheist socialist radicalism to a conservative upholding of tsardom and Russian Orthodoxy. This is a caricature; the transformation was much more nuanced and more gradual, taking place over many years and not only the Siberian years. Its complexity is reflected in *The House of the Dead* itself. Dostoevsky makes it clear there that the transformation he underwent was not a matter of a dramatic discovery of God (perhaps through reading the New Testament), still less of the legitimacy of conventional Russian religio-political authority. The discovery that *was* decisive, according to *The House of the Dead*, was a discovery of human nature, an uncovering of what human beings are through the penetrating observation of people living at the extremes of life. Dostoevsky entered Omsk with a secular humanist vision of human nature, rooted in his youthful utopian socialism; it was a Rousseauian view of the innate goodness of humanity, rendered corrupt by unjust social institutions that, if altered for the better, would liberate that innate goodness. It was for these idealized human beings, identified as the poor and the oppressed people of Russia, that Dostoevsky had been willing to sacrifice his life. Now, in Omsk, he was among them and saw them up close—and the sight was not pretty. He was appalled, first by the absolute, unyielding hostility of the peasant convicts toward the educated, upper-class political prisoners such as Dostoevsky (who were a small minority). As he put it in his letter to his brother: "Their hatred for the gentry knew no bounds. . . . They would have eaten us alive, given the chance."[11] He was appalled also at the coarseness and violence, approaching the level of bestiality, that he saw in his fellow prisoners. Indeed, Dostoevsky's greatest hardship for much of his term in the camp was simply the close proximity of these people, with their perpetual shouting, fighting, gambling, drinking (where possible), obscene language, and constant bickering.[12] Yet most profoundly disturbing for him was his encounter with criminals, including murderers and violators of children, who showed no remorse for their crimes, no evidence of a moral conscience.[13] This discovery of the ugliness, darkness, and evil of human beings utterly shattered Dostoevsky's secular humanitarian faith, what he later called his "Schillerism." This is the discovery that so enthralled Nietzsche when he read *The House of the Dead*, the discovery of what seemed to be a human nature driven by the will to power, beyond the categories of good and evil.

Yet this is not all that is portrayed in *The House of the Dead*. The shattering of Dostoevsky's humanitarian faith did not leave him mired in nihilism, for he made another, even more difficult discovery about his fellow inmates. He learned somehow to see through the brutalized exterior to the beauty of the human image beneath, to "discover

---

11. Dostoevsky, *Pisma I*, 135–37.
12. See the February 1876 section of Dostoevsky, *Writer's Diary*.
13. See, for instance, Dostoevksy, *House of the Dead*, 82–83, 104–6.

diamonds in this filth." This was for Dostoevsky a profoundly Christian discovery, because it was the Christianity of the convicts that was most evidently linked with the beautiful image sometimes showing through their "alluvial barbarism." Dostoevsky witnessed this Christianity, for instance, during the Easter services attended by the convicts:

> The convicts took their prayers very seriously, and each time they came to church each one of them would bring his widow's mite with which to buy a candle or contribute to the collection. . . . We took communion at early mass. When, with the chalice in his hands, the priest came to the words "receive me, O Lord, even as the robber," nearly all the convicts fell kneeling to the ground with a jangling of fetters, apparently interpreting the words as a literal expression of their own thoughts.[14]

The discovery of the beautiful image (*obraz*) in the most unlikely of places was a Christian discovery for Dostoevsky also, and more profoundly because it was related to the whole meaning of Christ as the transcendent ideal incarnate in reality. Indeed, this discovery was to become a leading element of Dostoevsky's vocation as a Christian artist. As an artist at the center of whose aesthetic was the image of Christ, his concern and struggle was to show the beautiful and the good incarnate in and transformative of reality, *without falsifying or sentimentalizing that resistant reality*. Thus his subject is so often the lowly human being; not according to some simplistic formula that the lowly, the downtrodden, the marginal *is* the beautiful, but in an attempt to reveal the presence of the beautiful in even the most fallen human beings.

Aleksandr Solzhenitsyn

Aleksandr Solzhenitsyn, too, underwent a transformation of heart and mind in Siberia, and in a direction analogous to Dostoevsky's, from secular humanism to Orthodox Christianity. When he joined the Red Army in 1941 to fight Hitler, he was an ardent communist (according to his first wife, Natasha, Lenin was his "idol"), but when he emerged from the gulag in 1957, he was embarked on the path that would lead him to embrace Orthodoxy publicly and, in an interview a few years before his death, to maintain that the only hope for the modern world is "a return to religion." Nor did Solzhenitsyn, like Dostoevsky, shy away from apocalyptic thought: in the same interview he notes that "in the Scriptures . . . that which predicts the future always talks of the road towards the anti-Christ."[15]

The primary sources for Solzhenitsyn's Siberian experience are his fictionalized account of his time as a bricklayer in the hard labor camp of Ekibastuz, *One Day in the Life of Ivan Denisovich* (first published in Russia in 1962 with Khrushchev's express permission), and of course, the monumental three-volume *Gulag Archipelago* (first published in the West in the 1970s), which laid bare in exhaustive detail the various dimensions of the

---

14. Ibid., 275.

15. For his early admiration of Lenin, see the biography by Thomas, *Alexander Solzhenitsyn*, 75–76. The later interview is found in Orthodoxy Today.org, August 12, 2005; also published as Pearce, "An Interview with Alexander Solzhenitsyn."

Soviet concentration camp system. Solzhenitsyn's memoir is to some extent continually in dialogue with that of Dostoevsky's; one can note, for instance, the repeated comparisons that Solzhenitsyn makes between camp conditions under the Soviets in regard to food, accommodation, work, punishment, and so on, and those that existed in the tsarist nineteenth century. The comparison is invariably to the advantage of the tsarist camps; one might say, in summing it all up, that Ivan Denisovich's "good day" under Stalin would have been a terrible day for Dostoevsky.

Out of all the overwhelming wealth of detail in the *Gulag Archipelago*, I will here only focus on the question of memoir writing itself, starting with the practical challenges faced by Solzhenitsyn. As was the case in Dostoevsky's camp, access to books, especially those not officially approved, was extremely limited; and in a way that is again reminiscent of Dostoevsky, Solzhenitsyn notes in *One Day* that Ivan Denisovich's bunkmate was a Baptist who kept a copy of the Gospels hidden in a hole in the wall near their bunk, which he would take out to read whenever the opportunity presented itself. Writing materials were even harder to come by, though it was not impossible for prisoners with the will to find a way to scavenge pieces of paper and pencil ends. In a fascinating chapter of *Archipelago Three* called "Poetry under a Tombstone, Truth under a Stone," Solzhenitsyn describes the means the would-be writer had to adopt to get around the strict prohibition against prisoners *keeping* anything in writing, even where writing materials were allowed. In the face of this prohibition, he did not even dare to do as Dostoevsky had done and keep a secret notebook hidden somewhere. His only recourse was to keep his manuscripts hidden in his head, by committing them to memory. He informs us that his procedure was first to compose on paper, so he could see what he had written in front of him, then quickly memorize it and burn the evidence. Since it was easier to memorize verse than prose, he would deliberately cast his work in verse form.

Solzhenitsyn also employed other mnemonic devices. As the number of verse lines grew day by day in his memory, he would repeatedly recite them to himself, keeping track of the lines, for instance, by breaking wooden matches into little pieces and arranging them in rows, then taking them away one by one as he worked his way through the verses. When he noticed that some Catholic Lithuanians among the prisoners were making rosaries for themselves from bits of bread, he asked them to make one for him, with certain precise specifications; he told them that in his religion he needed one hundred beads, that every tenth bead must be cubic and every fiftieth immediately distinguishable at a touch. The Lithuanians were apparently impressed by his devotion. By the end of his sentence, Solzhenitsyn had accumulated 12,000 lines of verse in his memory (twice the length of Pushkin's *Eugene Onegin*). This method of writing naturally had immense drawbacks, as Solzhenitsyn notes:

> The more you have written, the more days in each month are consumed by recitation. And the particular harmful thing about these recitals is that you cease to see clearly what you have written, cease to notice the strong and weak points. The first draft, which in any case you approve in a hurry, so that you can burn it,

> remains the only one. You cannot allow yourself the luxury of putting it aside . . . and then looking at it with a fresh critical eye.[16]

Revision was impossible. On at least two occasions, moreover, he was not able to burn what he had written before a search. He also barely escaped detection, once through lying about the meaning of what he had written to a badly educated guard, and the other time by throwing the paper away, fortunately to find it again the next day in order to destroy it properly.

Solzhenitsyn, no less than Dostoevsky, was relentless in his determination to remain a writer against all the odds. He too regarded his situation as also an extraordinary opportunity, and for the same reason—it was an opportunity to find the true human image, the *imago Dei*, within the apparently inhuman, and moreover, to find in the midst of suffering spiritual renewal through writing. Indeed, Solzhenitsyn came to see the gulag situation as a unique opportunity for creative discovery unprecedented in world literature. For the first time in history, educated insight and the lives of the lowly came together in a complete merger, so that the former did not merely *observe* the latter with compassion and pangs of conscience but actually *became* what had been formerly only observed from a distance. As he puts it, millions of Russian intellectuals were thrown there—not for "a joy ride, but to be mutilated, to die, without any hope of return. For the first time in history, such a multitude of sophisticated, mature and cultivated people found themselves, not [only] in imagination and once and for all, inside the skin of slave, serf, logger, miner."[17]

Solzhenitsyn did not regard his *Gulag Archipelago* as the final word on the Soviet camp system. In his afterword to the third and final volume, he laments its imperfections of style (noting that he never dared to have the entire manuscript in front of him at one time so he could revise it from beginning to end), and its omission of important details and facts. For instance, it is worth noting that in the vast index of the 1,800-page work, there are references to Polish and Lithuanian Catholics, central Asian Muslims, Russian Old Believers and Baptists, Romanians, Greeks, and Germans, but not to Mennonites. Yet Solzhenitsyn always insisted that it remained for his account to be completed by other memoirs, which he was convinced were composed in secret desperation throughout the Stalinist gulag. "How many of us were there? Many more, I think, than have come to the surface in the intervening years. Not all of them were to survive."[18] Among those that did survive and can help to complete the picture of that period of vast human suffering are the Mennonite memoirs to be discussed in part 2.

II: Mennonite Memoirs in Stalinist Siberia (Travis Kroeker)

The path of suffering in the gulag strips away the idolatries of identity, whether culturally and ethnically formed or merely ego-driven. What is revealed in these Siberian camps of exiles is both the bestial animality of human life and the true *imago Dei* within the most

---

16. Solzhenitsyn, *Gulag Archipelago*, 3:101.
17. Solzhenitsyn, *Gulag Archipelago*, 2:490–91.
18. Solzhenitsyn, *Gulag Archipelago*, 3:105.

destitute and appalling of human circumstances. What is revealed is the basic spiritual and ethical crisis of the human condition at all times and places, which is only made evident in the path of suffering. Aron Toews begins his "Siberian Diary" (1936–38)[19] with a meditation on 1 Corinthians 13:12 ("Now I know in part; someday I will know as I have been known") and 1 Corinthians 8:3 ("If one loves God one is known by God"), in which conventional human knowing is radically problematized: "The ways which God bids us go often seem dark and unclear. Many times we feel things could have been different and better. Our knowledge is imperfect, i.e. incomplete. We know neither God nor ourselves" (April 19 '36, 91). In eternity we will know as we are known, but in the meanwhile God tarries and we suffer in dark, entangled paths. Two days later Toews reflects on the reason for divine tarrying and human suffering: grace.

> Forbearance! Love to all mankind! It is Grace versus Justice. Compassion versus Righteousness. . . . My dear Maria and children, take note of how we so often look out only for our own wellbeing, our enjoyment. We do not like to go through "hard times," but would rather live for ourselves and then be received by our Lord and Saviour! . . . That is not a Christian attitude. . . . How patiently God had to wait before he found you and me. He also wants to redeem others—He looks for them and is still looking. That is why we have hard times. (April 21 '36, 92–93)

This is the messianic martyrdom theology of the early Anabaptists and indeed of the early Christians, who were well acquainted with political persecution. It is an engaged ethical stance of witness, not victim, that draws upon the spiritual disciplines and resources of the Christian tradition—a tradition not conceived as triumphal possession but as a training in suffering that refines the *imago Dei* through affliction and patient endurance of hard times. In what follows I will examine two Mennonite Siberian memoirs: Hans Harder's *No Strangers in Exile* is a literary and therefore fictional memoir of Mennonites in the Siberian forest camps on the Mezen River east of Archangel.[20] It is fictional but closely based on fact, and was written by Harder to alert Westerners to the plight of Mennonite colonists in Russia under Stalin's vicious policy of "de-kulakization" (euphemistically known as "voluntary resettlement") begun in 1929.[21] The *Siberian Diary of Aron P. Toews* was written by a former teacher and then (after 1924) minister ("elder," or "Ohm") in the old Chortitza colony during his exile in Goltjavino and other places at the edge of the *taiga* in Siberia in the years between 1936 and 1938 (he was arrested in 1934 and exiled in 1935). Written in solitude, it is addressed both to family and his congregation, taking the form not only of diary entries but also sermons, meditations,

---

19. Toews, *Siberian Diary of Aron P. Toews*. I cite dates and page references in parentheses in the body of the essay.

20. Harder, *No Strangers in Exile*. Page references cited in parentheses in the body of the essay.

21. It should be acknowledged that Hans Harder's fictional memoir has a different status than Dostoevsky's fictional memoir, insofar as Harder did not personally experience life in the gulag. While he endured hardships and dislocation during this period, his literary depiction of the Siberian prison camp is a work of imagination based on the experiences of people he knew. Part of the argument of this essay is that each of these very different memoirs—rooted in particular experiences and in different perspectives, written in varying circumstances—nevertheless shares the conviction that the divine image in the human is deeply revealed in suffering love, especially evident in conditions such as the gulag.

stories, and poetry/prayer. Toews was able to get the diary to his family, disappearing without a trace soon after.

Hans Harder and the "University of the North"

Hans Harder's narrator, Alexander Harms, a former village teacher exiled to the Siberian *taiga* with a group of fellow Mennonites but also Russian exiles drawn from various ethnic and regional backgrounds, reflects that these exiles "share a common identity now which transcends ethnic and cultural identities. In exile there are no strangers—only brothers known or not yet known" (*No Strangers*, 10; cf. 96). This common human and even familial identity is forged in the shared unspeakable degradation of suffering in which mental and spiritual discipline is crucial to survival. "To an exile hatred and grief are more dangerous than hunger and cold" (14), says Harms, and he struggles to forget the remembered images of his pregnant wife being raped by the drunken Cossacks of the White army and her subsequent death after the stillbirth. Ohm Jasch Peters, the devout, unpretentious Mennonite minister whose "simple faith is our pillar of fire in this dark night," is important for Harms, but it is the layman Waldemar Wolff whose open-hearted humanity is "like finding a diamond in a manure pile" (32). Wolff calls their Siberian work camp the "University of the North" and the question is, what is the subject of their shared training in this school of suffering? There is of course the isolation, monotony, weariness, hunger, and exposure to the elements. There is the drunkenness, debauchery, cynicism, brutality, and bestiality of other human beings. There is the ironic experience of spiritual disembodiment by a vast, harsh, frozen landscape devoid of human civilization, in which the exiles "become separate atoms floating alone and silent and aimless in a void" (29), the "sheer physical insensibility" of the north (34). And yet, as Harms sees it, "The most insidious enemy in camp life is the kind of spreading indifference which begins as callousness towards fellow sufferers and ends as a general apathy so pervasive one's very soul is frozen into it. Indifference to one's own fate is the camp disease from which no one recovers" (41).

The "brutally elemental" world of camp life demands an equally elemental faith of the sort expressed by the Mennonite Ohm Peters and the Russian Orthodox priest Father Nikolai, which fights the deadening acedia, the sin of apathy, of camp life (58). There is the burial sermon of Ohm Peters meditating on the strange Pauline words "by your rejoicing which I have in Christ Jesus our Lord, I die daily" (81), the free inner renunciation of this life in the recognition that life in this world is but a "way," not a homeland (cf. 15–16). There is the spiritual counsel Peters gives the despairing Sasha Harms when he returns to the camp after his failed escape attempt:

> God is a mysterious God, Alexander. By nature we are all fainthearted grumblers. . . . Do you know when all that will cease? . . . When we finally grasp the truth that the righteous One is waiting for us at the end of the road. Now it's true our road is very hard, but He expects us to look beyond our own miseries to Him. God can't smooth that road for us, Sasha. He can only wait for us at the end of it." (104)

Gulag Ethics: Russian and Mennonite Prison Memoirs from Siberia

In the end, says Ohm Peters, we either give in to despair and become scoffers, or give in to the suffering, waiting God and become praisers (106)—that is the crucial choice and only the latter produces the inner spiritual strength that is able to withstand the spiritual disease that blasphemes against the divine image within the human. In Harder's fictional memoir, such spiritual strength is also expressed in the ministry of the Orthodox priest Father Nikolai, who has asked to be accepted into the suffering family of Mennonite exiles, since "we are all travelling the same road" (17). "This is a time of exile," he says, and persecution, as in the early church, has again become the mark of the Christian. He says of his fellow Russians: "We are a nation of spiritual thieves" (and here he has in mind not so much the ideological Bolsheviks so much as the degradation of selfish drunken peasants). "And what if these times finally change us from spiritual thieves into real disciples," (18) through the shared school of suffering? Like Ohm Peters (40), Father Nikolai considers the question of God to be far more important than the question of land (though Russian peasants and Mennonite kulaks alike are so destructively attuned only to the possession of the latter). Like Mennonites, the Orthodox consider the congregation to be essential in the humanizing process, "otherwise we'll all topple individually, like the trees we cut. The true faith can exist only within the Church" (51). This gets expressed liturgically in the nighttime Easter Vigil and Mass conducted by Father Nikolai with the suffering peasants, in which the climax is expressed as a prayer, by the power of the resurrection, to "forgive those who hate us," followed by the priest's powerful admonition:

> Be of courage even when you are forced to sacrifice your lives in the savage wilderness of the north. We have borne witness to His Resurrection, even here. You may be forced to perish, but not one of you will be lost—for Christ is risen! Go back to your harsh routine, ready to die but still happy, rich in your poverty as lost lambs found by the Lord. (54)

Yet these literary icons of religious saints, Mennonite Ohm Peters and Russian Orthodox Father Nikolai, do not finally articulate the existential heart of gulag ethics in Harder's novel. That is left to the "diamond in a manure pile," Waldemar Wolff, who answers the examination questions posed by the "University of the North"—"What have you got left? And what are you?"—and offers them as words of comfort to his beloved Marfa Preuss, who is plagued by her sister's debauched betrayal of her fellow Mennonite exiles for her own personal benefit. Wolff states:

> When our existence here—after the loss of our former prosperity and social status—has torn the last shred of self-respect out of us, then and only then, will we arrive at the second question. When we finally understand the implications of

> that question we won't want to answer it. . . . we won't even want to admit that we are Mennonites, or claim any status or identity for ourselves at all. The only proper and permissible answer to the question will consist of just one word. That word will turn out to have been the real subject of our studies here. It will sum up the ultimate meaning of all this painful nonsense. The word is *Nothing—nothing at all!* Do you follow me? (76)

There is a "secret message of love" in Wolff's speech, says Harms, and it is related to the mysterious messianic secret of exilic faith, the hidden divine wisdom expressed by Paul in 1 Corinthians 1:27–30.: "But God chose what is foolish in the world to shame the wise, God chose what is weak in the world to shame the strong, God chose what is low and despised in the world, even things that are not to bring to nothing things that are, so that no human being might boast in the presence of God. He is the source of your life in Christ Jesus." It is Wolff who suggests that Father Nikolai and Ohm Peters are saints whose lives have no private meaning apart from the underlying divine life enlivening the church in the world: "The mystery that surrounds their personalities is God's mystery. It's the mystery of self-sacrificing love. It's a love that demands nothing for itself, and so does not feed the kind of ego we identify as individual personality" (122). Wolff's prayer ends the memoir: "God in his mercy grant that our world beyond the frozen Mezen be remembered as a real world with ordinary, decent, suffering and praying people in it . . . people who lived and loved and hoped in the midst of despair—as long as they could. . . . Many of us fell from despair to apathy to nothing" (123). The epilogue reflects on this "nothing" as in fact the precondition *in extremis* of true spiritual liberty—the freedom to bless the people, even enemies, in a spiritual condition that "surpasses all understanding." This is the *imago Dei* that reveals how the Mennonites of the gulag are not just victims. This identity of *imago Dei* goes beyond all egoistic personal identity in a sacrificial imitation of the kenotic Christ. I turn now to the diary of Ohm Aron Toews to spell this out in greater detail.

Aron Toews's Siberian Diary

Early in his diary (May 17 '36, 95), Toews reflects on Jeremiah 3:3, "I have loved you with an everlasting love; therefore I have drawn you with loving kindness," and he states that the footprints of divine love are found on the pathways of all humankind—an attempt to plant the vineyard of love. He meditates on the parable of the vineyard in Isaiah 5 (cf. Mark 12), stating that people may respond to the initiatives of divine love with ingratitude, resulting in their bearing not good fruit but rather wild grapes. This, he suggests, happened to the Mennonites in the late nineteenth and early twentieth centuries in the passion to acquire land and greater wealth, especially among the already rich, and it resulted in community-rending disparities:

> Some had one, two, even three farms, others had no land. . . . By 1905 non-resistant Mennonites had become landlords, guarded by Cossacks. The bank manager placed native guards before the door of his idol. What's more, entire villages hired armed Cossacks to guard their possessions, their mammons. The landless workers, poor widows and orphans remained! (98)

Furthermore the *Selbstschutz* (Mennonite self-defense force), which was established to protect villages from the incursions of anarchists such as Makhno, resulted only in burned villages and mass graves of murdered victims.[22] Without love and the disciplined practices of love, violence and devastation ensues, and it is the consequence of serving mammon. The only alternative is to "become silent and bow deeply in repentance and humility" (99). Like ancient Israel and the early Christians, Russian Mennonites will have to enter the wilderness of suffering, a wilderness largely created by their own idolatrous practices, in order to be given themselves as a beloved people again, in imitation of the suffering, self-emptying messianic *imago Dei*.

For Ohm Toews, this is very much a matter of cultivating the *imago Dei* so as to burnish the true image and fight idolatry within the self, and herewith he returns to the theme of "knowing":

> God and Self: these are the great antitheses which can never be combined. As long as mankind has existed, the struggle has raged under the watchword of the Serpent: "I will be like God, knowing good from evil." To be like God is the aspiration of mankind. The "Self" is the idol who has the most servants. This idol is strong, much stronger than you and I can know. (May 27 '36, 103)

Only the conversion to the divine image away from egoism, self-love, and self-honor can accomplish the true, non-idolatrous "coming to self" entailed in being known by God. The path of this conversion is that of the kenotic Christ who "emptied himself, taking the form of a servant" (Phil 2). This is not a conversion to a system, a person, or a church; Ohm Toews comments on how the idol "Self" can be well-versed in Scripture and devoted to the church, how it has managed "to create many churches, sects, confessions and fellowships" (105), and goes on to provide many negative examples of both Mennonites and also Russian clergy in exile (106). The process of conversion will entail a radical penitence for the Mennonite people, given their "shattering demoralization"; they will need to remember in deep humility their true spiritual estate revealed in the suffering servant Christ, the exemplary *imago Dei*:

> Our people have fallen deeply, ethically and morally. Even during the war, or perhaps already a decade earlier, this decline already existed. "Land, land" and "money, money" and "business and education" were corrupt watchwords of the time. The old staunch steadfastness gave way to a puffed-up enlightenment. The quiet Mennonite has become a contentious faction-monger and partly

---

22. Note also the harsh words in Neufeld, *Russian Dance of Death*: "When the occupation Revolutionary forces disarmed the local peasants to create order and gave the arms to the German colonists, the Mennonites also allowed themselves to be armed in order to protect their lands. Militarization always ends in provocation, not reconciliation, and the landless peasants were provoked even as the Mennonite communities suffered spiritual damage" (69–70). Mennonites are to be doubly blamed: "First, it was politically unwise. Then again it was in glaring contradiction to their hitherto professed concept of non-resistance. The Russian peasants pointed out this contradiction and called them hypocrites. A bitter truth was held up to the colonists: 'When our Russia,' so it went, 'our women and children, were threatened with attack in 1914, then you refused to take up arms for defensive purposes. But now that it's a question of your own property you are arming yourselves.' Certainly it was a crying shame that the colonists' actions were inspired neither by a desire to protect the state nor by a true Christian spirit" (79). Cf. Baerg, *Diary of Anna Baerg*, 42ff.

a supporter for ideas he doesn't understand; or for money. Our faith in God's defense, which through the centuries has protected our people, our fathers, is replaced by "Self-defense." (Aug. 2–9 '36; 115)

Here lies the heart of the gulag experience for the Mennonite people. Suffering is not only or always a form of punishment (as Job's friends mistakenly thought) but is "often our redemption," as "the token of love" in which human beings may learn that strength is made perfect in weakness—that messianic Pauline conundrum (2 Cor 12:9–10) (Aug. 16 '36). The path of suffering in imitation of Christ is the path, as Ohm Toews suggests in his Epiphany meditation of January 6, 1937, that dispossessed the first heathen worshippers (the spiritual representatives of the entire pagan world, including Mennonites) of their idolatrous worldly wisdom that cannot fulfill the longing of the human heart. This longing can only be fulfilled in worship of and ethical conformity to the true *imago Dei* who did not count equality with God a thing to be grasped, but emptied himself in order to become the instrument of divine love in the world even unto death.

Conclusion

The Mennonite authors, like Dostoevsky and Solzhenitsyn, vividly depict the coarseness, violence, and physical suffering of the Siberian prison camps and reflect on the transforming effects of the camp experience upon their religious and moral self-understanding and understanding of the human condition. In each case this is expressed in terms of a Christian interpretation of the *imago Dei*, a discovery of the profound truth and beauty of the suffering Christ in conditions of extreme deprivation and inhumanity. However, unlike Dostoevsky, whose transformation was from the secular humanism of his youthful utopian socialism, and Solzhenitsyn, who turned from ardent atheistic communism to an embrace of messianic Orthodoxy, the Mennonites sent to the gulag were for the most part not intellectuals and were already deeply shaped by a messianic Christian identity not part of the cultural mainstream. This is not to say that the transforming effects of the gulag experience were less radical for them, since in both Harder's fictional memoir and Toews's Siberian diary the school of suffering drives them to a deeper understanding of the profound truth of the *imago Dei* as one that transcends and indeed negates all lesser cultural, social, vocational, and ethnic identities. In this situation of exile each finds the conditions for a renewed understanding of the underlying human community constituted by the suffering, self-emptying Christ who images God in human form and humanity in the divine image. It is in these regards that their written lives bear witness no less than those of the famous Russian authors do to the divine authorship of all of life, disclosed even, and perhaps most vividly, in the extremity of Siberian prison camps.

12

Mennonite and Métis

Adjacent Histories, Adjacent Truths?
(with Carole Leclair)

EVERYWHERE, IN ALL TIMES and places, human beings have appropriated one another's cultures, lands, and religious practices. It may be argued that these are always colonizing acts, but there is in any case a great variety in kinds of appropriation, ranging from appreciative imitation to violent imposition and all manner of syncretisms in between. Our focus in this essay concerns the interreligious and cross-cultural exchanges between indigenous peoples and settler cultures in what has come to be called "North America." In much of the cultural appropriation literature, at issue are specific acts of appropriation of religious symbols and ceremonies—such as sacred sweats, pipe rituals, sun dances, vision quests—by non-natives, whether deep ecologists and "new agers" or those with more commercial interests. The issue here is the public representation of these religious practices when they are detached from their traditional contexts. This is especially problematic when those traditions have themselves been obliterated or diminished by law and government policies, and the peoples of those traditions stripped of their own practices and ceremonies—as is the case for First Nations.

This suggests that the larger ethical issue is the cultural context in which appropriation as destructive domination has stripped indigenous peoples of their heritage and identity, including the religious ceremonies and practices that have nurtured and sustained them. This is not only a question of whether or not to allow such ceremonies and practices, and under what conditions, but entails the larger issue of sovereignty—the rulings about property, rights of land ownership, and access that assume a modern European statist model of political and legal authority. That model already violates traditional indigenous understandings rooted in completely different cosmologies and religious visions of the human relation to the land and to particular places. Religious ceremonies and practices are not just "data" or "artifacts" or aesthetic-emotional rituals. They are also religious duties by which the land, the creation given as gift from sacred powers, is made holy and offered back by humans whose task it is to do so. These ceremonies are the sacred exchange of gifts and responsibilities that relate more broadly to a culture, a coherent way of life in the land. Vine Deloria puts it this way:

> Removing an Indian tribe from its aboriginal territory, therefore, results in the destruction of ceremonial life and much of the cultural structure which has made ceremony and ritual significant . . . Although the loss of the land must be seen as a political and economic disaster of the first magnitude, the real exile of the tribes occurred with the destruction of ceremonial life. People became disoriented with respect to the world in which they lived.[1]

The life of the people now comes to be defined not ceremonially and dramatically but technologically and litigiously in continuous adjustment to technological innovation, articulated in the legal terminology of a materialist commodity political economy and individual, contractual rights. At this point we ought to catch a glimpse of the enormity of the problem, one that threatens to call into question from the outset a basic assumption of these kinds of research projects, namely, that there are ethics experts who reside in modern industrial research universities who can sort all this out.

In other words, if we are to take up the question of the ethics of cultural appropriation with honesty, we will need to be willing to call into question the privileged status of normative ethical concepts and theories that define (a) culture, cultural engagement, respect, and so on; (b) property, representation, appropriation; (c) religion, the sacred (and the secular); (d) rational, rationality, and publicly acceptable reason. Indeed, the very notion that ethics may be abstracted from religion and from experiential, contextual dwelling in the land and its lived narratives is already a radical contradiction of traditional indigenous knowledges and practices—and not only of First Nations but also of the indigenous knowledges and practices of the biblical tradition that has shaped the ethical forms of habitation of particular countercultural peoples (such as Mennonites), even in contemporary Western, "European" contexts. The very idea of ethics as a discourse of normative control and technical conceptual expertise is problematic, tied performatively to a commodified culture informed by Hobbesian models of political sovereignty and legal authority (with their own rootedness in religious and political traditions of a distinctive kind).

We are convinced, however, that ethics should not be seen as a matter of problem-solving or of finding the correct theoretical or policy framework. We believe it is important to begin more gropingly in stories and in the difficult, vulnerable journey toward respect rooted in attending personally to divided worlds of experience. What we offer in this essay is such a path, the halting narrative beginnings of such a journey.

I: "Mennonite" (Travis Kroeker)

I was born in Steinbach, the main town of the East Reserve of the Manitoba Mennonite settlement, three generations removed from the Manitoba Act of 1870 that fostered

---

1. Deloria, *For This Land*, 244–45.

group colonization of the prairies. My ancestors arrived from Imperial Russia in 1874, a few short years after the Canadian government's Treaty 1 (1871) had extinguished Indian land titles and "opened up" the region for agricultural settlement. Having been born on a "reserve," perhaps it is not so odd that my first language was the Mennonite Low German and that when we moved to cosmopolitan Winnipeg when I turned five, beginning English kindergarten that autumn, I experienced culture shock—a shock from which I have never fully recovered. The shock was to my identity, my sense of self, as I experienced myself as an alien, an "other" with a strange, unwritten language and an odd cultural-religious formation. This wound to the spirit continued, as I grew older, to raise painful questions about negotiating cultural and religious differences—as of course I also discovered that I no longer truly belonged in my former world, either. Such wounds are an opportunity as well, and indeed this essay is but another step in what I expect will be a life-long journey toward healing.

At the age of three or four, as I recall, colorful strangers arrived on my grandparents' farmstead (where I too lived with my parents) with wares to sell. I say colorful because I had never seen people dressed in such bright shirts, large shiny belt buckles, and cowboy boots. My grandfather conversed with them in his broken English, a conversation I'm sure I did not understand. Afterward I was told these were "Indiauna"—though I expect they were really Métis, who neither lived on their own reserve nor on Métis homesteads but rather, as Carole Leclair memorably described to me, on the road allowance. I do not know whether or not my grandfather bought any of what they were selling, nor do I remember being told anything about the significance or historic importance of these intriguing strangers. I'm sure my parents and grandparents had never themselves been taught or thought much about it. They would not have known that in the 1870 Manitoba census, fully one-half the population was French-speaking Métis, another one-third English-speaking Métis, and that while the various treaties provided land reserves and colonial payments for various Aboriginal groups, the Métis land question was never resolved. Of course, neither my grandparents nor these Aboriginal visitors would have considered this ignorance an issue—they lived separate lives and for the most part probably preferred it that way. My "little church" (*Kleine Gemeinde*) Mennonite ancestors were not proselytizers, and indeed many of them fled Manitoba for Central America in the mid-twentieth century, in partial response to the government's "reinterpretation" of the historic agreement that had allowed Mennonites to self-school their children, thus now enforcing Mennonite acculturation to a dominant Canadian society.

When I moved to Winnipeg as a child we attended a small inner-city Mennonite church made up of recent emigrants from Mennonite reserves to the multicultural city—part of the rural-urban migration that accelerated Mennonite acculturation to the Canadian mainstream. Here again I encountered indigenous people, though now largely in terms of the demeaning caricature of the "drunk Indian." Unlike the many upwardly mobile Mennonites seeking and finding prosperity in their new setting "off the reserve," it seemed evident that many indigenous peoples were living out the despair of a subjugated and defeated culture. Clearly, as white Europeans, Mennonites "fit in" and indigenous peoples did not. I knew then even as I (more consciously) know now that there is something deeply troubling about this from both ends. That is, to me it was and is no less disturbing that acculturating Mennonites fit in so well, despising their own traditional ancestors and their Aboriginal neighbors—easily internalizing the grotesque caricatures and prejudices of the wider dominant culture—than it was and is distressing to see the visible oppression and despair in indigenous cultures. I knew in my bones (though I did not necessarily welcome this knowledge) that to be true to my own peoples' spiritual narrative would require me not to "fit in" but to remain deliberately marginal and alien to such marginalizing and alienating cultural patterns of colonizing oppression. This is not a stance of private, individual purity or neutral detachment, but one of engaged resistance to a cultural conformity of diminishment.

Breaking out of my Mennonite subculture in order to explore such disturbing questions meant for me attending a centrally dominant Canadian institution of acculturation, the university—about which our traditional elders had been deeply suspicious (*Je jeleada, je vetjeada*; "The more learned, the more perverted"). There, interestingly, on the recommendation of a Mennonite professor (one of the *vetjeada*, no doubt), I read a book that deeply affected me—*Black Elk Speaks* (1932), the autobiography of an Oglala Lakota holy man (1863–1950) as mediated through the literary telling of a white poet of the Great Plains, John Neihardt. This text may be interpreted as a parable of the ethics of cultural appropriation, in all of its perilous possibility. It is itself a literary record of an indigenous religious life lived in transition from the traditional ways to the colonizing arrival of the Wasichus on the Great Plains. While mediated in the language and literary form of a Wasichu poet, it nevertheless also preserves an indigenous account of the meaning of life experienced in the wake of this colonizing encounter, structured according to the sacred cosmology of the Lakota peoples.[2]

This book showed me two crucial things about dialogue in the face of difference and, indeed, a history of damaging colonization and appropriation: self-criticism (or, less academically, penitential lamentation) and generosity. Black Elk bears powerful witness to the conquest of the land by European Christendom colonizers. As such, it is a bitter truth also for Mennonites, themselves historical victims of European Christendom—having been persecuted for their difference in the practices of adult (not infant) baptism, a free (not state) church, and nonviolence in imitation of Jesus—that they too became willing and highly successful participants in this colonizing mission. And yet, in Black Elk's account, there is also a generosity toward the "other" that does not remain within exclusivist conventional categories of any kind—whether that of victim and oppressor or Aboriginal and Wasichu or Lakota and Christian. There is a dramatic openness of engagement and permeable identity displayed in Black Elk's story that allows for vulnerable exchange across cultures, that points to a path beyond ideologies (and ideology critiques) and power politics (whether statist, tribal, ecclesial, or academic), where movements toward healing may occur.

This healing path speaks to me of a willing dispossession of security—whether of moral self-justification or academic methodologies of various kinds or religious or political self-righteousness. This path is one of opening one's heart to pain, the pain of

---

2. Vine Deloria therefore suggests, as an articulation of the existential, liturgical, and theopolitical substance of the Lakota tradition, it has become (for better and for worse) something like a "bible of tribes," a pan-Indian vision for all kinds of First Nations peoples. Deloria, *For This Land*, chap. 23.

diminishment, the pain of one's own complicity in the diminishment of other peoples and cultures, and the pain of the great ignorance, complacency, and despair such diminishment produces in all who are involved. This pain, like all pain, is a gift that opens us to what is broken, damaged, and in need of repair. So also are guilt, anxiety, and regret—all forms of penitential lamentation for the failure to acknowledge, accept, and dwell with this pain—to be treated as gifts. Such gifts are intrinsic to the movement of spiritual and cultural freedom away from damaging and diminishing forms of prideful possession.

When I first met Carole Leclair I came armed with an academic essay draft that self-consciously displayed its unconventional and narrative approach to the ethics of religion and cultural appropriation. Carole likened it to a high-powered, finely tuned intellectual machine clicking on all cylinders (and, though she didn't say it, I imagine with all the windows closed and the stereo turned up to comfortable music). Despite its self-avowed vulnerability, Carole audaciously and generously showed me that it offered little room for her or for a truly open human exchange on what is at stake in this question. She opened me up to new dimensions of engagement, beginning in a more personal and groping attention to the stories that make up our different perspectives and experience. This personal attention entails for her a willingness to be reconnected to the history of the land that we share (not a meeting on more abstract intellectual, academic terrain) so as not to forget the possibility in generosity of a new kind of critical, mutual, and engaging dwelling in this suffering land.

What I come to see through Carole's tenacious "no bullshit" engagement is that ethics in this matter is neither a matter of constructing frameworks or paradigms (whether of the theoretical or the policy kind), nor of problem-solving. It is in the first instance a willingness to sit and walk together in the uncomfortable "between" of a cultural divide, where we neither see very clearly where the exchanges will take us nor are able to detach or abstract ourselves from the painful narratives and challenges we there encounter. Our first task is a disciplined, open attention. The academy, like the wider dominant culture, has not fostered such vulnerable attention very well. We have often instead developed mechanisms of control, cultivated exclusive and exclusionary disciplinary specialisms, and approached knowledge as "information processing," "data analysis," and methodological sophistication. By such paths wisdom will not allow herself to be seen or approached; such paths produce only terminal creeds/beliefs/ ideologies that violate reality through enforced conformity.

For myself, I have found a glimmering of the possibility of another path—not colonizing or controlling but penitential and open to otherness—in my own biblically formed tradition. It is well expressed in the words of the secular Jewish culture critic Walter Benjamin, deeply critical of European state sovereignty: "Like every generation that preceded us, we have been endowed with a *weak* messianic power, a power to which the past has a claim and that claim cannot be settled cheaply."[3] Settling cheaply is not primarily an economic matter, but a spiritual one—where is the spirit in our culture? Benjamin is very wary of a widespread progressivism in modern Western culture which assumes that everything belongs to it, is simply standing reserve for its own appropriation. Such is our techno-globalist age that piles up cultural conquests and appropria-

---

3. Benjamin, "Theses on the Philosophy of History," 254.

tions like so many trinkets in a multicultural boutique. Benjamin believes that our only possible redemption from such violent colonial politics lies in remembering again that we did not make the world, nor therefore do we measure it. Such practices of remembering will open us critically and generously to different notions of "tradition": oral and not only literary; ritual and not primarily monumental (ritual is alive and lived, whereas monuments terminally memorialize the captured dead); cosmological and not only sociological; liturgical and not primarily litigious; existential and not only creedal.

Only such spiritually disciplined cultural practices by people in their own particular times and places will enable resistance to the tremendous pressures to conform to the global progressivism that requires the oblivion of many forms of life and knowledge crucial for the flourishing of human dwelling in the land. Such lives lived on the margins are not a retreat from cultural engagement. For example, while Carole and I have each expressed serious criticisms of the academy and its practices, neither of us (so far as I know) is about to resign our university positions. But we each in our own way are calling for a more open and vulnerable way of being in the academy by accepting marginality and a greater range of cultural-linguistic expression and experience through the willing dispossession of security and dominance. This enlivening of both self-criticism and generosity will entail a movement from intellectual control to relinquishment, from dominion to more vulnerable dwelling, from possession to the exchange of (often painful) gifts, from fear toward love. In my own Mennonite tradition of messianic love patterned after Jesus, this marginality is expressed first of all in the dispossession of tradition as "one's own," since life is not "one's own." Paul the apostle expresses it as a messianic calling to live *hōs mē* (as if not):

> I mean the time has become contracted; in what remains let those who mourn live as if not (*hōs mē*) mourning, and those who rejoice as if not (*hōs mē*) rejoicing, and those who buy as if not (*hōs mē*) possessing, and those who use the world as if not (*hōs mē*) fully using it. For the outward form of the world is passing away. (1 Cor 7:29–30)

There is a particular kind of "making use" of the world that treats it in a non-proprietary manner, not tied to juridical ownership. It takes its ethical bearings from the non-possessive biblical vision of a creation in which human creatures dwell in the world vulnerably, in a manner that opens it up to being made new by the ever-new agency of the sovereign Creator. Such an ethic can never claim sovereignty for its own cultural or religious identity. The living "as if not" possessing one's cultural or religious identity is not abandoning it for an "elsewhere" but dwelling within it as in exile, in dispossession, in all of its embodied particularity. This transforms it in keeping with its true condition, its "passing away" toward an "end" that lies beyond it and remains unknown, open. Such a messianic identity is not a new universalism that somehow transcends or escapes difference. Indeed it is not to be related to a form of universal "knowing" of any sort. Paul says, "Anyone who claims to know something does not yet have the necessary knowledge; but anyone who loves God is known by God" (1 Cor 8:2–3).

This reversal suggests a relinquishment of human sovereignty and subverts a colonizing mindset. An "as if not" messianic ethic does not possess an ideal that makes humans the universalizing masters of their own moral and political destinies. It is rooted in a self-emptying movement of dispossession that cannot become yet another act of controlling legislation in the name of a merely human sovereignty. The "as if not" relinquishes its moral striving and its hold—whether of the technological means of progressive liberation from the decay and bondage of nature, or the political means of liberating particular identities from the burdens of their oppressive traditions and conditions. The point is rather to open all worldly callings and conditions to the transfiguring passage of love. And in love it is necessary to get beyond possessive identities and aspirations altogether via the gift of a healing rooted in penitence—for Mennonites, a penitence for participating in the destructive domination and appropriation of peoples and lands. Such healing will also require Mennonites to wrestle self-critically with the messianic paradigm in a suffering love that chooses to pass through and not merely leave behind or "replace" the groaning weight of past cycles of victimization, violence, and retribution. There is no path to salvation and shalom except through self-losing service to what passes away.

What could this mean for the question of appropriation? Perhaps it is easier to say what it would *not* mean. It would not mean bringing the Bible and taking the land, but rather, in the first instance, relinquishing the clinging to control in cultural exchange. It would not require the subordination of another culture to my own, nor the desire to possess that culture or even to preserve my own. It would not construct an ethic of universal principles or of universalizing procedures, nor a theory of universal political sovereignty, but would begin more humbly by honoring particular agreements made with particular indigenous peoples, allowing the pain of cultural wounds to open us to new, particular paths of dwelling together in our differences in this suffering land.

II: "Métis" (Carole Leclair)

> I will tell you something about stories, [he said]
> They aren't just entertainment.
> Don't be fooled.
> They are all we have, you see,
> all we have to fight off illness and death.
> You don't have anything
> If you don't have the stories.
> *Ceremony*—Leslie Marmon Silko[4]

Following a series of emails, Travis Kroeker and I agreed to meet at a local donut shop to discuss a possible collaborative essay. I admit it: I was skittish. I had almost made up my mind to refuse this task. I was wary of the assumption held by many that academic pursuit of indigenous religious and cultural knowledge is inherently positive. The outpouring of published texts on indigenous literary and spiritual life, by Native and non-Native writers, confuses issues of appropriation. What knowledge ought to be kept sacred?

---

4. Silko, *Ceremony*, 2.

PART 3: MESSIANISM AND DIASPORA ETHICS

What knowledge can be commercialized, and how do the communities who create this knowledge benefit from this process? Indigenous cultures have deep ties to storytelling, but the stories we tell bear little resemblance to the dominant cultural concepts of the literary Indian, the noble savage, the dying races.

Historian Winona Wheeler notes that Western-based academics place a high value on procuring "knowledge" or the "truth" as a goal in and of itself, whereas in indigenous thought, "you can't just go and take it, or even go and ask for it. Access to knowledge requires longterm commitment, apprenticeship and payment."[5] It is never enough simply to learn the facts of indigenous spirituality; the seeker must first learn how to respect its practices, its ways of living. The Department of Religious Studies at my university refused me permission to teach Native spirituality there because I am not an academic specialist in that discipline. Some doors remain closed. In my university there is a glimmer of discussion about the importance of space and place for indigenous knowledge, witnessed by the fact that our fledgling Indigenous Studies Program exists.

Travis and I reflected on how and why we should have a conversation, a Métis professor of Indigenous Studies and a professor of Religious Studies. The answers began to unfold for me when I learned that Travis, a Mennonite, was born near my Métis village of Vassar, Manitoba. Just look at this coincidence. Travis and I were born in the same neighborhood, in villages less than fifty kilometers apart. Both of us became academics in Ontario, but otherwise our worlds seemed not to intersect at all. I wanted to take a closer look at the idea of divided worlds, not with a view to finding comfortable parallels in our experience (a perspective that flirts with appropriation) but to find a way to come to easier terms with our differences. The land itself connected us. I trust the land as my mother and my teacher. And so, tobacco in hand, Travis came to visit and our conversations began. As we walked together on his bush property I could see that he felt a caring connection to the trees, the plants, and animals that live in that place. The connection Travis feels for the land is not the same as mine. Our cosmologies originate in difference. But as we walked the narrow trails, I began to relax and smile with him. What forces are at work to keep our worlds separate? Can "dialogue" accomplish change? I'll come back to these questions.

I am a Red River Métis, a descendant of many generations of Saulteaux, Dakota, Montagnais, and French peoples who traveled this land and who sometimes made their homes in those precarious little villages like St. Vital, St. Boniface, and Vassar. My grandfather Joachim was one of a number of Métis who emigrated from Red River, south and eastward, creating settlements along the way in places like Marchand, Thibaultville, and Woodridge. Marcel Giraud describes my family when he writes the following:

> Beyond the immediate bonds of the Red River, the situation is noticeably worse. . . . there survives a society without any breadth. A considerable proportion of its members lack any possibility of adapting to the methods or the mentality of the whites. Many families who were incapable of becoming incorporated into the economy of the Red River and of retaining their lands retreated here to

---

5. Wheeler, "'Every Word is a Bundle'"; quoted in Smith, *Conquest*, 133.

seek, in this primitive environment which so abruptly succeeds the agricultural zone of the colony, a way of life in keeping with their past.[6]

The term Métis usually refers to a particular group, primarily the French descendants of the fur trade era, those who developed their own ethnicity and language in Western Canada. Today the term is used throughout Canada and increasingly in the United States to identify any mixed Aboriginal/non-Aboriginal person. It is this practice of using the term Métis in a generic sense that Saskatchewan Métis leader Clem Chartier argues against.

> While Indian Nations and the Inuit have been here for a very long time, the Metis are a young nation. We have grown from the Indian Nations, particularly the Cree and Ojibway. Initially we were of "mixed blood" but since those beginnings, we have evolved and developed into a specific nation of our own. It's not correct, and we object, when people say the Metis are mixed-blood people.[7]

Métis, like First Nations people, are not one homogenous group. Our cultural and linguistic differences divide us as surely as geographic distance. For me, even more important than these cultural distinctions are the things we concern ourselves with as Aboriginal peoples—such as the land, the turn of the seasons, the telling of how we came to be and what will be our shared fate as living beings on this earth. I recall Laguna writer Leslie Marmon Silko's words, "You don't have anything / If you don't have the stories."

Feasting is a fine old Métis tradition. Eating together speaks to the communal, to trust, to the circle completed when all the food is eaten, the songs sung, the stories told. When I teach a course, my students host at least one social. I cart my plug-in fry pan, flour, and blueberries to many meetings. Once we held a bannock-making contest in the university corridors. Several hungry scholars peeked out of their tiny offices, sniffing the air, searching out the source of the delicious and seditious aromas.

> Hot bannock, fried slices of bologna, and a cup of tea. And, of course, blueberry jam for bannock dunking. After a while we are smiling with blue teeth, black mouths, and sparkling eyes, laughing at each other.[8]

I tell you this story because this is how we inhabit the space of the university, precariously, with difficulty. We invade with our smells of baking bannock, with our talk and our too-loud laughter. We set up a kitchen table in the very heart of the academy to acknowledge that the institution of academic research is alienating; it perpetuates colonizing structures. The process of encapsulation of indigenous peoples began with the fur companies' attempts at total economic control, with the government's legal and political control, and the church's replacing indigenous theologies with Christianity. Our talking does not yet gain us recognition, respect, or credentials in universities. The academy holds power to designate what is useful knowledge and to engage thoughtful people in critical discussions. Flux and adaptation is woven into our indigenous cultures, and it

---

6. Giraud, *Métis in the Canadian West*, 480–81.
7. Chartier, "Métis Perspectives on Self-Government."
8. Slipperjack, "Blueberry Days."

would be a mistake to see our use of skidoos and televisions, cell phones and academic posts as evidence of total conformity to the dominant society.

My grandmother remembered how it all began, the life of our little village. She told of arriving as a child from somewhere near Argyle, Minnesota, at the place that would become Vassar, a place she described as "that desolate place, all poor, with only a few log cabins." She recalled the men cutting the logs, dragging them by oxen to a portable sawmill and making nice big wide boards of Norway and jack pine. Last summer my mother, sister, and I went back to Vassar, possibly for the last time. We stood in the graveyard that cradles our ancestors; we walked around the crumbling foundations of grandmother's house, which now sits on land owned by strangers. Wonderfully strange, we found the old railway station house had been moved onto this land and there it sits, out of place. The Mennonite community refused this railway as a danger to their way of life. For many Métis, it was a way out of poverty and exclusion. The railway also brought nuns, and harsh assimilation, and loss of the Michif language, a loss that my mother still grieves.

I admit that I began my conversation with Travis with an attitude of suspicion and resentment, an attitude which I considered historically justified. I felt a familiar fear of being hurt, being humiliated. I charged him with the 1870s migration of Russian Mennonites to America, of bargaining with the Dominion for the best free Métis land settlements on the prairies, and of having initiated the great grab of Indian land in the Oklahoma Territory! He responded with words like repentance and regret. I didn't care for this response. Too Christian, I thought, and unlikely to address the grinding poverty in indigenous communities, poverty linked directly to unresolved land claims. What I was hoping for was a cooperative reflection, as allies, on solutions we might imagine when confronted by the displacement and disempowerment of Native peoples. There is a fine balance between setting out the boundaries of a discussion and being accusatory. Occasionally I lose my balance.

My grandparents were born into turbulent times. They were part of a generation of Métis whose lives and communities were deeply affected by the economic juggernaut of capitalism and the aftermath of the failed uprisings of 1885. All his life, grandfather was terrified of "la police" and in awe of priests. For many generations, Métis rebellion and loss in my family hardened to produce what Métis writer Gerald Vizenor calls "terminal creeds" and "terminal believers." Kim Blaeser offers Vizenor's definition in these terms:

> In "I know What You Mean" he defines "terminal believers as "those believing in only one vision of the world." . . . "Terminal creeds," claims a character in Bearheart, "are terminal diseases." . . . Whether sacred or secular, tribal or nontribal, terminal creeds destroy.[9]

Misogyny, threats of Christian hellfire, and concern for his family name motivated my grandfather to make virtual prisoners of his six daughters. Marriage was the only permanent way through the front gate. My mother, the most stubbornly resistant, most rebellious of his daughters, fled to Winnipeg and later to Ontario, after giving birth to

---

9. Blaeser, *Gerald Vizenor*, 49.

two Métis daughters *à la façon du pays*,[10] long after that fashion had faded from history. Grandfather, a "terminal believer," refused to see us. We did not travel back to Vassar until he died. I search for traditional dreams and visions in order to refashion my grandfather's fate, that of being trapped within any terminal creed that ultimately isolates and destroys love. As an adult, my mother chose the path of resistance to Christianity. She chose the "red road," learning what she could of the spirituality of her Saulteaux and Assiniboine heritages. She gave these teachings to us, and she gave us a persistent desire for freedom.

So, am I free today? Let me tell you another story. Recently I went to visit a lawyer in order to draw up a trust fund. Just before the meeting, I checked out his website and discovered that he was launching a class action suit on behalf of the townsfolk of Caledonia, a town where Six Nations peoples are attempting to reclaim lost lands. I asked him about the language he chose to describe the situation, with words like "angry native protesters" and "terrorists." He responded with fixed, banal, clichéd justifications and lack of historical knowledge, ideas I hear repeatedly from those who live in a world apart from indigenous peoples. I left the meeting feeling angry and cynical. To me this meant a closing down of spirit, the abandonment of kindness. Mutual accusations begin with conflict, over land and belief and sovereignty. The managers of such conflicts (government, police, church and tribal leaders) dictate the language, the slogans and stories that are most easily digested. In a recent speech to Latin American and Caribbean bishops at the end of a visit to Brazil, the pope said the church had not imposed itself on the indigenous peoples of the Americas. They had welcomed the arrival of European priests at the time of the conquest, as they were "silently longing" for Christianity, he said.[11] Without intellectual vigilance, we can become trapped within the crude generalizations and superstitions, the "terminal creeds" we use to imagine others' truths. We accuse each other, both within our indigenous communities and across the common Canadian culture. Political and ideological forces work to keep our worlds separate.

My conversations with Travis take a different turn. True, there is a small sadness, a certain lack of understanding, the difficulty of cross-cultural communication, but there is also a widening space of mutual respect. This is an important part of what our talks have produced. With increasing trust, we can speak of our memories, our beliefs and religious histories, without being forced by shallow rhetoric to choose the victim or aggressor roles. We can acknowledge one another's just claims without relinquishing any part of our unique identities. It was Travis who reminded me (several times) that our knowledge of each other's heritage and personal viewpoints is always partial, interested, and potentially oppressive. Our mutual histories on this land dictate this fact. The "old ones," the grandmothers, brought me to the academy to work for them. I am to play a small part in "getting the story right—telling the story well,"[12] a research model rooted in our indigenous ways of thinking, being, and knowing. For this reason, I insisted that

---

10. A fur trade term for liaisons with Native women outside church-sanctioned marriage.

11. http://www.nowpublic.com/aboriginals_in_brazil_deeply_offended_by_pope_benedicts_recent_statements_on_immaculate_genocide.

12. Smith, "Getting the Story Right."

PART 3: MESSIANISM AND DIASPORA ETHICS

Travis set aside his discipline-based approach to research and tell me some of his small stories, maps across generations, maps of devastation and also of hope.

Dialogue alone cannot create the kind of changes needed if first peoples are to prosper again in this land. Aboriginal "days of action" bring strident voices and political defensiveness to the podium rather than real change. Talking with Travis will not change the heart-wrenching statistics of teenage suicide in our indigenous communities. Have our conversations been simply an academic exercise? I will allow Travis to answer this for himself. For me, personal healing has been an important point of our encounters, not surrendering politics or ignoring the weight of history. These healing talks work against estrangement and indifference. As an Aboriginal scholar/activist, my first responsibility is to my own people. My work is for them. My heart is for them. But our elders tell us repeatedly that kindness is the simplest and most difficult teaching we have. It brings peace, and the confidence and courage to tell our stories without rancor or bitterness. In all our words together, Travis displayed this kindly spirit. Still I say, "Not enough."

At the heart of the appropriative impulse is what literary critic Arnold Davidson describes as a "double temptation."[13] Canadians often display a fascination with Aboriginal worldviews and the outward symbols of our various beliefs, while determined to hold on to their own cultural securities. Elders describe this tension as "walking with a shoe and a moccasin," of being off-balance. In an attempt to resolve this desire/refusal, some of us (academics in particular) are tempted to retreat to an imagined neutral corner, covering our escape in blankets of critical inquiry and intellectual reserve. Our stories, our historical narratives, are not objective and unbiased. They are constructed out of personal and ideological interests, as are all human narratives. Events in our histories have caused our cultures to become "split at the root,"[14] which produces a multiplicity of voices both traditional and contemporary.

The truth is, there is no neutral clearing in the thickets of current Aboriginal political and theoretical play, no safe place for academics, activists, or political leaders to position themselves with respect to competing truths. In this land now called Canada, Aboriginal peoples are not safe, nor are their sovereignty issues respected. To acknowledge this and to work for change does not require us to abandon cherished convictions if these include such values as social justice, empathy, and the refusal of a convenient historical amnesia with respect to first peoples.

---

13. Davidson, *Coyote Country*, 22.
14. Peterson, "Haunted America," 30.

13

Rich Mennonites in an Age of Mammon

Is a Messianic Political Economy Possible?

I

IN 1977 A CANADIAN teaching at Messiah College in the United States published a groundbreaking book, *Rich Christians in an Age of Hunger*, in which he argued that North American Christians were failing to discern or attend to the offensive proclamation of the Gospel on the dangers of wealth. Ronald Sider, the author, bluntly asserted: "The ever more affluent standard of living is the god of twentieth-century North America and the adman is its prophet."[1] Affluent Christians, he went on to argue at the heart of the book—"A Biblical Perspective on the Poor and Possessions"—have allowed economic self-interest to distort their interpretation of Scripture.[2] In contrast to certain liberation theologians who talked about God's preferential option for the poor, Sider made the interesting argument that God is not partial; it only appears that way to those seduced by the God of affluence and success:

> By contrast with the way you and I, as well as the comfortable and powerful of every age and society, always act toward the poor, God seems to have an overwhelming bias in favor of the poor. But it is biased only in contrast with our sinful unconcern. It is only when we take our perverse preference for the successful and wealthy as natural and normative that God's concern appears biased.... The God of the Bible is on the side of the poor just because he is *not* biased, for he is a God of impartial justice.[3]

---

1. Sider, *Rich Christians*, 46.
2. Ibid., 77.
3. Ibid., 84.

PART 3: MESSIANISM AND DIASPORA ETHICS

These striking words came from the pen of a Brethren in Christ farm boy from Stevensville, Ontario, who after taking his first degree at the University of Waterloo went on to complete a Yale PhD in history, and whose book was declared by *Christianity Today* to be one of the one hundred most influential books on religion in the twentieth century,[4] going through five editions and selling more than 350,000 copies. (Sider is also the author of twenty-two more books and one hundred articles, and founding president of "Evangelicals for Social Action."). Do we think that only accountants and entrepreneurs measure success, influence, and productivity? Perhaps it is no surprise that in a 1997 interview in *Christianity Today*, on the occasion of the twentieth-anniversary edition of his famous book,[5] Sider tried to set the record straight: he favors democratic politics and the market economy. He supports democratic capitalism because it is more compatible with human freedom and dignity and more efficient in the production of wealth.

I do not begin this way out of cynicism, but rather to point out some of the tensions endemic in a theological consideration of the theme "Mennonites and Money." North American Mennonites in the twentieth and twenty-first centuries have lived and continue to live in a culture in no doubt about the god it worships and that shapes all manner of decisions and strategies, from personal lifestyle to household acquisitions to corporate mergers, university governance, church growth, and political platforms: that god is mammon. Where does this name, this theological term "mammon," come from? From the lips of the Messiah Jesus, of course, who uses it in the Sermon on the Mount to indicate contrasting types of vision: "So, if your eye is sound, your whole body will be full of light; but if your eye is not sound, your whole body will be full of darkness. If then the light in you is darkness, how great is the darkness!" (Matt 6:22–23). He goes on to make the famous pronouncement that "no one can serve two masters, for either he will hate the one and love the other or he will be devoted to the one and despise the other," and of course these two masters are Yahweh and mammon.

"Mammon" is no less mysterious sounding to our ears than is "Yahweh," and its origins are obscure. It is a Semitic word signifying money, wealth, property, possessions.[6] Jesus here personifies it as a rival lord or god and suggests that the devotion it demands is no less total than that demanded by Yahweh, which is why it has everything to do with vision, with what is brought into view and what is kept out of view. This is very hard to see, it seems, even for the disciples, Jesus's closest followers. After Jesus's encounter with the upstanding and very righteous rich young man who seems to lack nothing, when he tells his disciples that "it is easier for a camel to go through the eye of a needle than for a rich person to enter the kingdom of God," they say in astonishment, "Who can get in then?" (Matt 19). The political economy of Yahweh is messianically opposed to the political economy of mammon, it seems, and this apocalyptic opposition is something the early Anabaptists took with deadly seriousness, as they did the entire Sermon on the Mount (in contrast to the more compromising ethical theories of the magisterial

4. *Christianity Today*, April 24, 2000.

5. Miller, "Conversations: The Rich Christian: How Ron Sider Has Changed."

6. Davies and Allison, *Critical and Exegetical Commentary*, 1:643. The etymology of the term is uncertain, though usually explained as deriving from *mn*, "to trust/believe in," which renders it appropriate as a term of idolatry.

reformers). Nowhere more radically, perhaps, than in the writings of the sixteenth-century Tyrolian Peter Walpot, who became leader of the Moravian Hutterites after Peter Riedemann and who initiated the *Bruderhof* economic experiment that continues to this day. Writing in 1577 in his treatise "True Yieldedness and the Christian Community of Goods," Walpot says,

> Humanity will hold a great Sabbath (Isa. 66). Yes, they will have a continual Sabbath and will lead a most holy life on earth, when they rid their nature of two words—"mine" and "yours." These words have been and are today the cause of many wars. From where comes war and bloodshed, quarrelling and fighting, envy and hatred, disunity and disruption, if not from private possessions and greed? For whoever deals in mine and yours, that is, with possessions, becomes a friend of avarice.... Whoever wants much feels the lack of much, and whoever covets much is left wanting much. That is actually the most poverty-stricken and dissatisfied kind of life on earth. And Christ, at home with those who walk in the true Sabbath, Pentecost and Easter, will have none of it.[7]

The rejection of the distinction between "mine" and "yours" has a long history in European messianic radicalism.[8] Walpot's messianic political economy calls for a community of the "poor in spirit," the dispossessed and humble ones:

> You cannot serve God and Mammon, for like a lock, the love of and concern for money occupies the heart. Therefore you should not strive for surplus and then seek to justify it. For Christ said that it is impossible to serve and nurture both of these two masters. So don't say that it is possible! For one master commands you to deny yourself . . . the other says you should be selfish and possessive.[9]

According to Walpot, the life of the messianic community must be the narrow gate, the needle's eye, "an oven of yieldedness in which the person is tried like gold in the fire."[10] Only in the community of messianic discipleship can one attend to the needed conformity of inner and outer, spiritual and material life—precisely those things divided by Luther's two kingdoms.

Menno Simons, like Walpot, held to the singular and undivided conformity of Christians to the messianic body, internal and external, though he was less convinced than Walpot that private property in itself is contrary to nature and the shalom of Yahweh's creation.[11] Nevertheless, the sacraments of the messianic body must be practically enacted, which requires members of the messianic community to serve their neighbors "not only with money and goods, but also after the example of their Lord and Head, Jesus Christ, . . . with life and blood."[12] Menno attacks the luxurious hypocrisy of those

---

7. Walpot, "True Yieldedness," 139.
8. See also Kierkegaard on the "eternal forgetting" of this distinction in his *Works of Love*, 269ff.
9. Walpot, "True Yieldedness," 145.
10. Ibid., 147.
11. See Ibid., 191.
12. Simons, "Reply to False Accusations," 558. In his confessional statement, "True Christian Faith," Menno articulates his Christology as follows: "We teach and believe, and this is the thrust of the whole Scriptures, that the whole Christ is from head to foot, both inside and outside, visible and invisible, God's first-born and only begotten Son; the incomprehensible, eternal Word, by whom all things were

PART 3: MESSIANISM AND DIASPORA ETHICS

religious and political leaders who are persecuting the Anabaptists for, among other things, practicing the community of goods:

> O preachers, dear preachers, where is the power of the Gospel you preach? Where is the thing signified in the Supper you administer? . . . Shame on you for the easygoing gospel and barren bread-breaking, you who have in so many years been unable to effect enough with your gospel and sacraments so as to remove your needy and distressed members from the streets.[13]

The political economy of violence, undergirded by an easygoing and luxurious Christianity, is tied to the worship of mammon, which renders the sacraments empty.[14] Menno especially laments the existence of a paid clergy—ministers who are corrupted by salaries become hirelings of the rich, seduced by the profit motive, and the mainline churches, he suggests, are full of such avaricious, selfish, and carnal leaders who aid and abet religious cynicism in the wider culture.[15]

This same apocalyptic teaching pervades Ron Sider's *Rich Christians*, where he argues that Jesus established a visible messianic community characterized by an *oikonomia* of economic sharing that Sider describes as "unlimited liability and total availability" grounded in eucharistic sharing.[16] Such a discernment of the lived and shared body of Christ can only conclude that "present economic relationships in the worldwide body of Christ are unbiblical, sinful, . . . a desecration of the body and blood of Jesus Christ."[17] The attempt to replace communion with the Creator, for which human beings are made, with the desire to possess the creation leads to ever-more frantic and desperate lifestyles of consumption rooted in *pleonexia*, an obsessive, anxious compulsion for more. This is the punitive end result of the idolatrous worship of mammon: a constant intake and output that is not truly human at all. The only possible response is penitence, a radical turning away from the disordered desire of insatiable possessiveness toward my neighbor in messianic community.

There is a similar account of the politics of Jesus by John Howard Yoder, perhaps the most significant Mennonite theologian of the twentieth century. In his *Politics of Jesus* (ranked number 5 in the *Christianity Today* list of the one hundred most influential Christian books of the twentieth century), Yoder suggests that the messianic mission of Jesus is the annunciation of the Jubilee as a visible sociopolitical and economic restructuring of all human relations. This is neither an impossible counsel of perfection nor a

---

created, the first-born of every creature" (335–36). See also his "Brief and Clear Confession" where he rejects any separation between the eternal Word of God and the incarnate Son of God: "He was not divided nor separated as being half heavenly and half earthly, half of the seed of man and half of God . . . but an unmixed, whole Christ, namely, spirit, soul, and body, of which, according to Paul, all men are constituted." The fact that Christ took the "form of the servant" (Phil 2), therefore, requires his followers to do the same in all ways. Here, as throughout his writings, there are many pointed warnings against avarice—the worship of mammon, external carnality, the profit motive.

13. Simons, "Reply to False Accusations," 559.
14. See Simons, "Foundation of Christian Doctrine," 176ff., 194ff., 207ff.
15. Simons, "True Christian Faith," 404–5.
16. Sider, *Rich Christians*, 103.
17. Ibid., 110.

constitutional law for a utopian state: it is the communal establishment of a material, ordinary, everyday messianic practice rooted in servanthood that is completely revolutionary, that breaks the sovereignty of fallen idolatrous powers. Yoder's claim, in keeping with the apocalyptic messianic vision of the early Anabaptists, is that the primary social structure through which the Gospel works to transform other structures is the messianic community that patterns itself after Christ. Such a community represents not a withdrawal from society but a cosmic challenge to the fallen powers by transforming life in the everyday from below, in new practical forms of life. Like Sider and the early Anabaptists, Yoder reads the eucharistic practice of the New Testament as a political economy, a communal sharing that extends the table fellowship of Jesus to the wider world.[18] He points to the economic pattern of the *Bruderhof* as the display of messianic poverty: not the renunciation of all property but the renunciation of personal or private possessiveness. It is best understood not as a flight from the world but as the messianic, monastic life of sharing and hospitality practiced in the everyday world.

II

What has this got to do with political economy? It just confirms what we already know, that theology is abstract, pious theorizing about biblical ideas and does no real analysis of the material social and political conditions in which we live. Historians can do better by examining what actually happens in the lived world, to see just how these ideas are enacted and what happens when real people and communities live them out temporally and spatially. James Urry's excellent book *Mennonites, Politics and Peoplehood*, for example, can show us how apocalyptic Mennonite separation from the world in a context of religious persecution actually leads to a social strategy of seeking special political privileges and the protection of autocratic rulers for living a quiet life in the land. He can also show the tensions faced by ethnic Mennonite communities from the end of the eighteenth century on, as they increasingly have to face new secular political forces that want to integrate Mennonites into secular nation-states as useful and productive citizens, calling for the subordination of Mennonite identity to those larger sociopolitical ones articulated in constitutional democracies: all citizens are equal under one law, which allows for religious commitment as a personal, emotional, and private activity largely disconnected from social practice.[19]

I suggest that this is not the only possible account of Mennonite messianic political economy. Yoder and Sider are examples of a theological and also a political-ethical resistance to understanding Mennonite or Anabaptist identity in terms of ethnicity. Yoder in particular would consider the "Mennonite commonwealth" established in nineteenth-century Russia—the Johann Cornies model, we could call it—no less a Constantinian failure of the church than the mainline Christendom versions. Perhaps we could offer a theopolitical account of the "Corniesian fall" of the Anabaptist vision. Furthermore, what do historians who casually use terms such as "conservative" and "progressivist" to

---

18. Yoder, *Body Politics*, chap. 2.
19. Urry, *Mennonites, Politics, and Peoplehood*.

describe less and more conformist (to the mainstream culture) Mennonite communities do with the continued existence of radical Amish and Old Order Mennonites in North America, who are neither "integrated" into the secular global economy (though certainly related to it) nor constitute a "Mennonite commonwealth"? I think of David Kline, for example, an Amish farmer friend of the radical agrarian social critic Wendell Berry,[20] who articulates an Anabaptist theology for living that cares for creation and witnesses to the wider culture by resisting the lures and blandishments of industrial capitalism and all its works.[21] For Kline the spirituality of this messianic political economy, this agrarian monasticism in the world, is articulated in the Amish evening prayer to be read daily, one line of which reads: "Und lasz uns deine Creaturen and Geschoepf nicht verderben sondern dasz wir zur ewigen Seligkeit moegen gebracht und erhalten warden," which he translates as, "And help us be gentle with your creatures and handiwork so that we may abide in your eternal salvation and continue to be held in the hollow of your hand."[22] David Kline certainly has not published twenty-two books, nor are his publications considered to be in the top one hundred most influential on any consumerist Christian booklist, nor are the communities out of which he writes considered to be relevant. But what if they are in fact bearing witness to the messianic body politic and political economy in our time? What if the Amish and Old Order Mennonites are the two faithful witnesses, the two olive trees and lamp stands (Rev 11:3–4) that bear cruciform witness in the midst of the destroyers of the earth? How would that be measured or even discerned?

I am aware that what I am saying embodies a tension between a non-ethnic Mennonite theology that cannot underwrite a politics of identity and that seems to entail a critique of the separatist agrarian, ethnic communities of the Amish and Old Order Mennonites, and a suggestion that these ethnic communities continue to bear an important messianic economic witness in our contemporary global context. So let me try to clarify what I am trying to say, and let me do so with reference to another excellent historical study that helps me make sense of my own life experience and the question of messianic political economy, namely, Royden Loewen's *Diaspora in the Countryside*. Loewen gives us a compelling, textured account of the capitalization of agriculture and urban migration of *Kleine Gemeinde* Mennonites in the mid- to late twentieth century, one of the last North American early ethnic immigrant groups to become integrated participants in the progressivist industrial vision of capitalist modernization. I am a living folklore fossil of this shift: born in 1957 in Steinbach, my mother tongue was *Plautdietsch* (Low German) until the age of five, when my father moved us off the family farm to urban, multicultural Winnipeg for a construction company job, and I remember feeling like a complete alien. Indeed the experience of being an alien, neither at home in the city nor in Steinbach, led me to pursue the academic study of religion, and here I am a product of industrial higher

---

20. See Kline's essay, hyperbolically entitled "How Wendell Berry Single-Handedly Preserved Three Hundred Years of Agrarian Wisdom." Berry returns the compliment in many places, but no more evocatively than in his novella *Remembering*, where the Amish as a community materially enact the agrarian messianic political economy.

21. Kline, "God's Spirit and a Theology for Living."

22. Ibid., 61–62.

education, even though it is more of the University of Chicago humanist variation than that of the medical engineering university at which I teach. The tensions abound—but my brief here today is not autobiographical; it is theological.

Therefore I am charged with offering a normative rejoinder to Loewen's impressive descriptive account, though of course it is impossible to do so properly here. I am compelled to choose a representative anecdote and to offer a few suggestive comments. My critical rejoinder takes issue with using the sociopolitical term "conservative" to describe those who nurture a local, village-based agrarian culture by focusing on household-produced goods and selective participation in the wider democratic capitalist marketplace. I wonder, if we shifted the focus from protecting an ethno-religious identity to discerning this as a non-violent resistance of globalizing capitalism, would we be able to discern here the possibility of a radical messianic political economy, where technological innovation is not mindlessly adopted but subjected to a community rule? Will this particular technology or economic practice or innovation destroy or enhance our community of shared goods, the shared pursuit of the kingdom of God? It should also be noted that Menno Simons's exemplars of the messianic community in "True Christian Faith" include the Centurion of Capernaum, the Malefactor on the cross, the Woman who was a sinner, the Syrophoenician Woman, and other nameless penitents. None of these are great, heroic Christians whose names are remembered for their exceptional individual accomplishments. They are rather anonymous witnesses to the power of divine grace and they bear witness to this power through anonymous humility. Until the mid-twentieth century, as Loewen shows, this model of exemplarity was characteristic of both men and women in the largely rural Mennonite communities of Manitoba and Kansas, communities that were largely self-sufficient, skeptical of the consumer lifestyles and individualist ideals of urban capitalism, and committed to the pacifist communitarian Christianity of their forebears. This changed in the 1950s and 1960s as the authority of the farmer-bishop/preacher as community leader and an emphasis on humble community service in everyday life gave way to the community authority of ambitious individual achievers whose names were emblazoned on the profitable businesses they built through aggressive and shrewd commercial development.

There is a representative anecdote in Loewen's book displaying the shift from agrarian humility in the everyday world to the ambitious industrial capitalism of the dominant North American culture. It involves a mid-century Steinbach car dealer, entrepreneur, and mayor, the poster-boy purveyor of the individualist values of conspicuous capitalist consumption and progressivist Mennonite masculinity: none other than A. D. Penner.[23] Loewen's book includes an evocative photograph of the symbolic spanking of the entrepreneurial A. D. by his eighty-four-year-old mother, dressed in traditional "conservative" Mennonite garb, on the occasion of his bulldozing of the last traditional Steinbach house-barn in 1960 to pave the way for progress. Loewen paints the scene vividly:

> When Steinbach had been founded as a farm village in 1874, the wooden framed house-barn built especially for easy access of women to livestock signaled pioneer success. By 1960 the town's only house-barn was an abandoned, sagging, unpainted, shingle-sided building located at the corner of Main Street and

23. See Loewen, *Diaspora in the Countryside*, 156ff.

> Victoria Avenue, the gateway to Steinbach's commercial center. Significantly, the rotting building sat just across the road from A. D. Penner's ultramodern Chrysler car dealership . . . In May 1960 Penner, who also owned a road construction company, announced that one of his huge D9 Caterpillar bulldozers was in town and he intended to demolish the old house-barn. . . . With typical flare Penner . . . crossed the road with his elderly mother to offer a photo opportunity. As cameras clicked, the huge D9 crushed the building and a grinning A. D. bent over to allow his mother to mock spank him. The message was clear: while the historical society might think him a reckless "boy," the massive, masculine D9 would do its work in the name of progress.[24]

Of course even asses and dominators may have a place in the kingdom of God, but only as humble penitents who give up their worship of mammon and of making a name for themselves in Babel-like fashion, according to the New Testament gospels. If Mennonites are to work toward a messianic political economy today, when globalizing technological and economic forces and relations are conscripting people and places everywhere into the service of an abstract industrial economy, it will be necessary to seriously reconsider this question of worship.

By way of conclusion, I shall try to suggest briefly what this might mean. In his book *Home Economics*, Wendell Berry writes of a conversation with his friend Wes Jackson about the causes of the modern ruination of farmland, including the money economy. Berry suggested that "an economy based on energy would be more benign because it would be more comprehensive." Jackson didn't agree, suggesting that an energy economy wouldn't be comprehensive enough. "Well," said Berry, "then what kind of economy *would* be comprehensive enough?" Jackson hesitated, then said with a grin, "The Kingdom of God."[25] This is of course the heart of the matter in a messianic political economy, rooted as it is in the teaching of Jesus: seek first the Kingdom of God means, among other things, seek and receive the shalom of Yahweh daily in all the gifts of creation that are always coming into being and passing away; this is what Berry calls the "Great Economy." If one lives in this way rather than being driven by the anxieties of human insecurity about the adequacy of one's own possessions, everything else will follow from it. If Jesus's teachings have nothing to do with worldly economics and our daily life in this world, then they are completely out of touch with reality. If his teachings are in fact true, then they also have tremendous practical implications for the real nature of worldly economies—including everything from households to neighborhoods to cities, nations, and global exchange. Wendell Berry's work on this holds great significance for those seeking a messianic political economy, including perhaps those Mennonites, whether urban or rural, ethnic or not, pietistic or secular, who turn in penitence from the destructive daily worship of mammon in our culture and begin to seek another way.

Berry's essays provide a moral and political economic challenge to dominant cultural practices, but his novels display what is at stake both historically and spiritually. Berry's novella *Remembering* tells the story of Andy Catlett, who has devoted his life to a rural community made up of small-scale family farms, but who, in the loss of his right

---

24. Ibid., 157–58.
25. Berry, "Two Economies," in *Home Economics*, 54.

hand to a corn-picking machine, finds he has "lost his hold" on his motivating vision of an alternative political economy. The story begins in a state of profound disorientation that represents Andy's spiritual condition as he awakes from a disturbing technological nightmare in the strange San Francisco hotel room to which he has fled, a nightmare in which bulldozers are enrubbling farms and destroying farmland to build the great causeway of progress where industrial human artifice dominates all nature. Andy will find no liberation from his problems by escaping his community and reshaping his identity through the commodified procurements of industrial urban capitalism. Only by remembering who he is, the defining moments of the life history of his soul, the tangled pattern of embodied memories, will he recover his purpose, the true direction of his bodily and spiritual desire. Andy's movement of penitence and return is described as follows:

> He is held, though he does not hold. He is caught up again in the old pattern of entrances: of minds into minds, minds into place, places into minds. The pattern limits and complicates him, singling him out in his own flesh. Out of the multitude of possible lives that have surrounded and beckoned to him like a crowd around a star, he returns now to himself, a mere meteorite, scorched, small, and fallen. He has met again his one life and one death, and he takes them back. It is as though, leaving, he has met himself already returning, pushing in front of him a barn seventy-five feet by forty, and a hundred acres of land, six generations of his own history, partly failed, and a few dead and living whose love has claimed him forever.[26]

What Andy recovers is the memory of why he chose to resist the siren voices of technological and economic "progress" in order to cultivate another way of life on the land. This other way has been given to him as a choice by the people of his community, who have fostered it through the disciplines of love. It is a radically traditional vision of agrarian life in which fidelity to family, farmland, community, and God are richly woven in a demanding pattern of skill and trust that our dominant urban technological culture views with either sentimentality or disdain. When Andy, as a young aspiring agricultural journalist (thereby trading on his rural experience to advance his own individual career) dares to voice his preference for the Amish farm he visits over hi-tech agribusiness, he realizes this is more than an argument about agriculture—it is a cultural battle, a struggle over the meaning of a good life and a bad one. Agribusiness, says Andy at an academic conference on "The Future of the American Food System," is an abstract "agriculture of the mind"[27] that cannot think humanly and spiritually about what it does, and therefore lacks good judgment. It produces death, not life. In the Mennonite rush to join a "progressive" mainstream culture, eager to cash in our hard-earned countercultural identities for careerist success, have we become willing to lose our embodied Mennonite souls? This is not to say that moving from the village to the city is necessarily soul-destroying, but neither is it true that to be the humble, agrarian *Stillen im Lande* is somehow an abdication of human cultural, economic, and political responsibility. It may be that such a life preserves a crucial set of cultural, social, and spiritual disciplines rooted

---

26. Berry, *Remembering*, 57–58. I reflect further on this novel in chapter 5, above, and in Kroeker, "Sexuality and the Sacramental Imagination."

27. Berry, *Remembering*, 23.

PART 3: MESSIANISM AND DIASPORA ETHICS

in a vision of existence that our culture desperately needs in order to bring it back from a headlong rush toward spiritual—and ecological, civil, and economic—suicide. At the very least this means that assimilated urban Mennonites dare not cut off dialogue with our theological and political economic past and with those "backward" and "conservative" traditional communities who continue to give visible, embodied cultural testimony to a radically different way of life that judges our own simply by being what it is.

14

On the Difference between Torture and Punishment

Theology, Liturgy, and Human Rights

IN HIS GIFFORD LECTURES, *The Lesser Evil: Political Ethics in an Age of Terror*, Michael Ignatieff seeks to argue the case for emergency measures in the face of global terrorism and asks what role human rights should play in deciding public policy during terrorist emergencies. While he holds that under such circumstances "neither rights nor necessity should trump" the other, he nevertheless argues that torture is a test case for the dilemma of liberal democracies' war on terror. It raises the question of what are the legitimate limits on the violation of human dignity rooted in the "necessities" of the security state. At what point, for example, does interrogation move from legitimate coercion and punishment to illegitimate torture? Ignatieff's extended defense of a "lesser evil" ethic advocates the development of democratic societies designed "to cope with tragic choice" required to ensure security in the face of terror and thus seeks a balance between "liberty" and "necessity."

Such ethical abstractions, however, are themselves of very limited value since precisely the line between (legitimate/warranted) punishment and (illegitimate/unwarranted) torture is largely a conventional one. What is human dignity anyway? At the very least it is hard to define, predicated on complex judgments about the inner meaning of human life, the relations between body and soul, and between individual embodied souls in relation to the body politic. How are these judgments themselves to be related to views about visibility and invisibility of interrogation, the embodied and/or psychological character of such interrogations, and the larger meaning of the juridical subject who bears rights in relation to "state security," the institutionalized relations of power and knowledge in a given society, and so on?

Michel Foucault's famous study, *Discipline and Punish*,[1] is so valuable precisely because it puts the genealogy of such complex judgments on dramatic display. The graphic opening scene of part 1 on "Torture," the gruesomely detailed eyewitness account of the

---

1. Foucault, *Discipline and Punish*.

horrible execution of the regicide (also called "parricide") Damiens in eighteenth-century Paris, is quite uncontroversially labeled torture by Foucault, as most non-psychopathic modern Westerners would automatically call it that—an unacceptably gratuitous violation of the bodily rights of a human being through the infliction of long-lasting and extended ordeals of intense pain. Most of us have difficulty reading the account, never mind imagining how anyone could stand to watch it as a public spectacle, as many apparently did on March 2, 1757. In contemporary Western societies we have become unaccustomed to *any* forms of corporal punishment. Witness the recent case of the removal of children from their parental homes in a small southern Ontario Mennonite community by Ontario social services authorities, because their parents advocated the use of strapping with a belt as a normal, though socially invisible, disciplinary practice. And yet anyone who observed the media images of traumatized children being forcibly extracted from their traumatized parents by police officers bearing weapons could not help but be struck by the ironies. How are we to make good judgments about such complex judgment scenes?

Oliver O'Donovan offers a fine generic definition of punishment that is designed to liberate us from the unhelpful abstractions of *theories* of punishment when he calls it "a judgment enacted on the person, property, or liberty of the condemned party."[2] As such, punishment is best understood as an expressive communication defending the order of society, an act of social definition that represents the truthful response to offense by a society (113). Hence it cannot but represent in symbolic terms a judgment on suffering that has been unjustly caused by communicating that suffering both to the offender and to the wider society. On O'Donovan's view, then, the problem with acts of torture is this: "They are performed in secret, without due process, without legal specifications as to duration or intensity; and in no way seek to tell the truth about the crimes they punish" (122). In this way are acts of torture subversive rather than expressive of social norms. It would seem that on O'Donovan's definition the execution of Damiens may not be considered an act of torture, insofar as it is public, governed by due judicial process that specifies each ordeal of pain as expressive of the enormity of the crime he committed against society—in this sense it is not "cruel or unusual" punishment. Indeed, it might even be possible to be moved by the extraordinary dignity displayed by Damiens in his consent and self-restrained subordination to his own punishment, especially in relation to his confessors and his executioners in the eyewitness account recounted by Foucault.

Finally, to take a more modern example of capital punishment, who can fail to be moved by the journey toward moral responsibility by the condemned murderer Matthew Poncelet in the film *Dead Man Walking* (1995)—a movement that is unimaginable without his impending execution and the loving, shriving presence of Sister Prejean, who, ironically, judges the death penalty itself to be immoral (and thus, it would seem, a form of torture). In the film it is only as the moment of death actually approaches that glimpses of the horrible crimes committed by the offender come to visible consciousness. The implication is that the offender can only acknowledge these deeds and confess them by confronting his own imminent punitive death. The judgment in conscience is

---

2. O'Donovan, *Ways of Judgment*, 107. Further references will be given parenthetically in the body of the essay.

clearly symbolized by the judicially authorized punishment and is existentially enacted in the complex expression of the sentence—though the film is nicely ambiguous about whether the violent punishment is indeed necessary, or whether simply the persistent caring rigor of Sister Prejean might suffice to facilitate the moral and indeed spiritual movement.

Is capital punishment torture? It seems Sister Prejean might think so, though she is no less horrified by the terrible murders committed by the offender. And what are we to make of the distinction between the execution of Damiens—with its drawn-out public infliction of grotesque ordeals of pain—and the hidden, rather clinical execution of Matthew Poncelet in *Dead Man Walking*—an execution designed to *appear* painless (not least by the medical administration of paralysis-inducing chemicals) and therefore more "humane." Both Oliver O'Donovan and Elaine Scarry make the connection between pain or suffering and mortality or death. O'Donovan argues that the basis of all retributive practice (and thus all punishment, which is always by definition also, among other things, retributive) is found here: "We are all mortal, and our life has a limited expectancy. That fact gives all crime and punishment its meaning" (122). The horizon of all punishment, then, is death itself. Every punishment is an assault on the offender's life, in return for assault on the victim's life. In Scarry's account of the structure of torture, she argues that "pain is the equivalent in felt-experience of what is unfeelable in death. Each only happens because of the body"[3]—and, of course, because of the human self-awareness of bodily mortality, the pain of death, the ultimate experience of "un-worlding."

In Scarry's account the speech enacted in torture, far from being the expression of true speech (a necessary condition in O'Donovan's definition of punishment), is precisely false. Both the speech of the torturer (rooted in the false motive of "information-gathering") and the speech of the tortured (the voice of pain, simply giving the answers sought by the torturer, without regard for truth) are therefore false. The effect of torture is thus to unmake the world in the shattering of language, in order to remake the world in the fictitious image of the torturer's power. Hence the covert disdain for the confession (often labeled "self-betrayal") of torture victims by their torturers. The interrelation of the infliction of pain and the interrogation in torture is designed precisely to create instability and disorientation in victims between the "real world" and "fiction," ultimately to prepare the way for the construction of a "second reality"—the power of the regime—as the only real or true one. All claims that challenge, threaten, or deny the truth of this reality must be eliminated. Such is the sovereignty of the absolutist or terrorist regime.

Here it may be instructive to return again to Foucault's *Discipline and Punish*. His thesis is that not only has the *context* of modern punishment shifted from public visibility to institutional hiddenness, but its *focus* has shifted attention away from the primacy of the body (and the infliction of pain upon it) to the primacy of the soul or subject and its reconstituting self-discipline. This entails an entirely different set of punitive and disciplinary practices, a new political technology that enforces a quite distinct—and ultimately more invasive and pervasive—sovereignty or regime of truth/power. Foucault's analysis suggests that the old public liturgy of bodily punishment displaying sovereign power—a liturgy both juridical and military, focusing on the punishment of evildoers

---

3. Scarry, *Body in Pain*, 31.

as "enemies"—has gone underground in sociopolitical mechanisms that exercise more powerful ordering influence on the social body. These mechanisms are less personal, less immediate, and less visible, and yet very effectively deployed in the reformative rise of the "scientific-juridical complex."[4]

The power of this sovereignty is displayed less in a visible physical terror (that is reinforced in ceremonies of public torture as punishment) than in a pervasive disciplinary administrative regime, a "school" of inner interpretation or "apparatus of knowledge" that governs conduct.[5] It does this through a calculated economy using instruments of hierarchical observation, normalizing judgment and examination in a "carceral" regime modeled after "panopticism"—the subjection of all citizens to a sovereign surveillance that establishes truth through a regime of control and inquisition that no longer needs to inflict pain upon the body in order to control its subjects, but in fact consolidates its power precisely through the promise to eliminate all such pain through comprehensive security. It would seem that Foucault would regard the discourse of universal human rights as yet another potential "knowledge apparatus" enforcing such a carceral sovereignty.

I do not wish to take up the details of Foucault's account of "normalization" and sovereign state control here. My concern has been to point up the ambiguities that exist between torture and punishment that render the making of moral judgments about them, including those rooted in human rights language, highly problematic. In order to begin to explore the thicket of possibilities theologically, I have found it helpful to turn to two nineteenth-century writers who have thought about the complex relationships between bodily punishment, the body politic, and the moral constitution of the agential practice of judging (sometimes called "conscience") from quite different theological and anti-theological perspectives—Friedrich Nietzsche and Fyodor Dostoevsky.

Nietzsche

Nietzsche, of course, is the great forerunner to Foucault in developing a "genealogy of morals" that unmasks the conventions of truth in our culture to be precisely that—the fictions of human language willfully imposed upon reality. Truth is always the imposition of perspectival conventions by the powerful, and punishment is the bodily-spiritual reinforcement of these conventions in rituals that express sovereign human power. Nietzsche's compelling account of the role of crime and punishment in constituting moral conscience is provided in the second essay of his *Genealogy of Morals*.[6] Human beings have bred into themselves the conditions of "answerability" (*Verantwortlichkeit*), namely, a memory related to promises they have made, a "memory of the will" by which human beings become "calculable [*berechenbar*], regular [*regelmässig*], necessary [*notwendig*]" (1). Such a responsible self is precisely a sovereign individual, one who has an independent will and has the right to make promises, to speak for him/herself in what has come

---

4. Foucault, *Discipline and Punish*, 19.

5. Ibid., 125.

6. Nietzsche, *On the Genealogy of Morals*. References to the second essay, "'Guilt,' 'Bad Conscience' and the Like," will be made by section number in parentheses in the body of the essay.

to be called the "conscience [*gewissen*]" (2–3). According to Nietzsche, the history of human responsibility is tied to the human animal's evolutionary development of the faculty of memory—promises made for calculable action in the future, a necessary feature of ordered human communities of speech. The beginning of the inner life of moral consciousness in which instinctual drives are countered and controlled, then, is dictated by social needs and is imprinted by rituals of punitive pain. The essence [*Wesen*] of human consciousness is memory grounded in pain—a "mnemotechnics" (3) of cruelty, the cruellest of which are religious.[7]

That is, in contrast to Kant's autonomous moral agent, Nietzsche's sovereign will is formed not by seeking universal moral ends given in the invisible structure of reality, but through the struggle to realize *my* aims and values in an agonistic world. The origins of memory are to be located in the history of human punishment, in which the demands of social existence are imprinted upon the instincts in legal promises, judgments, and enactments (5ff.). Instincts are thus ordered with reference to legal obligations, moral laws of behavior, "soaked in blood and torture" (6). These are not simply retributive relations—punishment is also rooted in the pleasure of imposing suffering on another, a "genuine *festival*." Indeed, says Nietzsche, "Without cruelty there is no festival: thus the longest and most ancient part of human history teaches—and in punishment there is much that is *festive!*" (6). Part of the enjoyment of violation in administering punishment is the experience of the free exercise of sovereign power, and this experience has been deeply sublimated in the cruel religious spectacles of divine punishment that undergird the moral conscience of the European West (7).

The two distinctive features of punishment according to Nietzsche are (a) its customary, dramatic character, which is relatively enduring, and (b) the meaning, purpose, or expectation associated with the performance of the dramatic act, which is fluid (13). The concept "punishment," therefore, cannot be reduced to one meaning but rather has a whole range of meanings related to particular performative acts: deterrence, preventing harm, recompense, isolation of a disturbance, inspiring fear, repayment, expulsion, festivity, mnemonesis, revenge, declaration of war, and so on. Thus is punishment overdetermined by various utilities, but Nietzsche insists that "bad conscience" did not grow on the soil of punishment. Rather, the effect of punishment is a heightening of prudent memory that tames human desires and instincts (15).

Nietzsche's hypothesis about the origin of "bad conscience" is related to a kind of Hobbesian evolutionary account of the origin of the security state (16) as the most fateful evolutionary shift in the human animal from a creature of instinct to a creature of consciousness. This is the "internalization" of the human in the development of "soul" or psyche, and it is coincident with the birth of the religious consciousness. Only through the invention of divine spectators and "otherworldly eyes" could the external violence of active instinct be internalized in the inner agon of the divided, self-lacerating, suffering soul. That is, the taming process of political sovereignty is accompanied by a religious self-surveillance that internalizes the conflictual drama of pleasurable punishment, the

---

7. Nietzsche writes, "Life operates *essentially*, that is in its basic functions, through injury, assault, exploitation, destruction and simply cannot be thought of at all without this character" (11); and again: "Thus the essence of life [*das Wesen des Lebens*] is *will to power* [*Wille zur Macht*]" (12).

PART 3: MESSIANISM AND DIASPORA ETHICS

"war of all against all." This inner war becomes the condition for social peace. In a self-regulating, self-punishing, self-torturing society, the more natural punishment of the body may be safely minimized as people are able to enjoy their own self-imposed punitive suffering:

> You will have guessed what has really happened here, beneath all this . . . this man of the bad conscience has seized upon the presupposition of religion so as to drive his self-torture to its most gruesome pitch of severity and rigor. Guilt before *God*: this thought becomes an instrument of torture to him. He apprehends in "God" the ultimate antithesis of his own ineluctable animal instincts: he reinterprets these animal instincts themselves as a form of guilt before God . . . he stretches himself upon the contradiction "God" and "Devil" . . . . In this psychical cruelty there resides a madness of the will which is absolutely unexampled [*nicht seines Gleichen hat*]: the *will* of man to find himself guilty and reprehensible to a degree that can never be atoned for [*Unsühnbarkeit*] . . . his *will* to infect and poison the fundamental ground of things [*untersten Grund*] with the problem of punishment and guilt . . . . what *bestiality of thought* [*Idee*] erupts as soon as he is prevented just a little from being a *beast in deed* [*Tat*]." (22)

We are familiar enough with this Nietzschean account of modern human beings as the "heirs of the conscience-vivisection and self-torture [*Selbsttierquälerei*] of millennia," possessors of an "evil eye [*bösem Blick*]" for natural inclinations, ultimately hostile to life. But what does it mean for interpreting the relation between punishment and torture? Surely at a minimum it requires a critique of the kind of conformist humanism that underlies the bourgeois citizens of modern security states devoted to the unnatural, nihilistic taming of the truly human—the desire for a perfect carceral society of equal rights for all that "overcomes" (bodily) suffering by domesticating and destroying human beings through taking over their consciences and taking away the freedom of their wills by imposing a civil religious "evil eye" of moral surveillance. Ultimately, for Nietzsche, it will require an agonistic effort to overcome the great juridical straitjacket that characterizes the "sovereignty" (in theory and practice) of modern statist humanism. Modern justice will itself have to be "overcome" through a mercy that goes beyond the law (10).

Dostoevsky

There is of course another, quite different yet equally penetrating and critical nineteenth-century approach to interpreting conscience in relation to crime, punishment, and torture, offered by Fyodor Dostoevsky, particularly in his great novels such as *Demons* and *Crime and Punishment*. His last and greatest novel, *The Brothers Karamazov*, is about the political and religious meanings of justice, and at the heart of this lies the discernment of conscience—an insight shared but differently resolved by the novel's two central ascetic figures, the Grand Inquisitor and the elder Zosima. Interestingly, it is precisely the punitive, indeed tortuous suffering of conscience that the Inquisitor seeks to relieve in his regime of external state power rooted in a Christian civil religion. Such a regime promises a secure and painless existence for all who submit to its authority. According to the elder, on the contrary, such relief is not a human prerogative, since conscience is not finally socially constituted or guided by the conventional norms and authorities of a community (*pace* both Nietzsche and the Grand Inquisitor). Conscience is a knowledge constituted also "before God," whose divine law measures human beings—a divine law that is not primarily understood in juridical or retributive terms but rather as the messianic law dramatically enacted in the restorative practices of "active love" (56).[8] The "security" of the Inquisitor can only result in ongoing psychic and bodily suffering, as the "second reality" it constructs is destructive of the human spirit and of human social life; indeed, on the elder's view, it is destructive of justice itself. Richard Peace, however, misses the mark when he suggests that Zosima "points to the individual conscience as the only true instrument of punishment,"[9] since for the elder conscience is neither simply "individual" nor "instrumental"—punishment is not extrinsic to the relational, embodied life of human society. Nor is conscience the "mnemotechnical" internalization of contractual power relations rooted in rituals of pain. The pain and punishment of conscience is rooted in the memory or consciousness of divine love (not acts of human or divine violation), which exposes one's (willed) separation from its fullness. Pain is an important symptom of a deeper illness that is ignored or dulled at peril of death. As such, conscience cannot work mechanically or instrumentally. Indeed, to treat conscience that way "only chafes the heart" (64).

Yet clearly the punishment related to conscience is also related by the elder (and Dostoevsky) to ritual sociopolitical contexts, and I wish to reflect on these here, as I believe they may be helpful in developing a distinction between punishment related to restorative justice and punishment related to forms of retributive justice that move inevitably toward torture. In some respects I have taken a cue from William Cavanaugh's argument in *Torture and Eucharist* that the failure of human rights language has been to construe torture primarily as an attack on individual bodies, and that "true resistance to torture depends on the reappearance of social bodies capable of countering the atomizing performance of the state."[10] He contrasts the liturgy of torture in the idolatrous state with the liturgy of the Eucharist in the Chilean church as the disciplined formation of two alternative social imaginations.

My argument is that the radicality in Dostoevsky's contrast between retributive and restorative justice is artistically depicted in the two central ritual settings of justice in *Brothers Karamazov*—the monastic cell of elder Zosima and the modern secular courtroom. It is no accident that the meeting between father and brothers Karamazov to mediate their dispute in the elder's cell early in the novel is a classic Dostoevskyan scandal scene, widely enjoyed for its sacrilegious buffoonery. Less well understood is the profound liturgical expression of spiritual discernment and restorative social justice it represents in the novel as a whole. The by contrast very lengthy and serious justice scene in the final third of the novel (by far the longest scene in a very long novel) is played

---

8. All parenthetical references in the remainder of the chapter are to Dostoevsky, *Brothers Karamazov*.
9. Peace, *Dostoyevsky*, 276.
10. Cavanaugh, *Torture and Eucharist*, 4.

out in the liturgical setting of the modern Russian courtroom, regarding the crime of parricide that gives the novel its central literal and symbolic dramatic movement. This scene is taken seriously, as Dostoevsky well knew, because we psychically "buy" the liturgical structure of the secular courtroom and we consider its rituals to be endowed with absolute political and religious authority. The courtroom, its liturgy, liturgical players, and icons—above all enshrining the sovereign rule of law understood as structuring and protecting the rights of contractual individuals—is the symbolic heart of one of the largest colonizing missions in human history: the global export of modern Western civilization as the model of the highest, happiest, most prosperous, and most just form of human life ever attained. Dostoevsky's scandalous claim is that this ritual of retributive justice travesties true justice.

The Elder's Cell

The monastic tradition is central to Eastern Orthodoxy, and in *Brothers Karamazov* it is the vision of the Russian monk that articulates and embodies the prophetic challenge and alternative to the orthodoxy of secular modernity.[11] This is for Dostoevsky not only a religious vision but a political one, and the institution of monastic elders founded upon the vows of complete obedience and self-renunciation stands in contrast to the secular path of absolute autonomy and self-realization. The root assumption of the monastic path is that freedom may be attained only through a "whole life's obedience" (27) to the rule of Christ and the difficult practices of serving, forgiving love. As the elder Zosima puts it: "Obedience, fasting, and prayer are laughed at, yet they alone constitute the way to real and true freedom," namely liberation "from the tyranny of things and habits" (314). Only one freed from the isolation of self-love can truly love others and build up the human community through deeds of humble love. The justice of this human community, moreover, is not to be found in the mechanics of procedural justice or in "rights" (313)—it is situated in the "consciousness of one's own conscience" (64). The elder states: "Remember that you cannot be the judge of anyone. For there can be no judge of a criminal on earth until the judge knows that he, too, is a criminal, exactly the same as the one who stands before him, and that he is perhaps most guilty of all for the crime of the one standing before him. When he understands this, then he will be able to be a judge" (320–21). Precisely such a posture of discernment is displayed by the elder in the opening scenes of the novel, and it is a posture of spiritual and political authority that stands in stark contrast to the Grand Inquisitor's.

The gathering of the Karamazov family in the elder's cell has a false pretext. The conflict over inheritance money between the father, Fyodor, and the eldest son, Dmitri, has intensified, and is of course complicated by their erotic pursuit of the same woman. Apparently as a joke Fyodor suggests they gather in the elder's cell—not for direct mediation but to see whether "the dignity and personality of the elder might be somehow influential and conciliatory" (32). Also attending is the relative of Fyodor's first wife and early guardian of Dmitri's, Miusov, a free-thinking atheist who is engaged in a lawsuit

---

11. This position is given extensive treatment in Kroeker and Ward, *Remembering the End*.

with the monastery (which borders his estate) over property and logging and fishing rights. Alyosha, the youngest Karamazov son, a monastic novice devoted to elder Zosima and the hero of the novel, suspects the motives of these various "quarrelers and litigants" but has hesitantly approached the elder with the request. The elder reluctantly agrees, citing (with a smile) the words of Luke 12:14—"Who has made me a judge over them?" (Jesus's response to a request that he settle an inheritance dispute). The visit therefore has both a litigious, juridical context and an explicitly religious context.

The meeting is set to follow immediately the late morning liturgy, and of course the guests show up *after* the liturgy. None but Alyosha truly orders his life under the authority of Christ or the disciplines of the church, and so the avoidance of the liturgical ritual that orders the elder's enactment of justice attests to the motives and predispositions of the claimants. Of course attendance at the liturgy, like consultations with the elder, is voluntary, not required. The foundation of the elder's authority is neither civically mandated nor based upon coercive state power. Hence the elder's words "Who has made me a judge?" echo his teachings on criminal justice rooted in the knowledge that is "the crown of the monk's path, and of every man's path on earth," namely, "that each of us is undoubtedly guilty on behalf of all and for all on earth, not only because of the common guilt of the world, but personally, each one of us, for all people and for each person on this earth" (164; cf. 289). Precisely such a personal penitential posture based upon eucharistic self-giving and the discernment of humble love is displayed by the elder in the meeting.

This also means, however, that the elder displays no sense of worldly honor and treats all his guests the same, whether important estate owners or poor peasant women, which offends the liberal-minded, worldly Miusov, who thinks he is being snubbed by the elder. The monks, moreover, greet one another ritually with deep bows and mutual blessings, which also offends Miusov and the secular guests, who scorn this as religious pretentiousness, in keeping with their scorn for the liturgy of the evening office. In effect, then, the ritual and liturgical setting of the practice of justice in the monastic cell is scorned by all of the guests except Alyosha. Furthermore, the monastic cell itself is small, the furniture, the narrator tells us, is crude and poor, and the room is dominated by icons—a large Mother of God lighted by an icon lamp, and a motley combination of expensive engraved prints of eighteenth-century Italian art alongside cheap Russian lithographs of saints, martyrs, and hierarchs, an egalitarian pluralism that offends Miusov's good taste. The liturgical and ritual setting, then, is lacking all conventional worldly markings of authority: wealth, power, high art, aesthetic formality. As Alyosha has feared, no reverence or even respect is paid either to the monastery or to the elder by family members. To the contrary, Fyodor's blasphemous buffoonery combined with Miusov's offended liberal vanity leads to a quintessentially Dostoevskyan scandal scene.

The elder Zosima, by contrast, is neither offended by the antics of his guests nor scornful of their impiety, and what follows cannot be easily summarized or represented, since it is really an extended informal conversation about theories of church and state and crime and punishment, as well as deeply personal revelations that expose the roots of the familial conflict, punctuated by vignettes involving the elder's acts of discernment with others seeking his counsel. In all it is a rather chaotic and disordered scene, and yet

PART 3: MESSIANISM AND DIASPORA ETHICS

Zosima manages to address the root causes of the familial conflict—pride, shame, false honor, habitual lying—offering both an interpretation and a prescribed cure: "Above all, do not lie to yourself" (44), he repeatedly tells Fyodor. Preserving the conscience from self-deception is the first step toward just discernment and fitting action in human beings. He also addresses Ivan's intellectual conflicts as the torments of an unresolved heart, a conflict of loves in the conscience that requires decision. Finally, in response to Fyodor's histrionic demand that in relation to the son "against whom I am seeking justice from you . . . Judge and save us!" (71) and the ugly exchange between father and son that follows, degenerating into talk of duels and parricide, the elder does a strange thing. He kneels deeply before Dmitri, even touching the floor with his forehead, and then begs forgiveness of all his guests. It is a gesture no one understands, and it evokes different responses in all his guests: Dmitri flees with his face in his hands, while Miusov takes it as a display of religious madness. Later Zosima explains it to Alyosha as a prophetic gesture: "I bowed yesterday to his great future suffering," in response to what he detected in Dmitri's eyes and non-self-justifying confession.

It may be useful here to recall what the elder says about crime and punishment in that same conversation. A true judgment ordered by Christ's law of love, which sees clearly the cause of the crime and how the criminal might be transformed, cannot "essentially and morally be combined with any other judgment, even in a temporary compromise. Here it is not possible to strike any bargains" (65). Hence Zosima's judgment on the "false consciousness" of the "establishment" churches of Western Christendom, in which the church's authorizing image (the law of Christ) has in some manner been falsely externalized and replaced by another form of rule (the juridical state)—symbolized in the sovereignty of the Grand Inquisitor. Ivan's Inquisitor covertly opposes the true authority of Christ (the freedom of the loving heart) in order to establish an external judicial political order that nevertheless claims the name of Christ. This is the founding "lie" of his sovereignty. It is a noble lie, claims the Inquisitor, premised on a "truer" image of human nature and history; but it is also a "lie in the soul" (Plato, *Republic* 382) that uses false images, speeches, and signs about the divine in the service of social order. On the Inquisitor's view, of course, human beings are not created in the divine image—they are merely clever beasts who must be tamed. For the elder, such lying is disastrous, as we may see in his account of the psychological anatomy of the liar (44, 58). Lying to oneself leads to a loss of discernment of truth, both within the self and in the world. This leads in turn to contempt, fear, disrespect—of self and others—and the inability to love. Such a self becomes the slave of changing passions and abstract, self-glorifying fantasies that can reach "complete bestiality" in a social order dominated by violence and fear, and the need for a security state.

The Secular Courtroom

It is Dmitri, of course, who will be formally (and falsely) charged with the murder of his father Fyodor, and this represents a kind of poetic justice, since he is of all the brothers the passionate sensualist most controlled by his desires. This gets him into trouble not only with women but also causes him to abuse physically three central fathers in the novel—Fyodor, Snegiryov, and Grigory the servant who treated him like a father. Yet book 12 of *Brothers Karamazov*, which concerns the courtroom trial of Dmitri, is entitled "A Judicial Error" and concerns not only a conventional miscarriage of justice on technical grounds but also provides Dostoevsky's display of the erroneous measure of justice embodied in the modern adversarial judicial process, which stands ritually and existentially over against the elder's understanding.

Let us note first of all some of the differences in this liturgical context of justice. The courtroom, in contrast to the elder's cell, is described by the narrator as "the best hall in town, vast, lofty, resonant" (659)—in keeping with its status as civic cathedral of public justice. At the center, in front of the presiding judges, is the table holding the objective "material evidence" of the crime committed, which will become the focus for the competing narratives interpreting the evidence. This particular trial has generated a great deal of public notoriety and journalistic attention both because of the nature of the crime, that of parricide in the context of complex erotic rivalries, and the fame of the defense lawyer Fetyukovitch. The gallery is filled with dignitaries and ladies whose faces exhibit "hysterical, greedy, almost morbid curiosity" (657) for an event that promises to deliver up sensational gossip and a gripping forensic contest between ambitious, articulate, and aggressive lawyers. The rivalries passionately displayed in the crime will be vicariously experienced by the spectators of the courtroom drama. The ritual legal performances will consciously exploit these rivalrous desires, though the lawyers will not be interested in them for any moral reasons. Their interests are focused on the contemporary legal and social significance of the case, to which their careers and public reputations are attached.

We should also note that there is nothing optional about attending the liturgy of the courtroom for its main participants. All are required to defer formally to its authority by standing for the judges, maintaining decorous silence, testifying under oath, wearing proper clothing, and allowing its designated ritual experts to follow a strictly formal procedure. In contrast to the elder's cell, for example, Dmitri's passionate and conscience-laden speechmaking is disallowed and immediately silenced, with threats. Above all this is to be a public contest between legal representatives about the objective data completely indifferent to, and in fact essentially abstracted from, any personal considerations. The thing most to be avoided in this liturgical ritual is spiritual discernment, which could only contaminate and render invalid the public and secular enactment of justice.

This does not mean that all kinds of appeals to "Christian values" will be disallowed, or that language of conscience is ruled out. But the ritual setting requires a quite different understanding of the meaning of such appeals and the ends to which they are dedicated. I do not have the time here to describe the liturgical performances in the courtroom. Suffice it to say that all of the legal liturgists share a commitment to Westernizing legal reforms. The detached, scientific exactitude of the secular progressivist judge stands in sharp contrast to the engaged spiritual disposition of the elder toward matters of justice. The role of medical, legal, and psychological experts in the adversarial construals of the evidence by opposing lawyers, and indeed the technical evidentiary process itself, are displayed by Dostoevsky as devoted to retributive ends, but not discerning the real relations of the human beings involved nor much concerned about the truth behind the evidence.

A frequent observer of criminal trials, Dostoevsky believed that the liturgical practices of modern adversarial justice often not only do not serve justice, but that their rituals and rhetoric actively corrupt it, breeding cynicism and lack of discernment in its practitioners and in the public observing the spectacle. He argued that the mechanisms of adversarial justice, which cater to appearance, external evidence, and spectacle, should be replaced by the disciplined pursuit of truly restorative justice. In *Brothers Karamazov* such an alternative set of rituals is offered in the practical institution of elders and the monastic disciplines. I have only been able to give a brief glimpse into Dostoevsky's rich artistic display of the correlation between ritual and justice in *Brothers Karamazov*. The point is that rights are related to rites, and ultimately to construals of the Right, which has implications for religion, ethics, and politics. Rites orient practitioners liturgically—in the etymological sense of *leitourgia* (*leitos*, public; *ergos*, performance or work/service)—and entail disciplines of speech and action that affect the enactment of political justice. Dostoevsky's alternative to the liturgy of retributive justice in the modern courtroom is the liturgy of restorative justice in monastic Christianity, which in *Brothers Karamazov* is taken out of the monastery and into the world by the novel's (anti)hero, Alyosha Karamazov. This establishes a very different context from Nietzsche's account for interpreting the meaning of punishment and torture.

Conclusion

I began this essay with reference to Michael Ignatieff's rather abstract consideration of the difference between punishment and torture "in an age of terror" in terms of a "balance" between liberty or rights and necessity. While I have argued that such abstractions are of very limited help (and indeed may be used to legitimate increasingly global "empire necessities") in making judgments about the differences between punishment and torture, I wish in conclusion to turn to the thinker who has perhaps most burdened Western political ethics with necessity language—namely, Augustine. In contrast to ethical abstractions, however, Augustine gives us in *City of God* 19.6 his vivid image of the anxious wise judge who is called upon to exercise public political responsibility to make judgments with the full awareness that in a sinful world those judgments will be flawed. They will entail a measure of evil necessity, evident in such practices as judicial torture, rituals of pain designed to evoke confessions of truth.

Augustine's image is both moving and deeply disturbing. It is moving not least for its uncompromising honesty (some call it "realism") about the presence of evil in the world and the dutiful necessity to act politically despite the necessary limitations on our capacities—for example, we cannot see into the souls of those we judge, and so have to do the best we can with the appearances of things (including bodily pain and interrogation). It is also moving because Augustine will advert repeatedly to what he calls the rallying cry of the Christian church in the midst of such miserable necessities: "forgive us our sins," and "deliver me/us from my/our necessities," a penitential disposition of humility. Yet Augustine's depiction is also disturbing in that it authorizes practices, such as various forms of corporal (and capital) punishment and judicial torture, that are not necessarily to be viewed as "necessary" but perhaps as strictly evil and thus avoided, even on Augustine's own account of messianic politics, which, though I do not have the space to argue it here, is finally not so different from Dostoevsky's.

While Augustine clearly envisions the ritual of judicial torture as a secular and civil, not ecclesial and religious, liturgy, his position is nevertheless problematic on several levels. The first is that it does not conform to Augustine's theological understanding of truth and lying—for him clearly not a bodily matter but a matter of the soul[12]—and this would pertain no less in the secular than in the ecclesial domain. In fact, Augustine's description of the "necessity" of judicial torture shows a clear awareness that innocents will often confess to crimes they have not committed under pain of torture: "And when [the accused] has been condemned and put to death, the judge still does not know whether he has slain a guilty man or an innocent one, even after torturing him to avoid ignorantly slaying the innocent. In this case, he has tortured an innocent man in order to discover the truth, and has killed him while still not knowing it."[13] The second problem is that judicial torture stands in egregious contradiction to the defining liturgical drama of his political theology, namely, the Eucharist—itself a sacrificial meal in which the church receives and offers itself in humble and penitential service to God and to the neighbor in an act of dispossessive self-giving. This is done in memory of another criminal torture and punishment, indeed under the sign of crucifixion, that both puts on cosmic display the sinful pretension of falsely sovereign human judgment and reveals the martyr form of the servant (not domination and coercive control) to be the sovereign and liberating form of God in a world of evil necessity. Clearly the torments of Augustine's judge derive from this more primary liturgical enactment. It is hard to see how appeals to "necessity" make any sense, then, with regard to the practice of judicial torture. Indeed, it is possible to see in Augustine's conscience-plagued figure the origins of the despised priest of Nietzsche's genealogy—one who is able to move adroitly between juridical inquisitorial torture (and why not use rituals of pain to evoke confessions also in an ecclesial setting where, even more, the eternal soul's salvation/condemnation, is at stake?) and the many possible pastoral uses of conscience-vivisection and tortuous self-surveillance to keep citizens and Christians in a state of moral conformity.[14]

---

12. For helpful discussions of Augustine's interpretation of truth and lying, see Rist, *Augustine*, 193–97, and Griffiths, *Lying*.

13. Augustine, *City of God*, 927. Augustine's reflections continue: "[The wise judge] does not consider it a wickedness [*nefas*] that innocent witnesses should be tortured in cases which are not their own, or that the accused are so often overcome by such great pain that they make false confessions and are punished in spite of their innocence. Nor does he think it wicked that, even if not condemned to die, they very often die under torture or as a result of torture . . . Witnesses may lie in giving testimony; the defendant himself may be obdurate under torture and refuse to confess; and so the accusers may not be able to prove the truth of their accusations, no matter how true those accusations may be, and the judge, in his ignorance, may condemn them." The key point, for Augustine, is that the wise judge's *intention* is not to do harm.

14. Here one finds the narrow opening for Connolly's Nietzschean-Foucauldian interpretation of Augustine's political theology in his *Augustinian Imperative*; see Dodaro's excellent critique of Connolly's too-narrow reading in "Augustine's Secular City," 231–59.

PART 3: MESSIANISM AND DIASPORA ETHICS

It is my view that Augustine cannot have it both ways. He cannot participate in the eucharistic liturgy and then advocate participation in the liturgy of judicial torture. If the former is true, the latter must be a lie—as the elder Zosima puts it, the messianic law of love may not "be combined with any other judgment, even in a temporary compromise." Furthermore, while I have not argued it here, I have assumed it is the case that the language of human dignity, rights, forgiveness, and the Right (I mean this as a synonym for the Good, not an ideological partisan political term) in the secular West is heavily indebted to religious practices and ideas. It is therefore important to draw analogically and comparatively upon these interrelations in thinking through the question of torture and punishment, and not simply in institutional or doctrinal terms. Above all, it would be dangerous to impose a strict institutional dualism (e.g., the church represents "mercy" while the state represents "judgment"[15]) upon these questions in a manner that precludes a fully critical analogical consideration.

Here, book 19 of *City of God* may itself provide a helpful structure. Augustine is convinced that the same existential relations of human love and justice hold true from the most intimate levels of self and household to the civic and international domains, from the most visible bodily level to the cosmic spiritual context concerning the origin and end of all things. No false boundaries will enable us to sort this out more simply. This does not mean that divine justice or judgment is transparent in the world, but it does mean that those ordered by the liturgical practices of penitence and self-offering may not presume to mediate divine judgment in anything but the servant form enacted therein. To the extent to which judicial torture and indeed any retributive judicial practices are devoted to the possessive and dominating "order" of the security state that claims to mediate a non-penitential justice, such practices are rooted in evil necessity and contribute to the "lie" of a strictly human sovereignty. They are subject to the Nietzschean critique of a Christianity that seeks coercively to impose its humble and confessional truth through internal and external disciplinary mechanisms of sovereign control. On the other hand, as I hope this essay has also shown, Nietzsche's reading of conscience, crime, punishment, and torture, is not the only possible reading—either of the Christian tradition or of the rise of the "sovereign" moral self in the modern (and postmodern) West. Dostoevsky (and Augustine) points to another possibility that is utterly pertinent to these questions, one that no less than Nietzsche and Foucault problematizes taken-for-granted assumptions about the difference between punishment and torture, and yet interprets and addresses them in a very different way. The sources I have drawn upon in this essay enable us to go beyond the often unhelpful abstractions of conventional technical ethics in order to wrestle theologically with the challenging lived complexities, including the religious ones, of our inherited moral discourses and practices concerning torture and punishment. The outcome of such a wrestling, just perhaps, may be a less confident limping through that nevertheless mediates political blessing.

---

15. This is the approach of O'Donovan in *Desire of the Nations*, 259ff.

15

Technology as Principality

The Elimination of Incarnation

IN AN EASTER OP-ED in the *New York Times*, Simon Critchley (Hans Jonas Professor of Philosophy at the New School for Social Research) makes an equation between the Christian hope of the resurrection and Prometheus the Titan, who stole fire from the gods and gave it as a gift to human beings.[1] In Aeschylus's version, not only is Prometheus thus responsible for the gift to humans of "technology" (all the arts of progressive human civilization), he is also responsible for a second, more "spiritual" gift: "I stopped mortals from foreseeing doom," says Prometheus, "I sowed in them blind hopes." According to Critchley, the apostle Paul inadvertently confirms this second Promethean gift in asserting that the Christian hope in resurrection is precisely a blind hope: "Now hope that is seen is not hope. For who hopes for what he sees?" (Rom 8:24; cf. Heb 11:1) The problem, Critchley implies, is that when blind hope of a spiritual kind is tied to civilizational arts and especially political ideals, we are in danger of being deluded by the most blatant and painful forms of unreality that prolong human bondage and suffering.

In this regard, of course, Critchley is in agreement with Nietzsche's scathing critique of Paul's spiritual causality, which Nietzsche considers to be "completely out of touch with reality."[2] The belief in resurrection puts the scandal of miracle at the very heart of reality: God creates the world *ex nihilo* at each moment; the world is not an immanent becoming according to causal laws of nature but is rather the gift of divine spirit, a gift given and revealed above all for Paul in the crucified Messiah, Jesus of Nazareth, who is sovereign over all worldly powers. It is Paul who gives us the language of "prin-

1. Critchley, "Abandon (Nearly) All Hope."
2. See Nietzsche, *Antichrist*, sec. 47. See my interpretation of Paul and Nietzsche on messianic political philosophy in chapter 1, above.

cipalities and powers" (*hai archai kai hai exousiai*) and, as G. B. Caird points out in his superb short study, this language pertains to three related domains of reality: politics, religion, and nature—all of which are related to causal language of "law" (*nomos*) of which an account is given by *logos*.³ The *logos* become flesh provides a different account of the causality of reality, one that (Paul claims) sets us free from the subjugating *nomoi* of worldly powers and authorities that have blinded human eyes to true reality and its (hidden, mysterious) causes. Thus is Critchley also in agreement with Paul, even though he doesn't see this. The question of technology is closely bound up with spiritual vision. This battle of science, religion, and politics continues unabated in our own time, a battle over an account of the true causes of disorder, suffering, and unhappiness in the world and of the true causes by which we might be liberated from those forms of bondage.

With technology, of course, we encounter another *logos* term. As we know from Aristotle, *technē* as a craft or art is always tied to a *logos*, or an account of something—and particular accounts are always related to larger causal accounts of the real. The term "technology" bears witness to this relationship within itself, as Heidegger's famous essay on "The Question Concerning Technology" makes profoundly clear.⁴ Good practice of these human crafts or arts is related to good *logoi* in what ethicists will call "virtue," by which we simply mean the proper human habituation of *technē* and *logos* so as to become "strong" human agents and communities—capable of good judgment and discernment, we might say, or practical wisdom, *phronēsis* (a kind of spiritual vision). Only this, for the ancient Greeks, can offer a hope that leads to happiness, freedom, a well-ordered community in body and soul. Arts or *technē* of the body such as medicine, gymnastics, and cooking require an account of health and its causes; arts or *technē* of the soul such as judging and legislating require an account of justice and its causes. And these accounts will be related. If this is so, and I will assume it is so also for Saint Paul and for Christian hope, we begin to see why religion (or worship) and politics (authority, sovereignty, power) and science (knowledge of the nature of things in the real world) are so closely related.

But as I have said, these relations are also deeply ambiguous and agonistic, as Paul's language of principalities and powers reveals. For Paul, as for Aeschylus and Plato, this agonism and ambiguity requires not merely a mathematical account of order rooted in external quantifying measurement but a dramatic one—what Heidegger also identifies as language of revelation, a "bringing forth" or a *poiesis*, a spiritual making that is not simply of our own human doing. Furthermore, the question of principalities in the ancient world raises the *political* question of sovereignty and therefore directs us above all to the philosophical and theological *governing* questions, the questions of *archē* (Latin: *princeps*), of beginnings and endings, the determining and terminal or "framing" questions, sometimes called foundational. But I simply want to note here again that for Paul and the New Testament, those foundational questions are fully dramatic and personal, not codified in doctrinal logics, juridical claims, or ethical systems. An interesting conjunction of the primary words in my title (technology and principality) appears in Paul's self-description in 1 Corinthians 3:10, where he calls himself a *sophos architekton*, a wise

---

3. Caird, *Principalities and Powers*.
4. In Heidegger, *Question Concerning Technology, and Other Essays*, 3–35.

architect, sometimes translated as "skilled master builder." We might remind ourselves here of Aristotle's designation of the political philosopher as an "architect of the end" (*Ethics* 1.1094b) who builds up happiness and the political good via *phronesis*.[5] Paul's efforts in this regard are devoted to building up (*oikodome*) the body of Christ, as a coworker (*synergos*) with God to build a structure envisioned as a messianic body whose foundation (*themelios*) is the messianic mind (*phronēte*, Phil 2; cf. the *nous* of 1 Cor 2:16, 1:10). This mind is for Paul tied to the revelation of the divine mystery (*mysterion*, Latin: *sacramentum*) that is spiritually or pneumatically—not "naturally" (and certainly not mechanically!)—revealed,[6] and it is attuned to a wisdom (*sophion*, 1 Cor 2:7) not understood by the *archontes* of this age who are governed by the "spirit of the world" (*to pneuma tou kosmou*, 2:12). Otherwise they would not have crucified the Lord of glory, an act of disincarnation that seeks to eliminate divine mystery from the world so as to control it on their own terms.

Perhaps here we can begin to see how modern technology comes into view as a worldly *archōn* of this age, and I now will attempt a theological and ethical account of this. The topic is of course vast. We could look at current technologies of the body, the ways in which we practice modern medicine, for example, in relation to a contemporary *logos* of health. If we were to do so, we might make the argument, as Ivan Illich and Barbara Duden do, that much of modern medicine is practiced in a culture of disincarnation, a denial of the flesh as reflecting divine mystery and a denial of the suffering of the cross as having anything to do with health.[7] Health, indeed, has come to be understood in terms of a global technological system or systems of "biomanagement" into which we are progressively integrated in a manner that disregards and disrespects our "personhood" (a term, we might note, that has increasingly been identified in legal terms with economic corporations to which our health care systems are closely tied). Is this good for our (personal or communal) health? Can it heal our diseases, or does it proliferate them? Does it console us in our suffering or intensify that suffering? To make a proper theological assessment would require us to interpret clinical rituals (and *technē* always appears in ritual settings) in relation to the whole liturgical practice of medicine, and compare this form of worship and authority to the sacramental practice of the Eucharist, for example, or the liturgical anointing of the sick or the administration of last rites.

Or, for example, we could examine technologies of the soul, such as the modern practices of justice in what we now call the "criminal justice system," which has exploded exponentially in the past half century, as attested to by the enormous sociopolitical and economic investments devoted to its expanding control and maintenance in building courts, appointing judges, and enhancing and training police, to say nothing of the incredible boom in building and filling prisons in an increasingly "carceral society."[8] Have these new technologies of judgment, discipline, and punishment led to a higher level of social justice and effective practices and institutions that make our communities safer,

---

5. See the discussion by Blumenfeld, *The Political Paul*.
6. See also Rom 8:5, 27 (*phronema*) and Rom 12:2 (*nous*).
7. Illich, *Medical Nemesis*; Duden, "Quest for Past Somatics"; and Duden, *Disembodying Women*.
8. This is Michel Foucault's terminology in *Discipline and Punish*. For Foucault this techno-social vision is symbolically depicted in the surveillance mechanism of Jeremy Bentham's "panopticon."

more peaceful, less violent and disordered? What kinds of virtues have they fostered? The answer to that of course depends on the *logos* of justice that is making judgments about *technē*. As Dostoevsky already saw in nineteenth-century Russia, the practice of judgment is closely tied to the rituals and liturgies that mediate the *logos* informing the *technē*. As I have argued elsewhere, Dostoevsky's last great novel, *The Brothers Karamazov*, concerns the political and religious meanings of justice.[9] The radicality in Dostoevsky's contrast between retributive and restorative justice (a justice of wrath and a justice of salvation) is artistically depicted in the two central ritual settings of justice in *Brothers Karamazov*—the monastic cell of elder Zosima and the modern secular courtroom. It is no accident that the meeting between father and brothers Karamazov to mediate their dispute in the elder's cell early in the novel is a classic Dostoevskyan scandal scene, widely enjoyed for its sacrilegious buffoonery. Less well understood is the profound liturgical expression of spiritual discernment and restorative social justice it represents in the novel as a whole. The serious justice scene in the final third of the novel (by far the longest scene in a very long novel), a scene that examines the crime of parricide that gives the novel its central literal and symbolic dramatic movement, is played out in the liturgical setting of the modern Russian courtroom. This scene will be taken seriously by readers, as Dostoevsky well knew, because we psychically and culturally "buy" the liturgical structure of the secular courtroom, and we consider its rituals to be endowed with worshipful political and religious authority. We swear solemn oaths to it on a closed Christian Bible. The courtroom, its liturgy, liturgical players, and icons—above all enshrining the sovereign rule of law understood as structuring and protecting the rights of contractual individuals—is the symbolic heart of one of the largest colonizing missions in human history: the global export of modern Western civilization as the model of the highest, happiest, most prosperous, and most just form of human life ever attained. Dostoevsky's scandalous claim is that this ritual of retributive justice makes a travesty of true messianic justice, and his wager in the novel is that only the monastic disciplines and practices of the messianic community (a "monasticism in the world" the elder Zosima calls it) will liberate us from the false sovereignty of modern technological desire. Only a messianic materialism will restore to us the divine mystery of our created embodiment, our "personhood." I will return to this.

Cybernetic Technology and Virtual Reality

I want now to move from these specific examples to a consideration of modern cybernetic technologies that have led us to the brink of the most extreme forms of death dealing and depersonalizing disembodiment under the aegis of liberating us from bondage to nature. "Virtual reality," we have come to call it, but it is really a death camp, without smoke stacks—well, at least we think we will eliminate the smoke stacks eventually through technological progress. Here I think we get a glimpse of "the god of this age" (2 Cor 4:4), the "archon of the authority of the air" (Eph 2:2) who blinds the eyes of those who worship the kind of power and the account of nature this principality represents.

---

9. See chapter 14, above.

What happens when the basic metaphors of nature, including human nature, are reduced to mechanistic process and technical information? I begin with a quotation from the well-known biologist Richard Dawkins, in *The Selfish Gene*: "We are survival machines—robot vehicles blindly programmed to preserve the selfish molecules known as genes. This is a truth which still fills me with astonishment," he gushes.[10] In case there were any doubt that this is no Socratic philosophical wonder (over whether the human being is a monster more complicated and furious than Typhon or a gentler, simpler creature related by nature to the divine; *Phaedrus* 230a), Dawkins clarifies his remark in his philosophical apologia: "But that was no metaphor. I believe it is the literal truth, provided key words are defined in the particular way favored by biologists."[11] This of course makes us curious about the favored linguistic preferences of biologists; as it stands, it seems an astonishing reductionism. Not only does it attribute a single moral intentionality (selfishness no less!) to the whole of life— it also uncritically names us "survival machines" or "robot vehicles," which one would have thought are strange metaphors for a biologist to choose. And yet this is not uncommon. For biologists, human nature has become revealed as techno-genetic standing reserves.

Dr. Robert Haynes, Yale professor and president of the 16th International Congress of Genetics (Toronto, 1988) states:

> For three thousand years at least, a majority of people have considered that human beings were special . . . It's the Judeo-Christian view of man. What the ability to manipulate genes should indicate to people is the very deep extent to which we are biological machines. The traditional view is built on the foundation that life is sacred . . . Well, not anymore. It's no longer possible to live by the idea that there is something special, unique, even sacred about living organisms.[12]

Machines, of course, are humanly made, artificial, engineered, usually not as a display of beauty or spiritual identity but as instruments—usually of control or procurement. Is it surprising that the *technē* of our culture takes on machine-like attributes when our primary metaphors are mechanistic? Increasingly not only our industrial economy but also our politics and our aesthetics take on the features of our primary linguistic metaphors, which are of course closely tied to a *logos*. Why else would people spend all that time and energy to make themselves look like the very muscle-building machinery they use to get them there? Why else are our lucrative fashion industries successfully marketing the hairless, well-oiled, "enhanced" body except that we literally are coming to see ourselves not as animal creatures but increasingly as biomechanical machines? Cyborgs? And who would not be willing to become a machine if it means avoiding a human death? The future markets in the cosmetic, therapeutic, and functional enhancement of the human machine (indeed the "nature machine") are vast indeed—and a great deal of research is being funded to exploit these opportunities and promote them in our public culture. To what extent is our technoscience guided by a morally laden *logos* of nature that denies its own moral judgments and assumptions as such (by assuming that the mechanistic

---

10. Dawkins, *Selfish Gene*, ix.
11. Dawkins, "In Defence of Selfish Genes," 572.
12. As quoted in Kimbrell, *Human Body Shop*, 283.

metaphor is objective rational description)? Of course, machines are not moral agents; hence if we are machines, are we moral agents? Or just power systems? Do we have a soul that is anything more than a ghost in the machine? Is the effort to enhance our machine-like efficiency a moral enterprise, and if so, what is the good it seeks and how will we speak about it?

In order to explore the good of technological research and development, we would do well to examine the cultural-linguistic (*logos*) history of modern science and its intimate connections with technology and the mechanistic paradigm.[13] As Carolyn Merchant's aptly titled book *The Death of Nature* argues, the modern vision of science has been closely tied to certain Baconian moral assumptions, most notably the commitment to relieve and benefit the human condition by liberating human beings from the constraints of nature and deliver control of nature, including human nature, into human hands.[14] "Knowledge is power," said Bacon, and by this he meant the power to *generate*, a power closely linking scientific research and technical development.[15] Bacon scoffed at the wisdom of the classical moral traditions and their language of the good, comparing it to prepubescent boyhood: "It can talk, but it cannot generate."[16] It is worth paying some attention to this language of "generating" because it is linked etymologically to an important family of words in our public culture: *genius, engine/engineer, gene/genetic*. All are linked to the Latin, *gigno/gignere*, to beget, and the Greek *gignomai*, to be born or to come into being. That is to say, such language is closely linked to central motives in a *logos* about *archē* as "origin," causality, bringing into being.

Genius is classically understood to be the tutelary or attendant spirit allotted to every person (or place or institution) at birth, influencing it for good or evil as that which gives moral form to the desires, the passions—that which we seek or love. Our coming into being is not only a biological but also a spiritual and moral begetting, by which our character or spirit or dispositions are shaped. Increasingly in the modern context, "genius" comes to be identified with inventive talent and technical ability of an externalized kind.

Engine or *engineer* (Latin: *ingenium/ingeniator*, linked to genius) traditionally referred to a natural quality, a person's disposition and moral character—that which *moves* a person: attitudes, pursuits, aims. In modern times, as we know, this is increasingly given a purely instrumental meaning and technical skill, to the point that the traditional meaning has disappeared. "Engines" are now mechanisms of external motion, and "engineers" are those professionals who design efficient machines that generate desired

---

13. We could do the same with politics and political theory, beginning with Hobbes's *Leviathan*. What Bacon did for modern science, Hobbes did for modern politics with his image of the great Leviathan as the gigantic artificial, mechanistic "human being writ large" that represents the body politic stripped of all spiritual causality. See chapter 4, above.

14. Merchant, *Death of Nature*, chap. 7. For Merchant's updated argument in the face of a spate of critical literature, see her "Violence of Impediments."

15. "*Ipse scientia potestas est*," said Bacon in *Meditationes sacrae* (1597), by which he was referring to divine creative power, related to his hope that science would enable human beings to restore the godlike power to dominate nature lost in the fall (*Novum organon*, bk. 2). Hobbes reduces this to "*scientia potentia est*," in contrast to the more traditional "*sapientia est potentia*," in *Leviathan* 1.10.

16. From the preface to *Instauratio magna*.

Technology as Principality

motions. The terms are, in effect, closely tied to technological power—as a profession, of course, "engineering" originated in a military context as the design and operation of engines of war and was, until the end of the eighteenth century, primarily a military career. The nineteenth and twentieth centuries saw the rapid expansion of civil engineering in the service of public works and then increasingly commercial enterprises, viewed as the engines of human liberation and control over nature and destiny.[17] In the late twentieth and twenty-first centuries engineering becomes intimately tied to the biomedical and information technologies, the latest locus of our hopes for human liberation and happiness.

Genes are units of heredity and biological transmission that shape the characteristics of offspring. Originally defined as ultimate units of mutation and recombination, they are now defined as sequences of DNA and increasingly described in images taken from the cybernetic and information sciences. It is, I suppose, not surprising that the instrument used to discover the DNA double helix—the computer—inspired the imagery of the new biology. Watson and Crick referred to the helix structure of the gene as a "code, programmed with chemical information to be deciphered."[18] The "cracking" of the genetic code that will unlock the secrets of life is a massive computational exercise in information processing.

Rather than focus here on particular ethical issues raised by this language and the action it generates—patenting of genetic information as intellectual property, the moral ambiguities entailed in various forms of genetic testing, cloning, and the new benevolent eugenics entailed in the biotech revolution that increasingly funds so much research in the life and health sciences—I want to consider the moral consequences of the shifts in language that I have briefly sketched. What happens when basic biological nature comes to be seen as information, and organisms as information-processing machines whose capacities can be progressively upgraded into increasingly efficient cybernetic survival systems?

I begin with Francis Bacon's own thought experiment, from his utopic *New Atlantis*, envisioning the future of modern scientific civilization. *New Atlantis* culminates in a vision of benevolent scientific empire communicated by the father of wise Solomon's House (a.k.a. the "College of Six Days' Work," instituted for the production of marvelous scientific works for human benefit), who comes in secret to give Bacon his blessing in a private conference. He states: "The end of our foundation is the knowledge of causes and secret motions of things; and the enlarging of the bounds of human empire, to the effecting of all things possible."[19] Thereupon follows a vision of technological empire that masters all of nature, including human nature, through a vast artificial infrastructure by which nature is subordinated to instrumental control, an order that respects not beauty but efficiency, says the father. It is a stunningly prescient vision: of novel plant

---

17. Herbert Hoover was the first civil engineer president of the United States. Of course, lest we forget, Adolf Eichmann was also an engineer by profession, and became highly proficient in the engineering of death camps—he considered himself, as his primary defense in his trial, to be simply "following orders" of his superiors.

18. Quoted in Rifkin, *Biotech Century*, 181.

19. Bacon, *Advancement of Learning*, 288.

species fashioned without seeds or natural generation, elaborate and extensive animal dissections and experiments that change them beyond species boundaries via artificial generation, an astonishing array of medicinal drugs and mechanical arts and penetrating diagnostic instruments. The last of the scientific powers listed are "houses of deceits of the senses" where the miracles of virtual reality are displayed; though of course as good scientists, the moral father hastens to add, "we do hate all impostures and lies" amongst fellow scientists who hold the power in this empire, so that to one another only nature "pure as it is, and without all affectation of strangeness" will be displayed.[20]

However, the question here quickly becomes distinguishing the "pure truths" of nature from mere conceits or dangerous deceits in the house of scientific culture. If nature is merely an information code to be cracked so that its various data might be reconfigured in endless different patterns, how might we distinguish true from false, benevolent from malevolent, healthy from harmful experiments, innovations, and developments? If there is no "good" in nature, including no moral goodness that can be commonly discerned, why even bother with ethics in scientific research and technological innovation?

I conclude this section with reference to another vision of technological empire as "posthumanism" that has, in effect, eliminated embodiment altogether—this one current and very influential right now in North American public life, represented here by Ray Kurzweil's *Age of Spiritual Machines*.[21] Ray Kurzweil is no flake; his work in artificial intelligence and pattern recognition technologies has led to the successful establishment of four high-tech companies (devoted, among other things, to pattern recognition technologies that aid the blind and the deaf), a number of influential books, and a host of academic and other national and international awards, including the U.S. National Medal of Technology (awarded him in 2001 by President Clinton). He is in many ways an icon of our culture's commercial and research aspirations; his books are the preferred reading of the political and business (and I suspect also certain academic) elites both in the United States and Canada.[22]

What is Kurzweil's vision? In a nutshell it is this: "Computation is the essence of order" (33). The evolutionary process that has begotten human intelligence is effectively generating an increasingly efficient information-processing machine. Kurzweil is convinced that human beings are the intermediate organic stage toward a new, essentially cybernetic technological stage of evolutionary development in which machine technology will eventually "take full control of its own progression" (32). This is indeed what human intelligence and consciousness really is, after all, when we get past "hard-to-define questions such as human dignity" (57). While the Human Genome Project is important as a scanning operation of DNA codes, it will ultimately be superseded by machine intelligence, according to what Kurzweil calls the "Law of Accelerating Returns," which interprets all reality on the model of increasingly complex information processing. This means that to adapt themselves to a changing natural—read "machine"—environment,

---

20. Ibid., 296.

21. Kurzweil, *Age of Spiritual Machines*. Further page references given in parentheses in the body of the essay.

22. Compare also the work of another such "visionary," UCLA bio-physicist Gregory Stock, in his books *Metaman* and *Redesigning Humans*.

in order to keep up with the evolutionary processes and maintain an evolutionary advantage, human beings will of necessity turn themselves into machines, gradually at first through genetic therapies, bioenhancement, and porting brains to computer intelligence. But "DNA-based evolution will eventually have to be abandoned" because "organisms created through DNA-based evolution are stuck with an extremely plodding type of circuitry" (101). Kurzweil's vision ends with the claim that "extremely little of the stuff on Earth is devoted to useful computation. This is even more true when we consider all of the dumb matter in the Earth's midst" (259). The aim of all life is to exploit nature for its computational intelligence (which is what Kurzweil means by "spirituality"), which will transform life into a shared machine consciousness, a posthuman virtual reality, where all things are possible—without God.

Kurzweil's book is filled with examples of what may be achieved through this biotechnological (and commercial) revolution he describes as "a road paved with gold . . . full of benefits that we're never going to resist" (130). For example, he is fond of speculating on the sexual possibilities that will open up when freed from the constraints of biological generation and conventional social norms. Sexual and spiritual activities can be reduced to information processing, not complex personal relations sustained through time or in nature, not educated through suffering and challenge and disciplined commitments between persons. Sex is merely the episodic manipulation of electronic data. Kurzweil celebrates the technological possibilities of virtual sex of every kind, which will no longer require moral censure because they will now be safely detached from the constraints of embodied nature. He imagines his fourth-grade son's ability to undress his fourth-grade teacher—and manipulate her in any way he desires—without affecting *her*; he imagines the ability to indulge many lovers at once, pleasuring himself by clicking on innumerable sites and partners at the same time (though I suppose eventually no real clicking will be required). So too the spiritual arts (music, poetry, painting) can easily be replicated by computer technology, and unfortunately Kurzweil cannot restrain himself from giving examples of his own design—all I can say is that if you love poetry and art, do not go there. The commodities on offer are at about the same level of moral wisdom and emotional intelligence as the fourth-grade sexual fantasies. We are now literally generating ("safe"!) sex for prepubescent boys, who no longer need either to talk or to generate.

How is it that our human quest for liberation and happiness ends up in such a tawdry and dehumanizing vision of totalitarian, mechanistic disembodiment that is nevertheless celebrated as the benevolent salvation of the future? I suggest it has something to do with the fact that we think we will magically crack the code of life through the collection of data. This is a Faustian bargain. Data lacks sanctity and goodness; to be sure, it takes attention away from our moral and spiritual sensibilities, which are developed and communicated through a different sort of language—the language of symbol, narrative, and the ordering of love, justice, beauty, and goodness. This classical moral language is attuned to a different kind of knowing than is the instrumental procurement and processing of data, and it is important to recognize this philosophically if we are to preserve a shared rational language (*logos*) that discloses to us spiritually and culturally who we truly are.

PART 3: MESSIANISM AND DIASPORA ETHICS

Now of course this reference to the spiritual raises the specter of pluralism. Especially in our so-called global culture there are many different traditions—religious, moral, philosophical—that try to tell us who we are or ought to be. Which one will we choose in order to guide our scientific and technological decisions? By now I hope you will anticipate at least the first part of my answer, namely, not by trying to find a single system or linguistic moral code that will sort out all possible conflicts and problems. Part of the problem in secular technological society is that we have sought precisely such solutions—another technical procedure, be it law or medicine or organizational theory. As T. S. Eliot says of modern human beings, in "Choruses from the Rock" (6):

> They constantly try to escape
> From the darkness outside and within
> By dreaming of systems so perfect
> that no one will need to be good.
> But the man that is will shadow
> The man that pretends to be . . .

What we need in the first place, rather, is an account of spiritual causality, if I may put it this way, in the language of poetic, dramatic experience, a return to our personhood—which is particular, limited, embodied, passing away, and yet inhabited, indeed inspired, by divine mystery.

The Messianic Annihilation/Reconciliation of "All Things"

How then are human beings to find life again in the midst of these disembodying and death-dealing principalities? I suggest it will require liberation from the pervasive language of "responsibility" in our public ethics. This is a language closely tied to worldly power, the power to control reality in a manner that overcomes the vulnerability of contingency, embodied particularity, and spiritual mystery.[23] Language of responsibility is also closely tied to the juridical codes of professional ethics, to which even an Adolf Eichmann could appeal with his *Nicht schuldig*: I was simply following professional orders and doing my responsible duty as one called upon to engineer the most efficient death camps possible. For the apostle Paul, too, the principalities and powers are closely correlated with juridical codes and legal dogmas—which are of no avail, he says, in liberating human beings from bondage to their false authority (Col 2:20–23). I note here that not only the *technē* of professional ethics but also the *technē* of religious authorities oriented toward control based on the possession of human knowledge have the effect, for Paul, of sinful disincarnation (1 Cor 8). They destroy rather than build up the body for which Christ died, a body rooted in the mystery of divine incarnation: suffering, death, and resurrection. This mystery only comes into view, we might say, through the *technē* of sacramental practices—*sacramentum* being the Latin term for the Greek word

---

23. See Carl Mitcham's essay, "Technology and the Burden of Responsibility"; and Mitcham, "Responsibility and Technology." See also Illich, *Rivers North of the Future*, chap. 21.

mysterion. This body, furthermore, includes "all things," all created reality that seeks its divine completion.

For Paul, this word *mysterion* can also be used with reference to the "mystery of iniquity" (2 Thess 2:7–8), the *parousia* of *anomia* (iniquity or "lawlessness") associated with Satan, and enacted with deceptively powerful "signs and wonders." The messianic *parousia* and the satanic *parousia* are "apocalypsed" together. As Ivan Illich points out, the mystery of this evil revealed in the heavenly places (as "Antichrist") is the corruption of the best, which happens when the incarnational Gospel is falsely institutionalized and turned into yet another universalizing global system that claims to bring salvation.[24] This is precisely a betrayal of the intimate truth of the embodied kenotic gospel, and it leads to the attempt to curse God's incarnation (even when it "blesses"). It builds up human empire in false godlikeness, in Babel-like fashion reducing culture to a single language, a univocal naming of reality "in order to make a name for ourselves" over against God. By contrast we note the "having become" (*genesthai* and its variants, 1 Thess 1:6, 7),[25] in which Paul is yoked together with the Thessalonians by receiving the apocalyptic word "in much affliction" and yet "with spiritual joy" (1:6).[26] For Paul this "becoming," this enactment of the truly human messianic body, is rooted in a "turning-around" (1:9) away from idols to serve "a living and true God, and to wait for his Son from heaven." But this waiting is not mere passivity related to "times and seasons" (5:1) of some future event. It is an entering into the "affliction" of the present time, the birthing of messianic love in the midst of false, destructive forms of "peace and security" (5:3ff.). For Paul this is not an otherworldly hope but the enactment of a hope that takes place in quiet, embodied service of others in everyday life (4:11).[27]

The demonic perversion of truth, as Ivan Illich shows, is not simply a violation of the laws of reality but a personal turning away from an intimate revelation of divine reality in whose image human beings are created. Its correlative is a turning in worship toward a false substitute, the apostatic *mysterium iniquitatis* Paul speaks about in 2 Thessalonians 2, revealed as anti-Messiah in the apocalypse of Messiah and characterized by mendacious power and wicked deception.[28] This is the personal, intimate character of sin that also has pervasive social and political consequences—the substitution of other-

24. Illich, *Rivers North of the Future*, chap. 2.

25. See the penetrating interpretation by Martin Heidegger in his early work on Paul, *Phenomenology of Religious Life*, 47–111.

26. The apostle Paul describes the intimacy of this union in "having become" when he says, "In all our distress and affliction we have been comforted about you through your faith; for now *we live*, if *you stand fast* in the Lord" (1 Thess 3:7–8). See also his strong language, where "having become" is linked to Jesus's messianic "coming" (*parousia*) in 1 Thessalonians 2:8, 2:19–20, 3:11–13.

27. For the contrast between "diaspora ethics" in the everyday to the globalizing ethics of Leviathan-Babel empire politics, see chapter 4, above.

28. Illich, *Rivers North of the Future*, chaps. 2, 14. Here is one of Illich's pithy formulations of what he means: "The Anti-Christ, or, let's say, the *mysterium iniquitatis*, the mystery of evil, is the conglomerate of a series of perversions by which we try to give security, survival ability, and independence from individual persons to the new possibilities that were opened through the Gospel by institutionalizing them" (169). Compare Augustine's reflection on 2 Thessalonians 2 and the possible meaning of the *Antichristo* as the "universal body" of the prince of apostasy, standing over against the messianic body as lie against truth (*City of God* 20.19). See chapter 3, above.

regarding personal love by self-securing institutional power. It may also be described as a turn away from the divine Spirit of love enfleshed in the person of Jesus toward a trust once again in the juridical, institutional constraints of external rules and codes of behavior—a shift from a community rooted in "con-spiratio" (personal faith, love, forgiveness inspired by the divine Spirit) to one rooted in "con-juratio" (the juridical state structure).[29] The impersonal, instrumental, and juridical character of modern social and political ethics, related to risk assessment and technical requirements of security systems (be they legal, educational, or medical), are the shared consequences of this shift in spiritual vision.

Let us return to the question of hope. In 1 Corinthians 15:24–28 Paul ties hope in resurrection with the messianic *katargēsis* of every principality and power in a passage in which "all" or "all things" (*pan, pantes, ta panta*) occurs ten times. The word *katargēsis* is sometimes translated destruction or "annihilation." Paul uses the same verb in 1 Corinthians 1:28 with reference to the wisdom and power of the cross: God chooses the things without being (*ta mē onta*) to bring to nothing (*katargēsē*) the things with being (*ta onta*). What does this mean, and how are cross and resurrection brought together in this verb that disarms the principalities and powers by setting aside their power to hold creation in the bonds of death (Col 1–2)? And how is it that through this agency of suffering the Messiah, now in his enfleshed body, reconciles a sinful, divided, and death-dealing creation with God? For Paul this is a divine mystery, one disclosed above all in the emptying movement of *kenosis* hymned in Philippians 2. It begins, of course, with God becoming enfleshed in the body of a young woman who accepts the begetting of her child as miraculous divine gift, and also a gift of suffering and mortality that requires her *kenosis*, her self-emptying.

Let me suggest in conclusion that this incarnational, personal technological vision is perhaps most importantly depicted for Paul in his experience of the resurrected crucified Messiah (which is where we began), an experience made visible in the sacraments, the embodied worship of the messianic suffering servant. This worship entails a sacrificial posture that breaks down dividing walls of hostility based on nature (male/female), religion (Jew/Greek), and socio-political status (slave/free), the three related domains of principalities mentioned by Caird. In proclaiming this hope Paul was quite aware of its scandalous claims with regard to visible human authority. In his famous address to the Athenians (Acts 17:16ff.) Paul relates the teaching that all human beings are generated by the divine as God's offspring to the teaching about the resurrection of the body. The resurrection is the vindication of the mystery of divine incarnation as dispossessive and kenotic, and it is celebrated in the sacrament of this enfleshment—not only a ritual liturgical event but also that which is liturgically enacted in all the *technēs* of charity, the serving works of love. As the elder Zosima proclaims, active love, unlike love in dreams rooted in isolated fantasies, is hard work requiring daily un-glorious, ascetic perseverance in the everyday.[30] It enters into affliction with joy. It requires death to the

---

29. Illich, *Rivers North of the Future*, chaps. 5, 15, 16.

30. Dostoevsky, *Brothers Karamazov*: "I am sorry that I cannot say anything more comforting, for active love is a harsh and fearful thing compared with love in dreams. Love in dreams thirsts for immediate action, quickly performed, and with everyone watching. . . . Whereas active love is labor and

self-desiring ego in order to be reborn in the "one mind" of messianic kinship, where in humility we work to build up communities in our shared mortal flesh.

We know from his diaries on *The Brothers Karamazov* that Dostoevsky worried mightily that the monastic path of the elder Zosima would not provide a compelling response to Ivan's techno-religious, demonic vision of the Grand Inquisitor in the novel. The current teaching of the world, says the elder, is the gratification and expansion of one's desires,

> for you have the same rights as the noblest and richest men. . . . But what comes of this right to increase one's needs? For the rich, *isolation* and spiritual suicide; for the poor, envy and murder, for they have been given rights, but have not yet been shown any way of satisfying their needs. We are assured that the world is becoming more and more united, is being formed into brotherly communion, by the shortening of distances, by the transmitting of thoughts through the air [remember, this is being written in the mid-nineteenth century!]. Alas, do not believe in such a union of people. Taking freedom to mean the increase and prompt satisfaction of needs, they distort their own nature, for they generate many meaningless and foolish desires, habits, and the most absurd fancies in themselves. They live only for mutual envy, for pleasure-seeking and self-display.[31]

By contrast, the elder articulates the monastic way: "Obedience, fasting, and prayer are laughed at, yet they constitute the way to real and true freedom: I cut away my superfluous and unnecessary needs, through obedience I humble and chasten my vain and proud will, and thereby, with God's help, attain freedom of spirit, and with that, spiritual rejoicing!"[32] Only one freed from the isolation of self-love can truly love others, and such freedom is made possible through spiritual rebirth in the image of Christ—conformity to the "form of the servant" that builds up the human community through embodied deeds of humble love.

---

perseverance, and for some people, perhaps, a whole science" (58)—a *technē*, we might say. "Brothers, love is a teacher, but one must know how to acquire it, for it is difficult to acquire, it is dearly bought, by long work over a long time" (319).

31. Dostoevsky, *Brothers Karamazov*, 313–14. For an extended discussion, see Kroeker and Ward, *Remembering the End*, chaps. 4 and 6.

32. Dostoevsky, *Brothers Karamazov*, 314.

Bibliography

Agamben, Giorgio. *The Kingdom and the Glory: For a Theological Genealogy of Economy and Government (Homo Sacer II.2)*. Translated by Lorenzo Chiesa (with Matteo Mandarini). Stanford: Stanford University Press, 2011.

———. "The Messiah and the Sovereign: The Problem of Law in Walter Benjamin." In *Potentialities: Collected Essays in Philosophy*, edited and translated by Daniel Heller-Roazen, 160–76. Stanford: Stanford University Press, 1999.

———. *The Time That Remains: A Commentary on the Letter to the Romans*. Translated by Patricia Dailey. Stanford: Stanford University Press, 2005.

Althaus, Paul. *The Ethics of Martin Luther*. Translated by Robert C. Schultz. Philadelphia: Fortress, 1972.

Arendt, Hannah. "The Concept of History: Ancient and Modern." In *Between Past and Future: Eight Exercises in Political Thought*, 41–90. New York: Penguin, 1958.

Auerbach, Erich. *Mimesis: The Representation of Reality in Western Literature*. Translated by Willard R. Trask. Princeton: Princeton University Press, 1953.

Augustine, Aurelius. *The City of God against the Pagans*. Edited and translated by R. W. Dyson. Cambridge: Cambridge University Press, 1998.

———. *Confessions*. Translated by Henry Chadwick. Oxford: Oxford University Press, 1991.

———. *On Christian Doctrine*. Translated by D. W. Robertson. Indianapolis: Library of Liberal Arts, 1958.

———. *Political Writings*. Edited by E. M. Atkins and R. J. Dodaro. Cambridge: Cambridge University Press, 2001.

———. *Teaching Christianity*. Translated by Edmund Hill. Works of Saint Augustine I/11. New York: New City, 1996.

———. *The Trinity*. Translated by Edmund Hill. Works of Saint Augustine I/5. New York: New City, 1991.

Bacon, Francis. *The Advancement of Learning and New Atlantis*. London: Oxford University Press, 1951.

———. *The Instauratio magna: Part 2, Novum organum and Associated Texts*. Edited by Graham Rees and Maria Wakely. The Oxford Francis Bacon 11. Oxford: Clarendon, 2004.

Badiou, Alain. *Saint Paul: The Foundation of Universalism*. Translated by Ray Brassier. Stanford: Stanford University Press, 2003. French: *Saint Paul: La Fondation de l'universalisme*. Paris: Presses Universitaires de France, 1997.

Baerg, Anna. *Diary of Anna Baerg: 1916–1924*. Translated and edited by Gerald Peters. Winnipeg: CMBC, 1985.

Balthasar, Hans Urs von. *The Theology of Henri de Lubac: An Overview*. Translated by Joseph Fessio and Michael M. Waldstein. San Francisco: Ignatius, 1991.

Barnes, Robin Bruce. *Prophecy and Gnosis: Apocalypticism in the Wake of the Lutheran Reformation*. Stanford: Stanford University Press, 1988.

Barth, Karl. *Epistle to the Romans*. Translated by E. C. Hoskyns. Oxford: Oxford University Press, 1968.

Becker, Adam H., and Annette Yoshiko Reed, eds. *The Ways That Never Parted: Jews and Christians in Late Antiquity and the Early Middle Ages*. Tübingen: Mohr Siebeck, 2003.

Benjamin, Walter. "Critique of Violence." In *Reflections: Essays, Aphorisms, Autobiographical Writings*, translated by Edmund Jephcott, edited by Peter Demetz, 277–300. New York: Schocken, 1978.

———. *Illuminations*. Edited by Hannah Arendt. Translated by H. Zohn. New York: Schocken, 1968.

Bibliography

———. "Theologico-Political Fragment." In *Reflections: Essays, Aphorisms, Autobiographical Writings*, translated by Edmund Jephcott, edited by Peter Demetz, 312–13. New York: Schocken, 1978. German: *"Theologisch-politisches Fragment."* In *Illuminationen: Ausgewahlte Schriften.* Frankfurt am Main: Suhrkamp, 1977.

———. "Theses on the Philosophy of History." In *Illuminations: Essays and Reflections*, edited by Hannah Arendt and translated by H. Zohn. New York: Schocken, 1968. German: *"Über den Begriff der Geschichte."* In Walter Benjamin, *In Illuminationen: Ausgewahlte Schriften.* Frankfurt am Main: Suhrkamp, 1977.

Berry, Wendell. *Remembering.* New York: North Point, 1988.

———. "Sex, Economy, Freedom, and Community." In *Sex, Economy, Freedom and Community: Eight Essays*, 117–74. New York: Pantheon, 1993.

———. "Two Economies." In *Home Economics: Fourteen Essays*, 54–75. San Francisco: North Point, 1987.

———. *What Are People For?* San Francisco: North Point, 1990.

Black Elk. *Black Elk Speaks: Being the Story of a Holy Man of the Oglala Sioux, as Told through John G. Neihardt.* Lincoln: University of Nebraska Press, 1961.

Blumenfeld, Bruno. *The Political Paul: Justice, Democracy and Kingship in a Hellenistic Framework.* Journal for the Study of the New Testament, Supplement series 210. Sheffield: Sheffield Academic, 2001.

Borgmann, Albert. *Technology and the Character of Contemporary Life: A Philosophical Inquiry.* Chicago: University of Chicago Press, 1984.

Boyarin, Jonathan, and Daniel Boyarin. *Powers of Diaspora: Two Essays on the Relevance of Jewish Culture.* Minneapolis: University of Minnesota Press, 2002.

Breidenthal, Thomas. "Jesus Is My Neighbor: Arendt, Augustine, and the Politics of Incarnation." *Modern Theology* 14 (1998) 489–503.

Breton, Stanislas. *Saint Paul.* Paris: Presses universitaires de France, 1988.

———. *The Word and the Cross.* Translated by Jacqueline Porter. New York: Fordham University Press, 2002.

Brueggemann, Walter. "Scripture: Old Testament." In *The Blackwell Companion to Political Theology*, edited by Peter Scott and William T. Cavanaugh. Oxford: Blackwell, 2004.

Buber, Martin. "Biblical Leadership." Translated by G. Hort. In *On the Bible: Eighteen Studies*, edited by Nahum N. Glatzer, 137–50. New York: Schocken, 1968.

———. "The Demand of the Spirit and Historical Reality." In *Pointing the Way,* translated and edited by Maurice Friedman, 177–91. New York: Schocken, 1957.

———. *Eclipse of God: Studies in the Relation between Religion and Philosophy.* New York: Harper & Row, 1952.

———. *I and Thou.* Translated by Walter Kaufmann. New York: Scribner's, 1970.

———. *The Origin and Meaning of Hasidism.* Edited and translated by Maurice Friedman. Atlantic Highlands, NJ: Humanities Press International, 1988.

———. "Plato and Isaiah." Translated by Olga Marx. In *On the Bible: Eighteen Studies,* edited by Nahum N. Glatzer, 151–59. New York: Schocken, 1968.

———. *The Prophetic Faith.* Translated by Carlyle Witton-Davies. New York: Macmillan, 1949.

Caird, G. B. *Principalities and Powers: A Study in Pauline Theology.* 1956. Reprint, Eugene, OR: Wipf & Stock, 2003.

Carter, Craig. *The Politics of the Cross: The Theology and Social Ethics of John Howard Yoder.* Grand Rapids: Brazos, 2001.

Cary, Phillip. *Augustine's Invention of the Inner Self: The Legacy of a Christian Platonist.* New York: Oxford University Press, 2000.

Cavanaugh, William. *Torture and Eucharist: Theology, Politics, and the Body of Christ.* Oxford: Blackwell, 1998.

Chartier, Clem. "Métis Perspectives on Self-Government." In *Continuing Poundmaker and Riel's Quest: Presentations Made at a Conference on Aboriginal Peoples and Justice,* edited by Richard James Goss, James Youngblood Henderson, and Roger Carter, 83–87. Saskatoon: Purich Publishing and the College of Law, University of Saskatchewan, 1994.

Clifford, James. "Diasporas." *Cultural Anthropology* 9/3 (August 1994) 302–38. Reprinted in *Routes: Travel and Translation in the Late Twentieth Century*, ch. 10. Cambridge, MA: Harvard University Press, 1997.

Cohen, Robin. *Global Diasporas: An Introduction*. Seattle: University of Washington Press, 1997.

Cohn, Norman. *The Pursuit of the Millennium: Revolutionary Millenarians and Mystical Anarchists of the Middle Ages*. New York: Oxford University Press, 1970.

Coles, Romand. "The Wild Patience of John Howard Yoder: 'Outsiders' and the 'Otherness of the Church.'" *Modern Theology* 18 (2002) 305–31. Also published as chap. 4 of Romand Coles, *Beyond Gated Politics: Reflections for the Possibility of Democracy*. Minneapolis: University of Minnesota Press, 2005.

Connolly, William. *The Augustinian Imperative: A Reflection on the Politics of Morality*. Thousand Oaks, CA: Sage, 1993.

Corbett, Margery, and Ronald Lightbown. *The Comely Frontispiece: The Emblematic Title-Page in England, 1550–1660*. London: Routledge and K. Paul, 1979.

Critchley, Simon. "Abandon (Nearly) All Hope." *New York Times*, April 19, 2014. http://opinionator.blogs.nytimes.com/2014/04/19/abandon-nearly-all-hope/?_r=0.

Davidson, Arnold E. *Coyote Country: Fictions of the Canadian West*. Durham: Duke University Press, 1992.

Davies, W. D., and Dale Allison. *A Critical and Exegetical Commentary on the Gospel According to Saint Matthew*. Vol. 1. Edinburgh: T. & T. Clark, 1988.

Davis, Grady Scott. "Tradition and Truth in Christian Ethics: John Yoder and the Bases of Biblical Realism." In *The Wisdom of the Cross: Essays in Honor of John Howard Yoder*, edited by Stanley Hauerwas, et al., 278–308. Grand Rapids: Eerdmans, 1999.

Davis, Kenneth R. *Anabaptism and Asceticism: A Study in Intellectual Origins*. Scottdale, PA: Herald, 1974.

Dawkins, Richard. "In Defence of Selfish Genes." *Philosophy* 56 (1981) 556–73.

———. *The Selfish Gene*. London: Granada, 1978.

Deleuze, Gilles. *Nietzsche and Philosophy*. Translated by H. Tomlinson. London: Athlone, 1983.

Deloria, Vine, Jr. *For This Land: Writings on Religion in America*. Edited by James Treat. New York: Routledge, 1999.

Derrida, Jacques. "Des Tours de Babel." In *Difference in Translation*, edited by Joseph Graham, 218–27. Ithaca: Cornell University Press, 1985.

Dillard, Annie. *Holy the Firm*. New York: Harper & Row, 1977.

Dodaro, Robert. "Augustine and the Possibility of Political Conscience." In *Augustinus: Ethik und Politik*, edited by Cornelius Mayer, 223–41. Würzburg: Augustinus-Verlag, 2009.

———. "Augustine's Secular City." In *Augustine and His Critics: Essays in Honour of Gerald Bonner*, edited by R. Dodaro and G. Lawless, 231–59. London: Routledge, 2000.

———. *Christ and the Just Society in the Thought of Augustine*. Cambridge: Cambridge University Press, 2004.

———. "'Christus Iustus' and Fear of Death in Augustine's Dispute with Pelagius." In *Signum Pietatis: Festgabe für Cornelius Petrus Mayer zum 60. Geburtstag*, edited by A. Zumkeller, 341–61. Würzburg: Augustinus-Verlag, 1989.

———. "*Ecclesia* and *Res Publica*: How Augustinian Are Neo-Augustinian Politics?" In *Augustine and Postmodern Thought: A New Alliance against Modernity?*, edited by L. Boeve, M. Lamberigts, and M. Wisse, 237–71. Leuven: Peeters, 2009.

———. "Eloquent Lies, Just Wars and the Politics of Persuasion: Reading Augustine's *City of God* in a 'Postmodern' World." *Augustinian Studies* 25 (1994) 77–138.

Dostoevsky, Fyodor. *The Brothers Karamazov*. Translated by Richard Pevear and Larissa Volokhonsky. New York: Vintage, 1990.

———. *Complete Letters*. Edited and translated by David Lowe and Ronald Meyer. Vol. 5. Ann Arbor, MI: Ardis, 1991.

———. *The House of the Dead*. Translated by David McDuff. London: Penguin, 1985.

———. *Pisma I*. Edited by A. S. Dolinin. Moscow, 1928–1959.

———. *A Writer's Diary*. Translated by Kenneth Lantz. Evanston: Northwestern University Press, 1994.

Duden, Barbara. *Disembodying Women: Perspectives on Pregnancy and the Unborn*. Translated by Lee Hoinacki. Cambridge, MA: Harvard University Press, 1993.

Bibliography

———. "The Quest for Past Somatics." In *The Challenges of Ivan Illich: A Collective Reflection*, edited by Lee Hoinacki and Carl Mitcham, 219–30. Albany: State University of New York Press, 2002.

Ebeling, Gerhard. *Luther: An Introduction to His Thought*. Translated by R. A. Wilson. Philadelphia: Fortress, 1970.

Eliot, T. S. "Choruses from the Rock." In *Collected Poems, 1909–1962*. London: Faber and Faber, 2002.

Feuerbach, Ludwig. *The Essence of Christianity*. Translated by G. Eliot. New York: Harper & Row, 1957.

Finger, Thomas N. "Anabaptism and Eastern Orthodoxy: Some Unexpected Similarities." *Journal of Ecumenical Studies* 31.1–2 (1994) 67–91.

Foucault, Michel. *Discipline and Punish: The Birth of the Prison*. Translated by Alan Sheridan. New York: Vintage, 1977.

———. "Nietzsche, Genealogy, History." In *Language, Counter-Memory, Practice: Selected Essays and Interviews*, edited by D. Bouchard, 139–64. Ithaca: Cornell University Press, 1977.

———. "Right of Death and Power over Life." Part 5 in *The History of Sexuality*, vol. 1. Translated by R. Hurley. New York: Vintage, 1980.

———. "Two Lectures." In *Power/Knowledge: Selected Interviews and Other Writings, 1972–1977*, edited by Colin Gordon. New York: Pantheon, 1980.

Frank, Joseph. *Dostoevsky: The Years of Ordeal, 1850–1859*. Princeton: Princeton University Press, 1983.

Fredrickson, Paula. "Tyconius and Augustine on the Apocalypse." In *The Apocalypse in the Middle Ages*, edited by Richard K. Emmerson and Bernard McGinn, 20–37. Ithaca: Cornell University Press, 1992.

———. "Tyconius and the End of the World." *Revue des Études Augustiniennes* 18 (1982) 59–71.

Friedman, Robert. *The Theology of Anabaptism: An Interpretation*. Scottdale, PA: Herald, 1973.

Friesen, Abraham. *Thomas Muentzer, a Destroyer of the Godless: The Making of a Sixteenth-Century Religious Revolutionary*. Berkeley: University of California Press, 1990.

Gadamer, Hans-Georg. *Dialogue and Dialectic: Eight Hermeneutical Studies on Plato*. Translated by P. Christopher Smith. New Haven: Yale University Press, 1980.

———. "Plato and the Poets." In *Dialogue and Dialectic: Eight Hermeneutical Studies on Plato*, translated by P. Christopher Smith, 39–72. New Haven: Yale University Press, 1980.

Giraud, Marcel. *The Métis in the Canadian West*. 2 vols. Translated by George Woodcock. Edmonton: University of Alberta Press, 1986.

Gooding-Williams, Robert. *Zarathustra's Dionysian Modernism*. Stanford: Stanford University Press, 2001.

Goosen, Rachel Waltner. "'Defanging the Beast': Mennonite Responses to John Howard Yoder's Sexual Abuse." *Mennonite Quarterly Review* 89 (2015) 7–80.

Grant, George. "In Defence of North America." In *Technology and Empire: Perspectives on North America*, 15–40. Toronto: Anansi, 1969.

———. *English-Speaking Justice*. Notre Dame: University of Notre Dame Press, 1985.

———. "Thinking about Technology." In *Technology and Justice*, 11–34. Toronto: Anansi, 1986.

Griffiths, Paul. *Lying: An Augustinian Theology of Duplicity*. Grand Rapids: Brazos, 2004.

Grislis, Egil. "Menno Simons on Sanctification." *Mennonite Quarterly Review* 69 (1994) 226–46.

Gritsch, Eric W. *Thomas Müntzer: A Tragedy of Errors*. Minneapolis: Fortress, 1989.

Gustafson, James. *Ethics from a Theocentric Perspective*. Vol. 1, *Theology and Ethics*. Chicago: University of Chicago Press, 1981.

Harder, Hans. *No Strangers in Exile*. Freely translated, edited, and expanded from the original by German by Al Reimer. Winnipeg: Hyperion, 1979. Published in 1934 in Germany as *In Wologdas weissen Wälder*.

Harink, Douglas. "The Anabaptist and the Apostle: John Howard Yoder as a Pauline Theologian." In *A Mind Patient and Untamed: Assessing John Howard Yoder's Contributions to Theology, Ethics, and Peacemaking*, edited by B. Ollenburger and G. Koontz, 274–87. Telford, PA: Cascadia, 2004.

———. *Paul among the Postliberals: Pauline Theology beyond Christendom and Modernity*. Grand Rapids: Brazos, 2003.

Hauerwas, Stanley. *With the Grain of the Universe: The Church's Witness and Natural Theology*. Grand Rapids: Brazos, 2001.

Hauerwas, Stanley, with James Fodor. "Remaining in Babylon: Oliver O'Donovan's Defense of Christendom." In *Wilderness Wanderings: Probing Twentieth-Century Theology and Philosophy*, 199–224. Boulder, CO: Westview, 1997.

Hauerwas, Stanley, et al., eds. *The Wisdom of the Cross: Essays in Honor of John Howard Yoder*. Grand Rapids: Eerdmans, 1999.

Hays, Richard. *The Moral Vision of the New Testament: A Contemporary Introduction to New Testament Ethics*. San Francisco: HarperCollins, 1996.

Heidegger, Martin. *Nietzsche*. Translated by David Krell. 2 vols. San Francisco: HarperCollins, 1991.

———. *The Phenomenology of Religious Life*. Translated by Matthias Fritsch and Jennifer Gosetti-Ferencei. Bloomington: Indiana University Press, 2004.

———. *The Question Concerning Technology, and Other Essays*. Translated by William Lovitt. New York: Garland, 1977.

———. "The Word of Nietzsche: 'God Is Dead.'" In *The Question Concerning Technology, and Other Essays*, translated by William Lovitt, 53–114. New York: Garland, 1977.

Heilke, Thomas. "Yoder's Idea of Constantinianism: An Analytical Framework toward Conversation." In *A Mind Patient and Untamed: Assessing John Howard Yoder's Contributions to Theology, Ethics, and Peacemaking*, edited by B. Ollenburger and G. Koontz, 89–125. Telford, PA: Cascadia, 2004.

Heschel, Abraham J. *The Prophets*. 2 vols. New York: Harper & Row, 1962.

Hobbes, Thomas. *Leviathan*. Edited by Edwin Curley. Indianapolis: Hackett, 1994.

Hofmann, Hans-Ulrich. *Luther und die Johannes-Apokalypse*. Tübingen: J. C. B. Mohr, 1982.

Holland, Scott. "Theology Is a Kind of Writing: The Emergence of Theopoetics." *Mennonite Quarterly Review* 71 (1997) 227–41.

Hunsinger, George. "Karl Barth and the Politics of Sectarian Protestantism: A Dialogue with John Howard Yoder." In *Disruptive Grace: Studies in the Theology of Karl Barth*, 114–30. Grand Rapids: Eerdmans, 2000.

Ignatieff, Michael. *The Lesser Evil: Political Ethics in an Age of Terror*. Edinburgh: Edinburgh University Press, 2004.

Illich, Ivan. *Medical Nemesis: The Expropriation of Health*. New York: Pantheon, 1976.

———. *The Rivers North of the Future: The Testament of Ivan Illich*. Toronto: Anansi, 2005.

Jaeger, Werner. *Paideia: The Ideals of Greek Culture*. Vol. 2, *In Search of the Divine Centre*. Translated by Gilbert Highet. New York: Oxford University Press, 1943.

Johnson, David. *The Rhetoric of Leviathan*. Princeton: Princeton University Press, 1986.

Kafka, Franz. "On Parables." In *The Basic Kafka*, 158. New York: Simon & Schuster, 1979.

Kamlah, Wilhelm. *Christentum und Geschichtlichkeit: Untersuchungen zu Entstehung des Christentums und zu Augustins Burgerschaft Gottes*. Stuttgart: W. Kohlhammer, 1951.

Kierkegaard, Søren. *The Concept of Anxiety: A Simple Psychologically Orienting Deliberation on the Dogmatic Issue of Hereditary Sin*. Edited and translated by Reidar Thomte and Albert Anderson. Princeton: Princeton University Press, 1980.

———. "The Difference between a Genius and an Apostle." In *The Book on Adler,* edited and translated by Howard V. Hong and Edna H. Hong, 173–80. Princeton: Princeton University Press, 1998.

———. *Fear and Trembling*. Edited and translated by Alastair Hannay. New York: Penguin, 1986.

———. *Philosophical Fragments*. Edited and translated by Howard V. Hong and Edna H. Hong. Princeton: Princeton University Press, 1985.

———. *Sickness unto Death: A Christian Psychological Exposition for Upbuilding and Awakening*. Edited and translated by Howard V. Hong and Edna H. Hong. Princeton: Princeton University Press, 1980.

———. *Works of Love*. Edited and translated by Howard V. Hong and Edna H. Hong. Princeton: Princeton University Press, 1995.

Kimbrell, Andrew. *The Human Body Shop: The Cloning, Engineering, and Marketing of Life*. Washington, DC: Regnery, 1997.

Klaassen, Walter, *Living at the End of the Ages: Apocalyptic Expectation in the Radical Reformation*. Lanham, MD: University Press of America, 1992.

Kline, David. "God's Spirit and a Theology for Living." In *Creation and the Environment: An Anabaptist Perspective on a Sustainable World*, edited by Calvin Redekop, 61–69. Baltimore: Johns Hopkins University Press, 2000.

Bibliography

———. "How Wendell Berry Single-Handedly Preserved Three Hundred Years of Agrarian Wisdom." In *Wendell Berry: Life and Work*, edited by Jason Peters, 60–65. Lexington: University Press of Kentucky, 2007.

Kreitzer, Beth. "Menno Simons and the Bride of Christ." *Mennonite Quarterly Review* 70 (1996) 299–318.

Kroeker, P. Travis. "Anabaptists and Existential Theology." *Conrad Grebel Review* 17 (1999) 69–88.

———. *Christian Ethics and Political Economy in North America: A Critical Analysis*. Montreal: McGill-Queen's University Press, 1995.

———. *Empire Erotics and Messianic Economies of Desire*. Winnipeg: Canadian Mennonite University Press, 2016.

———. "The Ironic Cage of Positivism and the Nature of Philosophical Theology." *Studies in Religion/Sciences Religieuses* 22 (1993) 93–103.

———. "On the Difference between Torture and Punishment: Theology, Liturgy, and Human Rights." In *Theology, University, Humanities: Initium Sapientiae Timor Domini*, edited by Christopher Brittain and Francesca Murphy, 19–38. Eugene, OR: Cascade, 2011.

———. "Overcoming Historicism: Weak Messianic Apocalpyticism." *Syndicatetheology.com* (June 2014). Print version in *Syndicate: A New Forum for Theology*, 1/1 (May/June 2014) 87–93.

———. "Sexuality and the Sacramental Imagination: It All Turns on Affection." In *Wendell Berry: Life and Work*, edited by Jason Peters, 119–37. Lexington: University Press of Kentucky, 2007.

———. "The Theological Politics of Plato and Isaiah: A Debate Revisited." *The Journal of Religion* 73 (1993) 16–30.

———. "The War of the Lamb: Postmodernity and John Howard Yoder's Eschatological Genealogy of Morals." *Mennonite Quarterly Review* 74 (2000) 295–310.

———. "Whither Messianic Ethics? Paul as Political Theorist." *Journal of the Society of Christian Ethics* 25 (2005) 37–58.

Kroeker, P. Travis, and Bruce K. Ward. *Remembering the End: Dostoevsky as Prophet to Modernity*. Boulder, CO: Westview, 2001.

Kurzweil, Ray. *The Age of Spiritual Machines: When Computers Exceed Human Intelligence*. New York: Penguin, 1999.

Labedz, Leopold, ed. *Solzhenitsyn: A Documentary Record*. Translated from the Russian. Harmondsworth, UK: Penguin, 1972.

Lednicki, Waclaw. *Russia, Poland, and the West*. New York: Roy, 1954.

Lee, Gregory W. "Republics and Their Loves: Rereading *City of God* 19." *Modern Theology* 27 (2011) 553–81.

Levenson, Jon D. *The Death and Resurrection of the Beloved Son: The Transformation of Child Sacrifice in Judaism and Christianity*. New Haven: Yale University Press, 1993.

Liddell, Henry George, and Robert Scott, compilers. *A Greek-English Lexicon*. Oxford: Clarendon, 1968.

Lilla, Mark. *The Stillborn God: Religion, Politics, and the Modern West*. New York: Knopf, 2007.

Loewen, Royden. *Diaspora in the Countryside: Two Mennonite Communities and Mid-Twentieth-Century Rural Disjuncture*. Toronto: University of Toronto Press, 2006.

Lowith, Karl. *Meaning in History*. Chicago: University of Chicago Press, 1949.

Lubac, Henri de. *Corpus Mysticum: The Eucharist and the Church in the Middle Ages*. Translated by Gemma Simmonds with Richard Price and Christopher Stephens. Edited by Laurence Paul Hemming and Susan Frank Parsons. Notre Dame: University of Notre Dame Press, 2006.

———. *The Splendor of the Church*. Translated by Michael Mason. San Francisco: Ignatius Press, 1999.

Luther, Martin. "The Estate of Marriage." Translated by Walther Brandt. In *Luther's Works*, 45:11–49. Philadelphia: Fortress, 1962.

———. "The Freedom of a Christian." In *Martin Luther: Selections from His Writings*, edited by John Dillenberger, 42–85. Garden City, NY: Doubleday, 1961.

———. "Secular Authority: To What Extent It Should Be Obeyed." In *Martin Luther: Selections from His Writings*, edited by John Dillenberger, 363–402. Garden City, NY: Doubleday, 1961.

———. "The Sermon on the Mount." Translated by Jaroslav Pelikan. In *Luther's Works*, 21:1–294. Philadelphia: Fortress, 1956.

———. "To the Christian Nobility." Translated by Charles Jacobs and revised by James Atkinson. In *Luther's Works*, 44:115–219. Philadelphia: Fortress, 1966.

Bibliography

MacIntyre, Alasdair. *Three Rival Versions of Moral Enquiry: Encyclopedia, Genealogy, and Tradition*. Notre Dame: University of Notre Dame Press, 1990.

Markus, Robert A. *Christianity and the Secular*. Notre Dame: University of Notre Dame Press, 2006.

———. *Saeculum: History and Society in the Theology of St. Augustine*. Cambridge: Cambridge University Press, 1970.

Martanyov, P. K. "V Perelome Veka." *I toricheskii Vestnik* 10–11 (1895).

Martens, Paul. "Anabaptist Ethics after Yoder: Accepting the Limits on the Freedom of a Christian Ethicist." In *The Freedom of a Christian Ethicist: The Future of a Reformation Legacy*, edited by Brian Brock and Michael Mawson, 107–26. London: Bloomsbury T. & T. Clark, 2016.

———. *The Heterodox Yoder*. Eugene, OR: Cascade, 2012.

Martin, Peter. *Martin Luther und die Bilder zur Apokalypse*. Hamburg: Friedrich Wittig, 1983.

McGinn, Bernard. *Antichrist: Two Thousand Years of the Human Fascination with Evil*. New York: HarperCollins, 1994.

Merchant, Carolyn. *The Death of Nature: Women, Ecology, and the Scientific Revolution*. New York: Harper & Row, 1980.

———. "Violence of Impediments: Francis Bacon and the Origins of Experimentation." *Isis* 99 (2008) 731–60.

Milbank, John. "A Closer Walk on the Wild Side." In *Varieties of Secularism in a Secular Age*, edited by Michael Warner, Jonathan VanAntwerpen, and Craig Calhoun, 54–82. Cambridge, MA: Harvard University Press, 2010.

———. *Theology and Social Theory: Beyond Secular Reason*. Oxford: Blackwell, 1990.

Miller, Kevin D. "Conversations: The Rich Christian; How Ron Sider Has Changed in the 20 Years since His First Book." *Christianity Today* 41.5 (April 28, 1997).

Mitcham, Carl. "Responsibility and Technology: The Expanding Relationship." *Philosophy and Technology* 3 (1987) 3–39.

———. "Technology and the Burden of Responsibility." In *Values and Ethics for the 21st Century*, edited by F. Gonzalez et al., 141–66. Madrid: BBVA, 2012.

Müntzer, Thomas. "Sermon before the Princes." In *Spiritual and Anabaptist Writers*, edited by G. Williams, 49–70. Philadelphia: Westminster, 1957.

Neufeld, Dietrich. *A Russian Dance of Death*. Translated and edited by Al Reimer. Winnipeg: Hyperion, 1977.

Newman, John Henry. *The Idea of a University*. New Haven: Yale University Press, 1996.

Niebuhr, H. Richard. *Christ and Culture*. New York: Harper, 1951.

Nietzsche, Friedrich. *The Antichrist*. In *The Portable Nietzsche*, edited and translated by Walter Kaufmann. New York: Penguin, 1968. German: *Der Antichrist*. In vol. 3 of *Nietzsche Werke: Kritische Gesamtausgabe*. Edited by Colli and Montinario. Berlin: de Gruyter, 1969.

———. *Daybreak: Thoughts on the Prejudices of Morality*. Edited by Maudemarie Clark and Brian Leiter. Translated by R. J. Hollingdale. Cambridge: Cambridge University Press, 1997.

———. *Ecce Homo*. In *The Anti-Christ, Ecce Homo, Twighlight of the Idols, and Other Writings*, edited by A. Ridley and J. Norman and translated by J. Norman. Cambridge: Cambridge University Press, 2005.

———. *The Gay Science*. In *The Portable Nietzsche*, edited and translated by Walter Kaufmann. New York: Penguin, 1968.

———. *The Gay Science*. Translated by Walter Kaufmann. New York: Vintage, 1974.

———. *On the Genealogy of Morals*. Translated by Walter Kaufman and R. J. Hollingdale. New York: Vintage, 1967. German: *Zur Genealogie der Moral*. Vol. 7 of *Nietzsche Werke*. Stuttgart: Alfred Kröner, 1921.

———. *Thus Spoke Zarathustra*. In *The Portable Nietzsche*, edited and translated by Walter Kaufmann. New York: Penguin, 1968. German: Vol. 4 of *Nietzsche Werke*.

———. *Twilight of the Idols, or How One Philosophizes with a Hammer*.In *The Portable Nietzsche*, edited and translated by Walter Kaufmann. New York: Penguin, 1968. German: Vol. 3 of *Nietzsche Werke*.

———. *Writings from the Late Notebooks*. Edited by Rüdiger Bittner. Translated by Kate Sturge. Cambridge: Cambridge University Press, 2003.

Northcott, Michael S. *A Political Theology of Climate Change*. Grand Rapids: Eerdmans, 2013.

Bibliography

Oberman, Heiko A. *Luther: Man between God and the Devil.* Translated by Eileen Walliser-Schwarzbart. New Haven: Yale University Press, 1989.

O'Daly, Gerard. *Augustine's "City of God": A Reader's Guide.* Oxford: Oxford University Press, 1999.

O'Donovan, Oliver. "Augustine's *City of God* XIX and Western Political Thought." *Dionysius* 2 (1987) 89–110. Also published in revised and lengthened form in Oliver O'Donovan and Joan Lockwood O'Donovan, *Bonds of Imperfection: Christian Politics, Past and Present,* 48–72. Grand Rapids: Eerdmans, 2004.

———. *Common Objects of Love: Moral Reflection and the Shaping of Community.* Grand Rapids: Eerdmans, 2002.

———. *The Desire of the Nations: Rediscovering the Roots of Political Theology.* Cambridge: Cambridge University Press, 1996.

———. "Karl Barth and Ramsey's 'Uses of Power.'" *Journal of Religious Ethics* 19 (1991) 1–30.

———. *The Ways of Judgment: The Bampton Lectures, 2003.* Grand Rapids: Eerdmans, 2005.

O'Donovan, Oliver, and Joan Lockwood O'Donovan, eds. *From Irenaeus to Grotius: A Sourcebook in Christian Political Thought, 100–1625.* Grand Rapids: Eerdmans, 1999.

Ollenburger, Ben C., and Gayle Gerber Koontz, eds. *A Mind Patient and Untamed: Assessing John Howard Yoder's Contributions to Theology, Ethics, and Peacemaking.* Telford, PA: Cascadia, 2004.

Oort, Johannes van. *Jerusalem and Babylon: A Study into Augustine's "City of God" and the Sources of His Doctrine of the Two Cities.* Leiden: E. J. Brill, 1991.

Pannenberg, Wolfhart. *Ethics.* Translated by Keith Crim. Philadelphia: Westminster, 1981.

Peace, Richard. *Dostoyevsky: An Examination of the Major Novels.* Cambridge: Cambridge University Press, 1971.

Pearce, Joseph. "An Interview with Alexander Solzhenitsyn." *St. Austin Review* 2.2 (February 2003). http://www.catholiceducation.org/en/culture/art/an-interview-with-alexander-solzhenitsyn.html.

Pecknold, C. C. "Migrations of the Host: Fugitive Democracy and the *Corpus Mysticum*." *Political Theology* 11 (2010) 77–101.

Peterson, Erik. *Theological Tractates.* Edited and translated by Michael J. Hollerich. Stanford: Stanford University Press, 2011.

Peterson, Nancy J. "Haunted America: Louise Erdrich and Native American History." In *Against Amnesia: Contemporary Women Writers and the Crises of Historical Memory,* 18–50. Philadelphia: University of Pennsylvania Press, 2001.

Pickstock, Catherine. *After Writing: On the Liturgical Consummation of Philosophy.* Oxford: Blackwell, 1998.

Planinc, Zdravko. *Plato's Political Philosophy: Prudence in the Republic and the Laws.* Columbia: University of Missouri Press, 1991.

Plato. *The Republic.* Translated by Allen Bloom. Second edition. New York: Basic Books, 1991.

———. *Symposium.* Translated by Seth Benardete. Chicago: University of Chicago Press, 2001.

Potok, Chaim. *My Name Is Asher Lev.* New York: Fawcett Crest, 1972.

Rad, Gerhard von. *Old Testament Theology.* Translated by D. M. G. Stalker. 2 vols. New York: Harper, 1962–65.

Reimer, A. James. "The Adequacy of a Voluntaristic Theology for a Voluntaristic Age." In *The Believers Church: A Voluntary Church,* edited by William Brackney, 135–48. Kitchener, ON: Pandora/Herald, 1998.

———. "'I came not to abolish the law but to fulfill it': A Positive Theology of Law and Civil Institutions." In *A Mind Patient and Untamed: Assessing John Howard Yoder's Contributions to Theology, Ethics, and Peacemaking,* edited by Ben C. Ollenburger and Gayle Gerber Koontz, 245–73. Telford, PA: Cascadia, 2004.

———. *Mennonites and Classical Theology: Dogmatic Foundations for Christian Ethics.* Kitchener, ON: Pandora, 2001.

Rifkin, Jeremy. *The Biotech Century: Harnessing the Gene and Remaking the World.* New York: Putnam, 1998.

Rist, John. *Augustine: Ancient Thought Baptized.* Cambridge: Cambridge University Press, 1994.

Rose, Gillian. *Judaism and Modernity: Philosophical Essays.* Oxford: Blackwell, 1993.

———. *Mourning Becomes the Law: Philosophy and Representation.* Cambridge: Cambridge University Press, 1996.

Rust, Jennifer R. "Political Theologies of the *Corpus Mysticum*." In *The Body in Mystery: The Political Theology of the Corpus Mysticum in the Literature of Reformation England*. Evanston: Northwestern University Press, 2014.

Said, Edward W. *Reflections on Exile, and Other Essays*. Cambridge, MA: Harvard University Press, 2003.

Scarry, Elaine. *The Body in Pain: The Making and Unmaking of the World*. Oxford: Oxford University Press, 1987.

Schindler, David L. "Religion and Secularity in a Culture of Abstraction: On the Integrity of Space, Time, Matter and Motion." *Pro Ecclesia* 11 (2003) 76–94.

Schlabach, Gerald. "The Christian Witness in the Earthly City: John H. Yoder as Augustinian Interlocutor." In *A Mind Patient and Untamed: Assessing John Howard Yoder's Contributions to Theology, Ethics, and Peacemaking*, edited by Ben C. Ollenburger and Gayle Gerber Koontz, 221–44. Telford, PA: Cascadia. 2004.

———. "Deuteronomic or Constantinian? What Is the Most Basic Problem for Christian Social Ethics?" In *The Wisdom of the Cross: Essays in Honor of John Howard Yoder*, edited by Stanley Hauerwas et al., 449–71. Grand Rapids: Eerdmans, 1999.

The Schleitheim Confession. Translated by John H. Yoder. Scottdale, PA: Herald, 1973.

Schmitt, Carl. *The Concept of the Political*. Translated by George Schwab. Chicago: University of Chicago Press, 1996.

———. *Political Theology: Four Chapters on the Concept of Sovereignty*. Translated by George Schwab. Cambridge, MA: MIT Press, 1985.

———. *Roman Catholicism and Political Form*. Introduction and translation by G. L. Ulmen. Westport, CT: Greenwood, 1996.

Sider, J. Alexander. "Constantinianism before and after Nicea: Issues in Restitutionist Historiography." In *A Mind Patient and Untamed: Assessing John Howard Yoder's Contributions to Theology, Ethics, and Peacemaking*, edited by Ben C. Ollenburger and Gayle Gerber Koontz, 126–44. Telford, PA: Cascadia, 2004.

Sider, Ronald. *Rich Christians in an Age of Hunger*. Downers Grove, IL: InterVarsity, 1977.

Silko, Leslie Marmon. *Ceremony*. New York: Penguin, 1977.

Simons, Menno. "Brief and Clear Confession." In *The Complete Writings of Menno Simons*, translated by Leonard Verduin and edited by John Christian Wenger, 419–54. Scottdale, PA: Herald, 1956.

———. "Foundation of Christian Doctrine." In *The Complete Writings of Menno Simons*, translated by Leonard Verduin and edited by John Christian Wenger, 103–226. Scottdale, PA: Herald, 1956.

———. "Reply to False Accusations." In *The Complete Writings of Menno Simons*, translated by Leonard Verduin and edited by John Christian Wenger, 541–77. Scottdale, PA: Herald, 1956.

———. "The True Christian Faith." In *The Complete Writings of Menno Simons*, translated by Leonard Verduin and edited by John Christian Wenger, 321–405. Scottdale, PA: Herald, 1956.

Skinner, Quentin. *Reason and Rhetoric in the Philosophy of Thomas Hobbes*. Cambridge: Cambridge University Press, 1996.

Slipperjack, Ruby. "Blueberry Days." In *An Anthology of Canadian Native Literature in English*, edited by Daniel David Moses and Terry Goldie, 1. Toronto: Oxford University Press, 1992.

Smith, Andrea. *Conquest: Sexual Violence and American Indian Genocide*. Cambridge, MA: South End, 2005.

Smith, Linda T. "Getting the Story Right—Telling the Story Well: Indigenous Activism—Indigenous Research." In *Pacific Genes and Life Patents*, edited by Aroha Te Pareake Mead and Steven Ratuva, 74–81. University of the South Pacific, Fiji: Call of the Earth Llamado de la Tierra and the United Nations University of Advanced Studies, 2007.

Solzhenitsyn, Aleksandr I. *The Gulag Archipelago, 1918–1956: An Experiment in Literary Investigation*. Vol. 2. Translated by Thomas P. Whitney. New York: Harper & Row, 1975.

———. *The Gulag Archipelago, 1918–1956: An Experiment in Literary Investigation*. Vol. 3. Translated by Harry Willetts. New York: Harper & Row, 1978.

Steinmetz, David C. "Luther and the Two Kingdoms." In *Luther in Context*, 112–25. Bloomington: Indiana University Press, 1986.

Stock, Gregory. *Metaman: The Merging of Humans and Machines into a Global Superorganism*. New York: Simon & Schuster, 1993.

———. *Redesigning Humans: Our Inevitable Genetic Future*. New York: Houghton Mifflin, 2002.

Bibliography

Stout, Jeffrey. *Democracy and Tradition*. Princeton: Princeton University Press, 2004.
Studer, Basil. "Le Christ, notre justice, selon saint Augustin." *Recherches Augustiniennes* 15 (1980) 99–143.
Taubes, Jacob. *Occidental Eschatology*. Translated by David Ratmoko. Stanford: Stanford University Press, 2009.
———. *The Political Theology of Paul*. Translated by Dana Hollander. Stanford: Stanford University Press, 2004.
Taylor, Charles. *A Secular Age*. Cambridge, MA: Harvard University Press, 2007.
———. *Sources of the Self: The Making of the Modern Identity*. Cambridge, MA: Harvard University Press, 1989.
Thielicke, Helmut. *Theological Ethics*. Edited by William H. Lazareth. Vol. 1. Grand Rapids: Eerdmans, 1966.
Thomas, D. M. *Alexander Solzhenitsyn: A Century in His Life*. New York: St. Martin's, 1998.
Toews, Aron. *The Siberian Diary of Aron P. Toews*. Translated by Esther Klaassen Bergen. Edited by Lawrence Klippenstein. Winnipeg: CMBC Publications, 1984. Original German edition entitled *Einer von Vielen*, edited by Gerhard Ens.
Toole, David. *Waiting for Godot in Sarajevo: Theological Reflections on Nihilism, Tragedy, and Apocalypse*. Boulder, CO: Westview, 1998.
Troeltsch, Ernst. *The Social Teaching of the Christian Churches*. Translated by Olive Wyon. Chicago: University of Chicago Press, 1931.
Urry, James. *Mennonites, Politics, and Peoplehood: Europe—Russia—Canada, 1525 to 1980*. Winnipeg: University of Manitoba Press, 2006.
Vessey, Mark, Karla Pollman, and Allan D. Fitzgerald, eds. *History, Apocalypse, and the Secular Imagination: New Essays on Augustine's "City of God."* Bowling Green, OH: Philosophy Documentation Center, 1999.
Voegelin, Eric. *Autobiographical Reflections*. Edited by Ellis Sandoz. Baton Rouge: Louisiana State University Press, 1989.
———. *The New Science of Politics: An Introduction*. Chicago: University of Chicago Press, 1952.
———. *Order and History*. 5 vols. Baton Rouge: Louisiana State University Press, 1956–87.
Voolstra, Sjouke. "True Penitence: The Core of Menno Simons' Theology." *Mennonite Quarterly Review* 42 (1988) 387–400.
Walpot, Peter. "True Yieldedness and the Christian Community of Goods." In *Early Anabaptist Spirituality: Selected Writings*, translated and edited by Daniel Liechty, 138–99. Classics of Western Spirituality. New York: Paulist, 1994.
Weil, Simone. *Gravity and Grace*. London: Routledge & K. Paul, 1972.
Westerholm, Stephen. *Perspectives Old and New on Paul: The "Lutheran" Paul and His Critics*. Grand Rapids: Eerdmans, 2004.
Wetzel, James, ed. *Augustine's "City of God": A Critical Guide*. Cambridge: Cambridge University Press, 2012.
Wheeler, Winona. "'Every Word is a Bundle': Cree Intellectual Traditions and History." Unpublished paper, 1998.
Wiebe, Rudy. "The Body Knows as Much as the Soul: On the Human Reality of Being a Writer." *Mennonite Quarterly Review* 71 (1997) 189–200.
———. *River of Stone: Fictions and Memories*. Toronto: Vintage, 1995.
Williams, Rowan. "Politics and the Soul: A Reading of the *City of God*." *Milltown Studies* 19 (1987) 55–72.
Wimbush, Vincent L., and Richard Valantasis, eds. *Asceticism*. New York: Oxford University Press, 1995.
Yoder, John Howard. *Body Politics: Five Practices of the Christian Community before the Watching World*. Nashville: Discipleship Resources, 1992.
———. *The Christian Witness to the State*. Newton, KS: Faith and Life, 1964.
———. *The End of Sacrifice: The Capital Punishment Writings of John Howard Yoder*. Edited by John Nugent. Harrisonburg, VA: Herald, 2011.
———. "Ethics and Eschatology." *Ex Auditu* 6 (1990) 119–28.
———. *For the Nations: Essays Public and Evangelical*. Grand Rapids: Eerdmans, 1997.
———. "How H. Richard Niebuhr Reasoned: A Critique of *Christ and Culture*." In *Authentic Transformation: A New Vision of Christ and Culture*, by Glen Stassen, D. M. Yeager, and John H. Yoder, 31–90. Nashville: Abingdon, 1996.

———. *The Jewish-Christian Schism Revisited*. Edited by Michael Cartwright and Peter Ochs. Grand Rapids: Eerdmans, 2003.

———. *Karl Barth and the Problem of War*. Nashville: Abingdon, 1970.

———, trans. and ed. *The Legacy of Michael Sattler*. Scottdale, PA: Herald, 1973.

———. "Meaning after Babble: With Jeffrey Stout beyond Relativism." *Journal of Religious Ethics* 24 (1996) 125–39.

———. "On Not Being Ashamed of the Gospel: Particularity, Pluralism, and Validation." *Faith and Philosophy* 9 (1992) 285–300.

———. "On Not Being in Charge." In *War and Its Discontents: Pacifism and Quietism in the Abrahamic Traditions*, edited by J. Patout Burns, 74–90. Washington, DC: Georgetown University Press, 1996.

———. *The Politics of Jesus: Vicit Agnus Noster*. 2nd ed. Grand Rapids: Eerdmans, 1994. First published in 1972.

———. *Preface to Theology: Christology and Theological Method*. Grand Rapids: Brazos, 2002.

———. *The Priestly Kingdom: Social Ethics as Gospel*. Notre Dame: University of Notre Dame Press, 1984.

———. *The Royal Priesthood: Essays Ecclesiological and Ecumenical*. Edited by Michael Cartwright. Grand Rapids: Eerdmans, 1994.

———. "See How They Go with Their Face to the Sun." In *The Jewish-Christian Schism Revisited*, edited by Michael G. Cartwright and Peter Ochs, 183–202. Grand Rapids: Eerdmans, 2003.

———. *To Hear the Word*. Eugene, OR: Wipf & Stock, 2001.

———. "To Serve Our God and to Rule the World." 1988 Presidential Address to the Society of Christian Ethics (SCE). In *The Royal Priesthood: Essays Ecclesiological and Ecumenical*, 127–40. Grand Rapids: Eerdmans, 1994.

Index of Subjects

A

academy. *See* university curriculum
Aboriginal peoples of North America. *See* indigenous peoples of North America
Agamben, Giorgio, 5, 20n24, 30, 31, 33–35, 70n21, 77
agapē (divine love), 26, 29
agrarian communities, witness of, 87–88, 216, 217, 219–20
Anabaptist/Anabaptism. *See* Mennonite/Anabaptist history and culture; Mennonite/Anabaptist theology
Antichrist, 16, 26, 49n11, 62, 70, 98–99, 100, 104, 115, 122n46, 128, 245
apocalyptic messianism, 54–56, 76
Arendt, Hannah, 74 110n2
Aristotle, 236, 237
asceticism (*ascesis*), Christian, 91–92, 96. *See also* monastic tradition
Auerbach, Erich, 20n24
Augustine
    apocalyptic political theology, 48–50, 53–56, 57–60, 61–63
    City of God (*civ. Dei*), 6–7, 15, 51–53, 55–63, 69, 154, 156, 159–60, 180, 232, 234
    Confessions, 57
    existential theology, 84–85
    judicial torture, 60–62, 155, 232–34
    political theology, 2, 4, 6–7, 8, 12, 101n15, 120n37, 120n38
    and Plato, 56–57, 140–41
    saeculum, theory of, 15, 69, 180
    spiritual causality, 50–53, 57
    Teaching Christianity (*De doctrina christiana*), 58, 174, 175, 182
    Trinity, 53, 58, 159
    two cities, 53, 56, 58, 59–60, 100, 101, 111, 114, 120, 155, 156, 158, 159
    the wise judge, 60–61, 232
voluntas, 129n84 (*see also* voluntariety and Christian community)

B

Babel, tower of (Scattering of the Peoples), 2, 3, 75–76, 155–56, 169–70n85
Bacon, Francis, 176, 240, 241–42
Badiou, Alain, 17–18, 29, 32, 85
Barth, Karl, 32, 78, 79, 109n1, 121n43, 145, 146, 147–48
becoming
    human, 22, 23, 24
    messianic, 22, 23, 25–27, 28, 167–68, 245
Benjamin, Walter
    Jetztzeit (messianic time), 16, 20n24, 26, 27, 31, 34, 70
    "Theologico-Political Fragment, 25, 77
    "Theses on the Philosophy of History," 16, 20n24, 26–27, 32n78, 70
    "weak messianic power," 16–17, 23, 29, 32, 35, 70, 75, 203–4
Berry, Wendell
    critique of technology, 65, 68, 74–75, 174, 179n23, 216
    good stewardship, 7
    sexual love and community, 11n34, 74n32
    Remembering, 86–88, 216n20, 218–19
"binding and loosing." *See under* Yoder, John Howard
Black Elk, 202
Blumenberg, Hans, 57, 77
Borgmann, Albert, 65, 174,
Breton, Stanislas, 20n24, 21, 29–30, 33
Breughel, Pieter, 84
Bruderhof (Moravian Hutterites), 213, 215
Buber, Martin, reading of Plato, 34–35, 36–38

C

Caird, G.B., 5n12, 236
Calvin, Jean, 9

261

Index of Subjects

Carter, Craig, 145, 147, 148
Cartwright, Michael, 162–63, 164
causality
    spiritual, 32, 49, 50–53, 57, 59, 136, 140n32, 155, 178–79, 235–36, 244
    natural versus spiritual, 19, 20–21, 26, 140
    in Hobbes's *Leviathan*, 70, 78
Cavenaugh, William, 227
Chalcedonian creed, 151
Chartier, Clem, 207
Christendom political theology and ethics, 2, 4, 9, 16, 17, 23, 27, 110, 118–19n28
Coles, Romand, 80n39, 168–70
consicence development of, 224–27
Constantinianism. *See* Yoder, John Howard, critique of Christendom political theology
Continental philosophy, interest in Paul, 15, 16–18, 19
Critchley, Simon, 235, 236
cross and resurrection, scandal of, 17, 18, 20, 28, 29, 78, 88–89, 117, 168, 184, 235, 246

D

Davidson, Arnold, 210
Davis, Kenneth, 91
Davis, Scott, 147–48
Dawkins, Richard, 175, 239
de Lubac, Henri, 4, 5, 6, 11n34
Dead Man Walking, 222–23
death of God (Nietzsche), 28, 130
Deleuze, Gilles, 133n8, 134n10
Deloria, Vine, 200, 202n2
diaspora and the academy, 139
diaspora ethics, 1, 8, 12, 76–78, 113–15, 136, 148, 149, 154, 180–81
diaspora Judiasm, 161, 162
diaspora in sociological literature, 75n34
Dillard, Annie, 88
"disenchantement of the world," 48, 64, 66
disposession and exile, 78, 204–5. *See also* kenosis (self-emptying)/kenotic
Dodaro, Robert, 54–55, 60
Dostoevsky, Fyodor
    arrest and imprisonment, 186, 187–90
    Brothers Karamazov, 73n29, 90–94, 95–96, 226–31, 238
    Crime and Punishment, 226
    Demons, 226
    Grand Inquisitor (*Brothers Karamazov*) and Hobbes's Leviathan, 73–74
    The House of the Dead, 187
    penitence and messianic becoming, 28
    Siberian Notebooks, 188

E

Ebeling, Gerhard, 102–3
economist/s of the divine mystery, 5, 7, 12
ekklēsia, 4, 6, 30, 33, 34–35, 146, 163
    calling and vocation of, 31–32, 77, 78, 168
Eliot, T. S., 244
eschatology, sixteenth-century apocalyptic, 98–100, 103–8
eschatology, Christian
    critiqued by Neitzsche and Feuerbach, 97–98
    and political responsibility, 126–29
ethics
    of cultural appropriation, 199–200, 202, 205
    messianic, 1–4, 77–78, 79–80
    parable as proper discourse for, 32, 79
    as social practice, 74
    See also diaspora ethics
exile, Babylonian, 7n21, 60, 76, 84, 113–14, 120,
exile-exodus-diaspora, biblical significance, 2–4

F

Feuerbach, Ludwig, 97–98, 100, 107
Fingarette, Herbert, 147
Friedman, Robert, 83
Foucault, Michel, 74, 133n8, 221–22, 223–24, 237n8

G

galuth. *See* diaspora
genealogy of morals (Yoder), 131 133, 139. *See also* Nietzsche, *On the Genealogy of Morals*
generation, language of, 176–77, 178–79, 240–41. *See also* causality
Glaucon, 36, 37, 38, 41n20, 45
Grant, George, 64 65, 173, 174
gulag (Siberian prison camp) experience
    of Mennonites, 185, 192–98
    of Russian writers 185, 186, 187–92
Gustafson, James, 98n5, 144

H

Habermas, Jürgen, 66, 68, 77, 79
Harder, Hans, *No Strangers in Exile*, 193, 194–96
Harink, Douglas, 163
Haynes, Robert, 239
Hauerwas, Stanley, 68, 144–45
Heidegger, Martin, 17n9, 18, 21, 26, 236
Heschel, A.J., 41
Hobbes, Thomas, 111–12, 120n36, 200, 225

Index of Subjects

Leviathan, 70–74
Holland, Scott, 84n3
hōs mē ("as if not") ethics and Pauline messianism, 2, 30, 32, 33, 77, 78, 167, 204–5
"hyper-Augustinianism," 46–48

I

Ignatieff, Michael, 221, 232
Illich, Ivan, 1, 47–49, 51, 62, 245
imago Dei (image of Christ) in suffering, 185, 190, 192, 193, 196, 197, 198
imitation
    of Christ (*imitatio Christi*), 53, 57, 116, 136, 151, 159, 196, 198, 202,
    of God (*imitatio Dei*), 42
indigenous peoples of North America
    appropriation of land and culture, 199–200, 201, 208
    spirituality and knowledge, 206, 207–8
    storytelling as research model/knowledge, 209–10
    urbanization and assimilation, 201–2, 208
    See also Métis, Red River
Isaiah
    compared to Plato and Socrates, 34–36, 39, 43–45
    political theology and spiritual failure, 35–36, 39–43
Israel, election of, 30, 163, 164–65, 169

J

Joachim of Fiore, 111, 112
John the Baptist, 182–83
Jubilee, 113, 214
Judaism, Hasidic cosmology, 89n18
judicial torture (Augustine), 60–62, 155, 232–34

K

Kafka, Franz, 32, 78, 79
Kant, Immanuel, "as if" (*als ob*), 32, 78
Kantorowicz, Ernst, 4
kenosis (self-emptying)/kenotic
    of Christ, 59, 86, 94, 117, 134, 137, 146, 148, 149, 151, 196, 197, 246
    disposession, 32, 78, 204–5
    form of a servant, 22, 29, 59, 118, 121
    love, 33, 37, 88, 94
    mission of the church, 121, 124, 128, 138
    parody by Nietzsche's Zarathustra, 24,
Kierkegaard, Søren, 22, 22n36, 23, 25n52, 27–28
kingship, 113–14, 135–36, 157–58, 159–60
Kline, David, 216

Kurzweil, Ray, *Age of Spiritual Machines*, 177–78, 242–43

L

Leviathan (Hobbes) and the Grand Inquisitor (Doestoevsky, *Brothers Karamazov*), 73–73
liberalism, secular
    and messianic ethics, 79–80
    and pluralism, 66–67, 76, 85, 114, 136, 156–57
    and technology, 75, 173–74, 179–80, 244
Lilla, Mark, 1
liturgy (*leitourgia*)/worship, 3–4, 5, 7, 8, 13, 49, 53, 58, 59, 61, 62, 119
    eucharistic, 61–62, 227, 233, 234
    of penance and self-offering, 228– 229, 232, 246–47
liturgy of the courtroom, 228, 231–32, 238
logos, 40–41, 57, 58n36, 152n28, 243
    of modern knowledge and technology, 236–41
    of the *stauros* (word of the cross; Paul), 23, 29, 30
love, of enemy and neighbor, 16, 30, 51, 69, 101n17, 145, 165, 166, 167
Loewen, Royden, *Diaspora in the Countryside*, 216, 217–18
Luddism, 179
Luther, Martin
    apocalyptic eschatology and ethics, 98–100, 107–8
    "To the Christian Nobility of the German Nation," 99
    "Theses for the Heidelberg Disputation," 99
    two kingdoms model, 100–103 (^see also Augustine, two cities)
    view of marriage and sexuality, 107

M

mammon, worship of, 212, 214, 218
MacIntyre, Alasdair, 133n8
Markus, Robert A., 47n5, 54
marks of the Christian community (Yoder), 116–17, 118, 122n49, 136–37, 146–47
Martens, Paul, 9–10
McGinn, Bernard, 99
Melchizedek, priest-king of Salem, 4, 7, 159, 160
Mennonite/Anabaptist history and culture
    affluence, 196–97, 212
    appropriation of North American indigenous lands, 201, 208
    "commonwealth" model, 215

Index of Subjects

Mennonite/Anabaptist history and culture (*continued*)
  "de-kulakization" ("voluntary resettlement") under Stalin, 193
  East Reserve, Manitoba, 200–201
  gulag (Siberian prison camp) memoirs, 185, 192–98
  Kleine Gemeinde, 201, 216
  Selbstschutz (self-defense force), 197
  die Stillen im Lande, 88, 219
  urbanization and acculturation, 87–88, 90, 201–2, 216–18, 219

Mennonite/Anabaptist theology
  in Augustinian tradition, 6
  critique of, 9, 11
  and communal discipleship, 8
  and identity, 87, 215, 216
  engagement with traditional agrarian communities, 88, 216, 219–220
  and asceticism, 91, 93
  and restorative justice, 94
  apocalyptic eschatology, 106–7
  existential theology, 83, 90, 91, 96
  martyrdom theology, 193
  messianic political economy, 212, 213, 216
  Schleitheim Confession, 103, 105–6, 166

Merchant, Carolyn, 240
messianic body/community, 7, 9, 30, 33, 55–56, 58–59, 78, 83, 85, 146, 149, 154, 168–69, 184, 213–14, 237
messianic faith, 174–75, 180–81
messianic political economy, 2–3, 6–7, 12, 212–13, 214–15, 218
messianic political theology, 1–4, 7, 15, 16, 30, 75–79
  of John Howard Yoder, 144–45, 146–47, 157, 168–70
  of Paul, 5–6, 8–9, 19–21, 77–78
messianic time (*Jetztzeit*), 16, 20n24, 26, 27, 31, 70
messianism, Jewish, 145, 161
Métis, Red River, 201, 206–10
Milbank, John, 47–48, 134
modernity criticism, 110n3, 111n4, 117n25
monastic tradition
  continued by Anabaptism/Mennonitism, 8, 91, 215
  as alternative to secular modernity and justice, 92, 228–29, 238, 247
Müntzer, Thomas, 99, 103–4

N

Newman, John Henry, 181
Nicean creed, 153
Nietzsche, Friedrich
  The Antichrist, 15, 20, 97
  critique of Christendom political theology, 23
  critique of Christianity, 9, 28, 47, 62, 97–98, 130–31, 132–33, 139–40, 234
  critique of Paul, 15, 18–23, 27, 30–31, 141n33, 235
  Daybreak, 22
  "Dionysius versus the crucified," 133, 134n10
  Ecce Homo, 23
  On the Genealogy of Morals, 97, 131–32, 137n18, 224
  and postmodernism, 130–31, 133n8
  development of conscience, 224–26
  Twilight of the Idols, 21
  Übermensch, Dionysian, 21, 23, 25, 26, 28
  Zarathustra, becoming and the tragedy of time, 23–25
nomos (law), 2, 4, 9, 12, 19, 146, 165

O

Oberman, Heiko, 99, 101, 107
Ochs, Michael, 162
O'Daly, Gerard, 62
O'Donovan, Oliver, 2, 5, 119–20, 121–23, 136n16
  and Augustine's political theology, 54, 61, 120n37, 120n38
  and John Howard Yoder, 109–10, 112, 114–15, 117–20, 122n46, 124–26, 126–29, 138
  The Desire of the Nations, 123
oikos/oikia (household), 5–6, 8, 9
oikodomein, 5, 8n28, 237

P

paideia (education), 38, 45, 57
Pannenberg, Wolfhart, 103
parable, as discourse for ethics, 32–33, language of parable, 78, 79
parousia (becoming), 25
Paul
  address to the Athenians, 11, 246
  concept of *katargeō/katargēsis*, 19, 21–22, 26, 27, 246
  and Continental philosophy, 15, 17–18, 27, 31, 32
  cross and resurrection, scandal of, 17, 20, 28, 29, 78, 168, 184, 235, 246
  cross, wisdom of, 141–43
  as *doulos* (slave) of the Messiah, 31–32
  dying to the law, 24–25
  economic theology, 5, 17, 19, 24, 33–34
  figural reading of, 20n24, 26, 27, 33

pneuma (spirit), 19–20, 22, 25
   messianic becoming, 20, 21, 25, 26 28, 246
   messianic political theology, 5–6, 17–18,
      30–31, 77–78, 163–64, 169
   mysterium iniquitatis (Antichrist), 48, 245
   principalities and powers, 5, 235–37,
      244–45, 246
Peterson, Erik, 4, 5
phronēsis (prudent judgment), 35, 38, 236, 237
Plato, 37–39, 42n9, 42n10, 63–64
   and Christian theology, 139–40
   compared to Isaiah, 34–36, 43–45
   existential theology, 83–85
   Republic, 34–39, 40, 41–43, 71, 83–84, 179,
      182, 230
   Phaedo, 36–37, 178–79
political theology
   defined, 1
   of Augustine, 2, 4, 6–7, 8, 12, 101n15,
      120n37, 120n38
   biblical, in Yoder and Augustine, 157–60
   Christendom, 117–19
   economic, 5
   and Exodus narrative, 2–3
   and Henri de Lubac's *Corpus Mysticum*, 4–8
   of Isaiah and Plato, compared, 34–36, 37,
      39, 43–45
   liberal Catholic, 47
   messianic (*see* messianic political theology)
   of Oliver O'Donovan, 2, 5
political theory, Euclidean (Thomas Hobbes),
   71–72, 73
postmodernism and moral authority, 130–31
Potok, Chaim, *My Name Is Asher Lev*, 88–90
punishment and torture, 221–224, 232, 234

R

Rad, Gerhard von, 39
Rawls, John, 66, 68, 79
Reimer, James, 148, 149–50
ressentiment, 23, 29, 32, 53, 92, 97, 130, 134,
   142
resurrection, 13, 19, 21, 23, 24
retributive vs. restorative justice (Dostoevsky),
   227, 228, 232, 234, 238
Rose, Gillian, 140
Rust, Jennifer, 4

S

Said, Edward, 2
Sattler, Michael, 106–7, 166–67
Scarry, Elaine, 223
Schindler, David, 64, 173
Schlabach, Gerald, 150, 155

Schleitheim Confession, 103, 105–6, 166
Schmitt, Carl, 4, 5, 16, 69, 73, 166
secularization thesis (Max Weber), 31, 66, 77
Sermon on the Mount, 10, 101, 102, 105,
   106n32, 164, 212
servant, form of, 7, 10, 29, 64, 100, 105, 115,
   121, 135, 137, 141, 142, 149, 151, 157,
   159, 160, 185, 197, 213–14n12, 233, 234,
   247. *See also kenosis* (self-emptying)/
   kenotic
servant, suffering, 25, 29, 32–33, 62, 64, 78, 86,
   88, 92–93, 95, 117, 118, 168, 197, 246. *See
   also kenosis* (self-emptying)/kenotic
shalom, 76, 78, 79
Sider, Ronald, *Rich Christians in an Age of
   Hunger*, 211–12, 214
Silko, Leslie Marmon, *Ceremony*, 205, 207
Simons, Menno
   "Brief and Clear Confession," 213–14n12
   christology, 213n12
   messianic community, 213–14
   "Foundation of Christian Doctrine" 93, 96
   "Reply to False Accustaions," 213n12
   theology, 93–94, 96
   "True Christian Faith," 93, 213n12
Socrates, 35, 36–37, 38, 41n20, 57, 139–40,
   178, 179, 181
Solzhenitsyn, Aleksandr
   arrest and imprisonment, 186
   conversion, 190
   Gulag Archipelago, 190–91, 192
   One Day in the Life of Ivan Denisovich, 190
   experience in prison, 190–92
sovereignty
   empire, 3
   individual, 224
   as limit concept, 16, 69, 166
   (weak) messianic, 16–17, 19, 21, 33, 70
   of Yahweh, 17
   civil/secular state, 18, 19, 70–74, 111–12,
      120n36, 200, 225
   political/state, 166, 225, 226, 230
   messianic, 146, 167
Stout, Jeffrey, 66–68, 79
suffering love, 57, 148
suffering, transformation and conversion
   through, 189, 192, 194–95, 197, 198

T

Taylor, Charles, 46–48
Taubes, Jacob, 4, 17, 18–19, 20n24, 27, 30, 31,
   33–34, 77, 146, 164–66
technē and *logos*, 236–37, 240–41
technology
   as principality, 236–37

Index of Subjects

technology *(continued)*
    cybernetics, 176, 177–78, 239, 241, 242–43
    in secular liberal society, 64–65, 173–75, 179–80
    as globalizing culture, 67, 68–69, 72, 74, 75, 85, 173–74, 175–77, 181–82
    and scientific knowledge, 175–78
"terminal creeds" (Gerald Vizenor), 203, 208, 209
theology, existential
    Anabaptist/Mennonite, 83, 86, 87–88, 91, 93, 94–95, 96
    of Augustine, 84–85
    and asceticism, 91–92, 102, 105
    of Plato, 83–85
Thielicke, Helmut, 102n18
Toews, Aron, *Siberian Diary of Aron P. Toews*, 193, 196–98
Toole, David, 134n10

U

Übermensch, Dionysian (Nietzsche), 19, 21, 23, 25, 131
university curriculum
    and messianic model, 174, 180–81, 182–84
    and secular pluralism, 179–80
    and technological globalization, 174, 175–77, 181–82
Urry, James, 215

V

Varro, tripartite division of theology, 56
Vizenor, Gerald, 208
Voegelin, Eric, 110–11, 112, 114, 115, 117, 117n25,
    rereading of Isaiah, 34–35, 39–40
voluntareity and Christian community (Yoder), 110, 112, 115, 121, 124–25, 129, 137–38, 157, 163

W

Walpot, Peter, 213
Walzer, Michael, 69n19
Weber, Max, 31, 66, 77
Weil, Simone, 175
Wheeler, Winona, 206
Wiebe, Rudy, 84n5
Williams, George Huntston, 8
wise judge (Augustine), 60–61, 232

Wolin, Sheldon, 4n8
worship. *See* liturgy (*leitourgia*)/worship

Y

"Yes and Amen," 22, 26
Yoder, John Howard
    and Augustine, 150–51, 154–160
    Body Politics, 116
    "binding and loosing," 105, 116, 121, 122, 123, 146
    "body politics," 116, 118, 126, 163, 169
    Christology and messianic discipleship, 148, 151–53
    critique of Christendom political theology (Constantinianism), 117–18, 124–25, 127–28, 137–39, 140, 150, 158, 161, 162
    critique of "Mennonite commonwealth" model, 215
    critique of modernity/postmodernity/mainstream moralism, 132–34
    critical responses to his work, 138n26, 139n27, 144–46, 147–51, 153, 154, 162–64, 168–70
    For the Nations, 113, 145, 157
    genealogy of morals, 131, 133n10
    To Hear the Word, 145
    "Jeremian shift," 113–15, 124, 135–36, 161
    The Jewish-Christian Schism Revisited, 145, 149, 157, 158, 160, 162
    Jewish-Christian dialogue, 144, 145, 163
    and Karl Barth, 121n43
    marks of the Christian community, 116–17, 118, 122n49, 136–37, 146–47
    "middle axioms," 147n8
    and Oliver O'Donovan, 109–10, 112, 114–15, 117–20, 124–26, 126–29
    "Patience as Method in Moral Reasoning," 170
    Preface to Theology: Christology and Theological Method, 145, 148, 149, 157,
    The Politics of Jesus, 113, 144–45, 145, 163, 164, 170, 214
    slain Lamb (Christ), authority of 134–35, 136–37
    theology and behavior, 8–9, 10–11
    and Karl Barth, 145, 146, 147–48

Z

Zweig, Stephen, 113, 135, 162

Index of Scripture References

OLD TESTAMENT

Genesis
1–11	2–3
11	75–76, 156
14:17–18	7

Exodus
20:17	22

Deuteronomy
32:21–22	169

Job
28	72n27
41	71
41:24	72

Psalms
110:4	7

Isaiah
2	41, 42
7	41, 42
40	19

Jeremiah
29	76, 162, 181
29:7	113, 134, 154
31:31–34	4

Daniel
2	104

NEW TESTAMENT

Matthew
5:39	101
5:44	69
6:22–23	212
18	9
18:15–20	121, 123

Acts
17:16–31	12, 246

Romans
1	21
1:19–20	57
7	22
9–11	30, 169
12:2	7

1 Corinthians
	141–42
1	168, 184
1:20	27–28, 15
1:28	21
2	19
3:10	236
3:11	131
7:31	32n80, 79n38
7:29–31	77, 167, 204
7:29	31
8:1	8
8:3	193, 204
9:17	8
10	26
13	26
13:12	193
10:23	8
14:24ff	122n49
15:24	21, 246

2 Corinthians
3	122
3:12–18	22

Index of Scripture References

Galatians
3:13   27

Ephesians
2:19   6

Philippians
2   24, 134, 151, 197, 213–14n12, 246

Colossians
2:15   5

2 Thessalonians
2   49, 245

1 Timothy
4:3   107

Hebrews
5–7   7
8   3–4
11   175

Revelation
4:11   7
5   95
12–18   74
21   95

www.ingramcontent.com/pod-product-compliance
Lightning Source LLC
Chambersburg PA
CBHW081329230426
43667CB00018B/2873